LISTEN   SIXTH EDITION

LISTEN

SIXTH EDITION

JOSEPH KERMAN
University of California, Berkeley

GARY TOMLINSON
University of Pennsylvania

with
VIVIAN KERMAN

BEDFORD / ST. MARTIN'S
Boston ◆ New York

For Bedford/St. Martin's

Developmental Editor: Caroline Thompson
Senior Production Editor: Michael Weber
Senior Production Supervisor: Nancy Myers
Marketing Manager: Adrienne Petsick
Art Director: Lucy Krikorian
Cover Designer: Donna Lee Dennison
Text Design: Anna Palchik
Copy Editor: Edward B. Cone
Photo Research: Elaine Bernstein
Cover Art: Joseph Holston, *Cello Concerto.* Oil on linen. Collection of the Southern
   Alleghenies Museum of Art, Loretto, Pennsylvania.
Composition: Techbooks
Music Composition: A-R Editions, Inc.
Printing and Binding: R.R. Donnelley & Sons Company

President: Joan E. Feinberg
Editorial Director: Denise B. Wydra
Editor in Chief: Karen S. Henry
Director of Marketing: Karen Melton Soeltz
Director of Editing, Design, and Production: Marcia Cohen
Managing Editor: Shuli Traub

Library of Congress Control Number: 2006930987

Manufactured in the United States of America.

2   1   0   9   8   7
f   e   d   c   b   a

For information, write: Bedford/St. Martin's, 75 Arlington Street, Boston, MA 02116   (617-399-4000)

ISBN-10: 0-312-43419-7   ISBN-13: 978-0-312-43419-9   (paperback)

ISBN-10: 0-312-43425-1   ISBN-13: 978-0-312-43425-0   (hardcover)

Acknowledgments

Acknowledgments and copyrights are printed at the back of the book on pages 445–49, which constitute an extension of the copyright page.

Preface
To the Instructor

Instructors who adopted the original *Listen* back in 1972 may remember a soft plastic 5-inch LP packaged with the book, modeled on a cereal box giveaway and containing listening examples for the "Introductions" chapter. Incredibly, that first edition came out without any other recordings—though the publisher scrambled together a 6-LP set soon afterwards, and LP sets became a fixture with subsequent editions. In 1986 we wept as CD production slowly got underway, just as *Listen*, First Brief Edition, went to press; we were able to refer to upcoming CDs but couldn't issue our now-familiar 3- and 6-CD sets until the next time around. By 2004, *Listen* took advantage of new media to provide interactive resources on a CD-ROM and a companion Web site.

And *Listen*, Sixth Edition, which you have before you, draws on technology for new features that may improve music instruction more significantly than any other innovations of recent years. First, the companion disk included in every copy of the print book is no longer a CD-ROM but a DVD; now immediately accessible are video excerpts of operatic and orchestral works treated in the text, as well as additional audio tracks. Second, with this edition we introduce the e-book version of *Listen*. The e-book gives students an online version of the text that integrates the features of the *Listen* Web site and offers instructors more opportunities to customize the content. For both print and online versions of the book, new tutorials on music fundamentals and enhanced listening quizzes use streaming music clips to provide students with a streamlined interactive experience.

We try to follow the injunction of our title, and not only in musical matters—listening carefully to many thoughtful suggestions from readers, we have once again worked to improve the coverage of musical repertories at the heart of the book. Both small changes (a chanson by Josquin, a rondo by Francesca LeBrun) and large ones (a new Wagner selection) aim to bring clearer and more accessible examples to students. We've cut down the discussion of early modernism—without cutting out any of the selections— and drawn a new, more vivid picture of composers' stylistic choices at the end of the millennium. Film music makes its overdue debut, as does John Adams, welcomed with a video from his oratorio *El Niño* on the Companion DVD.

The publishers of *Listen,* no less than the authors, have always worked hard to make the book attractive to look at (one edition received a design award). But the real point of a good design is to make it easy to find your way around in a book and make the book inviting to use. In that respect, longtime users will notice some improvements: the streamlined design is easier to follow than before, and the book's many diverse elements or features are now easier to distinguish. In a number of unobtrusive but stylish ways, the new design highlights the most important parts of the book—the musical selections.

We have also redesigned, revised, and rechristened the abbreviated charts that go with the DVD's audio tracks in Unit I, "Fundamentals." The seven Listening Exercises, as they are now called, illustrate rhythm, melody, counterpoint, texture, and so on, and culminate in the redoubtable *Young Person's Guide to the Orchestra* by Benjamin Britten. We show students how to listen to this work both for instrumental sonority and as an informal summary of fundamentals at the end of the unit.

What has not changed is our basic coverage, organization, treatment, and style, which have proved so solid over many editions. For new users, we draw attention to the following strong features that we believe set *Listen* apart:

⁊ *Prelude* Many instructors work out a special introductory session to break the ice and interest students in the subject matter of their course. The *Prelude* to Unit 1 of this book is a specific suggestion for such an icebreaker—students can listen to a four-minute piece, the eventful orchestral Prelude to *The Valkyrie,* with a short commentary that will give them a taste of what the semester will be like. (An uncomplicated Listening Chart in the *Prelude* serves to introduce a feature that is essential to the book.) At this stage the emphasis is on direct impressions rather than on terminology, but some technical terms are introduced in passing, terms that will be presented formally in Unit I.

⁊ *Overall organization* The book's coverage is simple and clear, and evident at once from the listing of "Contents in Brief," on page xxi. (This may seem like an elementary, obvious thing, but in our judgment not a few texts give first impressions that are muddled and forbidding.) After "Fundamentals," the historical scheme goes from "Early Music"—in effect, everything before Bach and Handel, when the standard repertory begins—to the three great periods of Western classical music: the eighteenth and nineteenth centuries, and the twentieth century to the present. Each period is treated as a unit—Unit III, Unit IV, and Unit V—containing several chapters.

⁊ *Flexible coverage* Coverage—that perpetual (and probably insoluble) problem for instructors, and for textbook writers also! How much time or space does one devote to music of the so-called common-practice period, and how much to Early Music and music of the twentieth century? How much to popular music? Music from beyond Europe and America?

The main emphasis of *Listen* is on the common-practice repertory, basically for reasons of time. Only so much can be accomplished in a semester course, and most instructors will agree that students learn more from exposure to a limited amount of material in some depth than from overambitious surveys. Probably all agree that beginning courses in music should introduce students to the good music they will most likely hear in later life.

By the end of many a semester, the final pages of books like this one tend to be sacrificed because of time constraints. For those who would rather save time at the beginning, Unit II, "Early Music: An Overview," has been made *strictly optional* in the book's sequence. Nothing later in the book depends on having studied it, so if your course plan begins with Unit III, "The Eighteenth Century," no one will need to skip back for explanations of continuo texture, recitative, fugue, and so on. And for those who prefer to use some selections of early music without teaching the entire unit, the fairly modest amount of prose in Unit II should prove manageable as a general orientation for the music chosen.

❦   *Non-Western music*   The Global Perspectives segments of *Listen* are positioned so as to elaborate the European and American topics discussed around them. Three Global Perspectives come at the ends of the Early Music chapters; they take up sacred chant (at the end of the Middle Ages chapter), European colonialism (Renaissance), and ostinato techniques (early Baroque). Two items come at the ends of the eighteenth- and nineteenth-century units of the book and treat complexities of form in instrumental music and musical drama, respectively. Segments on African drumming and on global pop come in the last chapter, "American Music: Jazz and Beyond." We believe these materials broaden the coverage of *Listen* in a meaningful way, but we are certainly not offering them as a token survey of world musics. If they are a token of anything, it is the authors' belief that music-making worldwide shows certain common, deep-seated tendencies in which the European classical tradition has shared.

❦   *Cultural background*   The Baroque and Classical eras and the nineteenth and twentieth centuries are introduced by what we call, again, "Prelude" chapters. These summarize some features of the culture of the times, in particular those that can be seen to affect music. (Generously captioned color illustrations for these chapters, and others, are an original *Listen* specialty that has now become a standard textbook feature.) The Prelude chapters also contain concise accounts of the musical styles of the eras, so that these chapters furnish background of two kinds — cultural and stylistic — for listening to specific pieces of music in the chapters that follow.

Biography boxes segregate material on the lives of the major composers from discussions of their music — again, making the book easier to read and easier to work from. The boxes include portraits, concise lists of works that can serve for study or reference, and, under the heading "Encore," suggestions for further listening.

❦   *Recordings*   The main compositions studied in *Listen* are available in multiple recordings, and much time and effort has gone into searching for what seem to us the best ones. (The search becomes increasingly difficult as licensing rights are denied by more and more record companies.) It is gratifying to learn from market research that many users consider our choices superior. We hope that instructors and students will get the same charge out of our selections that we do, and it's our further fond hope that students may keep these recordings and keep listening to them in future years.

The eleven selections for the Listening Exercises in Unit I of the book are included as audio tracks on the Companion DVD. The remaining eighty-three selections discussed in the text appear on the accompanying 6-CD set, and thirty-six of those appear on the 3-CD set. Four selections have accompanying video clips on the DVD. (To allow for the maximum use of disc space, a few selections in the CD sets appear out of order: that is, not in the sequence of their appearance in the book. The Global Perspectives tracks have all been put at the ends of the CDs.) Icons tell the listener *which number* CD to select from

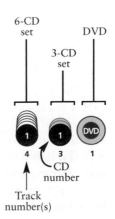

6-CD set

3-CD set

DVD

CD number

Track number(s)

the sets (this is the numeral inside the circle) and then *which track* to play (the numeral below it). The DVD has its own icon with track numbers marked below it.

❧   *Listening Charts*   One of the strongest features of *Listen,* instructors have always told us, is the format of its Listening Charts. They are especially important for the big instrumental works discussed in this book. Songs, operas, and other vocal works can be followed by listening to the words sung, words that we print in boxes with the simple title "Listen."

Look at the portion of Listening Chart 5 shown on p. xvii to see how these charts work. The charts all fit onto one page, visible at a glance, with concise descriptions and identifications. Off at the side, brief music tags can easily be consulted by those who read music—and just as easily ignored by those who don't. As to the timings, in selections divided into several CD tracks, the timings to the *left* of the vertical rule give the time elapsed from the start of the previous track, while those to the *right* of the rule give the total time from the start of the piece. (Interactive versions of all the Listening Charts can be found on the *Listen* Web site; many of them are enhanced with activities for second and third listenings.)

❧   *Appendices*   "Appendix A: Time Lines" groups the time lines that formerly appeared at the beginning of each unit. "Appendix B: Suggested Readings and Recommended Web Sites" provides students with recommendations for print and online materials for further study and (we hope, once again) reference for a lifetime of engagement with music. The readings are mostly standard reference works. Links to the recommended Web sites also appear on the *Listen* Web site with additional annotated links for every chapter.

Supplements Package

Recognizing how much the teaching and learning experience of this course may be enhanced through a mixture of media, we have updated and expanded the supplements for the Sixth Edition as follows:

For Students

❧   The **new Companion DVD,** packaged with each copy of the book, provides two valuable resources. First, it presents thirty-five minutes of video excerpts from performances of four opera and orchestral works discussed in the book. Second, it contains eleven audio recordings that form the basis of the Listening Exercises in Unit I, "Fundamentals." See the user guide at the back of this book for a complete list of the DVD's contents.

❧   The **Web site for students at bedfordstmartins.com/listen** includes listening and reading quizzes for every chapter, demos (real, not synthesized) and photographs of instruments of the orchestra, interactive Listening Charts, annotated research links organized by chapter, vocabulary flashcards, a hyperlinked glossary, and other resources. (See illustration on facing page.)

❧   The **new e-book** integrates the Interactive Listening Charts and other online resources, and includes helpful highlighting and note-taking features. With the custom e-book option, instructors can select chapters, rearrange chapters, and add their own text, images, and Web links.

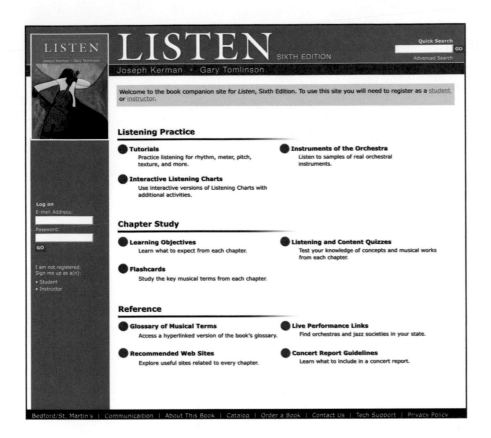

❦ The **new interactive tutorials** are designed to supplement Unit I, "Fundamentals," and the seven Listening Exercises in that unit by offering guided practice with detailed feedback so that students can hone their listening skills.

For Instructors

❦ The *Instructor's Resource Manual* (prepared by Mark Harbold) offers chapter outlines, important terms, teaching objectives, suggestions for lectures and class discussions, ideas for further listening, additional Listening Charts and song translations, ideas for using multimedia resources, and a useful bibliography. In addition, an index of thousands of musical examples from the *Listen* recordings is keyed to important terms from the textbook.

❦ The *Test Bank* (by Jane Viemeister) has more than 1,800 multiple-choice and essay questions. Use the print version with perforated pages for easy copying and distribution, or download Test Bank files from the *Listen* Web site to edit and customize your own tests.

❦ The *Overhead Transparencies* set includes acetates of each of the Listening Charts, with many other maps, charts, and listening guides from the book. These, too, can be downloaded from the Web site as Transparency Masters.

❦ The **Web site for instructors at bedfordstmartins.com/listen** includes downloadable PowerPoint presentations for each chapter, digitized scores, additional Listening Charts and song translations, and access to students' online quiz results. In addition, the Instructor's Resource Manual, Transparency Masters, and Test Bank are all available on the site.

❡ *Videos and DVDs of complete performances* of works discussed in this edition are available to qualified adopters. Contact your local Bedford/St. Martin's sales representative for more information.

❡ *Content for course management systems* helps instructors using *Listen* to develop custom Web sites with systems such as Web CT. In addition to the Test Bank and other resources from the *Listen* Web site, special handouts are included that present musical concepts from the book in a visual manner.

This is a long list of special features indeed, and it will be a rare instructor who draws on all of them for aid in teaching, reading, and listening. But in the end *Listen* owes its success less to features than to two basic attributes, which the authors have been grateful to hear about many times from instructors as well as students over the history of *Listen*. *Listen* is distinctive in its writing style and, related to that, in the sense it conveys of personal involvement with the music that is treated. The tone is lively and alert, authoritative but not stiff and not without humor. We sound (because we are) engaged with music, and we work to engage the student. We never condescend to students, and we don't begrudge them careful explanation of matters that we as musicians find elementary. "My music course used *Listen,* Third Brief Edition," an alum of a college in Colorado, now an attorney, wrote recently. "I cannot tell you how amazing it was to take that course. It opened my ears and my heart to hear and feel much more from music than I ever dreamed possible. To this day, I have the textbook and consult it frequently — it is one of the few that has had such an impact on my life."

The excitement and joy that the experience of music can provide — this, more than historical or analytical data about music — is what most instructors want to pass on to their students. This is the ideal goal of music teaching, so to speak, which is why technology will never replace live instructors. It's no easy undertaking, and most (though not all) of us turn to textbooks for support and assistance — or at best, collaboration. We have prepared every edition of *Listen* in this spirit, always in the hope of collaborating more closely and getting closer to that goal.

Acknowledgments

It remains to express our gratitude to the numerous battle-scarred "music apprec" instructors who have reviewed the book and its supplements and given us the benefit of their advice for this revision. Their criticisms and suggestions have significantly improved the text, as have the market surveys in which an even larger number of instructors have generously participated. In addition to the users of previous editions who over the years have given us suggestions, we wish to thank:

Wayne Bailey, Arizona State University
Paul Beaudoin, Northeastern University
Dominique Bellon, Arizona State University
Stephanie Berg Oram, Red Rocks Community College
Lester Brothers, University of North Texas
Jennifer Campbell, Central Connecticut State University
John Canarina, Drake University

Kathleen Cantrell, University of Louisville
Arthur Chankin, Baruch College
David Chapman, Modesto Junior College
John Cloer, University of North Carolina–Charlotte
Carmelo Comberiati, Manhattanville College
James Cunningham, Florida Atlantic University
Paul Davies, Foothill College

Andrew Dell'Antonio, University of Texas
Linda Dzuris, Clemson University
Lawrence Ferrara, City College of San Francisco
Craig Ferrin, Salt Lake Community College
Jeffrey Funderburk, University of Northern Iowa
Michael Haberkorn, Otterbein College
Christopher Hahn, Black Hills State University
Mark Hudson, Colorado State University–Pueblo
Stephen Jenkins, Grand Valley State University
Scott R. Johnson, Augustana College
Steven Johnson, Brigham Young University
Kimberley Jones, Columbia College of Missouri–Online
Jonathan King, Columbia University
Elisa Koehler, Goucher College
Orly Krasner, City College of CUNY
Jamey Lamar, Boise State University
Anatole Leikin, University of California–Santa Cruz
Bliss Little, Arizona State University
Mary Macklem, University of Central Florida
Martin Marks, Massachusetts Institute of Technology
Kevin McCarthy, University of Colorado–Boulder

Lawrence Mitchell, University of South Dakota
Charlotte Mueller, Lee College
David Murray, Butler University
Stephen Noble, University of Louisville
Francis Osentowski, North Lake College
Thomas B. Payne, College of William and Mary
Richard Porterfield, City College of CUNY
Jana Rader, San Jacinto College South
Judith Rosenberg, Mills College
Michael Samball, Boise State University
Ronald Sherrod, Columbus State University
Ruth Solie, Smith College
David Tracek-King, University of Nebraska–Omaha
Floyd Vasquez, Albuquerque TVI Community College
Cynthia Verba, Harvard University–Extension
Scott Warfield, University of Central Florida
William Watson, Community College of Baltimore County
Phyllis White, Oakland University
Edward Zeliff, Saddleback Community College
Katrina Zook, University of Wyoming

The production of a major textbook is a complex, arduous process drawing on professionals from many areas. Many of them, by necessity, the authors don't know personally, but we are very grateful to them all, starting with Art Director Anna Palchik, who was as imaginative as she was patient, working with us on the design indirectly, from a distance. Art Director Donna Dennison designed the cover. Thanks go to Dr. Jane Viemeister, for writing questions for the Test Bank and online quizzes; Vicki Curry, for writing the interactive tutorials; and to Tom Millioto, for reviewing every track timing in the text. Fletcher Moore and Andrew Dell'Antonio created the original Interactive Listening Charts, which have been updated for the present edition. We wish to acknowledge Permissions Assistant Krista Peutherer; Editorial Assistant Katherine Bouwkamp; the cartographers at Mapping Specialists Limited; and Rick Barker at NBDtv for DVD licensing.

Those whom we do know have worked with us directly on previous editions—a high-powered, innovative team that is bringing *Listen* to more and more readers and listeners edition by edition. We again express our appreciation to Joan Feinberg of Bedford/St. Martin's for her enthusiastic, very substantial support all along, and Editor in Chief Karen Henry for her wise and deft guidance over many years. Other old friends are layout expert DeNee Reiton Skipper, picture consultant Elaine Bernstein, and—seemingly unfazed by current craziness in the recording industry—Tom Laskey of Sony BMG. We are delighted that Professor Mark Harbold has undertaken the *Instructor's Resource Manual* for the current edition, as he has done so successfully in the past.

Finally, there are new friends—Development Editor Caroline Thompson, Managing Editor Shuli Traub, Production Editor Michael Weber, Editor David Mogolov, New Media Editor Harriet Wald, and Editorial Assistant Blake Royer. They are the ones who work down and dirty with the authors and not only turn the book and the Web site into realities but also make them better in more ways than you might think. We (and you) have Carrie Thompson to thank for the video tracks on the *Listen* Companion DVD.

And we are grateful and fortunate indeed that Davitt Moroney agreed to perform two works specially for the CD sets. He recorded the Frescobaldi Passacaglia and Suite for Unit II on the seventeenth-century Spanish organ by Greg Harrold at the University of California, Berkeley (in meantone tuning), and the LeBrun sonata for Unit III on the university's fortepiano. Robert Shumaker was the recording engineer.

The high quality of *Listen* is a tribute to the expertise, dedication, and artistry of all of these people. We are indebted to them all.

J. K.

G. T.

Berkeley and Philadelphia, 2007

Introduction
To the Student

Classical music: just what is meant by that? The ordinary meaning of "classical" or "classic" is something old and established and valued on that account. The term can be applied to many things, as we know: classic cars, Classic Coke, classic jazz, classic rock, even classic rap. Classical music itself can be very old indeed; it covers more than a thousand years of music as practiced and heard in the upper strata of society in Europe and America. Other names for it that you may encounter are art music, Western music, or music of the Western tradition.

Classical music continues to flourish today; it's very likely that musical composition in the classical tradition is being taught this semester at your own college or university. The coverage in this book extends to music composed in 2000, the multicultural oratorio *El Niño* by American composer John Adams. But nobody doubts that the great age of classical music is in the past. (Some would say the same for poetry, painting, and even jazz.) Listening to classical music is listening to history. Why do that?

Ultimately, because classical music has stayed the course. Over history, it has provided generations (dozens of generations, to push the point) with pleasure, joy, inspiration, and solace. So they have said, repeatedly. It can do the same for us today. It may be true, as someone has said, that if we do not understand the past, we are doomed to repeat its mistakes—in history and politics, that is, not art. There are no mistakes in music, poetry, and painting, only successive manifestations of the human spirit. With art, if we do not understand the past, we are only doomed to living in the present.

When we dip into the past, it's important to acknowledge the "otherness" of people in history, the differences between them and us, between people then and people today. Nonetheless, we relate to them; they are recognizably us—as we can tell from their diaries and their poems, their portraits, their political aspirations, and indeed also from their philosophical reflections, if we are prepared to give them the time it takes to really grasp them. We treasure our Declaration of Independence, written more than two hundred years ago, and it will be a bad day when we lose touch with the Constitution. There is a case to be made for also staying in touch with the poetry, art, and music of what one historian has called the "usable past."

On one level, music serves as entertainment, of course, and is none the worse for that. On another level, it provides knowledge or, if not exactly knowledge, insight into human experience and feeling as they extend over time. How music manages to do this is a famous philosophical problem. The best short hypothesis is that music, which on a basic level is a strange and wonderful way of filling up time, vividly represents the way time feels as we actually live through it.

Music and History

The era of Classical music extends over more than a thousand years. Naturally, music changed vastly over that time — not only in its sound but also in its function and its institutions in society, its basic support system. Classical music is not monolithic. Record stores that carry "classical" need to separate their stock into several categories. In addition to an untitled section organized by composer, you will probably find smaller sections labeled Early Music and Contemporary. In this book, indeed, Early Music is set apart as an optional topic of study. We should try to explain why.

In sociological terms (very quickly, now!), Western musical history can be said to fall into three great phases. The later phases overlap, as forces underlying the earlier phases decay over long periods of time and other forces take their place.

❧   In the first millennium C.E., European culture was the culture of Christianity. All musicians (or at least all musicians that we know about) were churchmen, and all their music was sung in churches, abbeys, convents and cathedrals. The function of music was to stimulate and enhance worship. Music makes prayer more fervent, and music makes church services more solemn and impressive.

❧   Around 1100, music manuscripts of a new kind began to appear — often richly illuminated manuscripts, transmitting music composed for princely courts, as well as music for the Church. Slowly the Church was yielding power to kings and nobles. Courts furnished the locale for instrumental and vocal music for many centuries. Music was now entertainment for court society, and indeed there were some very famous monarchs who were keen musicians: Henry VIII of England is one example, and Frederick the Great of Prussia is another. Increasingly over time, the function of court music was to glorify kings and princes.

Note also that court music included music for the court chapels, which not only praised the Almighty in lavish terms but also celebrated the mighty rulers who could put on such lavish services.

❧   As aristocratic power declined and the middle classes (the bourgeoisie) gained more and more strength, public opera houses and concert halls were invented and became the new social spaces for

Music at court, 1540: King Henry VIII of England playing the harp, posing as a modern King David. Only his court jester Will Sommers was allowed to pull long faces about this.

Music at court, 1750: Frederick II of Prussia, an accomplished flutist. His court composer
J. J. Quantz composed over three hundred flute concertos.

music. The first opera house opened around 1650; the first concert hall around
1750. From then on concert music was in principle available to all who cared
to buy tickets and could afford them. Courts and court music remained important for some time, but music was becoming more generally available, at
least for the well-to-do.

Meanwhile European music took a big leap to Latin America and then to
North America — first in the California missions and then in the English
colonies. In the twentieth century it also became a major presence in Japan and
other non-European countries.

Today classical music has entered a new phase. Now a worldwide phenomenon,
it is played and heard more and more via digital recordings, on aluminum-
and-plastic discs or simply downloaded. However, the concert still counts as
classical music's main site and paradigm, so for this reason it seems right to concentrate on music of the concert hall in a book of this kind, rather than music
of the Church and music at court. Concert music all dates from within the span
of United States history, plus about seventy-five years at the beginning — from
around 1700 to the present.

Music earlier than that had mostly died out until the twentieth century.
Many old scores slumbered in libraries, but they were hard to decipher and
nobody was much interested in singing or playing the music. But especially
after the middle of the twentieth century, Early Music experienced a significant
revival, thanks to efforts by imaginative musicologists and performers — and

thanks also to recordings, which (as never before) spread the word with instant efficiency. People now listen to Early Music widely, and we include this topic as a concise optional unit at the beginning of this book.

Global Perspectives   The main concern of this book is European classical music and its offshoots in the United States, which remained a cultural colony of Europe for many years after our declaration of political independence.

But in an era of instantly available recorded sound, we have easy access to much more than European music alone. All through this book we will take stock of the multiplicity of musical traditions ("musics") around the world, by engaging a number of traditions outside the European classical heritage: China, Japan, Islam, and others. Though our glimpses of these other musics will be brief, they will not be arbitrary or superficial, because the Global Perspectives inserts are connected to the European issues in the chapters around them. Our inserts point out broad similarities between Western/European and non-Western music, similarities sometimes of musical technique, sometimes of social uses of music, and sometimes of both together.

By making such sweeping *comparisons,* we mean at the same time to highlight the real *differences* between European and other traditions. This is, basically, the kind of approach anthropologists take. Our instinctive sense of common human aims and interests attracts us and draws us near to foreign cultures. Then a finer sense of precise differences—of a crucial strangeness, in fact—deepens our understanding of them. It can also deepen our understanding of ourselves.

Listening

Say "music" and many people will think at once of recordings on an iPod or downloaded onto a computer. Yet many of those same people know music as something rather different—from playing in marching bands (or garage bands), from singing, from actually *performing* music, as distinct from *experiencing* it. Virtually all music, it seems, is available on recordings, and the recorded sound of music from many different eras and many different cultures is an integral feature of this textbook. But of course, total recall has only been achieved at a price. No one should forget that recordings are abstractions, at some distance from the experience of actual live music. Music is human communication, and human presence is leached out of a recorded performance. Missing is the physical pleasure of doing music, missing the immediacy, the empathy that springs up between listener and performer. Missing, too, is the special push that performers deliver when they feel that an audience is with them.

People probably tend to supply these feelings imaginatively when listening to recordings, by extrapolating them from their own experience of live performance occasions. Be that as it may, a classroom is not a concert site, and recorded music is there to be played again and again. If the abstractness of recordings encourages us really to *listen* to music, and not treat it as a background to some other activity, some good will have come of it.

For often you just *hear* music—out of the corner of the ear, as it were. The center of your attention is elsewhere—on the chemistry equation you are balancing, or the car ahead of you cutting in from the other lane, or your date at a restaurant. Instead it's necessary to make a listening commitment to music, comparable to the dedication on the part of composers and performers that goes into its making. Background listening won't do. Real listening means recognizing specific events in the music as it goes by in time, holding them in the memory, and relating them to one another in the mind. Just as you do with events in a novel. Classical music requires full attention if it is to yield its full rewards.

Listening to individual pieces again and again is the basic activity that leads to the understanding and love of music; that is why this book is called *Listen.* Focused listening, whether live or through earphones, is the one essential thing.

Listening Charts   Therefore, Listening Charts that focus listening are an integral feature of this text. Look at the portion of Listening Chart 5 below to see how they work (the complete chart is found on page 141). Identify the logo for your recording set at the top right corner of the chart; it will show six red or three black stacked CDs for the 6-CD or the 3-CD sets. The numeral inside

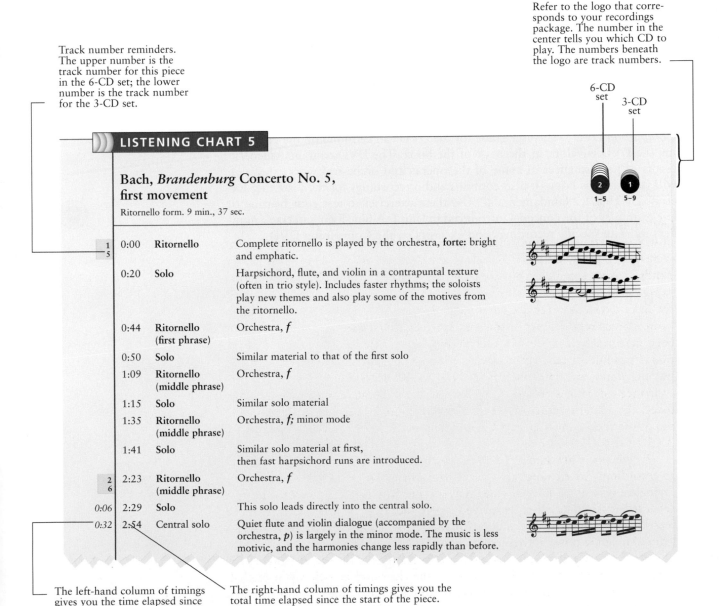

Refer to the logo that corresponds to your recordings package. The number in the center tells you which CD to play. The numbers beneath the logo are track numbers.

6-CD set

3-CD set

Track number reminders. The upper number is the track number for this piece in the 6-CD set; the lower number is the track number for the 3-CD set.

LISTENING CHART 5

Bach, *Brandenburg* Concerto No. 5, first movement

Ritornello form. 9 min., 37 sec.

2 / 1-5   1 / 5-9

1/5	0:00	Ritornello	Complete ritornello is played by the orchestra, **forte:** bright and emphatic.
	0:20	Solo	Harpsichord, flute, and violin in a contrapuntal texture (often in trio style). Includes faster rhythms; the soloists play new themes and also play some of the motives from the ritornello.
	0:44	Ritornello (first phrase)	Orchestra, *f*
	0:50	Solo	Similar material to that of the first solo
	1:09	Ritornello (middle phrase)	Orchestra, *f*
	1:15	Solo	Similar solo material
	1:35	Ritornello (middle phrase)	Orchestra, *f*; minor mode
	1:41	Solo	Similar solo material at first, then fast harpsichord runs are introduced.
2/6	2:23	Ritornello (middle phrase)	Orchestra, *f*
0:06	2:29	Solo	This solo leads directly into the central solo.
0:32	2:54	Central solo	Quiet flute and violin dialogue (accompanied by the orchestra, *p*) is largely in the minor mode. The music is less motivic, and the harmonies change less rapidly than before.

The left-hand column of timings gives you the time elapsed since the start of the current CD track.

The right-hand column of timings gives you the total time elapsed since the start of the piece.

the logo indicates *which number* disk to choose from the set. The numeral below the logo indicates *which track* to play on that disk. For long selections with multiple tracks, small boxes on the vertical line running down the Listening Charts show where each new track begins. In these boxes, track numbers from discs in the 6-CD set are printed in red, and those from the 3-CD are set in black.

In essence this Listening Chart is a table of the main musical events in Bach's *Brandenburg* Concerto ("Ritornello," "Solo," and so on) with brief explanatory notes where needed. As you listen, follow down this list with the timing figures. To the *left* of the vertical line are the timings that appear on the CD display, starting anew with each track. The timings to the *right* of the line give the total time from the beginning of the composition.

For the benefit of those who are able to read music, the charts include a few brief notations of the main themes, directly across from the timing indications and the reference to the musical event. They are an extra; it is not necessary to read musical notation or even follow it in a general way to use these charts. Even people who think they are tone deaf (there's no such condition) can follow the music with the help of the timings.

The Listening Charts are also available in an interactive format on the companion Web site at **bedfordstmartins.com/listen.** The interactive charts work in conjunction with the recordings, indicating when each new section of a piece begins and allowing you to play back specific themes or motives with a single mouse click.

Companion DVD   The user guide for the DVD can be found on the page facing the DVD envelope at the back of the book. The DVD contains video excerpts of performances of some of the operas and orchestral works that you will study in this book. It also contains audio recordings for the Listening Exercises in Unit I, "Fundamentals." Use these exercises to test your hearing of live examples of the concepts introduced in Unit I. A blue logo and track numbers indicate specific recordings and excerpts on the Companion DVD.

DVD
1

J. K.

G. T.

About the Authors

Joseph Kerman and Gary Tomlinson are leading musicologists and music educators. Kerman, who with his wife, Vivian Kerman, was *Listen*'s original author, served for two terms as chair of the Music Department at the University of California at Berkeley, and Tomlinson has done the same at the University of Pennsylvania. Both are known as inspirational and wide-ranging teachers; between them, their course offerings encompass harmony and ear training, opera, world music, interdisciplinary studies, seminars in music history and criticism, and—many times—Introduction to Music for nonmajor students.

Kerman's books include *Opera as Drama* (second edition, 1988), *Contemplating Music* (1985), *The Art of the Fugue* (2005), and studies of Beethoven and William Byrd. His lectures as Charles Eliot Norton Professor of Poetry at Harvard in 1997–1998 were published as *Concerto Conversations* (1999). Tomlinson, a former MacArthur Fellow, is the author of *Monteverdi and the End of the Renaissance* (1987), *Music in Renaissance Magic* (1993), *Metaphysical Song: An Essay on Opera* (1999), and *The Singing of the New World* (2007). He has also published on jazz and music historiography.

Contents in Brief

Global Perspectives

Maps

Listening Charts

Contents

LISTEN   SIXTH EDITION

Fundamentals

U nit I, the introductory unit in this book, covers music fundamentals and their standard terminology. We start right away with a piece of music, the Prelude to The Valkyrie by the nineteenth-century composer Richard Wagner. Chapter 1 presents the basic concepts of sound and time — pitch, dynamics, tone color, and duration — and introduces the terms used by musicians for these phenomena. Chapter 2 explains how, in music, time is organized into rhythm and meter, and how pitch is deployed in scales. Then Chapter 3 deals with melody and harmony in Western music, and other combinations of the basic elements that have already been treated. Chapter 4 carries the discussion one stage further, to a discussion of musical form and style. Our "Interludes" treat musical instruments and musical notation.

Listening

The basic activity that leads to the love of music and to its understanding — to what is sometimes called "music appreciation" — is listening to particular pieces of music again and again. Such, at least, is the premise of this book. Its pages are filled mostly with discussions of musical compositions — symphonies, concertos, operas, and the like — that people have found more and more rewarding as they have listened to them repeatedly. These discussions are meant to introduce you to the contents of these works and their aesthetic qualities: what goes on in the music, and how it affects us.

The kind of hands-on knowledge of music that is necessary for a music professional — for a composer or a performer — is of no special use to you as a nonprofessional listener. But familiarity with musical concepts and musical terms can be useful, helping you grasp more clearly what you already hear in music. Analyzing things, pinpointing things, even simply using the right names for things all make us more actively aware of them. Sometimes, too, this process of analyzing, pinpointing, and naming can actually assist listening. We become more alert, as it were, to aspects of music when they have been pointed out. And greater awareness contributes to greater appreciation of music, and of the other arts as well.

Since our emphasis is on music, this is where we start — with an actual listening experience, our "prelude" to this book. It will exemplify in a general way some of the concepts introduced in the following chapters, and make understanding the terminology of music, when we come to explain it, seem less abstract and mysterious, more immediate and alive.

An Orchestral Prelude by Richard Wagner

L isten, then, to what we are calling the Prelude to Unit 1. In fact its composer also called it that; it is the orchestral prelude that begins the opera *The Valkyrie (Die Walküre)* by Richard Wagner, which we will take up further in Chapter 17. *The Valkyrie* comes from a huge, four-opera cycle Wagner composed on stories from Norse mythology. The cycle as a whole is called *The Nibelung's Ring,* and what with its gods, heroes, giants, dwarfs (Nibelungs), dragons, talking birds, and magic swords and cloaks and potions, *The Nibelung's Ring* has served as a source of many mythic tales since Wagner—most famously J. R. R. Tolkien's *Lord of the Rings.* The title *The Valkyrie* refers to one of the "wish-maidens" of Wotan, king of the gods; they chose the souls of slain heroes to be carried off to Valhalla, heavenly home of the gods.

In the following discussion, we introduce a few of the musical terms that will be defined and discussed later and used throughout this book. The idea is not to learn these terms now but to get a feel for their use in the context of a piece of music. So the most important thing to do here is to *listen* to the music in one or, preferably, all of these three ways: (1) cold, (2) while at the same time following the prose discussion below, and (3) while following the Listening Chart on page 5.

Preliminaries Music, as we listen to it, often presents an unstable, changing profile, as Wagner's Prelude certainly does. The shifting sounds seem almost to summon up a story before our ears—a story of a general sort, to be sure, as the music is for instruments alone and has no words to make it specific. What story do you hear in this brief piece for orchestra? Whatever the story, it is certainly not calm or serene. This music is unlikely to conjure up images of a placid spring morning or a lingering sunset over a lake. Instead the music tells of turbulence, storminess, even violence. Is it the natural turmoil of a thunderstorm, or a purely internal, psychological trouble? Both at once, as Wagner will show us—but we'll save that story for later.

So the first thing to notice in listening to this Prelude is that it stamps in our minds a definite, by no means bashful, expressive *character.* Much music does the same, and we value this expressive force. (Music lacking it we often tend to write off as subpar; indeed, we have a special word for such unobtrusive, inexpressive music: Muzak.) The next thing to note is that the violence of this particular music does not come upon us all at once. Wagner carefully builds up to a big orchestral climax and then falls away from it. Let's examine how he manages this.

Scale Theme   The Prelude to *The Valkyrie* opens with a distinct musical idea, or *theme*. It is played by low *stringed instruments,* or *strings,* and takes the form of a repetitive melody marching up and down the scale. It marches to a clear *beat,* arranged in a regular pattern, or *meter,* by threes (count: ONE *two three* | ONE *two three*); and it marches at a fairly fast speed, or *tempo.* Above this repeating theme we hear other strings, playing a single *pitch* in an anxious, trembling manner.

First Climax   Gradually, with much repetition, the scale theme begins to move higher in pitch. Finally its *dynamic* level, or loudness, also increases; this effect is called a *crescendo* (from Italian for "growing"). When the scale theme reaches its first highpoint, *brass instruments* and *woodwinds* are heard for the first time. Especially prominent are the French horns, playing a new theme. It is two notes long and sounds like a musical lightning stroke: DA-**DAAA.**

Second Climax   After this first climax—a brief, preliminary climax with a very short theme—the strings are left alone again, and the scale theme falls back in pitch. The dynamic level of the music also diminishes (*diminuendo*)—but not for long, for the storm is about to break out in all its fury. Now after another quick *crescendo* all the strings take up the scale theme. The music swirls up, and the full brass section weighs in with titanic effect. The instruments enter from low to high, first tubas, then trombones, finally trumpets, at higher and higher pitch levels. They shout out an extended version of the lightning theme first played by the horns: no longer DA-**DAAA** but now DA-**DAAA**-**DA**-**DA**-**DA**-**DAAA.**

Collapse   Suddenly, at its loudest moment, the bottom drops out of the orchestra. All that is left is a thunderous roll on the kettledrums, or *timpani.* The full orchestra returns to play, sporadically, the lightning theme. Now its melody has even taken on the jagged shape of a lightning bolt. While the timpani roll continues, this melody is heard four times, each time softer in dynamic level and lower in pitch. In its wake comes a survivor—the scale theme from the beginning, gradually subsiding and moving lower in pitch.

Continuity   The Prelude does not truly come to an end; there is no full and clear stopping point, or *cadence.* Instead it leaves us on an unexpected pitch; a pitch that halts the motion of the scale theme as the curtain rises and the action of the opera begins. The stage shows the inside of a gloomy, rough house

LISTENING CHART 1

Wagner, Prelude to *The Valkyrie*

3 min, 13 sec.

0:00	A	Scale theme in low strings; *crescendo* and rise in pitch
0:58	B	Preliminary climax: Lightning theme in horns and woodwinds
1:11	A	Scale theme, briefly subsiding; then *crescendo*
1:36	B′	Main climax: Lightning theme, extended, in full brass
2:07		Collapse: timpani roll; sporadic lightning strikes; *diminuendo*
2:35	A	Scale theme

The forest dwelling where Siegmund finds refuge from the storm (*The Valkyrie*, Act I). There is a sword in the tree, planted by Wotan, king of the gods. Siegmund will pull it out, and another famous old myth will find its way into Wagner's great epic *The Nibelung's Ring*.

in a forest, and sure enough, as the door swings open we see the storm that we have just been hearing about from the orchestra. As it winds down, a man (Siegmund) stumbles exhausted out of the storm and into an unfamiliar home; there he will meet, and fall in love with, Sieglinde. Neither of them knows yet that they are brother and sister, separated when they were young children. We follow up on this fateful turn of events on page 287.

Musical Form   This music is certainly stirring in its chaotic climax; Wagner was a master at using his large orchestra to such dramatic effect. But underneath the chaos his prelude reveals a clear organization, or *musical form*, built around its two main themes, the scale theme and the lightning-stroke theme:

Scale theme	Preliminary climax: Lightning theme	Scale theme	Main climax: Lightning theme extended	Scale theme

We could simplify this diagram by using letters to represent the main elements of the form, **A** for the scale theme and **B** for the climaxes: **A B A B′ A.** Throughout this book musical forms will be represented by letter diagrams of this kind.

bedfordstmartins.com/listen
▶ Interactive Listening Chart 1

CHAPTER 1

Music, Sound, and Time

Music is the art of sound in time. We start with an outline of the basic properties of sound when it is produced, each of which corresponds to an effect that we experience when sound is heard. The scientific terms for sound all have their analogues in the terminology of music.

1 Sound Vibrations

As everyone who has taken a course in physics knows, sound is produced by vibrations that occur when objects are struck, plucked, stroked, or agitated in some other way. These vibrations are transmitted through the air, or another medium, and picked up by our ears.

For the production of sound in general, almost anything will do—the single rusted hinge on a creaky door as well as the great air masses of a thunderstorm. For the production of musical sounds, the usual objects are taut strings and membranes, columns of air enclosed in pipes of various kinds, and silicon chips. These produce relatively simple vibrations, which translate into clearly focused or, as we say, "musical" sounds. Often the membranes are alive: They are called vocal cords.

Sound-producing vibrations are very fast; the range of sound that can be heard extends from around 20 to 20,000 cycles (that is, our vocal cords warble close to that many times every second). The vibrations are also very small. Look inside a piano while it is being played: You will not detect any movement in the strings, except possibly for some blurring of the very longest ones. To be heard, sound vibrations often need to be *amplified,* either electronically or with the aid of something physical that echoes or *resonates* along with the vibrating body. In a piano, this is the entire wooden soundboard. The resonator in a guitar is the hollow box that the strings are stretched across.

Pitch (Frequency)

The term for the rate of sound vibration is <u>frequency</u>. Frequency is measured in cycles (per second). On the level of perception, our ears respond differently to sounds of high and low frequencies, and to very fine gradations in between.

Early musical instruments often have resonators that are found in nature: gourds in a pair of Mexican maracas, and a tortoiseshell in the ancient Greek lyre, a small harplike instrument.

Indeed, people speak about "high" and "low" sounds quite unselfconsciously, as though they know that the latter actually have a low frequency—relatively few cycles—and the former a high frequency.

The musical term for this quality of sound, which is recognized so instinctively, is **pitch**. Low pitches (low frequencies) result from *long* vibrating elements, high pitches from *short* ones—a trombone sounds lower than a flute. Tap on a (tall) glass of water as you fill it up, and the pitch gets higher as the column of vibrating air gets shorter.

Noises, with their complex, unfocused vibrations, do not have pitch. And the totality of musical sounds, as distinct from noises, serves as a kind of quarry from which musicians of every age and every culture carve the exact building blocks they want for their music. We hear this totality in the sliding scale of a siren, starting low and going higher and higher.

But musicians never (or virtually never) use the full range of pitches. Instead a limited number of fixed pitches is selected from the sound continuum. These pitches are calibrated scientifically (European-style orchestras these days tune to a pitch with a frequency of 440 cycles), given names (that pitch is labeled A), and collected in *scales*. Scales are discussed in Chapter 2.

The experience of pitch is gained very early; babies only a few hours old respond to human voices, and they soon distinguish between high and low ones. They seem to prefer higher pitches naturally—those in their mothers' pitch range. At the other end of life, it is the highest frequencies that older people find they are losing.

2 Dynamics (Amplitude)

In scientific terminology, *amplitude* is the level of strength of sound vibrations—more precisely, the amount of energy they contain and convey. If you have ever been next to a big guitar amplifier, you know that very small string vibrations can be amplified until the energy in the air transmitting them rattles the eardrums. Amplitude is measured in *decibels*.

In musical terminology, the level of sound is called its **dynamics**. Musicians use very subtle dynamic gradations from very soft to very loud, but they have never worked out a calibrated scale of dynamics, as they have for pitch. The terms used are only approximate. Because all European music looked to Italy when this terminology first came into use, the terms used for dynamics are in Italian.

The main categories are simply loud and soft, **forte** (pronounced fór-teh) and **piano**, which may be qualified by expanding to "very loud" or "very soft" and by adding the Italian word for "medium," **mezzo** (med-zo):

pianissimo	*piano*	*mezzo piano*	*mezzo forte*	*forte*	*fortissimo*
pp	*p*	*mp*	*mf*	*f*	*ff*
very soft	soft	medium soft	medium loud	loud	very loud

Other terms are **più forte** and **meno forte**, "more loud" and "less loud" (pyo͞o, méh-no). Changes in dynamics can be sudden (*subito*), or they can be gradual—a soft passage swells into a loud one, or a powerful blare fades into

LISTENING EXERCISE 1

11

For explanation of this icon, see page xviii.

Pitch and Dynamics

In Unit I of this book, we will illustrate the concepts that are introduced with listening examples drawn from the enclosed DVD. Follow the timings on these Listening Exercise charts, which are simplified versions of the Listening Charts provided for complete compositions. The charts are explained on page xvii.

High and low *pitch* and loud and soft *dynamics* are heard so instinctively that they hardly need illustration. Listen, however, to the vivid way they are deployed in one of the most famous of classical compositions, the "Unfinished" Symphony by Franz Schubert. Symphonies usually consist of four separate big segments, called movements; musicologists are still baffled as to why Schubert wrote two superb movements for this work and started but never finished the rest.

		PITCH	DYNAMIC
0:00	Quiet and mysterious	Low range	*pp*
0:15	Rustling sounds	Middle range	
0:22	Wind instruments	High	
0:35	Single sharp accent		*sf*
0:47	Gets louder	Higher instruments added	Long *crescendo,* leading to *f*, then *ff*, more accents
1:07	Sudden collapse		*piano* followed by *diminuendo*
1:15	New tune	First low, then high	(Marked *pp* by Schubert, but usually played *p* or *mp*)
1:52	Cuts off sharply; big sound		*ff*, more accents
	(Similar pitch and dynamic effects for the rest of the excerpt)		
3:07	Sinking passage	Individual pitches, lower and lower	
3:43	Ominous	Lowest pitch of all	*pp*

quietness. Below are the terms for changing dynamics and their notational signs (sometimes called "hairpins"):

crescendo (**cresc.**)

decrescendo (**decresc.**), or *diminuendo* (**dim.**)

gradually getting louder   gradually getting softer

3 Tone Color: Overtones

At whatever pitch, and whether loud or soft, musical sounds differ in their general *quality*, depending on the instruments or voices that produce them. <u>**Tone color**</u> and <u>**timbre**</u> (tam-br) are the terms for this quality.

Tone color is produced in a more complex way (and a more astonishing way, it must seem, the first time you learn about it) than pitch and dynamics.

Piano strings and other sound-producing bodies vibrate not only along their total length, but also simultaneously in half-lengths, quarters, eighths, and so on.

STRING VIBRATIONS

FULL-LENGTH: HALF-LENGTH: HALF-LENGTH
AND QUARTER-LENGTH
SIMULTANEOUSLY:

The diagrams above attempt to illustrate this. The amplitudes of these fractional vibrations are called **partials** by scientists and <u>overtones</u> by musicians. They are much lower than the amplitudes of the main vibrations; for this reason, overtones are not heard as distinct pitches, but somehow as part of the string's basic or fundamental pitch. The amount and proportion of overtones are what give a sound its characteristic tone color. A flute has few overtones. A trumpet has many.

Musicians make no attempt to tally or describe tone colors; about the best one can do is apply imprecise adjectives such as *bright, warm, ringing, hollow,* or *brassy.* Yet tone color is surely the most easily recognized of all musical elements. Even people who cannot identify instruments by name can distinguish between the smooth, rich sound of violins playing together, the bright sound of trumpets, and the banging of drums.

Listen to orchestral tone colors with the Listening Chart on page 55, after following the discussion of European musical instruments in Interlude B (pages 37–47). Look forward to hearing many more non-European instruments in connection with the Global Perspectives sections of this text. The variety of devices invented for the different tone colors that people have desired for their music, in all societies, is almost unbelievable.

The most distinctive tone color of all, however, belongs to the first, most beautiful, and most universal of all the sources of music—the human voice.

4 Duration

Sound exists in time, and any sound we hear has its <u>duration</u>—the length of time we hear it in minutes, seconds, or microseconds. Though duration is not an actual property of sound, like frequency, amplitude, and other of sound's attributes that are taught in physics courses, it is obviously of central importance for music, which is the art of sounds in time. The broad term for the time aspect of music is <u>rhythm.</u>

The primacy of rhythm in the experience of music is practically an act of faith in our culture—and in most other cultures as well. Rhythm is the main driving force in music both popular and classical, music of all ages and all cultures, and rhythm is where we begin our discussion of the elements of music in Chapter 2.

The singing voice, "the most universal of all sources of music": Among the newest stars in opera, Russian soprano Anna Netrebko and Mexican tenor Rolando Villazón have made a mark playing across from one another as lovers in various operas—here, *Rigoletto* by Giuseppe Verdi (see page 279).

Rhythm and Pitch

We start this chapter by discussing *rhythm*, the way musical time is organized by the use of durations of various magnitudes. We then go on to the organization of pitch into *scales* and *intervals*.

1 Rhythm

As we have seen, the term **rhythm** in its broadest sense refers to the time aspect of music. In a more specific sense, "*a* rhythm" refers to the actual arrangement of durations—long and short notes—in a particular melody or some other musical passage. Of course, the term is also used in other contexts, about golfers, quarterbacks, poems, and even paintings. But no sport and no other art handles rhythm with such precision and refinement as does music.

The term *rhythmic* is often used to describe music that features simple patterns, such as ONE *two* | ONE *two*, repeating over and over again, but that is not really correct (think about what a golfer or tennis player means by rhythm). Such patterns should be described as *metrical*, or strongly metrical, not rhythmic. See the section "Rhythm and Meter" on page 13.

Beat

Beats provide the basic unit of measurement for time in music; if ordinary clock time is measured in seconds, musical time is measured in beats. When listening to a marching band, to take a clear example, we surely sense a regular recurrence of short durational units. These units serve as a steady, vigorous background for other, more complicated durational patterns that we discern at the same time. We can't help beating time to the music, waving a hand or tapping a foot, following the motion of the drum major's baton and the big-drum players' drumsticks. The simple durational pattern being signaled by waving, tapping, or thumping is the music's beat.

Accent

There is, however, an all-important difference between a clock ticking and a drum beating time. Mechanically produced ticks all sound exactly the same,

66 Music has four essential elements: rhythm, melody, harmony, and tone color. These four ingredients are the composer's materials. He works with them in the same way that any other artisan works with his materials."

From what is still one of the best books on "music appreciation," What to Listen for in Music by composer Aaron Copland, 1939 (see page 362)

The beat: There are times when the drummers in a band do little more than bang it out.

but it is virtually impossible for people to beat time without making some beats more emphatic than others. This is called giving certain beats an **accent**.

And accents are really what enable us to beat time, since the simplest way to do this is to alternate accented ("strong") and unaccented ("weak") beats in patterns such as ONE *two*|ONE *two*|ONE *two* . . . or ONE *two three*|ONE *two three*|ONE *two three*. . . . To beat time, then, is not only to measure time but also to organize it, at least into these simple two- and three-beat patterns. That is why a drum is a musical instrument and a clock is not.

Accents are not usually indicated in musical notation, since in most types of music they are simply taken for granted. It's only when composers want a particularly strong accent that they put the sign > above or below a note. A pattern of alternating very strong and weak beats is indicated as shown to the right. An even stronger accent is indicated by the mark *sfz* or *sf*, short for *sforzando*, the Italian word for "forcing."

strong weak strong weak

Meter

Any recurring pattern of strong and weak beats, such as the ONE *two* and ONE *two three* we have referred to above, is called a **meter**. Meter is a strong/weak pattern repeated again and again.

Each occurrence of this repeated pattern, consisting of a principal strong beat and one or more weaker beats, is called a **measure**, or **bar**. In musical notation, measures are indicated by vertical lines called **bar lines**. The meter indicated schematically in the margin above is notated as shown to the right.

In Western music there are only two basic kinds of meter, called **simple meters**: duple meter and triple meter. **Compound meter** involves a subdivision of one of the simple meters.

In duple meter the beats are grouped in twos (ONE *two*|ONE *two*). Duple meter is instantly familiar from marches—such as "Yankee Doodle"—which

Bar line   Bar line

tend always to use duple meter in deference to the human anatomy (LEFT *right,* LEFT *right,* LEFT *right*).

Duple meter   *Triple meter*

❡ In triple meter the beats are grouped in threes (ONE *two three*|ONE *two three*). Two of our national songs, "The Star-Spangled Banner" and "My Country, 'Tis of Thee," are in triple meter. "My Country, 'Tis of Thee" starts on the strong beat ONE of the triple meter; "The Star-Spangled Banner" starts on the weak beat *three*. Two other national songs, "America the Beautiful" and "God Bless America," are in duple meter.

ONE	two	three
My	coun -	try
'tis		of thee,
Sweet	land	of
li - - - -		ber - ty,
Of	thee	I
sing.		

❡ Not infrequently, there is a clearly marked subdivision of the main beats into threes, resulting in *compound meters* with six or nine beats:

ONE		two		three
ONE *two three*	FOUR *five six*	ONE *two three*	FOUR *five six*	SEVEN *eight nine*

Compound meters are really best thought of as subtypes of duple and triple meter. The round "Row, row, row your boat" is in compound meter, 6/8, but while the first voice is moving at a fast six-beat clip at the words "Merrily, merrily, merrily, merrily," the second voice comes in pounding out the basic duple meter, "ROW, *row,* ROW":

first voice:

Row,	row,	row your	boat	gently	down the	stream,		Merrily,	merrily,	merrily,	merrily,
1 2 3	4 5 6	1 2 3	4 5 6	1 2 3	4 5 6	1 2 3	4 5 6	1 2 3	4 5 6	1 2 3	4 5 6
ONE	*two*	ONE	*two*	ONE	*two*	ONE	*two*	ONE	*two*	ONE	*two*

						second voice:		Row,	row,	row . . .	
								ONE	*two*	ONE	*two*

❡ Meters with five beats, seven beats, and so on have never been used widely in Western music, though they are found frequently enough in some other musical cultures. It was an unusual tour de force for Tchaikovsky to have provided his popular Sixth Symphony with a very convincing waltzlike movement in *quintuple* meter (five beats to a bar).

Tchaikovsky, Symphony No. 6

Rhythm and Meter

We have already seen that *rhythm* in the most general sense refers to the entire time aspect of music and, more specifically, that *a* rhythm refers to the particular arrangements of long and short notes in a musical passage. In most Western music, duple or triple *meter* serves as the regular background against which we perceive music's actual rhythms.

As the rhythm first coincides with the meter, then cuts across it independently, then even contradicts it, all kinds of variety, tension, and excitement can result. Meter is background; rhythm is foreground.

Musical notation has developed a conventional system of signs (see pages 21–22) to indicate relative durations; combining various signs is the way of indicating rhythms. Following are examples of well-known tunes in duple and triple meters. Notice from the shading (even better, sing the tunes to yourself and *hear*) how the rhythm sometimes corresponds with the meter and sometimes departs from it. The shading indicates passages of rhythm-meter correspondence:

❝ Rhythm might be described as, to the world of sound, what light is to the world of sight. It shapes and gives new meaning."

Edith Sitwell, poet and critic, 1965

The above diagrams should not be taken to imply that meter is always emphasized behind music's rhythms. Often the meter is not explicitly beaten out at all. It does not need to be, for the listener can almost always sense it under the surface. People will even imagine they hear a duple or triple meter behind the steady dripping of a faucet or the ticking of a clock.

Naturally, meter is strongly stressed in music designed to stimulate regular body movements, such as marches, dances, and much popular music. The connection between strongly metrical music and sex is acknowledged by the uninhibited gesturing of rock stars and lots of imagery on MTV.

At the other extreme, there is *nonmetrical* music. The meandering, nonmetrical rhythms of Gregorian chant contribute to the cool, otherworldly, and spiritual quality that devotees of this music cherish. Sometimes these two different kinds of rhythmic organization are joined together. In the classical music of India, for example, most performances begin with a long section of nonmetrical music, and then proceed to music with a clearly defined meter.

> **❝** The most exciting rhythms seem unexpected and complex, the most beautiful melodies simple and inevitable.**❞**
>
> *Poet W. H. Auden, 1962*

Syncopation

One way of obtaining interesting, striking effects in music is to displace the accents in a foreground *rhythm* away from their normal position on the beats of the background *meter*. This may seem counter-intuitive, but not at all. In **syncopation**, as it is called, accents can be displaced so they go *one* TWO|*one* TWO instead of ONE *two*|ONE *two*. Or the syncopation can occur in between beats ONE and *two*, as in this Christmas ballad:

Ru-*dolf* __	the	red -	nosed	rein -	deer _____
ONE	*two*	ONE	*two*	ONE	*two*	ONE	*two*

If you know the George M. Cohan classic "Give My Regards to Broadway," you know that it starts with the same syncopation as in "Rudolf," and has another syncopation in its second line:

Give *my* __ re-	gards	to	Broad - - -	way,	Re - member	me to	Her*ald* ___	Square
ONE	*two*	ONE	*two*	ONE	*two*	ONE	*two*	one	*two*	ONE	*two*	ONE

The consistent use of syncopation is the hallmark of African American–derived popular music, from jazz to world beat. This we take up in Chapter 23.

))) LISTENING EXERCISE 2

Rhythm, Meter, and Tempo

For samples of *duple*, *triple*, and *compound meters*, listen to the following tracks on the DVD.

12, 15	Duple meter **2/4** or **2/2**	Count ONE *two*|ONE *two* . . . etc., for about half a minute.
17	Duple meter **4/4** or **4/8**	Count ONE *two* THREE *four*|ONE *two* THREE *four* . . . etc.
11, 20	Triple meter **3/4**	Count ONE *two three*|ONE *two three* . . . etc.
18	Compound meter **6/8**	Count ONE *two three* FOUR *five six*|ONE *two three* FOUR *five six* . . . etc.
13	*Tempo* is best illustrated when tempo changes, as in passages from 0:30–1:00 and from 3:40–4:10 in track 13.	
12	*Syncopation:* In Scott Joplin's "Maple Leaf Rag," listen to the piano left hand, with its steady ONE *two*	ONE *two* beat in duple meter, while the right hand is cutting across it with syncopations in almost every measure.	

Tempo

Our discussion so far has referred to the *relative* duration of sounds — all beats are equal; some notes are twice as long as others, and so on — but nothing has been said yet about their *absolute* duration, in fractions of a second. The term for the speed of music is **tempo**; in metrical music, the tempo is the rate at which the basic, regular beats of the meter follow one another.

Tempo can be expressed exactly by such indications as ♩ = 60, meaning 60 quarter-note beats per minute. These indications are called **metronome marks**, after the metronome, a mechanical or electrical device that ticks out beats at any desired tempo.

When composers give directions for tempo, however, they usually prefer approximate terms. Rather than freezing the music's speed by means of a metronome mark, they prefer to leave some latitude for different performers, different acoustical conditions in concert halls, and other factors. Like the indications for dynamics, the conventional terms for tempo are Italian:

An early metronome owned by Beethoven, who was a friend of the inventor, Johannes Maelzel. A clockwork mechanism made the bar swing back and forth, ticking, at a rate determined by a little movable weight on the bar.

COMMON TEMPO INDICATIONS		LESS COMMON TEMPO INDICATIONS	
adagio:	slow	*largo, lento, grave:*	slow, very slow
andante:	on the slow side, but not too slow	*larghetto:*	somewhat faster than *largo*
moderato:	moderate tempo	*andantino:*	somewhat faster than *andante*
allegretto:	on the fast side, but not too fast	*vivace, vivo:*	lively
allegro:	fast	*molto allegro:*	faster than *allegro*
presto:	very fast	*prestissimo:*	very fast indeed

It's interesting that in their original meaning many of these Italian words refer not to speed itself but rather to a mood, action, or quality that can be associated with tempo only in a general way. Thus, *vivace* is close to our "vivacious," *allegro* means "cheerful," and *andante,* derived from the Italian word for "go," might be translated as "moving along steadily."

The most important terms to remember are those listed under "common tempo indications" above. When they appear at the beginning of a symphony movement or the like, they usually constitute its only heading. People refer to the "Andante" of Beethoven's Fifth Symphony, meaning a certain movement of the symphony (the second), which is played at an *andante* tempo.

Other terms indicate irregularities of tempo and tempo changes:

accelerando (acheleráhndo) (accel.):	gradually getting faster
ritardando (rit.) or rallentando (rall.):	gradually getting slower
più lento, più allegro:	slower, faster
⌒ (fermata symbol):	a hold of indefinite length on a certain note or rest, which for a moment suspends the tempo
a tempo:	back to the main tempo

2 Pitch

As we noted in Chapter 1, music generally does not use the total continuous range of musical sounds. Instead, it draws on only a limited number of fixed pitches. These pitches can be assembled in a collection called a **scale**. In effect, a scale is the pool of pitches available for making music.

But the exact pitches that make up a scale differ from culture to culture. Twelve basic pitches have been fixed for most of the music we know — and so people tend to think of the Western scale as "natural." This is a mistake. Five pitches were once used in Japan, and as many as twenty-four have been used in Near Eastern countries; and Western Europe itself originally used seven.

Intervals (I): The Octave

The difference, or distance, between any two pitches is called an **interval**. Of the many different intervals used in music, one has a special character that makes it particularly important. This is the **octave**.

LISTENING EXERCISE 3

13

Rhythm, Meter, and Tempo

A more advanced exercise: our excerpt, from the middle of *Rhapsody on a Theme by Paganini,* for piano and orchestra, by Sergei Rachmaninov, consists of four continuous segments in different meters and tempos, here labeled A, B, C, and D. (If you note a family likeness between the segments, that is because they are all variations on a single theme. See page 190.)

0:00	A	The piano starts in *duple meter.* The loud orchestral interruptions are *syncopated.* (After the interruptions the meter is somewhat obscured, but it gets clearer.)
0:33		Clear duple meter by this time; then the music comes to a stop.
0:49	B	No meter. The piano seems to be engaged in a meditative improvisation, as if it is dreaming up the music to come.
1:45		Orchestral instruments suggest a slow *duple meter?* Not for long.
2:24	C	Slow *triple meter*
3:47		*Ritardando* (getting slower)
3:56	D	Fast *triple meter,* marchlike (note one or two syncopated notes)
4:26		Faster *triple meter*

Choral singing, the route by which millions of people come to know and love music.

If the successive pitches of a scale are sounded, one after another—say, running up the white keys on a keyboard—there comes a point at which the pitch seems in some sense to "duplicate" an earlier pitch, but at a higher level. This new pitch does not sound identical to the old one, but somehow the two sounds are very similar. They blend extremely well; they almost seem to melt into each other.

What causes the phenomenon of octaves? Recall from Chapter 1 that when strings vibrate to produce sound, they vibrate in partials; that is, not only along their full length but also in halves and other fractions (page 10). A vibrating string that is exactly half as long as another will *reinforce* the longer string's strongest partial. This reinforcement causes the duplication effect of octaves.

As strings go, so go vocal cords: When men and women sing along together, they automatically sing in octaves, duplicating each other's singing an octave or two apart. If you ask them, they will say they are singing "the same song"—not many will think of adding "at different octave levels."

As a result of the phenomenon of octaves, the full continuous range of pitches that exists in nature (and that is covered, for example, by a siren starting low and going up higher and higher) falls into a series of "duplicating" segments. Human ears are able to detect about ten of these octave segments. Two or three octaves is a normal range for most instruments and voices (from the low *bass* voice to the medium-low *tenor*, medium-high *alto*, and high *soprano*). A large pipe organ covers all ten octaves and a piano covers about seven. Two octaves are shown in our next diagram.

The Diatonic Scale

The set of seven pitches originally used in Western music is called the **diatonic scale**. Dating from ancient Greek times, it is still in use today. When the first of the seven pitches is repeated at a higher duplicating pitch, the total is eight—hence the name *octave,* meaning "eight span."

Anyone who knows the series *do re mi fa sol la ti do* is at home with the diatonic scale. You can count out the octave for yourself starting with the first *do* as *one* and ending with the second *do* as *eight*. The set of white keys on a keyboard plays this scale. Shown below is a keyboard and diatonic scale notes running through two octaves, marked with their conventional letter names (see page 22).

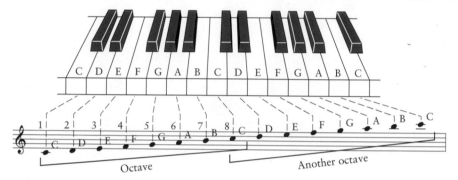

The Chromatic Scale

The diatonic scale was the original, basic scale of Western music. At a later period, five more pitches were added between certain of the seven pitches of the diatonic scale, making a total of twelve. This is the **chromatic scale**, represented by the complete set of white and black keys on a keyboard.

However, the chromatic scale did not make the diatonic scale obsolete. For centuries Western composers used the chromatic scale freely while favoring the diatonic scale that is embedded in it. Keyboards reflect this practice, with their chromatic notes colored differently from the diatonic ones, set back and thinner. (On medieval church organs, designed to accommodate the diatonic scale only, the keyboards had no "black notes," or at most just one.)

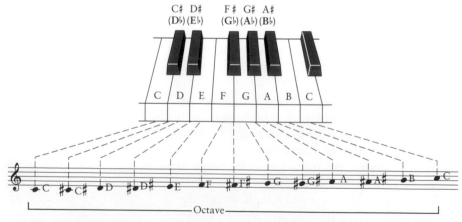

These extra pitches caused a problem for musical notation. The pitches of the diatonic scale are indicated on the lines and spaces of the staff; there are no positions in between, so symbols such as those shown to the right were introduced. B♭ stands for B **flat**, the pitch inserted between A and B; C♯ stands for C **sharp**, the pitch between C and D, and so on.

Intervals (II):
Half Steps and Whole Steps

As previously noted, the difference, or distance, between any two pitches is called the interval between them. Look at the chromatic scale in the diagram on page 18. Besides the C-to-C octave interval marked with a bracket, eleven other kinds of intervals exist between C and the other notes of the scale.

For our purposes, there are only two additional interval types that need be considered:

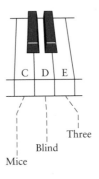

֍ The smallest interval is the **half step**, or semitone, which is the distance between any two successive notes of the chromatic scale. ("Step" is a name for small intervals.) On a keyboard, a half step is the interval between the closest adjacent notes, white or black. The distance from E to F is a half step; so is the distance from F to F sharp (F♯), G to A flat (A♭), and so on.

As the smallest interval in regular use, the half step is also the smallest that most people can "hear" easily and identify. Many tunes, such as "The Battle Hymn of the Republic," end with two half steps, one half step going down and then the same one going up again ("His truth is *march-ing on*").

֍ The **whole step**, or whole tone, is equivalent to two half steps: D to E, E to F♯, F♯ to G♯, and so on. "Three Blind Mice" starts with two whole steps, going down.

The chromatic scale consists exclusively of half steps. Therefore—though this may seem rather abstract—the chromatic scale can be described as "symmetrical," in the sense that one can start on any of its pitches and sing up or down the scale by half steps with exactly the same effect as if one had started anywhere else. The diatonic scale is *not* symmetrical in this sense because it includes both half steps and whole steps. Between B and C and between E and F, the interval is a half step, but between the other pairs of adjacent notes the interval is twice as big—a whole step. We come back to this point in the discussion of **mode** on page 32.

Music is made out of these scales, and the diatonic and chromatic scales differ in the intervals between their constituent pitches—hence the importance of intervals. In the diagram below, the two scales are lined up in order to show the differences in their interval structure.

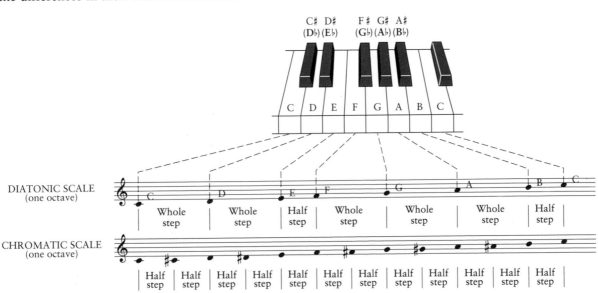

A pioneer of modern design, the German-American painter Josef Albers (1888–1976) produced twenty-seven of these wonderful treble clefs, all in different color combinations.

Scales and Instruments

Until fairly recently, Western music used the twelve pitches of the chromatic scale, duplicated through all the octaves, and in principle no other pitches. Features of many instruments are designed to produce these particular pitches exactly: frets on guitars, carefully measured holes in flutes, and the tuned sets of strings of harps and pianos.

Other instruments, such as the violin and the slide trombone, have a more continuous range of pitches available to them (as does a police siren or the human voice). In mastering these instruments, one of the first tasks is learning to pick out exactly the right pitches. This is called *playing in tune;* singing in tune is a big concern for vocalists, too.

It is true that many instrumentalists and all singers regularly perform certain notes slightly out of tune for important and legitimate artistic effects. "Blue" notes in jazz are an example. However, these "off" pitches are only small, temporary deviations from the main pitches of the scale—the same twelve pitches that, on keyboard instruments, are absolutely fixed.

bedfordstmartins.com/listen
▶ Tutorials

INTERLUDE A: Musical Notation

Many cultures around the world employ different notations for writing their music down. It is never necessary, obviously, to read these notations in order to understand the music or to love it; indeed, many cultures have no notation at all. However, written music examples can help clarify many points about musical style—even ones not written down by their creators—and it will help if you can learn to follow the music examples in this book in an approximate way. The following brief survey of Western musical notation can be used for study or review or reference.

As we have seen in our discussion of musical elements, *time* and *pitch* are really the only ones that can be specified (and therefore notated) with any precision. Think of pitch and time as coordinates of a graph on which music is going to be plotted. The resulting pitch/ time grid is quite close to actual musical notation, as shown in the diagrams below.

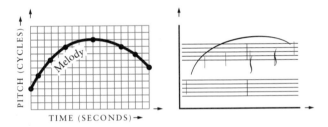

Notes and Rests

The longest note in common use is the *whole note* (o). A half note (♩) lasts for half the time of a whole note, a quarter note (♩) lasts for a quarter of the time, an eighth note (♪) for an eighth, a sixteenth (♬) for a sixteenth, and so on. (We are dealing here with proportional lengths; how long any note lasts in absolute time depends on the tempo: see page 15).

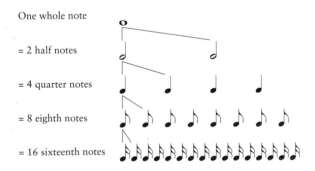

One whole note

= 2 half notes

= 4 quarter notes

= 8 eighth notes

= 16 sixteenth notes

When the shorter notes come in groups, they can also be notated as shown at the top of the next column.

The *flags*—they look more like pennants—at the sides of the note *stems* have been connected into horizontal *beams* for easier reading:

Rests   To make rhythms, composers use not only sounds but also short silences called *rests*. The diagram below shows the relation between rests, which are equivalent in duration to their corresponding notes. (Compare the whole-and half-note rests, which are slugs beneath or atop one of the lines of the staff.)

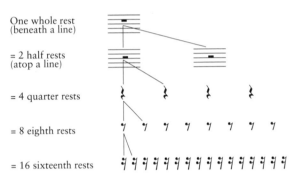

One whole rest (beneath a line)

= 2 half rests (atop a line)

= 4 quarter rests

= 8 eighth rests

= 16 sixteenth rests

The shorter rests have their own sort of flags. As with notes, more flags can be added to rests, with each flag cutting the time value in half. Thus, three flags on a rest (𝄾) make it a thirty-second rest.

Rhythmic Notation

Beyond the notation of basic notes and rests, a number of other conventions are necessary to indicate the combining of notes and rests into actual rhythms.

Dotted Notes and Dotted Rhythms   A dot placed after a note or rest lengthens its duration by 50 percent. Thus a dotted half note lasts as long as a half note plus a quarter note: ♩. = ♩ + ♩ And a dotted quarter-note rest equals a quarter plus an eighth: 𝄽. = 𝄽 + 𝄾 Even simple tunes, such as "Yankee Doodle," make use of the dot convention.

A *dotted rhythm* is one consisting of dotted (long) notes alternating with short ones:

Ties   Two notes of the same pitch can be connected by means of a curved line called a *tie*. This means they are played continuously, as though they were one note of the combined duration. Any number of notes of the same pitch can be tied together.

Ties

Beware: The same sort of curved line is also used to connect notes that are *not* of the same pitch. In this case it means that they are to be played smoothly, one following the next without the slightest break (*legato* or "bound" playing). These curved lines are called *slurs*.

Slurs: legato

To indicate that notes are to be played in an especially detached fashion (*staccato*), dots are placed above or below them.

Staccato dots

Triplets Three notes bracketed together and marked with a 3 (♩ ♩ ♩) are called a *triplet*. The three notes take exactly the same time that would normally be taken by two. A quarter-note triplet has the same duration as two ordinary quarter notes: ♩ ♩ ♩ = ♩ ♩

The convention is occasionally extended to groups of five notes, seven notes, etc. For an example, see page 266.

Meter: Measures and Bar Lines A *measure* (or *bar*) is the basic time unit chosen for a piece of music, corresponding to the meter of the piece (see page 12). Measures are marked in musical notation by vertical *bar lines*. Each measure covers the same time span. In the following example, the time span covered by each measure is one whole note, equivalent to two half notes (measure 1), or four quarter notes (measure 2), or eight eighth notes (measures 3, 4).

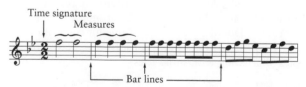

Time Signatures In the example above, the meter is indicated by means of a *time signature*. Time signatures are printed on the staffs at the beginning of pieces of music (they are not repeated on later staffs).

In spite of appearances, time signatures are not fractions. The top digit shows *how many beats* are in each measure, and the bottom digit shows *what kind of note* represents a beat. If the bottom digit is 2, the beat is represented by a half note; if 4, by a quarter note, and so on.

In our example, the 2 at the top indicates there are two beats in each measure (duple meter), and the 2 at the bottom indicates that the beats are half-note beats. This time signature can also be indicated by the sign ¢.

Pitch Notation

The letter names A B C D E F G are assigned to the original seven pitches of the diatonic scale. Then the letters are used over and over again for pitches in the duplicating octaves. Octaves are distinguished by numbers (c^1, c^2) or prime marks (A′, A″); so-called middle C (c^1) is the comfortable note that virtually any man, woman, or child can sing and that can be played by the great majority of instruments. On a keyboard, middle C sits in the middle, right under the maker's name—Casio, Yamaha, Steinway.

The Staff: Ledger Lines For the notation of pitch, notes are placed on a set of five parallel lines called a *staff*. The notes can be put on the lines of the staff, in the spaces between them, or right at the top or bottom of the staff:

Above and below the regular five lines of the staff, short extra lines can be added to accommodate a few higher and lower notes. These are called *ledger lines*.

Clefs Nothing has been said so far about which pitch each position on the staff represents. To clue us in to precise pitches, signs called *clefs* (French for "key" or "clue") are placed at the beginning of each staff. Clefs calibrate the staff; that is, they connect one of the five lines of the staff to a specific pitch.

Thus in the treble clef, or G clef (𝄞), the spiral in the middle of this antique capital G curls around line 2, counting up from the bottom of the staff. Line 2, then, is the line for the pitch G—the first G above middle C. In the bass clef, or F clef (𝄢), the two dots straddle the fourth line up. The pitch F goes on this line—the first F below middle C. Complicated! But not too hard to learn.

Adjacent lines and spaces on the staff have adjacent letter names, so we can place all the other pitches on the staff in relation to the fixed points marked by the clefs:

D E F G A B C D E F G   F G A B C D E F G A B

There are other clefs, but these two are the most common. Used in conjunction, they accommodate the maximum span of pitches without overlapping. The treble and bass clef staffs fit together as shown in Figure 1 below.

The notation of six A's, covering five octaves, requires two staffs and seven ledger lines (see Figure 2).

Sharps and Flats; Naturals The pitches produced by the black keys on the piano are not given letter names of their own. (This is a consequence of the way they arose in history; see page 18.) Nor do they get their own individual lines or spaces on the staffs. The pitch in between A and B is called A sharp (or A♯, using the conventional sign for a sharp), meaning "higher than A." It can also be called B flat (B♭), meaning "lower than B." In musical notation, the signs ♯ and ♭ are placed on the staff just *before* the note that is to be sharped or flatted.

Which of these two terms is used depends partly on convenience, partly on convention, and partly on theoretical considerations that do not concern us here. In the example below, the third note, A♯, sounds just like the B♭ later in the measure, but for technical reasons the composer (Béla Bartók) notated it differently.

The original pitches of the diatonic scale, played on the white keys of the piano, are called "natural." If it is necessary to cancel a sharp or a flat within a measure and to indicate that the natural note should be played instead, the natural sign is placed before a note (♮♩) or after a letter (A♮) to show this. The following example shows A sharp and G sharp being canceled by natural signs:

Key Signatures In musical notation, it is a convention that a sharp or flat placed before a note will also affect any later appearance of that same note *in the same measure* — but not in the next measure.

There is also a way of specifying that certain sharps or flats are to be applied throughout an entire piece, in every measure, and in every octave. Such sharps and flats appear on the staffs at the very beginning of the piece, even prior to the time signature, and at the beginning of each staff thereafter. They constitute the *key signature*:

is equivalent to:

Scores

Music for a melody instrument such as a violin or a trumpet is written on one staff; keyboard instruments require two—one staff for the right hand, another for the left hand. Music for two or more voices or instruments, choirs, bands, and orchestras is written in *scores*. In scores, each instrument and voice that has its own independent music gets its own staff. Simultaneously sounding notes and measure lines are aligned vertically. In general, high-sounding instruments go on top, the low ones on the bottom.

Shown on page 24 is a page from Mozart's "Jupiter" Symphony, with arrows pointing to the various details of notation that have been explained above.

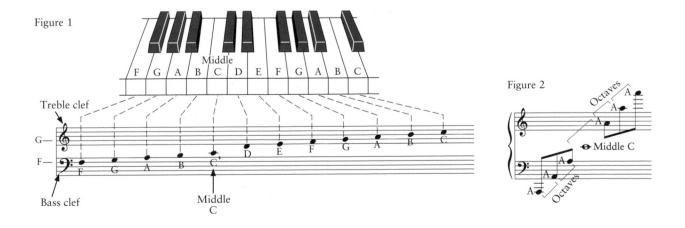

Figure 1

Figure 2

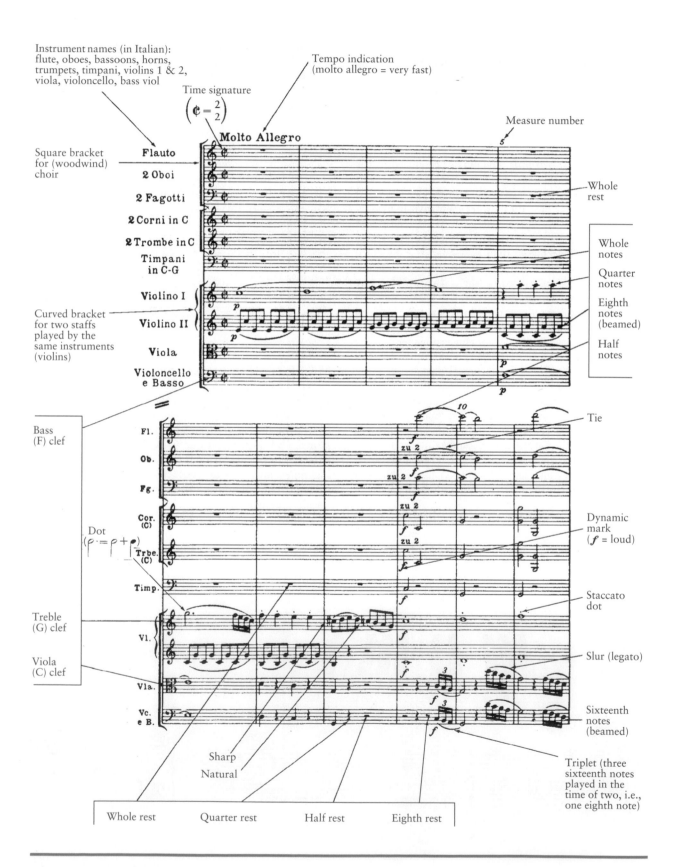

CHAPTER 3

The Structures of Music

In this chapter we take up musical concepts that combine the basic elements discussed in Chapters 1 and 2. Listening to an actual piece of music, we obviously don't experience its rhythm, pitch, tone color, and dynamics in isolation from one another. Rhythms, pitches, and the rest are seldom experienced one at a time. Rather, music consists of simple and complex "structures" built from these elements.

1 Melody

A **melody** is an organized series of pitches. Think for a moment, if you can, of pitch and time as the two coordinates of a graph on which music is going to be plotted. A series of single pitches played in a certain rhythm will appear as dots, high or low, on the pitch/time grid, and the dots can be connected by a line (see the marginal diagram). Musicians commonly speak of "melodic line" (or simply "line") in this connection.

Just as an actual line in a painting or a drawing can possess character — can strike the viewer as forceful, graceful, or tentative — so can a melodic line. A melody in which each note is higher than the last can seem to soar; a low note can feel like a setback; a long series of repeated notes on the same pitch can seem to wait ominously. The listener develops a real interest in how the line of a satisfactory melody is going to come out.

In such a melody, the notes seem to be holding together in a meaningful, interesting way — interesting, and also emotional. Of all music's structures, melody is the one that moves people the most, that seems to evoke human sentiment most directly. Familiar melodies register simple qualities of feeling instantly and strongly. These qualities vary widely: martial in "The Battle Hymn of the Republic," mournful in "Yesterday," serene and assured in "Amazing Grace," extroverted and cheerful in "Happy Birthday."

Tunes

A simple, easily singable, catchy melody such as a folk song, or a dance, or a Christmas carol is a **tune**. A tune is a special kind of melody. *Melody* is a term that includes tunes, but also much else.

"The Star-Spangled Banner," which everyone knows, illustrates the general characteristics of tunes. See the box on the next page.

❝ Always remember that in listening to a piece of music you must hang on to the melodic line. It may disappear momentarily, withdrawn by the composer, in order to make its presence more powerfully felt when it reappears. But reappear it surely will . . ."

Aaron Copland, *What to Listen For in Music*

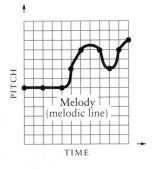

25

Characteristics of Tunes

The best way to grasp the characteristics of tunes is by singing one you know, either out loud or in your head, or along with your MP3 player.

❡ *Division into Phrases* Tunes fall naturally into smaller sections, called **phrases**. This is, in fact, true of all melodies, but with tunes the division into phrases is particularly clear and sharp.

In tunes with words (that is, songs), phrases tend to coincide with poetic lines. Most lines in a song lyric end with a rhyming word and a punctuation mark such as a comma. These features clarify the musical phrase divisions:

> And the rockets' red *glare,*
> The bombs bursting in *air*

Singing a song requires breathing—and the natural tendency is to breathe at the end of phrases. You may not need to breathe after phrase 1 of our national anthem, but you'd better not wait any longer than phrase 2:

Oh _ say can you see   By the dawn's ear-ly light

❡ *Balance between Phrases* In many tunes, all the phrases are 2, 4, or 8 measures long. (The *measure,* or bar, is the basic time unit of music; see page 22.) Blues tunes, for example, usually consist of three four-measure phrases, hence the term *twelve-bar blues.*

Most phrases of "The Star-Spangled Banner" are two measures long (see phrase 1 and phrase 2, above). But one phrase broadens out to four measures, with a fine effect: "Oh say, does that star-spangled banner yet wave." You don't want to breathe in the middle of this long phrase.

Other phrase lengths—three measures, five, and others—can certainly occur in a tune and make for welcome contrast. For a good tune, the main requirement is that we sense a balance between the phrases, in terms of phrase lengths and in other terms, too, so that taken together the phrases add up to a well-proportioned whole.

❡ *Parallelism and Contrast* Balance between phrases can be strengthened by means of *parallelism.* For example, phrases can be exactly parallel except for the words ("Oh, say can you see," "Whose broad stripes and bright stars"). Others have the same rhythm but different pitches ("Oh say can you see," "By the dawn's early light").

Sometimes phrases have the same general *pattern of pitches,* but one phrase is slightly higher or lower than the other ("And the rockets' red glare," "The bombs bursting in air"). Such duplication of a phrase at two or more different pitch levels, called **sequence,** occurs frequently in music, and is a hallmark of certain musical styles.

Composers also take care to make some phrases *contrast* with their neighbors—one phrase short, another

long, or one phrase low, another high (perhaps even *too* high, at "O'er the land of the *free*"). A tune with some parallel and some contrasting phrases will seem to have logic, or coherence, and yet will avoid monotony.

❡ *Climax and Cadence* A good tune has *form:* a clear, purposeful beginning, a feeling of action in the middle, and a firm sense of winding down at the end.

Many tunes have a distinct high point, or **climax,** which their earlier portions seem to be heading toward. Feelings rise as voices soar; a melodic high point is always an emotional high point. The climax of our national anthem foregrounds what was felt to be the really crucial word in it—"free." Patriot Francis Scott Key put that word in that place (Key wrote the words of "The Star-Spangled Banner"—the words only, adapted to an older melody).

Then the later part of the tune relaxes from this climax, until it reaches a solid stopping place at the end. Emotionally, this is a point of relaxation and satisfaction. In a less definite way, the music also stops at earlier points in the tune—or, if it does not fully stop, at least seems to pause. The term for these interim stopping or pausing places is **cadence.**

Composers can write cadences with all possible shades of solidity and finality. "And the home of the brave" is a very final-sounding cadence; "That our flag was still there" has an interim feeling. The art of making cadences is one of the most subtle and basic processes in musical composition.

LISTENING EXERCISE 4

Melody and Tune

Division into phrases, parallelism and *contrast* between phrases, *sequence, climax,* and *cadence:* These are some characteristics of tunes that we have observed in "The Star-Spangled Banner." They are not just inert characteristics—they are what make the tune work, and they are present in tunes of all kinds. Our example is a song by George Gershwin from the Depression era, which was also the jazz era: "Who Cares?" from the musical comedy *Of Thee I Sing* (1932).

In "The Star-Spangled Banner" the *climax* matches the text perfectly at "free." Here "jubilee" makes a good match for the climax, and a melodic *sequence* fits the words "I care for you/you care for me" neatly. "Who cares?" comes at 0:57 on our recording by the great jazz singer Ella Fitzgerald, after an introduction (called the *verse*) typical of such songs—a sort of subsidiary tune, with words that will not be repeated.

0:12	**Verse:** Let it rain and thunder . . . (eight more lines)	Includes a long *sequence*
0:48		Tempo changes
0:57	**Tune:** Who cares if the sky cares to fall in the sea?	First phrase of the tune
	Who cares what banks fail in Yonkers?	*Contrasting* phrase
	Long as you've got a kiss that conquers.	*Parallel* phrase—starts like the preceding, ends higher
	Why should I care? Life is one long jubilee,	Threefold *sequence* ("should I care/life is one/jubilee")
		Climax on "jubilee"
	So long as I care for you and you care for me.	Free *sequence* ("I care for you"/ "You care for me")—*cadence*
1:55	**Tune** played by the jazz band, today's "big band" (with saxophone *breaks:* see page 396)	

Motives and Themes

Tunes are relatively short; longer pieces, such as symphonies, may have tunes embedded in them, but they also contain other musical material. Two terms are frequently encountered in connection with melody in longer pieces of music: <u>motive</u> and <u>theme</u>.

A *motive* is a distinctive fragment of melody, distinctive enough so that it will be easily recognized when it returns again and again within a long composition. Motives are shorter than tunes, shorter even than phrases of tunes; they can be as short as two notes. Probably the most famous motive in all music is the four-note DA-DA-DA-**DAAA** motive in Beethoven's Fifth Symphony. It is heard literally hundreds of times in the symphony, sometimes up front and sometimes as a restless element in the background.

DA DA DA   DAAA

The second term, *theme*, is the most general term for the basic subject matter of longer pieces of music. *Theme* is another name for "topic": The themes or topics of a political speech are the main points that a politician announces, repeats, develops, and hammers home. A composer treats musical themes in much the same way.

Since the term *theme* refers to the *function*, not the *nature*, of musical material, in principle almost anything can serve as a theme. A melody can perform this function, or a phrase, a motive, even a distinctive tone color. It depends on the kind of music. The theme of the last movement of Beethoven's Ninth Symphony is the tune we will hear several times on the DVD, track 15 (see page 31).

The theme of Beethoven's Fifth Symphony consists of the DA-DA-DA-**DAAA** motive played in sequence. Many of the themes of Richard Wagner's operas are closely identified with a particular tone color and instrument (the love theme for cellos and double basses, in the excerpt discussed on page 290).

2 Harmony

A single melodic line in time is enough to qualify as music: sometimes, indeed, as great music. When people sing in the shower and when parents sing to their babies they are producing melody, and that is all, to everyone's full satisfaction. The same was true of the early Christian Church, whose music, Gregorian chant, consisted of over two thousand different (sometimes only slightly different) melodies, sung without instruments or any kind of harmonizing.

Today, however—and this is the outcome of a long and complicated historical development—it seems very natural to us to hear melodies together with other sounds, which we call *accompaniments*. A folk singer singing and playing a guitar is performing a song and its accompaniment. In church, the congregation sings the hymns; the organist plays the accompaniment.

The folk singer uses a number of standard groupings of simultaneous pitches that practice has shown are sure to work well in combination. These groupings are called <u>chords</u>. Imaginative players will also discover nonstandard chords and unexpected successions of chords in order to enrich their accompaniments. The song is said to be <u>harmonized</u>; the changing chords provide a sort of constantly shifting sound-background for the song.

Any melody can be harmonized in different ways using different chords, and the overall effect of the music depends to a great extent on the nature of these chords, or the <u>harmony</u> in general. We can instinctively sense the differences in harmony between Mozart and Wagner, or between New Orleans jazz and salsa. However, to characterize the differences requires technical language, and we shall not make the attempt in this book.

Melody and harmony: singer Joni Mitchell playing the Appalachian dulcimer.

Consonance and Dissonance

A pair of terms used in discussions of harmony is <u>consonance</u> and <u>dissonance</u>, meaning (roughly speaking) chords that sound at rest and those that sound tense, respectively. *Discord* is another term for dissonance. These qualities depend on the kinds of intervals (see pages 16–19) that are sounding simultaneously to make up these chords. Octaves are the most consonant of intervals. Half steps are among the most dissonant.

In everyday language, "discord" implies something unpleasant; discordant human relationships are to be avoided. But music does not avoid dissonance in its technical meaning, for a little discord supplies the subtle tensions that are essential to make music flow along. The listener may not know it, but a dissonant chord leaves a feeling of expectation; it requires a consonant chord following it to complete the gesture and to make the music come to a point of stability. This is called *resolution;* the dissonance is said to be <u>resolved</u>. Without dissonance, music would be like food without salt or spices.

Important cadences—say, at the ends of pieces of music—are almost always helped by the use of dissonance. Movement from tension (dissonance) to rest (consonance) contributes centrally to a sense of finality and satisfaction.

> “ Medicine, to produce health, must know disease; music, to produce harmony, must know discord."
>
> *Plutarch, c. 46–120 C.E.*

3 Texture

<u>Texture</u> is the term used to refer to the blend of the various sounds and melodic lines occurring simultaneously in music. The word is adopted from textiles, where it refers to the weave of the various threads—loose or tight, even or mixed. A cloth such as tweed or denim, for instance, leaves the different threads clearly visible. In fine silk or percale, the weave is so tight and smooth that the constituent threads can be impossible to detect.

Thinking again of the pitch/time graph on page 21, we can see that it is possible to plot more than one pitch for every time slot. Melody exists in the horizontal dimension, texture in the vertical dimension. For the moment, we leave the lower dots (below the melody) unconnected.

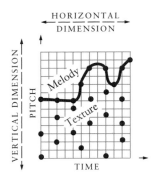

Monophony

Monophony is the term for the simplest texture, a single unaccompanied melody: Gregorian chant; singing in the shower; "Row, Row, Row Your Boat" before the second person comes in:

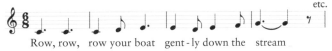

Simple as this texture is, some very beautiful and sophisticated **monophonic** music has been composed, just as artists have done wonderful things with line drawings: See page 335.

Heterophony

A special kind of monophonic texture, not much used in the European classical tradition but more prominent elsewhere, is called **heterophony**. This is a texture in which subtly different versions of a single melody are presented simultaneously. We will hear several examples of heterophony in the non-European musics discussed throughout this book.

Homophony

When there is only one melody of real interest and it is combined with other sounds, the texture is called **homophonic**. A harmonized melody is an example of homophonic texture; for instance, one person singing the tune of "Row, Row, Row Your Boat" while playing chords on a guitar:

We might indicate a chord on the pitch/time graph by a vertical box enclosing the dots. The sum of these boxes represents the harmony. Homophony can be thought of as a tight, smooth texture—like silk, among the textiles.

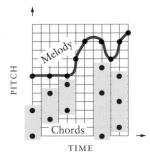

Polyphony

When two or more melodies are played or sung simultaneously, the texture is described as **polyphonic**. In polyphony, the melodies are felt to be independent and of approximately equal interest. The whole is more than the sum of the parts, however; the way the melodies play off against one another makes for the possibility of greater richness and interest than if they were played singly. In the textile analogy, polyphony would be compared to a rough texture where the strands are all perceptible, such as denim.

It's also important to recognize that polyphonic music automatically has harmony. For at every moment in time, on every beat, the multiple horizontal melodies create vertical chords; those chords make harmony.

A word often used for polyphonic texture is *contrapuntal,* which comes from the word **counterpoint,** the technique of writing two or more melodies that fit together. Strictly speaking, polyphony refers to the texture and counterpoint to the technique of producing that texture—one *writes* counterpoint to *produce* polyphony—but in practice the two terms are used interchangeably.

Imitation

In fact polyphonic texture, like so many other musical elements, cannot be categorized with any precision. It is impossible to distinguish all the kinds of polyphony found in European music, to say nothing of the enormously intricate kinds in music from other societies.

One useful and important distinction, however, is between *imitative polyphony* and *non-imitative polyphony.* **Imitative polyphony** results when the various lines sounding together use the same or fairly similar melodies, with one coming in shortly after another. The simplest example of imitative polyphony is a round, such as "Row, Row, Row Your Boat" or "Frère Jacques"; the richest kind is a fugue (see Chapter 9). When people sing a round, by singing the same tune at staggered time intervals, the result is imitative polyphony:

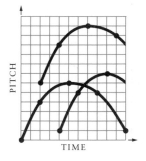

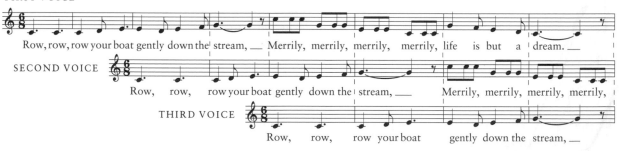

Non-imitative polyphony occurs when the melodies are essentially different from one another. An example that many will know is the typical texture of a New Orleans jazz band, with the trumpet playing the main tune flanked top and bottom by the clarinet and the trombone playing exhilarating melodies of their own. Here is a made-up example of non-imitative polyphony, with a new melody added above the tune of "Row, Row, Row Your Boat":

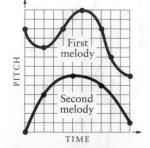

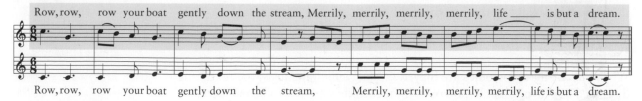

LISTENING EXERCISE 5

Texture

15, 16

A famous passage from Beethoven furnishes a clear example of *monophonic, polyphonic,* and *homophonic textures*—the initial presentation of the so-called Joy Theme in Symphony No. 9, the "Choral" Symphony. The theme, a tune known around the world, takes its name from the words it is set to, an enthusiastic ode to the joy that comes from human freedom, companionship, and reverence for the Deity. The words are sung by soloists and a chorus.

But before anyone sings, the theme is played several times by the orchestra, in a way that suggests that joy is emerging out of nothingness into its full realization. Beginning with utterly simple monophony, and growing successively higher and louder, it is enriched by *polyphony* and then reaches its grand climax in *homophony*.

15	0:00	Joy Theme	Low register	*Monophony:* a single melodic line; cellos and double basses playing together, with no accompaniment whatsoever
	0:49	Theme	An octave higher	*Polyphony, non-imitative:* the theme with two lines of *counterpoint,* in low strings (cello) and a mellow wind instrument (bassoon)
	1:36	Theme	Two octaves higher	
	2:21	Theme	Three octaves higher	*Homophony:* full orchestra with trumpets prominent

Our example of *imitative polyphony* comes from the *Symphony of Psalms,* another symphony with chorus, a major work by the twentieth-century composer Igor Stravinsky. For brief characterizations of the instruments that play the contrapuntal lines, see Interlude B starting on page 37.

	00	A slow, winding melody, unaccompanied, played by a wind instrument (oboe)
	25	The same melody enters in another instrument (flute), as the oboe continues with new material; this produces two-part *imitative counterpoint.*
	58	Third entry, second flute plays in a lower register—three-part counterpoint
	19	Fourth entry, second oboe—four-part counterpoint

Fugue in Two Colors, an imaginative portrayal of counterpoint, by the modernist artist Franz Kupka (1871–1957). Fugue is one of the most contrapuntal of musical genres: See page 142.

4 Tonality and Modality

Tonality and modality are aspects of harmony, and as such they could logically have been taken up at an earlier point in this chapter. We have deferred them till last because, even more than the other basic structures of music, they require careful explanation.

Tonality

We start with a basic fact about melodies and tunes: Melodies nearly always give a sense of focusing around a single "home" pitch that feels more important than do all the other members of the scale. Usually this is **do** in the *do re mi fa sol la ti do* scale (C D E F G A B C). This pitch feels fundamental, and on it the melody seems to come to rest most naturally. The other notes in the melody all sound close or distant, dissonant or consonant, in reference to the fundamental note, and some of them may actually seem to lean or lead toward it.

This homing instinct that we sense in melodies can be referred to in the broadest terms as the feeling of **tonality**. The music in question is described as **tonal**. The home pitch (*do*) is called the *tonic pitch,* or simply the **tonic**.

The easy way to identify the tonic is to sing the whole melody through, because the last note is almost invariably *it*. Thus "The Star-Spangled Banner" ends on its tonic, *do:* "and the home of the *brave*." (It also includes the tonic pitch in two different octaves as its first two accented notes: "Oh, *say* can you *see*.") An entire piece of music, as well as just a short melody, can give this feeling of focusing on a home pitch and wanting to end there.

Modality: Major and Minor

Turn back to page 18 and the diagram for the diatonic scale, the basic scale of Western music. This diagram, of course, showed only a portion of a longer scale extending all the way up the octaves, from the lowest limits of hearing to the highest. Our portion, covering two octaves, started from C because most melodies are oriented around C (*do*), as we've just explained.

The diagram below shows another portion of the diatonic scale, starting on A (*la*), because another class of melodies in Western music is oriented around A, not C:

> **6** The difficulty of describing the facts of tonality is not the difficulty of describing red to the color-blind. It is the difficulty of describing red to anybody; you can only point to red things and hope that other people see them as you do. It is even more like trying to describe the taste of a peach. . . ."
>
> *Sir Donald Tovey, pianist, conductor, and educator, 1935*

If you look carefully at the diagram you will see that, moving up through the octave from C to C, you encounter a different sequence of whole- and half-steps than you do moving from A to A. This difference gives melodies oriented around A a quality different from those oriented around C. The term for these different ways of centering or organizing the diatonic scale is **modality**; the different tonic pitches are said to determine the different **modes** of music. We will discuss the actual listening experience of the modes in a moment. Music with the *do* center is in the **major mode.** Music with the *la* orientation is in the **minor mode.**

Keys

Mode and key are concepts that are often confused. Let us see if we can clarify them.

We have just seen how the two modes, the major with its tonic or home note on C and the minor on A, are derived from the diatonic scale (and this was the way it happened in history). However, if you avail yourself of all the twelve notes of the *chromatic* scale, you can construct both the major and the minor modes starting from any note at all. Whichever note you choose as tonic, starting from there you can pick out the correct sequence of half steps and whole steps. (This is because the chromatic scale includes all possible half steps and whole steps.) If C is the starting point, the major mode comes out all on the white notes; if the same mode is started from D, two black notes are required, and so on.

Thanks to the chromatic scale, then, major and minor modes can be constructed starting on any pitch. These different positions for the modes are called **keys.** If the major mode is positioned on C, the music is said to be in the key of C major, or just "in C"; positioned on D, the key is D major. Likewise we have the keys of C minor, D minor, and—as there are twelve pitches in the chromatic scale—a grand total of twenty-four different major and minor keys.

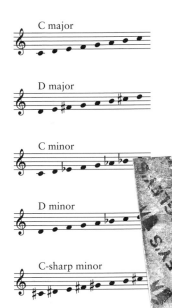

Hearing the Major and Minor Modes

On paper, it is easiest to show the difference between major and minor if we compare a major and minor key that has the same tonic. So yet another diagram, below, compares C major with C minor. C minor is derived by duplicating, above the pitch C, the minor-mode arrangement of whole- and half-steps that we saw in the diagram on page 19.

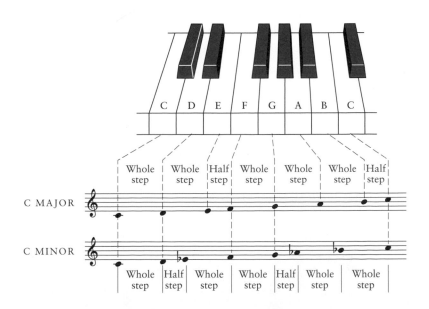

Is it fair to represent the major and minor modes by comedy and tragedy masks? Yes, but only in a very general sense—there are many "delicate nuances," as the composer Robert Schumann once put it.

The difference between the modes is easy to see: Three of the scale degrees are lower in the minor (hence the term *minor,* of course). The arrangement of intervals is not the same when you sing up the scale, and this in turn makes a great difference in the feel of the modes.

Easy to see—but *hearing* the difference is another matter. This comes easily to some listeners, less easily to others. As a result of the three lower scale degrees, music in the minor mode tends to sound more subdued, more clouded than music in the major. It is often said that major sounds cheerful and minor sounds sad, and this is true enough in a general way; but there are many exceptions, and in any case people can have different ideas about what constitutes sadness and cheerfulness in music.

Learning to distinguish the major and minor modes requires comparative listening. Listen especially for the third scale degree up from the tonic. "Joshua Fit the Battle of Jericho," "Summertime," and "We Three Kings of Orient Are" are all in the minor mode. Singing them through, we should come to recognize the characteristic minor-mode sound involving the third scale degree at the final cadence.

Joshua Fit the Battle of Jericho

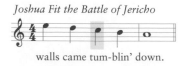

walls came tum-blin' down.

Summertime

don't ___ you cry. ___

We Three Kings

fol-low-ing yon - der star.

Compare this with the third note up from the tonic at the end of major-mode songs such as "Happy Birthday," "Row, Row, Row Your Boat," "The Star-Spangled Banner," and many others. It sounds brighter, more positive.

Happy Birthday

Hap-py birth-day to you!

Row, Row, Row Your Boat

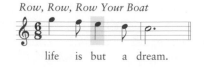

life is but   a dream.

The Star-Spangled Banner

home   of   the   brave.

And here is the whole of "Row, Row, Row Your Boat" once again — but this time in an altered version, with the mode switched from major to minor. Can you sing it?

Hearing Keys and Modulation

The major and minor modes can be said to differ from one another intrinsically, for in each mode the pitches form their own special set of intervals and interval relationships. As we have seen, C major and C minor, while sharing the same central or tonic note, have their own individual arrangements of half- and whole-step intervals.

Different keys, however, merely entail the same set of intervals moved to a new position within the pitch continuum. This is a significant difference, but not an intrinsic one. First base is different from second base, but only because the same sort of bag has been put in a significant new place.

As for actually *hearing* keys — that is, recognizing the different keys — for some listeners this presents an even greater problem than hearing modality, though to others it comes more easily. The latter are the fortunate ones born with perfect pitch, the innate faculty of identifying pitches the way most people can identify colors.

However, this is not the great boon of nature it is sometimes thought to be. The important thing is not to be able to identify keys in themselves, but rather to be able to hear when keys change. For changing the key of music changes its mood or the way it feels; generations of composers have used this resource for some of their most powerful effects, as we shall see. Such changes of key — that is, changes of the tonic or home note — are called **modulations**. In large compositions we can hear them whether or not we were born with perfect pitch.

Indeed, we hear modulations even in shorter compositions. If you know "The Twelve Days of Christmas," you will remember the modulation at the words "Five gold rings." (Try singing this cumulative carol all the way through leaving out the fifth gift with its modulation — the result is utter monotony.) In another Christmas carol, "Deck the Halls," modulation causes an agreeable little lift at the end of the third line, "Don we now our gay apparel, *Fa-la la, la-la la, la la la.*"

At hard-fought baseball and basketball games the organist plays a little musical figure over and over, higher and higher, louder and louder. This is brute-force modulation, and like all modulations, it changes the mood and the way you feel — it makes you feel *excited*.

The structures of music we have discussed in this chapter apply particularly to Western classical music. Two points need to be made regarding other musical traditions, outside of the European orbit.

First, questions of melody, texture, harmony, and tonality are fully as important in understanding most of these other musics as they are in understanding music closer to home. This will be clear from our discussions in the Global Perspectives sections throughout the book. But second, each musical tradition tends to have its own characteristic ways of approaching the structures of music. What counts as a tune, which textures are preferred above others, how

LISTENING EXERCISE 6

Mode and Key

Modality is probably most obvious when you hear a minor-mode melody (or phrase of melody) and then hear it with the mode changed to major. A short passage from the String Quartet in A Minor by Franz Schubert is a lovely illustration of this change.

17 | 0:00   *pp* A melancholy melody in the *minor mode.* Listen to the first violin above the rustling accompaniment in the lower string instruments.

0:47   The beginning of the melody returns, changed to the *major mode.*

Listen to more of the Schubert quartet for a change in *key:*

1:04   *ff* Agitated; back in the minor mode. Lower instruments alternate with the solo violin.

1:39   *p* A quiet cadence, still in the same key, but followed by *modulation*

1:56   *p* Reaching a *new key,* for a new theme. This theme is in the major mode, calm and sunny.

For a series of *modulations* to several different keys, go to a passage from Beethoven's Piano Concerto No. 5, the "Emperor" Concerto. Here the key changes stand out clearly because the modulations are carried out so brusquely — a Beethoven specialty — and also because the music in between them is harmonically quite simple.

18 | 0:00   Lively music for the piano, *f,* followed by a *f* response from the orchestra

0:28   Modulation (French horns)

New key: Similar music for piano, but *pp,* followed by the same orchestral response, *f*

1:03   Similar modulation (French horns). The music seems to be searching for a place to settle.

Another new key: piano, *p,* and orchestra, *f,* as before

1:36   The piano bursts in, *f,* in the same key but in the *minor mode.* It begins modulating to further new keys in a more complicated way than before.

tonality is asserted, which combinations of pitches are considered consonant or dissonant — all these differ widely from tradition to tradition. They may even differ from style to style within a single tradition.

As a result, the vocabulary we develop here for Western music cannot, in its most specific form, encompass all this variety. But the general issues raised in this vocabulary are issues that you will meet also in musics from around the world.

bedfordstmartins.com/listen
▶ Tutorials

INTERLUDE B: Musical Instruments

Listen to The Young Person's Guide to the Orchestra *by Benjamin Britten: See pages 54–55.*

20–25

View the orchestral performance of The Rite of Spring *by Igor Stravinsky: See page 336.*

1

Different voices and different instruments produce different tone colors, or timbres. Over the course of history and over the entire world, an enormous number of devices have been invented for making music, and the range of tone colors they can produce is almost endless.

This interlude will discuss and illustrate the instruments of Western music that make up the orchestra, and a few others. Later, in our Global Perspectives sections, we will meet many instruments from other musical traditions.

Musical instruments can be categorized into four groups: *stringed instruments* or *strings, woodwinds, brass,* and *percussion.* Musical sound, as we know, is caused by rapid vibrations. Each of the four groups of instruments produces sound vibrations in its own distinct way.

Stringed Instruments

Stringed instruments produce their sound by means of taut strings attached to a *sound box,* a hollow box containing a body of air that resonates (that is, vibrates along with the strings) to amplify the string sound.

The strings themselves can be played with a bow, as with the violin and other orchestral strings; the bow is strung tightly with horsehair, which is coated with a substance called rosin, so that the bow grips the strings to produce continuous sound. With guitars and harps, the strings are plucked or strummed by the fingers or a small pick.

Strings can be plucked on bowed instruments, too, for special effects. This is called **pizzicato**.

The Violin and Its Family The **violin** is often called the most beautiful instrument used in Western music. Also one of the most versatile of instruments, its large range covers alto and soprano registers and many much higher pitches. As a solo instrument, it can play forcefully or delicately, and it excels in both brilliant and songlike music. Violinists also play chords by bowing two or more of the four strings at once, or nearly so.

As in a guitar, the (four) violin strings are *stopped* with a finger — that is, pressed down on the neck of the violin under the strings — to shorten the string length and get different pitches (see the illustrations below). Unlike a guitar, a violin has no frets, so the player has to feel for the exact places to press.

The violin is an excellent ensemble instrument, and it blends especially well with other violins. An orchestra violin section, made up of ten or more instruments playing together, can produce a strong, yet sensitive, flexible tone. Hence the orchestra has traditionally relied on strings as a solid foundation for its composite sound.

Like most instruments, violins come in *families,* that is, in several sizes with different pitch ranges. Three members of the violin family are basic to the orchestra.

The **viola** is the tenor-range instrument, larger than a violin by several inches. It has a throaty quality in its lowest range, from middle C down an octave; yet it fits especially smoothly into accompaniment textures. The viola's highest register is powerful and intense.

The violin family: violin, viola, and cello

Violin

❡ The **cello,** short for *violoncello,* is the bass of the violin family. Cellists play seated with the instrument propped on the floor between their knees. Unlike the viola, the cello has a rich, gorgeous sound in its low register. It is a favorite solo instrument, as well as an indispensable member of the orchestra.

Bass Viol Also called **string bass, double bass,** or just **bass,** this deep instrument is used to back up the violin family in the orchestra. (However, in various details of construction the bass viol differs from members of the violin family; the bass viol actually belongs to another, older stringed instrument family, the *viol* family.)

   Played with a bow, the bass viol provides a splendid deep support for orchestral sound. The bass viol is often (in jazz, nearly always) plucked to give an especially vibrant kind of accent and to emphasize the meter.

Harp **Harps** are plucked stringed instruments with one string for each pitch available. The modern orchestral harp is a large instrument with forty-seven strings covering a range of six and a half octaves. A pedal mechanism allows the playing of chromatic (black-key) as well as diatonic (white-key) pitches.

   In most orchestral music, the swishing, watery quality of the harp is treated as a striking occasional effect rather than as a regular timbre.

Woodwind Instruments

As the name indicates, woodwind instruments were formerly made of wood, and some still are; but today certain woodwinds are made of metal. Sound in these instruments

Cellist Yo-Yo Ma—perhaps this country's preeminent instrumentalist, certainly the most versatile and most honored.

◄ Orchestral harp

Orchestras usually have two or three *oboes:* See page 40.

Flutist James Galway

Clarinetist Sabine Meyer

is created by setting up vibrations in the column of air in a tube. A series of precisely spaced holes are bored in the tube, which players open or close with their fingers or with a lever device. (This channels the air into columns of different lengths, thus producing all the different pitches of the scale.)

Of the main woodwind instruments, *flutes, clarinets,* and *oboes* have approximately the same range. All three are used in the orchestra because each has a quite distinct tone quality, and composers can obtain a variety of effects from them. It is not hard to learn to recognize and appreciate the different sounds of these woodwinds.

The Flute and Its Family The **flute** is simply a long cylinder, held horizontally; the player sets the air vibrating by blowing through a side hole. The flute is the most agile of the woodwind instruments and also the gentlest. It nonetheless stands out clearly in the orchestra when played in its high register.

❦ The **piccolo,** the small, highest member of the flute family, adds special sparkle to band and orchestral music.

❦ The **alto flute** and **bass flute**—larger and deeper flutes—are less frequently employed.

❦ The **recorder,** a different variety of flute, is blown not at the side of the tube but through a special mouthpiece at the end. Used in older orchestral music, the recorder was superseded by the horizontal, or *transverse,* flute because the latter was more agile and stronger.

In the late twentieth century recorders made a comeback for modern performances of old music using reconstructed period instruments. The instrument is also popular (in various family sizes) among musical amateurs today. The recorder is easy to learn and fun to play.

Clarinet The **clarinet** is a slightly conical tube made, usually, of ebony (a dark wood). The air column is not made to vibrate directly by blowing into the tube, as with the flute. The player gets sound by blowing on a reed—a small piece of cane fixed at one end—in much the same way as one can blow on a blade of grass held taut between the fingers. The vibrating reed vibrates the air within the clarinet tube itself.

Compared to the flute, the clarinet sounds richer and more flexible, more like the human voice. The clarinet is capable of warm, mellow tones and strident, shrill ones; it has an especially intriguing quality in its low register, below middle C.

❦ The small **E-flat clarinet** and the large **bass clarinet** are family members with a place in the modern orchestra. The tube of the bass clarinet is so long that it has to be bent back, like a thin black saxophone.

Oboe The **oboe,** pictured on page 38, also uses a reed, like the clarinet, but it is a double reed — two reeds lashed together so that the air must be forced between them. This kind of reed gives the oboe its clearly focused, crisply clean, and sometimes plaintive sound.

❦ The **English horn** is a larger, lower oboe, descending into the viola range. (Scores often give the French equivalent, *cor anglais;* in either language, the name is all wrong, since the instrument is not a horn but an oboe, and it has nothing to do with England.)

Bassoon The **bassoon** is a low (cello-range) instrument with a double reed and other characteristics similar to the oboe's. It looks somewhat bizarre: The long tube is bent

double, and the reed has to be linked to the instrument by a long, narrow pipe made of metal. Of all the double-reed woodwinds, the bassoon is the most varied in expression, ranging from the mournful to the comical.

❦ The **contrabassoon,** also called the **double bassoon,** is a very large member of the bassoon family, in the bass viol range.

Saxophone The **saxophone** is the outstanding case in the history of music of the successful invention of a new instrument family. Its inventor, the Belgian instrument maker Adolphe Sax, also developed saxhorns and other instruments. First used around 1840 in military bands, the saxophone (or "sax") is sometimes included in the modern orchestra, but it really came into its own in jazz.

Saxophones are close to clarinets in the way they produce sound. Both use single reeds. Since the saxophone tube is wider and made of brass, its tone is even mellower than that of the clarinet, yet at the same time more forceful.

Bassoon, double bass, accordion (*not* an orchestral instrument!), and violin

French horn and timpani

The long saxophone tube has a characteristic bent shape and a flaring bell, as its opening is called.

Most common are the **alto saxophone** and the **tenor saxophone.** But the big family also includes *bass, baritone, soprano,* and even *contrabass* (very low) and *sopranino* (very high) members.

Brass Instruments

The brass instruments are the loudest of all the wind instruments because of the rather remarkable way their sound is produced. The player blows into a small cup-shaped mouthpiece of metal, and this actually sets the player's lips vibrating. The lip vibration activates vibration of the air within the brass tube. This is easy to do.

All brass instruments have long tubes, and these are almost always coiled in one way or another. This is easy to do with the soft metal they are made from.

Trumpet   The **trumpet,** highest of the main brass instruments, has a bright, strong, piercing tone that provides the ultimate excitement in band and orchestral music alike. Pitch is controlled by three pistons, or valves, that connect auxiliary tubes with the main tube or disconnect them, so as to lengthen or shorten the vibrating air column.

French Horn   The **French horn** has a lower, mellower, thicker tone than the trumpet. It is capable of mysterious, romantic sounds when played softly; played loudly, it can sound like a trombone. Chords played by several French horns in harmony have a specially rich, sumptuous tone.

Trombone   The **tenor trombone** and the **bass trombone** are also pitched lower than the trumpet. The pitch is controlled by a sliding mechanism (thus the term *slide trombone*) rather than a valve or piston, as in the trumpet and French horn.

Less bright and martial in tone than the trumpet, the trombone can produce a surprising variety of sounds, ranging from an almost vocal quality in its high register to a hard, powerful blare in the low register.

Tuba   The **bass tuba** is typically used as a foundation for the trombone group in an orchestra. It is less flexible than other brass instruments. And like most other deep bass instruments, it is not favored for solo work.

Other Brass Instruments   All the brass instruments described so far are staples of both the orchestra and the band. Many other brass instruments (and even whole families of instruments) have been invented for use in marching bands and have then sometimes found their way into the orchestra.

Among these are the *cornet* and the *flügelhorn,* which resemble the trumpet; the *euphonium, baritone horn,* and *saxhorn,* which are somewhere between the French horn and the tuba; and the *sousaphone,* a handsome type of bass tuba named after the great American bandmaster and march composer, John Philip Sousa.

Finally there is the *bugle.* This simple trumpetlike instrument is very limited in the pitches it can play because

French horns

Trombone

it has no piston or valve mechanism. Buglers play "Taps" and military fanfares and not much else.

Buglers get different pitches by *overblowing,* that is, by blowing harder into the mouthpiece so as to get strong partials (see page 10). Overblowing is, indeed, a basic, important resource of all wind instruments.

Percussion Instruments

Instruments in this category produce sound by being struck (or sometimes rattled, as with the South American maraca). Some percussion instruments, such as drums and gongs, have no fixed pitch, just a striking tone color. Other percussion instruments, such as the vibraphone, have whole sets of wooden or metal elements tuned to regular scales.

Timpani The **timpani** (or *kettledrums*) are large hemispherical drums that can be tuned precisely to certain low pitches. Used in groups of two or more, timpani have the effect of "cementing" loud sounds when the whole orchestra plays, so they are the most widely used

Drum kit with cymbals

percussion instruments in the orchestra. As with most drums, players can obtain different sounds by using different kinds of drumsticks, tapping at different places on the drumhead, and so on.

Timpani are tuned by tightening the drumhead by means of screws set around the rim. During a concert, one can often see the timpani player, when there are rests in the music, leaning over the drums, tapping them quietly to hear whether the tuning is just right. Also available is a pedal mechanism to retune the timpani instantaneously.

Pitched Percussion Instruments Pitched percussion instruments are *scale instruments,* capable of playing melodies and consisting of whole sets of metal or wooden bars or plates struck with sticks or hammers. While they add unforgettable special sound effects to many compositions, they are not usually heard consistently throughout a piece, as the timpani are. They differ in their materials:

❦ The **glockenspiel** has small steel bars. It is a high instrument with a bright, penetrating sound.

❦ The **xylophone** has hardwood plates or slats. It plays as high as the glockenspiel but also lower, and it has a drier, sharper tone.

❦ The **marimba,** an instrument of African and South American origins, is a xylophone with tubular resonators under each wooden slat, making the tone much mellower.

❦ The **vibraphone** has metal plates, like a glockenspiel with a large range, and is furnished with a controllable electric resonating device. This gives the "vibes" a flexible, funky quality unlike that of any other instrument.

❦ Also like the glockenspiel, the **celesta** has steel bars, but its sound is more delicate and silvery. This instrument, unlike the others in this section, is not played directly by a percussionist wielding hammers or sticks. The hammers are activated from a keyboard; a celesta looks like a miniature upright piano.

❧ **Tubular bells,** or **chimes,** are hanging tubes that are struck with a big mallet. They sound like church bells.

Unpitched Percussion Instruments In the category of percussion instruments without a fixed pitch, the following are the most frequently found in the orchestra:

❧ **Cymbals** are concave metal plates, from a few inches to several feet in diameter. In orchestral music, pairs of large cymbals are clapped together to support climactic moments in the music with a grand clashing sound.

❧ The **triangle**—a simple metal triangle—gives out a bright tinkle when struck.

❧ The **tam-tam** is a large unpitched gong with a low, often sinister quality.

❧ The **snare drum, tenor drum,** and **bass drum** are among the unpitched drums used in the orchestra.

The Orchestra

The orchestra has changed over the centuries, just as orchestral music has. Bach's orchestra in the early 1700s was about a fifth the size of the orchestra required by ambitious composers today. (See pages 127, 177, and 248 for charts showing the makeup of the orchestra at various historical periods.)

So today's symphony orchestra has to be a fluid group. Eighty musicians or more will be on the regular roster, but some of them sit out some of the pieces on many programs. And freelancers have to be engaged for special compositions in which composers have imaginatively expanded the orchestra for their own expressive purposes. A typical large orchestra today includes the following sections, or *choirs:*

❧ *Strings:* about thirty to thirty-six violinists, twelve violists, ten to twelve cellists, and eight double basses.

❧ *Woodwinds:* two flutes and a piccolo, two clarinets and a bass clarinet, two oboes and an English horn, two bassoons and a contrabassoon.

❧ *Brass:* at least two trumpets, four French horns, two trombones, and one tuba.

❧ *Percussion:* one to four players, who between them manage the timpani and all the other percussion instruments, moving from one to the other. For unlike the violins, for example, the percussion instruments seldom have to be played continuously throughout a piece. If a composition uses a great deal of percussion—and many modern compositions do—more players will be needed.

There are several seating plans for orchestras; which is chosen depends on at least two factors. The conductor judges which arrangement makes the best sound in the particular hall. And some conductors feel they can control the orchestra better with one arrangement, some with another. One such seating plan is shown on page 44.

A fantastically ornamented Victorian square piano

ORCHESTRAL SEATING PLAN

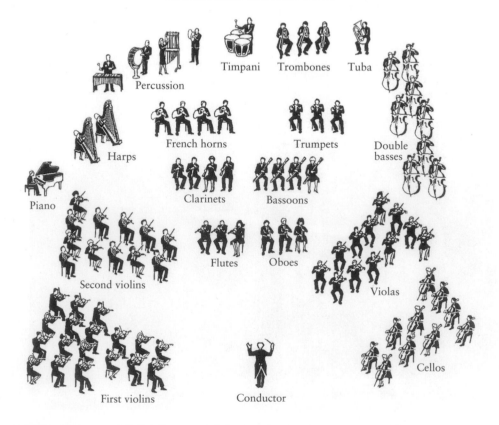

instrument without requiring any other musicians at all. Consequently the solo music that has been written for piano, harpsichord, and organ is much more extensive than (accompanied) solo music for other instruments—more extensive, and ultimately more important.

Piano The tuned strings of a **piano** are struck by felt-covered hammers, activated from a keyboard. Much technological ingenuity has been devoted to the activating mechanism, or *action*.

The hammers must strike the string and then fall back at once, while a damping device made of felt touches the string to stop the sound instantly. All this must be done so fast that the pianist can play repeated notes as fast as the hand can move. Also, all possible shades of loudness and softness must lie ready under the player's fingers. This dynamic capability is what gave the piano its name: *piano* is short for *pianoforte*, meaning "soft-loud."

In the nineteenth century, the piano became *the* solo instrument. The list of great virtuoso pianists who were also major composers extends from Frédéric Chopin to Sergei Rachmaninov. At the same time, every middle-class household had a piano. Obligatory piano lessons served and still serve for millions of young people as a magical introduction to the world of music (we hope).

Harpsichord The **harpsichord** is an ancient keyboard instrument that was revived in the 1900s for the playing of Baroque music, in particular.

Like the piano, the harpsichord has a set of tuned strings activated from a keyboard. The action is much simpler, however. There is no damping, and instead of hammers striking the strings, little bars flip up with quills that pluck them. (The inside of the harpsichord is shown on page 56.) This means, first, that the tone is brittle and ping-y. Second, it means that the player cannot vary

An elaborately painted eighteenth-century harpsichord

Keyboard Instruments

Though most orchestras today include a pianist, the piano is a relatively new addition to the symphony orchestra. In earlier times, the orchestra regularly included another keyboard instrument, the harpsichord.

The great advantage of keyboard instruments, of course, is that they can play chords and full harmony as well as melodies. One can play a whole piece on a keyboard

A five-manual organ. The player pulls out *stops* (or *stop knobs*) to change the sets of pipes that sound.

Artists loved to paint lutes and lutenists: This is *A Young Man Playing a Lute* by the great early Baroque painter Caravaggio (1573–1610).

dynamics; when a string is plucked in this way, it always sounds the same.

Harpsichord makers compensated for this limitation in dynamics by adding one or two extra full sets of strings, controlled by an extra keyboard. One keyboard could be soft, the other loud. A mechanism allowed the keyboards to be coupled together for the loudest sound of all.

In spite of its brittle tone and its lack of flexibility in dynamics, the harpsichord can be a wonderfully expressive instrument. Good harpsichord playing requires, first and foremost, great rhythmic subtlety.

Clavichord   Another ancient keyboard instrument, the **clavichord,** was strictly for private use. Small and relatively inexpensive, its strings (only one set) are struck by simple metal levers. The clavichord has a very sensitive but also very quiet sound—it cannot be heard across a large room, let alone a concert hall.

Organ   Called "the king of instruments," the pipe organ is certainly the largest of them. This instrument has to provide enough sound to fill the large spaces of churches and cathedrals on a suitably grand scale. The organ has a great many sets of tuned pipes through which a complex wind system blows air, again activated from a keyboard. The pipes have different tone colors, and most organs have more than one keyboard to control different sets of

pipes. A pedal board—a big keyboard on the floor, played with the feet—controls the lowest-sounding pipes.

Each set of tuned pipes is called a *stop*; a moderate-sized organ has forty to fifty stops, but much bigger organs exist. One organ in Atlantic City, New Jersey, has 1,477 stops, for a total of 33,112 pipes. A large organ is capable of an almost orchestral variety of sound.

The organ is not a member of the orchestra, but because the grandest occasions call for orchestra, chorus, vocal soloists, and organ combined (e.g., the *Messiah* at Christmastime; see page 161), a major symphony hall has to have its organ—usually an imposing sight.

Electronic Keyboard Instruments   Today *keyboard* or *organ* generally means an electronic instrument. Synthesizers simulate the sound of organs, pianos, and harpsichords. Electronic pianos look like acoustic ones and sound quite like them, though the feel is different. They cost a great deal less.

Modern concert music, from the 1960s on, has occasionally used electronic keyboards. On the whole, however, synthesizers have been used more to compose concert music than to play it.

Plucked Stringed Instruments

Plucked stringed instruments figure much less in art music of the West than in Asian countries such as India and Japan, as we shall see. One exception is the orchestral harp; see page 38. The acoustic **guitar** and the **mandolin** are used very widely in Western popular music, but only occasionally in orchestras.

However, a now-obsolete plucked instrument, the **lute,** was of major importance in earlier times. One of the most beautiful-looking of instruments, the lute sounds rather like a gentle guitar. It differs in its rounded sound box, and in the way its pegboard is set nearly perpendicular to the neck. Large members of the lute family were the **theorbo** and the **archlute.**

Like keyboard instruments, plucked stringed instruments have been revolutionized by electronic technology. The **electric guitars** of rock music have rarely found their way into concert music.

bedfordstmartins.com/listen
 ▶ Instruments of the Orchestra

The gawky archlute. Several other "early music" instruments are shown later in this book: **vihuelas** on pages 61 and 70; the **viola da gamba** on pages 132, 137, and 142; a splendid seventeenth-century organ on page 168; and the early piano or **fortepiano** on page 208.

CHAPTER **4**

Musical Form
and Musical Style

F*orm* is a general word with a long list of dictionary definitions. As applied
to the arts, **form** is an important concept that refers to the shape, arrangement, relationship, or organization of the various elements. In poetry, for
example, the elements of form are words, phrases, meters, rhymes, and stanzas;
in painting, they are lines, colors, shapes, and space.

1 Form in Music

In music, the elements of form and organization are those we have already discussed: rhythm, pitch and melody, dynamics, tone color, and texture. A musical work, whether a simple song or a symphony, is formed or organized by
means of repetitions of some of these elements, and by contrasts among them.
The repetitions may be strict or free (that is, exact or with some variation).
The contrasts may be of many different kinds—the possibilities are virtually
limitless—conveying many different kinds of feeling.

Over the centuries and all over the world, musicians have learned to create longer and more impressive pieces in this way: symphonies, operas, works
for the Javanese gamelan or Japanese gagaku orchestras, and more. Each piece
is a specific sound experience in a definite time span, with a beginning, middle, and end, and often with subtle routes between. Everyone knows that
music can make a nice effect for a minute or two. But how does music extend
itself—and hold the listener's interest—for ten minutes, or half an hour, or
three whole hours at a time?

This is one of the main functions of musical form. Form is the relationship
that connects those beginnings, middles, and ends.

Form and Feeling

Form in art also has a good deal to do with its emotional quality; it is a mistake to consider form as a merely structural or intellectual matter. Think of the
little (or big) emotional click we get at the end of a limerick, or a sonnet, where
the accumulated meanings of the words are summed up with the final rhyme.
This is an effect to which form—limerick form or sonnet form—contributes.
Similarly, when at the end of a symphony a previously heard melody comes

66 Keep two things in
mind, then. Remember the
general outlines of the
[outer form], and remem-
ber that the content of the
composer's thought forces
him to use that formal
mold in a particular and
personal way—in a way
that belongs only to the
particular piece that he is
writing."

Aaron Copland, What to
Listen For in Music

back, with new orchestration and new harmonies, the special feeling this gives us emerges from a flood of memory; we remember the melody from before, in its earlier version. That effect, too, is created by form.

How easy is it, actually, to perceive form in music and to experience the feelings associated with form? Easy enough with a short tune, such as "The Star-Spangled Banner"—that's what our analysis on page 26 was all about. The various phrases of this tune, with their repetitions, parallel features, contrasts, and climax, provide a microcosm of musical form in longer pieces. A large-scale composition like a symphony is something like a greatly expanded tune, and its form is experienced in basically the same way.

To be sure, a symphony requires more from the listener—more time and more attention—than a tune does. Aware of the potential problem here, composers scale their musical effects accordingly. The larger the piece, the more strongly the composer is likely to help the memory along by emphasizing the repetitions and contrasts that determine the musical form.

Form and Forms

Like the word *rhythm* (see page 11), the word *form* has its general meaning and also a more specific one. "Form" in general refers to the organization of elements in a musical work, but "*a* form" refers to one of many standardized formal patterns that composers have used over the centuries.

Forms in this latter sense can be referred to as "outer" forms; the ones treated later in this book are listed in the margin. The fixed elements in such forms provide a welcome source of orientation for listeners, but they are always general enough to allow composers endless possibilities on the detailed level.

Form in Poetry

Fleas:
Adam
Had 'em.

The poet creates rhyme and meter to add a little lift, and a smile, to the prose observation "Adam had fleas" (or "Ever since Adam, we've all suffered").

Form in Painting

A Madonna by Raphael Sanzio (1483–1520), built out of two cunningly nested triangles. To balance the boys at the left, the Virgin faces slightly to the right, her extended foot "echoing" their bare flesh. On a larger scale, the activity at the left is matched by a steeper landscape.

LISTENING EXERCISE 7

17, 19

Musical Form

"The Star-Spangled Banner" has one of the simplest forms, **a a b.** "Oh, say can you see . . . the twilight's last gleaming" is **a,** "Whose broad stripes . . . gallantly streaming" is the second **a,** and the rest of the anthem is **b.** Section **b** makes a definite contrast with **a** by means of its new melody and higher range, as we've seen on page 26.

When sections of music are not identical but are considered essentially parallel, they are labeled **a, a′, a″,** and so on. The first theme of Schubert's Quartet in A Minor is in **a a′ a″** form.

17	0:00	**a**	Melancholy
	0:21	**a′**	Begins like **a,** but the melody lasts longer and goes higher and lower than in **a**
	0:47	**a″**	The beginning now turns luminously to the major mode.

Smaller form elements (**a, b, a′**) can be nested in larger ones, marked with capital letters: **A, B, A′.** A more extended example comes from an all-time classical favorite, the Christmas ballet *The Nutcracker* by Piotr Ilych Tchaikovsky. Tchaikovsky used the Dance of the Sugar-Plum Fairy mainly to show off the celesta, a rare instrument (see page 42). The **A B A′** form of the dance breaks down into **a a′ b b a a′.**

19	0:00			Introduction: the 2/4 meter is previewed by low stringed instruments.
	0:08	**A**	**a**	Solo for celesta, with comments by a bass clarinet
	0:23		**a′**	Begins like **a,** but the ending is different—on a new pitch and harmony
	0:37	**B**	**b**	Contrasts with **a**
	0:44		**b**	
	0:51			Transition: the music has a preparatory quality.
	1:07	**A′**	**a**	Celesta an octave higher, with a quiet new click in the violins
	1:22		**a′**	The high celesta is a very striking sound.

The new orchestration is what gives this **A B A′** form its prime mark—not changes in melody or harmony, as is usually the case. More strictly, the form could be marked *introduction* **A (a a′) B (b b)** *transition* **A′ (a″ a‴),** but this level of detail is seldom needed.

The quality and feeling of works in the same outer form can therefore vary greatly. Or, to put it another way, any work adhering to a common outer form can also have an individual inner form of its own.

Musical forms, as standardized patterns, are conventionally expressed by letter diagrams, such as **A B A** or **a b a** (small letters tend to be used for shorter sections of music). They will be used again and again in this book. More complicated forms come about through "nesting":

A	B	A
a b a	c d c	a b a

Two basic factors create musical form: *repetition* and *contrast*. In **A B A** form, one of the simplest, the element of repetition is **A** and the element of contrast is **B.** Some sort of tune or theme or other musical section is presented at the beginning (**A**), then another section (**B**) that contrasts with the first, and then the first one again (**A**). If **A** returns with significant modification, a prime mark can be added: **A′.**

Form in Architecture

The central, contrasting unit of this building seems almost to flow into the unit at the right. The musical analogy would be to an interesting **A B A′** form, in which **A** comes back after **B** in an expanded version (**A′**), and that version includes some new rhythm or instrument that we first heard during **B**.

Seems clear enough. Yet the outer form tells us only so much. With any particular work, what about the inner form: Is **B** in a different mode? A different key? Does it present material that contrasts in rhythm, texture, or tone color—or does it work its contrast by ringing changes on the original material, on **A**? The returns to **A** material in **A B A′** form, too, can convey very different feelings. One return can sound exciting, another tricky, while yet another provides a sense of relief.

So identifying outer forms—getting the letters right—is just a first step in musical appreciation. The real point about great music is the way composers refine, modify, and personalize outer forms for their own expressive purposes.

Musical Genres

One often hears symphonies, sonatas, and operas referred to as "forms" of music. Actually this is loose terminology, best avoided in the interests of clarity, because symphonies and other works can be composed in completely different forms (outer forms)—that is, their internal orders or organizations can be of quite different kinds. Thus, the last movement of Joseph Haydn's Symphony No. 95 is in rondo form, whereas the last movement of Hector Berlioz's *Fantastic Symphony* follows no standard form whatsoever.

The best term for these general categories of music is *genre* (jáhn-ruh), borrowed from French. A genre can be defined by its text (a madrigal has Italian verses of a specific kind), or by its function (a Mass is written for a Roman Catholic service), or by the performing forces (a quartet is for four singers or instrumentalists). The main genres of Western music are listed in the margin. Other genres from other musical traditions will be encountered in the Global Perspectives sections.

2 Musical Style

Style, like *form*, is another of those broad, general words—general but very necessary. The style of a tennis player is the particular way he or she reaches up for the serve, swings, follows through on the forehand, hits the ball deep or short, and so on. A lifestyle means the whole combination of things one does and doesn't do: the food one eats, the way one dresses and talks, one's habits of thought and feeling.

The style of a work of art, similarly, is the combination of qualities that make it distinctive. One composer's style may favor jagged rhythms, simple harmonies, and tunes to the exclusion of other types of melody. Another may prefer certain kinds of tone color; still another may concentrate on a particular form. The type of emotional expression a composer cultivates is also an important determinant of musical style.

One can speak of the lifestyle of a generation as well as the lifestyle of a particular person. Similarly, a distinction can be made between the musical style of a particular composer and the style of a historical period. For example, to a large extent George Frideric Handel's manner of writing falls within the parameters of the Baroque style of his day. But some features of Handel's style are unique, and perhaps it is those features that embody his musical genius.

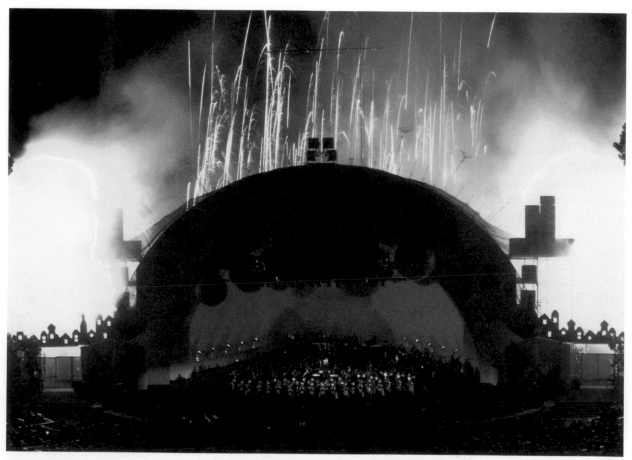

Even *where* people listen to music reflects their lifestyle. The Hollywood Bowl, which has been known to hold 26,000 people, flaunts both the superb topography of Los Angeles and the blockbuster mentality, hallmark of the movie industry.

Musical Style and Lifestyle

In any historical period or place, the musical style bears some relation to the lifestyle in general; this seems self-evident. Perhaps the point is clearest with popular music, where distinct (and distinctly different) worlds are evoked by rock, rap, and country music, to say nothing of earlier styles such as 1950s rhythm and blues or 1930s swing.

Older styles of music, too, relate to total cultural situations, though how this works in detail is not fully understood. We can, however, at least suggest some of these musical-cultural relationships for music of the various historical periods. For each period, we sketch certain aspects of the culture, history, and lifestyle of the time. We then briefly outline the musical style and, wherever possible, suggest correlations. Then the musical style is examined in more detail through individual composers and individual pieces of their music.

These individual pieces are our principal concern — not history, or culture, or concepts of musical style in the abstract. Learning the basic concepts of music (as we have tried to do in this unit) is useful only insofar as it focuses and sharpens the process of listening to actual music. This book is called *Listen*, and it rests on the belief that the love of music depends first and foremost on careful listening to particular pieces. But such listening never happens in a cultural vacuum; it takes place in a vivid, experienced context of some kind. The general information we present here on history, culture, styles, and genres is intended to remake, in some small way, our own listening contexts — and hence reshape our listening experiences.

Coming to the end of Unit I, after a lot of prose and a number of hasty musical excerpts, we should listen now to a whole composition at some length. Turn the page for an account of *The Young Person's Guide to the Orchestra* — the young of all ages — by Benjamin Britten, who was the leading English composer of the mid-twentieth century. Follow the audio from the Companion DVD with Listening Chart 2.

Benjamin Britten conducting a Promenade Concert at another locale that reflects a lifestyle — London's Albert Hall, capacity 8,000. For 112 years, droves of music-lovers have heard and learned music of all kinds at the "Proms," which are given every day during July and August. All the Proms are broadcast.

BENJAMIN BRITTEN (1913–1976)
The Young Person's Guide to the Orchestra (1946)

20–25

The *Young Person's Guide to the Orchestra* is *the* ideal piece for learning the tone colors of the Western orchestra. Britten, an English composer who wrote a lot of music for children, undertook this *Guide* as an educational responsibility — and as a challenge to his ingenuity — but he also set out to create a coherent and interesting musical composition. Listen to it primarily to come to know instrumental sounds, but also as a review of several of the concepts introduced in Unit I.

The work uses one basic *theme* — a short, rather bouncy tune by an earlier English composer, Henry Purcell (see page 105). After first displaying the grand sound of the full orchestra playing this *tune,* Britten has each of the four *orchestral choirs* play it: woodwinds, brass, strings . . . but he knew he had to cheat when he got to the percussion. (The main percussion instruments are pitch-impaired and can't play tunes.) It was clever, then, to prepare for the not-very-thematic percussion statement at 1:21 by freeing up the theme a little in the preceding brass and stringed statements, and afterward to remind us of the original tune, played verbatim by the full orchestra again. (Britten makes up for his cheat by a particularly brilliant percussion episode later.)

So far everything has been in the *minor mode* and in triple meter. But next comes a series of *variations* on the theme — versions of the theme varied in melody, rhythm, texture, mode, tempo, everything. We study variation form on page 190. The first section of the piece has given us a theme in the minor mode and its repetitions, but the first variations already switch to the major mode. Variation 3, in a swinging *triple meter,* is followed at once by a variation in *duple meter.* Many variations — variations 1, 3, and 4, to begin with — involve a great deal of repetition of a single *motive.* There are variations in fast *tempo* that last for hardly more than half a minute, and others in slow tempo that take nearly three times as long. Along the way, in keeping with Britten's teaching aims in the work, each variation features a particular instrument (or family of instruments) from the orchestra.

In variation form, variety is the order of the day. This central, variation section of the *Young Person's Guide* offers, in addition to the catalogue of instrumental sounds, an equally dazzling catalogue of the endlessly varied moods that can be represented in music.

At the end, Britten writes an extremely vigorous *fugue,* based on yet another version of the Purcell tune. We study fugue on page 142. For now, notice that this section of the *Young Person's Guide* provides an excellent example of *imitative polyphony.*

And our virtuoso composer has still one more trick up his sleeve: He brings the tune back triumphantly just before the end, unvaried, while the fugue is still going on. Both can be heard simultaneously. This is non-imitative polyphony. The return of the tune wraps up the whole long piece very happily as a unique variety of **A B A'** *form.*

theme, page 27

tune, page 25
orchestral choirs, page 43

major and minor mode,
   page 32

duple and triple meter,
   pages 12–13
motive, page 27
tempo, page 15

polyphony, page 29

form, page 48

bedfordstmartins.com/listen
▶ Interactive Listening Chart 2

))) LISTENING CHART 2

Britten, *The Young Person's Guide to the Orchestra*

17 min., 13 sec.

DVD
20–25

20	0:00	**THEME**	Full orchestra	Note the prominent *sequence* in the middle of the Purcell tune. You will hear snatches of this in some of the variations.
	0:19	Transition		*Diminuendo* (getting softer). Further transitions occurring between thematic statements and variations will not be indicated on this chart.
	0:23	Theme	WOODWIND choir	
	0:45	Theme	BRASS choir	Ending is changed.
	1:04	Theme	STRING choir	Theme is changed further.
	1:21		PERCUSSION	"Theme" only in principle; only some rhythms remain.
	1:36	**THEME**	Full orchestra	Same as the first time
21	1:55	Variation 1	Flutes and piccolo	(harp accompaniment)
0:11	2:06			Piccolo and flute play in thirds.
0:35	2:30	Variation 2	Oboes	Beginning of the tune transformed into a slow, romantic melody in oboe 1; oboe 2 joins in two-part *polyphony.*
1:42	3:37	Variation 3	Clarinet family	Solos for bass clarinet (1:42), clarinet (1:57), and E-flat clarinet (1:46)
2:21	4:16	Variation 4	Bassoon	Typical qualities of the bassoon: *staccato* (comic effect) and *legato* (melodious)
22	5:15	Variation 5	Violins	With chordal accompaniment—particularly clear *homophonic* texture
0:33	5:48	Variation 6	Violas	Slower
1:53	7:08	Variation 7	Cellos	Another slow, romantic melody: falls into a a′ form (clarinet in the background)
2:53	8:08	Variation 8	Double bass	Solo—humorous
3:47	9:02	Variation 9	Harp	In the background is a string *tremolo,* caused by bowing a single note extremely rapidly, so that it sounds like a single trembling note.
23	10:01	Variation 10	French horns	
0:51	10:52	Variation 11	Trumpets	With snare drum, suggesting a fast military march
1:22	11:23	Variation 12	Trombones, tuba	Typical qualities of the trombone: humorously pompous, and mysterious chords
24	12:33	Variation 13	PERCUSSION	Timpani and bass drum (heard throughout the variation), cymbals (0:15), tambourine (0:26), triangle (0:29), snare drum (0:38), Chinese block (0:42), xylophone (0:48), castanets (1:00), gong (1:06), whip (1:14), marimba and triangle (1:40)
				Percussion instruments are described starting on page 42.
25	14:28	**FUGUE**	Full orchestra	*Imitative polyphony* starts with flutes, then oboe, clarinet (same order as above!).
1:53	16:21	**THEME**	Full orchestra	Climax: slower than before. The tune is superimposed on the fugue.

Early Music:
An Overview

W*estern art music extends from the great repertory of Gregorian chant, assembled starting around the year 600 C.E., to electronic compositions that were programmed yesterday and today. The sheer scope, variety, and richness of all this music is almost bewildering. Some of it was developed to maintain Christianity through centuries of barbarism, some to glorify great monarchs such as Queen Elizabeth I of England or Louis XIV of France. Some of it is being produced in today's recording studios for the enjoyment, mainly, of connoisseurs. The field ranges from music by mystic visionary Hildegard of Bingen in the twelfth century, through compositions by familiar masters such as Bach and Beethoven, to work in progress stored on hard drives at computer music centers around the world.*

Certainly there is too much here to cover in a single semester or quarter course—too much, that is, if one is going to do more than skim the music, picking up a few stray facts and figures about it without really listening. *It cannot be said often enough that listening to particular pieces again and again is the basic activity that leads to the love of music and to its understanding. A hurried survey does justice to none of the world's significant music; we need to make choices. We have: The essential coverage of this book begins in the eighteenth century, with Unit III and the music of Bach and Handel, who are the first composers with a long-standing place in the standard repertory of concert music.*

By standard repertory, *we mean a large but not limitless body of music from which concert artists and conductors usually draw their programs. As an optional introduction to all of this, Unit II presents a brief overview of music before the eighteenth century; so-called Early Music was forgotten for centuries and revived mainly in the second half of the twentieth century. Admittedly, the division we are making for this book is somewhat arbitrary, for concert life keeps changing, and by now many concert agencies and even opera companies—if not symphony orchestras—do include earlier music on their schedules. Through recordings especially, Early Music has found or is finding its way into the musical mainstream.*

CHAPTER 5

The Middle Ages

"The Middle Ages" is a catchall term for nearly a thousand years of European history, extending from the collapse of the Roman Empire in the fifth century C.E. to the advent of new learning, technology, and political organization in the age of Columbus. Even though life and culture changed slowly in those days, this is obviously too broad a span of time to mean much as a single historical period.

Nowhere is this clearer than in music. Music changed radically from the beginning to the end of the Middle Ages, more than in any other historical period. Two of the central features of later Western music, *tune* and *polyphony,* originated around the middle of this long period.

1 Music and the Church: Plainchant

The early history of Western music was determined by the Christian Church to an extent that is not easy for us to grasp today. The church cultivated, supported, and directed music as it did art, architecture, poetry, and learning. All composers were in holy orders, and all musicians got their training as church choirboys. (Exception must be made for popular musicians—called minstrels and **jongleurs**—but we know next to nothing about their lives or their music. The only people who wrote music down were monks and other clerics, who could not have cared less about preserving popular music.)

The music fostered by the church was the singing or chanting of sacred words in services, and we might pause for a moment to ask why singing was so important for Christian worship. One could point to traditions of singing in older religions from which Christianity borrowed much—especially the singing of psalms in the ancient Jewish synagogue. But this merely shifts the question: Why did ancient worshipers *sing* at all?

Singing is, first of all, a way of uttering words that sets them apart from ordinary speech. Words denote concepts, and singing words gives concepts in prayer or doctrine a special status, a step above merely speaking them. Music provides words with special emphasis, force, mystery, even magic. Throughout human history, this heightening by music has served the basic aim of religion: to bring humans into beneficial contact with unseen spirits, with deities, or with a single God. If you go to church, you don't need to be told this.

"God is gone up with a *shout*, the LORD with the *sound* of a trumpet. *Sing* praises to God, *sing* praises; *sing* praises unto our King, *sing* praises."

Psalm 47, 5–6 (italics added)

All the largest world religions—Islam, Hinduism, and Buddhism as well as Christianity and Judaism—possess and prize old and complex systems of chant. Most other, smaller religions do, too. (See Global Perspectives 1, page 73.)

Music and Church Services

Sacred texts were sung at church services—and the life of the church centered in its services. The music that has come down to us was sung in monasteries and cathedrals, not humble parish churches; the services were conducted by and for the higher ranks of Christendom: monks, nuns, and cathedral clergy. And monks and nuns spent an amazing amount of their time in prayer. Besides the Mass, a lengthy ceremony that might happen more than once a day, there were no fewer than eight other services through the day and night, known collectively as the Divine Office. Large portions of these services were sung.

Though each service had its standard format, many details in the verbal texts for them changed from day to day, according to the church calendar (Christmas, Easter, various saints' days, and so on). As a result, there were literally thousands of religious texts specified for the Mass and the Office throughout the year.

All these texts required music, but providing such music was less a matter of free invention than of small additions and adjustments to a sacrosanct, traditional prototype. And listening to it was not so much listening as worshiping, while allowing music to expand the devotional experience. Hearing Gregorian chant or later medieval music today, one feels less like a listener in the modern sense than like a privileged eavesdropper, someone who has been allowed to attend a select occasion that is partly musical, but mainly spiritual. The experience is an intimate and tranquil one, cool and, to some listeners, especially satisfying.

> " A psalm is the work of the Angels, the incense of the Spirit. Oh, how wise was that Teacher who found a way for us to sing psalms and at the same time learn worthwhile things, so that in some mysterious way doctrine is more deeply impressed upon the mind!"
>
> *St. Basil, fourth century* C.E.

Plainchant

The official music of the Catholic Church in the Middle Ages and far beyond was a great repertory of melodies designated for the many religious texts to be sung at services throughout the year. This is the system of **plainchant** (or plainsong), widely known as Gregorian chant.

Clerics singing plainchant, depicted within an illuminated initial letter *C* in a late medieval manuscript. The whimsical little string-instrument player is outside the *C*, for instrumental music was taboo in church.

It is called "plain" because it is unaccompanied, monophonic (one-line) music for voices. And it is called "Gregorian" after the famous pope and church father Gregory I (c. 540–604); Gregory is reputed to have assembled and standardized all the basic chants required for the church services of his time. Many medieval plainchants were composed later, however, and so cannot strictly speaking be called Gregorian. And even with truly Gregorian chant, we only know it by extrapolating backwards from later manuscripts. Notation to write down music of the Middle Ages did not begin to develop until around the ninth century C.E., long after Gregory.

Characteristics of Plainchant

Plainchant has many genres, differing widely in melodic style, depending on their religious function. Some plainchants consist of simple recitation on a monotone, with only slight deviations from that single pitch; in monasteries, the entire set of 150 psalms had to be sung in this fashion every week. Other chants are intricate songs with hundreds of notes ranging well over an octave. And still others count as the first real tunes that are known in Western music.

In whatever style or genre, all plainchants share two characteristic features. First, they are *nonmetrical;* they have no clearly established meter, and therefore the rhythm is free. Not only is a distinctive beat lacking in this music, but rhythms may change from one performance (rather, one service) to the next.

Second, plainchant is not construed in the major/minor system, but according to one of the **medieval modes**. (Medieval means from the Middle Ages.) As discussed in Unit I, the original scale of Western music was the diatonic scale, equivalent to the "white-note" scale on the piano. We still use this scale today, oriented around the pitches C or A as home or tonic (see pages 32–33). Oriented around C, the music is said to be in the major mode, oriented around A, in the minor mode.

Musicians of the Middle Ages organized the scale differently—not around C or A, but around D, E, F, or G. The result was music in other modes, different from the modern major or minor. These modes were given numbers or Greek names. (Medieval scholars traced them back to the modes of ancient Greek music, as discussed by Plato and others.) The medieval modes are these:

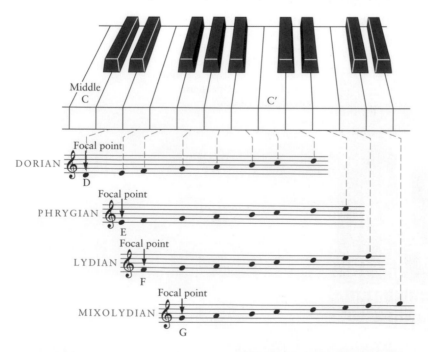

Multicultural medieval music: At a time when half of Spain was in Arab (Moorish) hands, a Moor and a Spaniard are shown playing large vihuelas together. Plucked stringed instruments like the vihuela, ancestors of the modern guitar, were an important novelty brought to medieval Europe from Arab countries.

The essential difference between the modern major and minor modes comes in the different arrangement of half steps and whole steps in their scales. The medieval modes provide four other arrangements. (Compare the preceding diagram with the one on page 32.) So medieval tunes sound different from modern tunes; in this respect medieval plainchant is actually richer and more subtle than music in the major/minor system. The artistic effect of plainchant — music without harmony or definite rhythm — is concentrated in melody, melody built on this rich modal system.

Gregorian Recitation

As we have said, the huge repertory of Gregorian chant ranges from simple recitation on a single pitch, with scarcely any variation, to long melodies that can make one dizzy by their endless, ecstatic twists and turns. Recitation was used for texts considered fairly routine in the services, such as lengthy readings from the Bible. Melody was used on more significant occasions, such as solemn church processions. (We will see an example of this use later.)

In Gregorian recitation, the pitch on which the text is sung, called the **reciting tone**, is held except for small, formulaic variations at beginnings and ends of phrases. These punctuate the text and make it easier to understand — and sing — since they give the singers time for a breath.

PLAINCHANT (c. ninth century)
Preface for Mass on Whit Sunday, "Vere dignum"

Our example is the music for a relatively minor text in the Mass, the Preface, which introduces a much more important element in the service.* This text consists of three sentences, recited in the same way. Each sentence is

*The Preface introduces the Elevation of the Host, where the priest celebrating Mass displays the bread and wine that is or represents the body and blood of Christ. By tasting these things, the faithful reaffirm their communion with Christ — the basic purpose of this service.

divided into phrases, and the last phrase changes to a new, second reciting tone, lower than the one at the start. All the phrases have a little opening formula sliding up to the reciting tone — launching it, in effect — and a closing formula sinking down again. These are indicated only approximately on the chart below.

| LISTEN | **Preface for Mass on Whit Sunday, "Vere dignum"** |

Since the sentences of the Preface text are quite long — the first of them has four phrases (a, b, c, d) and the others have three (a, b, c) — each sentence requires two lines on this listening diagram. The lines go up and down, with arrows, as an approximate indication of pitch levels. The reciting tone is shown in regular type, the opening and closing formulas *in italic*.

(The reciting tone arrives at 1d, 2c, and 3c.)

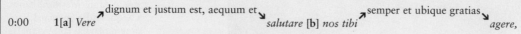

0:00   1[a] *Vere* ↗dignum et justum est, aequum et↘ *salutare* [b] *nos tibi* ↗semper et ubique gratias↘ *agere,*

[c] *Domine* ↗sancte Pater, omnipotens↘ *aeterne Deus,* [d] *per Christum*↘ *Dominum nostrum.*

0:48   2[a] *Qui* ↗post resurrectionem suam omnibus discipulis suis manifestus↘ *apparuit,*

[b] *et* ↗ipsis cernentibus est elevatus↘ *in coelum,* [c] ut nos divinitatis suae tribueret↘ *esse participes.*

1:30   3[a] *Et ideo cum* ↗Angelis et↘ *Archangelis,* [b] *cum*↗ Thronis et Dominationibus, cumque omnia militia caelestis↘

exercitus [c] hymnum gloriae tuae canimus↘ *sine fine dicentes:* [Sanctus, Domine Deus Sabaoth — not included in the recording]

1. It is truly meet and just, right and for our salvation, that we should at all times and in all places give thanks to Thee, O Lord, holy Father, almighty and eternal God, through Christ our Lord.

2. Who after His resurrection appeared openly to all His disciples, and while they looked on, was raised up into heaven, so that He might let us share in His own divinity.

3. And therefore with the Angels and Archangels, with the Thrones and Dominations, and with all the hosts of the heavenly army, we sing the hymn of Thy glory evermore, saying: ["Holy, holy, holy, Lord God of Sabaoth"]

Gregorian Melody

In addition to recitation, something we can recognize as melody abounds in many different genres of plainchant. One of the simplest genres is the **antiphon**.

PLAINCHANT (c. ninth century)
Gregorian antiphon, "In paradisum"

In the services for the dead, this antiphon is sung in procession on the way from the final blessing of the corpse in church to the graveyard where burial takes place. "In paradisum" is in the Mixolydian (G) mode. The special nature of this mode, which makes it different from the modern major mode, is heard twice in this melody, at cadences on the words "Chorus Ange*lo*rum" (line 4) and "quondam pau*pere*" (line 5).

The way to experience "In paradisum" is to set track 2 on repeat and imagine yourself a medieval monk or nun who has lost a brother or sister. Candles have all been extinguished in the church after the Requiem Mass (so called because you have prayed for the soul's eternal rest—in Latin, *requiem aeternam*). As the coffin is lifted up, the priest begins "In paradisum," and then the entire religious community joins in. You sing this brief antiphon again and again, for as long as it takes the slow procession to reach the graveyard.

Notice that the beginning of "In paradisum" reveals its ultimate derivation from recitation; afterwards the music grows more and more melodic. The melodic highpoint comes in line 5, where the text refers to Lazarus, the poor beggar in the Bible who went to heaven while a rich man went to hell—a point of identification for the mourners, all of whom had taken the vow of poverty, like the deceased. This haunting melodic figure was etched in the memory of the Middle Ages through an endless succession of last rites.

LISTEN | **Gregorian antiphon, "In paradisum"**

0:00	In paradisum deducant te Angeli: in tuo adventu suscipiant te Martyres, et perducant te in civitatem sanctam Jerusalem.	May the Angels lead you to paradise, and the Martyrs, when you arrive, escort you to the holy city of Jerusalem.
0:39	Chorus Angelorum te suscipiat, et cum Lazaro quondam paupere aeternam habeas requiem.	May the Angel choir sustain you, and with Lazarus, who was once poor, may you be granted eternal rest.

HILDEGARD OF BINGEN (1098–1179)
Plainchant sequence, "Columba aspexit"

Abbess Hildegard of the little convent of Bingen, in western Germany, was one of the most remarkable figures of the Middle Ages. Most famous for her book relating her religious visions, she also wrote on natural history and medicine; she gained such renown that popes and emperors sought her counsel.

Five hundred years after Gregory I, the first compiler of Gregorian chants, Hildegard composed plainchant melodies in her own highly individual style to go with poems that she wrote for special services. "Columba aspexit" honored one of the many minor saints venerated in those days, Saint Maximinus. It belongs to a late medieval plainchant genre called the **sequence**.

The sequence is a much more elaborate kind of melody than the antiphon. It consists of a series of short tunes sung twice, with some variation (and an extra unit at the end: **A A′ B B′ C C′ . . . N**). A soloist sings **A**, the choir **A′**, and so on. Modal cadences—Mixolydian, once again—at the beginning of the melody ("*fen*estrae," "*eius*") give it a deceptively humble quality that contrasts with its ecstatic soaring later.

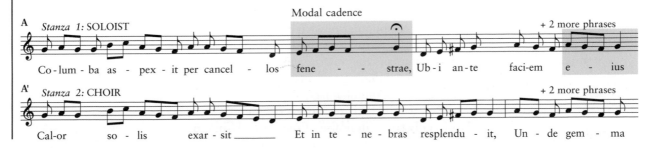

Hildegard of Bingen, "Columba aspexit"

0:02	A	Columba aspexit	The dove entered
		Per cancellos fenestrae	Through the lattices of the window,
		Ubi ante faciem eius	Where, before its face,
		Sudando sudavit balsamum	Balm emanated
		De lucido Maximino.	From incandescent Maximinus.
0:28	A′	Calor solis exarsit	The heat of the sun burned
		Et in tenebras resplenduit;	And dazzled into the gloom,
		Unde gemma surrexit	Whence a jewel sprang forth
		In edificatione templi	In the building of the temple
		Purissimi cordis benevoli.	Of the most pure loving heart.
0:56	B	Iste turis . . .	He is the high tower of Lebanon . . .
1:29	B′	Ipse velox . . .	The swift hart sped to the fountain . . .
2:03	C	O pigmentarii . . .	O you makers of incense . . .
3:15	D	O Maximine . . .	O Maximinus . . .

(two more stanzas)

A miniature illustration of Hildegard of Bingen, in one of her manuscripts, shows the miracle by which fire came down from heaven to engulf and inspire her. Her secretary, a monk named Volmar, looks on in wonder.

Our recording includes an instrumental *drone*—a single two-note chord running continuously. Drones are known from music around the world as well as from European folk music, and there is evidence that drones were sometimes used to accompany plainchant. The drone, the mystical words of Hildegard's poem, and the free, surging rhythm of her music work together to produce a feeling of serene yet intense spirituality.

2 Music at Court

Over the long span of the Middle Ages, kings and barons gradually gained political power at the expense of the church. They also came to assume leadership in artistic matters. In the later Middle Ages, the princely courts joined the monasteries and cathedrals as major supporters of music.

Troubadour and Trouvère Songs

Large groups of court songs have been preserved from the twelfth and thirteenth centuries, the Age of Chivalry. The noble poet-composers of these songs—who, we are told, also performed the songs themselves—were called **troubadours** in the south of France, **trouvères** in the north, and **Minnesingers** in Germany (Minne means ideal or chivalric love). Among them were knights and princes, even kings—such as the most famous of all chivalric heroes, Richard I of England, "the Lion-Hearted." Troubadour society (but not trouvère society) also allowed for women troubadours, such as Countess Beatriz of Dia, Maria di Ventadorn, and others.

Perhaps some of these noble songwriters penned the words only, leaving the music to be composed by *jongleurs,* the popular musicians of the time. The music is relatively simple—just a tune, in most cases, with no indication of any accompaniment. We hear of jongleurs playing instruments while the trouvères sang; they probably improvised some kind of accompaniment, or played a drone, such as we heard in Hildegard's "Columba aspexit."

There are some very beautiful troubadour poems—crusaders' songs, laments for dead princes, and especially songs in praise of the poets' ladies, or

My love and I keep state
In bower,
In flower,
Till the watchman on the
    tower
Cry:
    "Up! Thou rascal, Rise,
    I see the white
            Light
        And the night
                Flies.

— *Troubadour alba*

Left: Many German Minnesingers from around 1200 are pictured in a later manuscript. Here the jongleurs directed by Heinrich Frauenlob (Henry Praiselady) play medieval equivalents of a drum, flute, oboe, viola, violin, harp, and bagpipe (left to right).
Above: The Countess of Dia holding forth; she was one of a small number of women troubadours.

How Did Early Music Sound?

Because sound recording is only about a hundred years old, the hard truth is we do not really know how the music of Beethoven sounded in 1800, or the music of Bach in 1700. We have the scores, and it may be that tradition, writings, anecdotes, and surviving instruments allow us to extrapolate from score to sound with some confidence. But what about Early Music—music from 1500, 1300, 1100?

Obsolete instruments have come down to us in an imperfect condition, and we can try to reconstruct them; but figuring out how they were actually played is much more speculative. As for singing, who can guess what a cathedral choir sounded like in the Middle Ages, to take just one example? Since then, language itself has changed so much that it is hard enough to read a fourteenth-century poet such as Geoffrey Chaucer, let alone imagine how the words that he wrote were pronounced—or sung.

Another set of problems involves the way Early Music was written down. Its composers never indicated the tempo and rarely specified the instrumental or vocal forces that they anticipated for their music. With vocal pieces, they did not say whether a single singer or a whole choir was to sing. It has taken generations of patient research and experiment to "reconstruct" the probable sounds of Early Music.

The earliest music taken up in this book, Gregorian chant, is usually sung today in a performance style that was thought to be "historical" in the nineteenth century—this was the first of all Early-Music reconstructions, in fact. Our recording of "In paradisum" (page 63) adopts this smooth, respectful, rather gentle style.

Recent scholar-musicians have taken another look at history and proposed a different style—austere, less refined, and closer to other traditions of religious chanting that go back as far as the Gregorian, such as the Qur'anic chanting discussed on pages 73–74. We hear this new reconstruction in the Preface "Vere dignum" (page 62).

complaints of their ladies' coldness. One interesting poetic type was the *alba*, the "dawn song" of a knight's loyal companion who has kept watch all night and now warns him to leave his lady's bed before the castle awakes. Another was the *pastourelle*, a (typically unsuccessful) seduction dialogue between a knight on horseback and a country maid.

BERNART DE VENTADORN (c. 1135–1194)
Troubadour song, "La dousa votz"

Bernart was one of the finest troubadour poets and probably the most important musically; other troubadour and trouvère songs were derived from some of his pieces. Originally of humble background, he came to serve the powerful Queen Eleanor of Aquitaine, wife of Henry II of England.

Like hymns and folk songs, troubadour songs set all their stanzas to the same melody, resulting in what is called *strophic* form (**A A A . . .**); often each stanza is in **a a′ b** form. "La dousa votz" is in the G (Mixolydian) mode:

La dousa votz ai au-zi - da   Del rosin - ho-let sau - va-tge   Et es m'insel cor salhi - da   Si que tot lo co-si - rer

The performance on the recording stresses secular aspects of Bernart's song, including an imaginative reconstruction of a possible instrumental accompaniment to it. It sounds far removed indeed from the serene spirituality of Hildegard of Bingen.

The language the troubadours spoke and wrote was Provençal, now almost extinct. It combines elements from Old French and Old Spanish.

LISTEN | Bernart de Ventadorn, "La dousa votz"

0:07	*St. 1:* La dousa votz ai auzida	I have heard the sweet voice
	Del rosinholet sauvatge	Of the woodland nightingale
	Et es m'insel cor salhida	And my heart springs up
	Si que tot lo cosirer	So that all the cares
	E'ls mals traihz qu'amors me dona,	And the grievous betrayals love has given me
	M'adousa e m'asazona.	Are softened and sweetened;
	Et auria'm be mester	And I would thus be rewarded,
	L'autrui joi al meu damnatge.	In my ordeal, by the joys of others.
0:48	*St. 2:* Ben es totz om d'avol vida	In truth, every man leads a base life
	C'ab joi non a son estatge . . .	Who does not dwell in the land of joy . . .
1:28	*St. 3:* Una fausa deschauzida	One who is false, deceitful,
	Trairitz de mal linhage	Of low breeding, a traitress
	M'a trait, et es traida . . .	Has betrayed me, and betrayed herself . . .

The Estampie

A few—a very few—instrumental dances also survive from the same court circles that produced the chivalric trouvère repertory. Called **estampies,** they are unassuming one-line pieces in which the same or similar musical phrases are repeated many times in varied forms. (This suggests that these estampies may have been written-down jongleur improvisations.) Estampies are marked by lively and insistent rhythms in triple meter. Modern performers often add a touch of spice with the help of percussion instruments.

This is a modest beginning to the long and important history of European dance music. We will pick it up again in the next chapter.

3 The Evolution of Polyphony

Polyphony—the simultaneous combination of two or more melodies—must have arisen in early Europe because people took pleasure in the sensuous quality of music, in the rich sounds of intertwining melodic lines with their resulting harmony. Many cultures all over the world have developed some kind of improvised polyphony, polyphony that is made up on the spot without the aid of written scores. (If you and someone you know can sing in thirds together, that is improvised polyphony.) Some other cultures, also, have traditions of complex, preplanned polyphony involving little or no improvisation.

We know about early European polyphony only from its uses within the church (for, once again, all we know about very early music comes from the writing of monks and other clerics). And within the church, the sensuous aspect of polyphony had to be rationalized away. Polyphony was seen as a way of embellishing Gregorian chants—that is, as yet another way of enhancing the all-important services.

Organum

The earliest type of polyphony is called **organum** (plural *organa*). First described theoretically in treatises around 900 C.E., actual organum has survived in musical notation from around 1000. Organum consists of a traditional plainchant melody to which a composer/singer/improviser has added another melody in counterpoint, sung simultaneously to the same words.

The history of organum between about 1000 and 1200 C.E. provides a fascinating record of growing artistic ambition and technical invention. We can trace a number of steps:

꒚   Originally, each note of the chant was accompanied by another single note in the added melody (or *counterpoint*); the two melodies moved along with the same interval, or distance, between them. The rhythm of this early, so-called parallel organum was the free rhythm of Gregorian chant.

꒚   Soon the added melody (the counterpoint) was treated more independently — it would sometimes go up when the chant went down, and vice versa.

꒚   Next, the counterpoint began to include several notes at the same time as each single chant note. The embellishment process was growing richer. As more and more notes were crowded in, making richer and richer added melodies, the single chant notes were slowed down to surprising lengths, sounding finally like long drones.

꒚   The next step was a radical one. Two counterpoints were added to the chant. This required much more skill from the composer, since the second added melody had to fit both the chant and also the first added melody.

꒚   Equally radical was the idea of introducing definite rhythms controlled by meter. First the counterpoints and then the chant itself were set in simple rhythms. This development was probably necessary to synchronize the counterpoints with each other and with the chant.

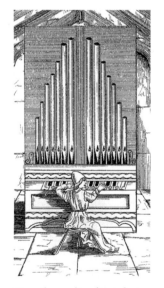

Does the medieval word *organum* imply that early polyphony was accompanied by the organ? We do not know; but churches of the time certainly had organs. The keyboard of this medieval organ seems to have heavy levers rather than keys.

Notre Dame Cathedral in Paris. Flying buttresses—the great medieval engineering feat that made such tall buildings possible—support the main structure (the nave). With its lofty front towers and its spire, Notre Dame seems to reach up to heaven itself.

Organum of these last, highly developed kinds flourished at the Cathedral of Notre Dame in Paris, which was built slowly over the period 1163–1345. The names of two composers of the so-called Notre Dame school are recorded: Master Léonin and his follower Pérotin (called "the Great"). Pérotin astonished thirteenth-century Paris by creating impressive organa for as many as four simultaneous voices.

PÉROTIN (c. 1200)
Organum, "Alleluia. Diffusa est gratia"

1

5

Many organa were composed for services devoted to the Virgin Mary, the patron saint of Notre Dame Cathedral. Our example is added to a lengthy chant for the Mass, "Alleluia. Diffusa est gratia." The music was probably written by Pérotin, though we cannot be certain.

At first the chant is sung—in the usual Gregorian way:

Phrase 1   Phrase 2   Phrase 3   Phrase 4

Al-le - - - - - lu - - - - - ia. (a)

The whole chant is much longer, but this opening "Alleluia" section is the most important part—it comes back twice before the chant is over—and the

most beautiful. The joyful exclamation "alleluia" is often set to **melismas**, passages of pure vocalism with many notes to a single syllable. The medi...

a. George Crumb.
b. Edgard Varese.
c. Steve Reich.
d. Phillip Glass.

An example of chance music is:

a. instructing the performer to place his or her hands inside the lid of the piano and strum the strings.
b. setting four radios to different stations and playing them for a specified duration, not knowing what is to be braodcast on each station.
c. using a synthesizer to produce sounds.
d. using the twelve tones of the chromatic scale in a fixed order.

0. Which one of the following is correct?

a. *Poeme electronique* was composed by George Crumb.
b. *4'33"* was composed by John Cage.
c. *Black Angel* was composed by Steve Reich.
d. *Tehillim* was composed by Edgard Varese.

After 1200 C.E. the most significant development in polyphonic music was its
gradual distancing from church services. Music's foundation was still Gregorian
chant; to this extent, the church still ruled. But the foundation was now handled

more abstractly. Composers of organum had already made up new rhythms for the plainchants they were using. Now they set only fragments of the chants, repeating them several times over.

In another radical development, the upper lines were now given their own words. This sort of polyphony is no longer an organum but a **motet**, from the French word *mot* ("word"). At first, motets were set to sacred poems in Latin, then to sacred poems in French. Later motets began to use love poems or political satires for their texts. It is clear that by now a church genre had been taken over by the courts; some motets even included bits of actual trouvère songs. But most motets still used a fragment of Gregorian chant for the notes of their bottom line.

Ars Nova

We are moving through history very rapidly. After 1300 the technical development of polyphony reached new heights of sophistication. Composers and music theorists of the time began to speak of an *ars nova*, a "new art" or "new technique." The organum and motets of the Notre Dame composers were now regarded as "ancient art," *ars antiqua*.

Some historians have compared the fourteenth century with the twentieth, for it was a time of the breakup of traditions—an age of anxiety, corruption, and worse. Bubonic plague, the "Black Death," carried away an estimated 75 million people, at a time when the papacy had been thrown out of Rome and two rival popes claimed the allegiance of European Christendom. The motet grew increasingly secular, intricate, and even convoluted, as did the painting, architecture, and poetry of the time.

The new intricacy of the motet was mainly in the area of rhythm. The *ars antiqua* composers had introduced fixed rhythms and meter into organum and the motet, as we have seen; the composers of the *ars nova* carried their innovations much further. Rhythm seems to have obsessed them. They superimposed complex rhythmic patterns in the various voices so as to produce extraordinary combinations. Rhythms of great complexity are standard in much African music, but in Europe we have to go all the way up to 1950 to find anything like the dizzy rhythms of the advanced "new music" of 1400.

The leading composers, Philippe de Vitry (1291–1361) and Guillaume de Machaut (c. 1300–1377), were both churchmen—Vitry ended his life as a bishop—but they were political churchmen serving the courts of France and Luxembourg. Machaut was also the greatest French poet of his time, admired (and imitated) by his younger English contemporary, Geoffrey Chaucer.

GUILLAUME DE MACHAUT (c. 1300–1377)
Motet, "Quant en moi"

Following tradition, Machaut based this motet on a repeated fragment of plainchant, taken from the Eastertide services. On the recording, it is played on an early bowed stringed instrument.

Above this, he wrote two faster counterpoints set to love poetry (very artificial and elegant poetry, in both form and content: see opposite page). To the medieval mind, there was nothing sacrilegious about combining these sacred and secular elements. Notice the exceedingly complicated rhythm of these upper voices, the nervous, hyperelegant way in which they utter the words, and the spiky harmonies they produce in combination:

> " Each sound is found always in its own row. And in order that you may better distinguish these rows, lines are drawn close together, and some rows of sounds occur on the lines themselves, others in the intervening intervals or spaces."
>
> — *Guido d'Arezzo, c. 1025, inventor of the staff (see page 22)*

Medieval musicians: The boy appears to be tuning his vihuela—a Spanish plucked stringed instrument—to the pitch being played by the older man (his teacher?).

> Of instrument of strings in accord
> Heard I so play a ravishing sweetness
> That God, that Maker is of all, and Lord,
> Ne heard never better, as I guess.
>
> — *Geoffrey Chaucer, 1375*

))) **LISTEN**   Guillaume de Machaut, "Quant en moi"

The soprano's poem and the alto's poem start together, and are sung simultaneously, stanza by stanza.

0:00   **SOPRANO POEM, STANZA 1**

Quant en moi vint premierement
Amours, si tres doucettement
Me vost mon cuer enamourer
Que d'un regart me fist present,
Et tres amoureus sentiment
Me donna avuec doulz penser,

When I was first visited by
Love, he so very sweetly
Enamored my heart;
A glance is what he gave me as a gift,
And along with amorous sentiments
He presented me with this delightful idea:

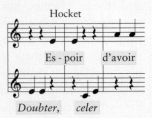

Hocket

0:19   Espoir   d'avoir

Merci sans refuser.
Mais onques en tout mon vivant
Hardement ne me vost donner.

To hope   to have

Grace, and no rejections.
But never in my whole life
Was boldness a gift he meant for me.

ALTO POEM, STANZA 1

Amour et biauté parfaite

Doubter,   celer

Me font parfaitement.

Thanks to love and consummate beauty,

Fearing,   feigning

Are what consume me entirely.

0:33   **SOPRANO POEM, STANZA 2**

E si me fait en desirant
Penser si amoureusement
Que, par force de desirer,
Ma joie convient en tourment
Muer, se je n'ay hardement.
Las! et je n'en puis recouvrer,

And if, in my passion,
He makes me think so amorously
That, thanks to desire
My joy turns into torment—
Must turn, since I am not bold.
Alas! I cannot save myself—

0:52   Qu'amours   secours

Ne me vuet nul prester,
Qui en ses las si durement
Me tient que n'en puis eschaper.

For Love   no help

Will lend me—
Love, who holds me so tightly
In his grasp that I cannot escape.

ALTO POEM, STANZA 2

Et vrais desirs, qui m'a fait

De vous,   cuer doulz

Amer sans finement,

And true desire, that has made me

Love you,   dear heart,

For ever and ever,

1:06   **SOPRANO POEM, STANZA 3**

Ne je me weil, qu'en attendant
Sa grace se weil humblement
Toutes ces dolours endurer.

Nor do I wish to escape, but awaiting
Your mercy, I humbly
Endure all these sorrows.

Je says   de vrai . . .

I know,   in truth . . .

ALTO POEM, STANZA 3

Et quant j'aime si finement,

Merci   vous pris . . .

And since I love you so perfectly,

For mercy   I pray you . . .

1:38   **SOPRANO POEM, STANZA 4**

Mais elle attend . . .

ALTO POEM, STANZA 4

Sans votre honeur . . .

Quant en moi   vint premierement   Amours,   si   tres doucette - ment   Me vost   mon cuer enamourer   Que d'un_regart

As the voices stop abruptly, rest, and start up again, they create an intriguing texture—perforated, sparkling, asymmetrical. To make things even more intricate, the two singers sing two different poems simultaneously—a longer poem sung by a soprano, and a shorter poem sung by an alto.

Each of these poems contains several stanzas with the same syllable counts and rhyme schemes, but Machaut (unlike a troubadour such as Bernart) does not repeat the same melodies for each stanza. A more esoteric system of repetition is at work. Successive stanzas are set to entirely different melodies in each voice—but these melodies have basically *the same overall rhythms*, complex patterns of over eighty notes in the soprano, forty in the alto.

This technique of writing successive lengthy passages in identical rhythms but with distinct melodies is called **isorhythm**. Motets that employ the technique are known as **isorhythmic motets**. Isorhythm represents the height of late medieval ingenuity, and it is hard to know whether anyone was expected to hear such purely rhythmic repetitions.

At a certain point in each stanza there are fast echoes between the soprano and the alto (see the shaded words below: "doubter—espoir—celer—d'avoir," etc.). This amusing device is called **hocket** (compare our word *hiccup*). Isorhythmic repetitions of rhythmic patterns are easiest to hear at hocket points.

> ❝ Hocket is a cut-up song, composed for two or more voices. This kind of song is pleasing to the hot-tempered and to young men on account of its fluidity and speed."
>
> *From a fourteenth-century treatise on music*

More scenes of medieval music making. These and other miniatures in this chapter are from *Songs of the Virgin Mary,* written (or perhaphs complied) by King Alphonso X of Spain, "The Wise" (1252–1284), renowed for his support of learning and the arts.

Global Perspectives 1

Sacred Chant

The vast number of societies that exist or that have existed in this world all generated their own music—or, as we say, their own different "musics." Often they are very different indeed; the first time South African Zulus heard Christian hymn singing they were amazed as much as the missionaries were when they first heard Zulu music. Yet for all their diversity, the musics of the world do show some parallels, as we are going to see in the Global Perspectives sections of this book. There are parallels of musical function in society, of musical technique, and sometimes of both together.

Often these parallels come about as the result of influences of one society on another—but influences are never accepted without modification and the blending of a foreign music with music that is indigenous. At other times parallels appear in musics that have nothing whatsoever to do with one another. Considering all these parallels, we have to believe that certain basic functions for music and certain basic technical principles are virtually universal in humankind.

One of these near-universal features—and one of the most fundamental—is the role of music in the service of religion. Singing serves across the world as an essential means of marking off the rituals of worship, signaling their special status and their difference from other, secular, pursuits. The repertory of Gregorian chant developed in the Christian Church of the Middle Ages (see pages 58–64) is only one of many traditions of monophonic religious chant, albeit one of the more elaborate.

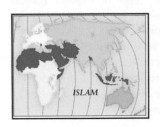

Islam: Reciting the Qur'an

Another highly elaborate tradition of chant is found in Islam, practiced today by about a fifth of the world's population, and the dominant religion in some fifty nations. Across all of Islam, the revelations of the prophet Muhammad gathered in the Qur'an (or Koran) are chanted or sung in Arabic. Muhammad himself is said to have enjoyed this melodic recitation.

Usually **Qur'anic recitation** is rigorously distinguished from all types of secular music making. It is thought of as "reading" the sacred text aloud, not singing it; it is not even considered to be the same sort of activity as secular singing or playing instruments. These nonreligious activities might be referred to as music (*musiqi*), but reading the Qur'an is not.

Given these distinctions, it is not surprising that Qur'anic recitation, like Gregorian chant, is monophonic and nonmetric, and does not involve instruments. It aims, above all else, to convey the Qur'anic text in a clearly comprehensible manner. Unlike plainchant, it has been passed along in oral tradition down to the present day; it has resisted the musical notation that came to be a part of the Gregorian tradition already in the Middle Ages. To this day, great Islamic chanters sing the whole 114-chapter Qur'an from memory.

Ya Sin

Our excerpt is the beginning of a long recitation of one of the most highly revered chapters from the Qur'an.

The azan: A muezzin high in a minaret calls the faithful to prayer in Cairo, Egypt.

It is titled "Ya Sin" and is recited in times of adversity, illness, and death. A skilled reciter, Hafíz Kadir Konya, reads the verses in a style midway between heightened speech and rhapsodic melody. His phrases correspond to lines of the sacred text, and he pauses after every one. He begins:

> In the name of Allah, the Beneficent, the Merciful.
> Ya Sin.
> By the wise Qur'an,
> Lo! thou art of those sent
> On a straight path,
> A revelation of the Mighty, the Merciful,
> That thou mayst warn a folk whose fathers were not
>   warned, so they are heedless.
> Already hath the word proved true of most of them, for
>   they believe not.

In his first phrases, Konya begins at a low tonic and gradually expands his range to explore pitches around it. By 0:38, he reaches a pitch central to his melody, higher than the tonic. The succeeding phrases circle around this pitch, reciting words on it and decorating it with ornamental melodic formulas of varying intricacy. In this regard, it is a bit like the Gregorian reciting tone we studied before (page 61), only more elaborate in its melodies.

The Azan

Like Gregorian chant, Islamic chanting has developed a wide variety of approaches and styles. The best-known type of Islamic chant employs a style related to recitation, though it does not take its words from the Qur'an: the singing of the *adhan*, or **azan**. This is a call to worship issued five times daily by a special singer called *mu'adhdhin,* or *muezzin.* That an entire society comes to a stop five times a day for prayer reveals the tremendous force of Islamic religion.

The muezzin traditionally delivers his azan from the minaret, a tower attached to the mosque, and later inside the mosque to begin the prayers. In Islamic cities today, the azan is often broadcast over loudspeakers to enable it to sound over modern urban noises.

Hawai'ian Chant

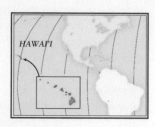

We should not be too surprised to find certain broad similarities between Qur'anic and Gregorian chant. Both Christianity and Islam emerged from the same region, the Middle East, and Muhammad drew on elements of Christian doctrine in forming his new religion. He counted Jesus Christ as one of the Islamic prophets.

It is more surprising to find some of the same features in religious chant from halfway around the globe, in Polynesia—in Hawai'ian prayer songs, or **mele pule** (mél-eh póol-eh). By reciting these prayers, Hawai'ians sought to bring to life images of their gods fashioned of wood, stone, or feathers, animating them with divine powers.

Our brief example shows a style similar in some general ways to our Gregorian Preface and Qur'anic recitation. It is monophonic, like all traditional Hawai'ian

Three Hawai'ian singers. They strike large, resonant gourds on the ground to accompany their song.

song. It is also almost monotonal, with only one prominent pitch other than the central reciting tone. In this it contrasts with more active melodic styles used in other Hawai'ian genres of song—especially love songs and *mele hula,* or hula-dance songs.

The mele pule takes its rhythms from the words and shows little trace of meter. Though nearly monotonal, it is ornamented subtly with various shifts of vocal delivery and divergences from its reciting tone. The most prominent of these is a clear, pulsating, almost sobbing *vibrato,* or wavering pitch, that the singer, Kau'i Zuttermeister, introduces on long syllables. This technique, called *i'i,* is a stylistic feature much prized in many types of traditional Hawai'ian song. It is felt to endow melodies with special, deep emotion.

A Navajo Song

NAVAJO TERRITORY

One more example of chant comes to us from Native American traditions. In these, too, singing is closely allied with the sacred. Song plays a role in healing, hunting, social rituals, and—embracing all these activities—in human relations with gods, spirits, and ancestors. Most Native North American song is monophonic, like the Hawai'ian, Arabic, and Western chants we have heard. Unlike them, it is usually accompanied by drums or rattles of one sort or another.

Our example comes from the Navajo nation of the Four Corners area of the American Southwest. It is called "K'adnikini'ya'," which means "I'm leaving," and it dates from the late nineteenth century.

Just as individual Gregorian chants have their assigned places in Catholic services, so this chant has its own special role. It is sung near the end of the Enemy Way ceremony, a central event of Navajo spiritual life. In this solemn ceremony, warriors who have come in contact with the ghosts of their enemies are purified and fortified. Such purification is still performed today, sometimes for the benefit of U.S. veterans of Vietnam or other wars.

"K'adnikini'ya'" falls into a group of Navajo sacred songs known as *ho'zho'ni'* songs, and you will hear the related word *ho'zhon'go* ("beautiful," "holy") sung alongside *k'adnikini'ya'* to end each of the seven central phrases of the song. Every phrase of the song begins with the syllables *hé-yuh-eh, yáng-a-ang-a.* These are *vocables,* syllables having no precise meaning. Vocables are sometimes called "nonsense syllables" and likened to the "tra-la-las" and "hey-diddle-diddles" of European nursery rhymes. But they are hardly

At a powwow in British Columbia

nonsensical. They can carry secret, venerable, and even mystical significance.

The melody of "K'adnikini'ya'," like the other chants we have examined, is organized around a prominent reciting tone (the pitch of *hé-yuh-eh*); each phrase turns upward at its end (on *k'adnikini'ya'*). The song's meter, given the regular drumstrokes, is more pronounced than in any of our earlier examples. The formal plan consists of a refrain at the beginning and end, with a group of parallel phrases in between.

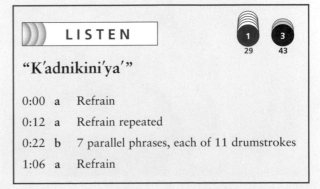

LISTEN

1 29   **3** 43

"K'adnikini'ya'"

0:00	a	Refrain
0:12	a	Refrain repeated
0:22	b	7 parallel phrases, each of 11 drumstrokes
1:06	a	Refrain

CHAPTER 6

The Renaissance

Renaissance ("rebirth") is the name given to a complex current of thought that worked deep changes in Europe from the fourteenth to the sixteenth century. It began in Italy. By rediscovering and imitating their ancient Greco-Roman civilization, Italians hoped they could bring about the rebirth of their glorious past. It was an unrealistic idea, which came to nothing in political terms. Instead of becoming a new Roman empire, Italy at the end of the Renaissance consisted of the same pack of warring city-states that had been at each other's throats all through the Middle Ages.

However, the revival of Greek and Roman culture provided a powerful model for new values, first in Italy and then the rest of Europe. In the words of a famous nineteenth-century historian, the Renaissance involved "the discovery of the world and of man." This was the age of Columbus and Magellan, Leonardo da Vinci, Copernicus, and Shakespeare. Medieval society was stable, conservative, authoritarian, and oriented toward God. The Renaissance laid the groundwork for the dynamic world we know today, a world in which human beings and nature, rather than God, have become the measure in philosophy, science, art, and sometimes even religion.

Accordingly, Renaissance artists strove to make their work more relevant to people's needs and desires. They began to reinterpret the world around them—the architect's world of space and stone, the painter's world of images, the musician's world of sound—in new ways to meet these ambitions.

> "Music is a thing which delighteth all ages and beseemeth all states; a thing as seasonable in grief as in joy. The reason hereof is an admirable facility which music hath to express and represent the very standing, rising, and falling, the very steps and inflections every way, the turns and varieties of all passions."
>
> *Anglican bishop and theologian Richard Hooker, 1593*

The church singers in these famous panels by Florentine sculptor Luca della Robbia (1400–1482) are handsome boys who seem to be taking the same sensuous pleasure in their singing as Luca did in sculpting them.

1 New Attitudes

A good indication of the Renaissance mindset, in the early fifteenth century, was a new way of treating plainchant in polyphonic compositions. Medieval composers writing organum or isorhythmic motets seem to have felt that so long as they used a traditional plainchant, there was nothing wrong with distorting it. They lengthened its notes enormously underneath the added counterpoints. They recast the meterless chant into fixed, arbitrary rhythms.

Renaissance composers no longer felt obliged always to use plainchants; but when they did they tended to treat them as melodies to listen to, not as rock-solid foundations for polyphonic structures. They embellished chants with extra notes, set them in graceful rhythms, and smoothed out passages that struck them as awkward or antiquated. This procedure is known as **paraphrase**. Here is a plainchant paraphrase from a fifteenth-century work we will examine below; dashed lines mark the notes taken directly from the chant, shown above the paraphrase:

Gregorian hymn, "Ave maris stella" (see page 78)

The emphasis is on the sonorous, sensuous aspect of the chant rather than on its function as structure and control — its authoritarian function, one might say. (Sonority means either tone color or, more loosely, rich tone color.) A new sensitivity to sonority and melody was one of the first signs of Renaissance attitudes toward music.

Having transformed plainchants into modern melodies with a more attractive profile, composers put them not at the bottom of the polyphony but on top, in the soprano, where they could be heard most clearly. And the soprano voice was probably already considered the most beautiful.

Early Homophony

The fifteenth century also saw the beginning of composed *homophony* — that is, music in a harmonic texture (see page 29). In the simpler plainchant paraphrases of the time, the melody is often highlighted by an accompaniment that does not really sound polyphonic. Though there are still several polyphonic voices, most of the time their independence vanishes because they move along together and form simple chords.

The result is a plainchant harmonization. Once again the emphasis is on sensuous effect, that of melody with chordal accompaniment, rather than on the more intellectual process of polyphony.

Guillaume Dufay (c. 1400–1474)

Guillaume Dufay (or Du Fay) was born and bred in the north of France near modern Belgium, a region that supplied the whole of Europe with musicians for many generations. For over twenty-five years he worked in Italy, where he came to know artists and thinkers of the Renaissance and (equally important!) the princely patrons who supported them. His later years were spent in a glow of celebrity at the important French cathedral of Cambrai.

> 66 There does not exist a single piece of music, not composed within the last forty years, that is regarded by the learned as worth hearing. Yet at this present time there flourish countless composers who glory in having studied the divine art under John Dunstable, Gilles Binchois, and Guillaume Dufay, recently deceased."
>
> *Composer and music theorist Johannes Tinctoris, 1477*

GUILLAUME DUFAY
Harmonized hymn, "Ave maris stella"

This is a homophonic setting of a Gregorian **hymn**, one of the most tuneful of plainchant genres. A short tune is sung through many stanzas, followed by an Amen—much like a modern hymn, in fact. One of the loveliest of Gregorian hymns, "Ave maris stella," was also one of the best known, because it was addressed to the Virgin Mary and sung on all of the many special feasts in her honor, and on most Saturdays, too. Note how line 1 contains the words AVE MARI(*s stell*)A.

"Ave maris stella" is in the D (Dorian) mode. You may be able to hear that the third note in the tune (the sixth note of the scale) is higher than would be normal in the modern minor mode. The hymn itself has six or seven stanzas; Dufay set only the even-numbered ones to his own music, leaving the others to be sung Gregorian-style in alternation. This makes it fairly easy to hear how he embellished the plainchant.

His music for stanzas 2, 4, and 6 is the same each time—almost entirely homophonic and quite suave. The top voice sings a paraphrased, somewhat longer version of the hymn tune, as shown here. The embellishment consists of a few extra notes and extensions, with the free rhythm of Gregorian chant channeled into a graceful triple meter.

Plainsong hymn, "Ave maris stella"

A - ve _ ma-ris _ stel-la, ____

De - i   Ma - ter   al - ma,

At - que sem-per Vir-go, ____

Fe - lix coe - li   por - ta.

| | **LISTEN** | Dufay, "Ave maris stella" |

7	0:00	STANZA 1: Plainchant	

Ave maris stella,   Hail, star of the ocean,
Dei Mater alma,   Kind Mother of God,
Atque semper Virgo,   And also still a virgin,
Felix coeli porta.   Our blessed port to heaven.

STANZA 2: Dufay's paraphrase

0:22   Sumens illud Ave   May that blessed "Ave"
       Gabrielis ore,   From Angel Gabriel's mouth
       Funda nos in pace,   Grant us peace,
       Mutans Hevae nomen.   Reversing the name "Eva."

STANZA 3: Plainchant

1:13   Solve vincla reis . . .

STANZA 4: Paraphrase

1:35   Monstra te esse matrem . . .

STANZA 5: Plainchant

2:26   Virgo singularis . . .

STANZA 6: Paraphrase

2:48   Sit laus Deo Patri,   Praise be to God the Father,
       Summo Christo decus,   To Christ on high,
       Spiritui Sancto,   To the Holy Spirit:
       Tribus honor unus,   Three honored as one.
         Amen.   Amen.

Dufay and another fifteenth-century composer, Gilles Binchois (c. 1400–1460), with a harp. Portable small organs (called *portatives*) were in use at the time.

"Ave maris stella": The Virgin Mary was the subject of special veneration in the late Middle Ages and the early Renaissance. Countless plainchants, motets, paintings, and sculptures were created to honor her. Lost in her own thoughts, this serene, childlike Virgin by the German artist Stefan Lochner (1400–1451) seems oblivious to Jesus, even to God the Father—and no doubt to the music played for her by the baby angels.

This counts as a rather simple composition for Dufay, whose fame was and is based on longer, more elaborate pieces; he wrote some of the first polyphonic Masses, for example. Still, plainsong harmonizations make up an appreciable proportion of his output, and they show the new Renaissance attitudes with particular clarity.

The Mass

The new treatment of traditional plainchant, as in the technique of paraphrase, shows Renaissance composers taking a relaxed attitude toward medieval authority. The same can be said of their reaction to medieval intricacy, as represented by that most intellectual of musical devices, isorhythm. Fourteenth-century composers such as Machaut had used isorhythm even when writing love songs. Composers now cultivated a much simpler style for their polyphonic songs, or **chansons**: simpler, gentler, and more supple. The modest style of these new chansons was sometimes used for sacred texts, including portions of the Mass.

The rejection of isorhythm did not mean, however, that composers abandoned the technical development of their craft, which had taken such impressive strides from the early days of organum. Rather, such efforts were focused on large-scale musical construction. For the first time, compositions were written to last—and to make sense—over twenty or thirty minutes.

The problem of large-scale construction that fascinated fifteenth-century composers was how to write music that would hold together throughout the **Mass,** the largest and most important of all church services. The Mass contains numerous items that were sung in plainchant, and as we have seen, for centuries—from the time of organum to the time of harmonized hymns—composers had been embellishing plainchants with polyphony to be sung in services. The next step was to set the words that had been chanted to new music, instead of embellishing the existing chant music. For reasons we need not go into here, composers settled on these five items of the Mass for their new music:

Kyrie	a simple prayer:	"Lord have mercy, Christ have mercy"
Gloria	a long hymn, beginning:	"Glory to God in the highest"
Credo	a recital of the Christian's list of beliefs, beginning:	"I believe in one God, the Father almighty"
Sanctus	another, shorter hymn:	"Holy, holy, holy, Lord God of hosts"
Agnus Dei	another simple prayer:	"Lamb of God . . . have mercy on us"

The polyphonic Mass thus was standardized into a five-section form, and it has retained this form down to the present day, in settings by Palestrina, Bach, Mozart, Liszt, Stravinsky, and many others.

One of the earliest ways to unify these disparate elements was simply to use the same music to open each movement. Another way was to base each movement on the same Gregorian chant—not one belonging to the Mass but perhaps to the liturgy of some special day on which the Mass was celebrated. This would make the Mass especially appropriate for Christmas or Easter or (as we will see shortly) Corpus Christi, a celebration of the Holy Eucharist held every year in springtime.

So large a structure presented composers with a challenge, and they took this up in a spirit of inventiveness and ambition characteristic of the Renaissance. What the symphony was to nineteenth-century composers and their audiences, the Mass was to their fifteenth-century counterparts: a brilliant, monumental test of artistic prowess.

2   The High Renaissance Style

Around 1500 a new style emerged for Masses, motets, and chansons that would hold sway for much of the sixteenth century. The chief characteristic of this High Renaissance musical style was a careful blend of two kinds of musical texture, *imitative counterpoint* and *homophony* (see pages 29–30).

Functional, commercial: Compare this Mass printed around 1500 with the manuscript on page 82. The circulation of music (as of books, maps, images, and data in general) skyrocketed with the great Renaissance invention of the printing press.

Imitation

Most polyphony at the beginning of the fifteenth century was non-imitative; most polyphony at the end of the century was imitative. This remarkable change is due partly to the fact that imitative polyphony, or imitation, reflects the ideals of moderation and balance that also characterize the visual arts of the High Renaissance. In the Madonna by Raphael on page 49, the calm, dignified repose expressed by the figures and faces is as striking as the beautiful balance among all the pictorial elements.

By its very nature, imitative texture depends on a carefully controlled balance among multiple voice parts. A first voice begins with a motive (see page 27) designed to fit the words being set. Soon other voices enter, one by one, singing the same motive and words, but at different pitch levels; meanwhile the earlier voices continue with new melodies that complement the later voices without swamping them. Each voice has a genuinely melodic quality, and all the melodies are drawn from a single source. None is mere accompaniment or filler, and none predominates for very long.

We can get an impression of the equilibrium of imitative polyphony from its look on the page, even without reading the music exactly. The following excerpt is from the score of Josquin Desprez's *Pange lingua* Mass:

Compare two Madonnas shown in this book: One (page 79) is a late medieval masterpiece from northern Europe, the other from the new world of Renaissance Italy (page 49; painted only fifty years later). Uncrowned, uncluttered, a mother holds her child, smiles, the children play . . . God and His angels do not encircle this Madonna by Raphael as they do Lochner's.

Homophony

Almost all polyphony involves some chords, as a product of its simultaneously sounding melodies. But in the music of Machaut, for example, the chords are more of a by-product. Late medieval composers concentrated on the horizontal aspects of texture at the expense of vertical ones (see page 29), delighting in the separateness of their different voice parts. Chordal sonority was a secondary consideration.

A major achievement of the High Renaissance style was to create a rich chordal quality out of polyphonic lines that still maintain a quiet sense of independence. Composers also used pure homophony—passages of *block chord* writing. They learned to use homophony both as a contrast to imitative texture and as an expressive resource in its own right.

Other Characteristics

The ideal tone color at this time, especially for sacred music, becomes *a cappella* performance—that is, performance by voices alone. Tempo and dynamics change little in the course of a piece. The rhythm is fluid, without any sharp accents, and shifting unobtrusively all the time, so that the meter is often obscured. The melodies never go very high or very low in any one voice; the ups and downs are carefully balanced. This music rarely settles into the easy swing of a dance rhythm or into the clear patterns of an actual tune.

Music in the High Renaissance style can sometimes strike modern listeners as vague, but if we listen more closely — and always listen to the words as well as the music — its flexibility, sensitivity, and rich expressive potential begin to come clear. Does it remind us of a wonderfully musical and subtle speaking voice? The sixteenth century would have been pleased to think so.

Josquin Desprez (c. 1450–1521)

The first master of the High Renaissance style was Josquin Desprez. Like Dufay, he was born in the north of France, and like Dufay and many other of his countrymen, in early life he traveled to Italy. The list of Josquin's patrons reads like a Renaissance *Who's Who*: Pope Alexander VI, the notorious Sforza family of Milan, the Estes of Ferrara, Louis XII of France.

An amazingly imaginative composer, Josquin brought the fifteenth-century Mass to a brilliant climax and pioneered whole new expressive genres, such as the sixteenth-century chanson and motet. He was famous both for his technical prowess and for his expressive innovations — for the childlike serenity of his motet "Ave Maria," as well as the grief-stricken accents of "Planxit autem David," a setting of King David's lament for his dead son Absalom.

Josquin Desprez

A Kyrie (one voice part) from a dazzling illuminated manuscript book of Mass music. Did singers actually sing from such precious books? The man who commissioned it is shown here praying with the help of an angel, who also (below) seems to be giving a seal of approval to the family coat of arms.

JOSQUIN DESPREZ
Pange lingua Mass (c. 1510)

Josquin wrote eighteen different settings of the Mass—all large pieces in the standard five-section form. The *Pange lingua* Mass, one of his masterpieces, derives its melodic material largely from a hymn called "Pange lingua" ("Proclaim the Mystery"). This is a Gregorian hymn of the same kind as "Ave maris stella," which we have heard in Dufay's harmonized setting. "Pange lingua" (and hence Josquin's Mass) is designed for Corpus Christi, a feast celebrating the Holy Eucharist.

This is a four-part Mass (that is, a Mass for a choir with four separate voice parts). In Josquin's day, boys sang the high parts and men the lower ones; Josquin probably started his musical career as a choirboy. Today women usually substitute for boys in music of this period.

We shall examine the first two sections of Josquin's *Pange lingua* Mass.

Kyrie The men in the choir sing line 1 of the hymn "Pange lingua," in simple monophony, before the first section of the *Pange lingua* Mass. This first section, the Kyrie, is an elemental prayer consisting of three subsections:

Kyrie I:	Kyrie eleison.	Lord have mercy.
Christe:	Christe eleison.	Christ have mercy.
Kyrie II:	Kyrie eleison.	Lord have mercy.

For Kyrie I, Josquin wrote a **point of imitation**—a brief passage of imitative polyphony covering one short phrase of a composition's verbal text, and using a single musical motive. This motive, which enters many times, is a paraphrase (see page 77) of line 1 of the hymn:

Plainsong hymn, "Pange lingua"

Pan-ge lin-gua _ glo-ri-o-si

Cor-po-ris mys-te-ri-um, _

San-gui-nis-que pre-ti-o-si,

Quem in mun-di pre-ti-um _

Fruc-tus ven-tris gen-ne-ro-si

Rex ef-fu-dit _ gen-ti-um.

Gregorian hymn, "Pange lingua"

TENORS Ky-ri-e e-le-i-son

(The order of the voice entries is tenor, bass, *wait*, soprano, alto, *wait*, bass, tenor, soprano.) Josquin did not invent this motive—it was derived from the plainchant hymn, as shown above—but his paraphrase is very beautiful, especially at the end.

The Christe section has two points of imitation, also derived from the hymn, for the words *Christe* and *eleison;* the motives of these points are rhythmically similar. Kyrie II has a new point of imitation for the words "Kyrie eleison," followed by free (that is, nonhymn) material—a descending sequence and, prior to the drawn-out final cadence, a powerful oscillating passage.

LISTEN | Josquin, *Pange lingua* Mass, Kyrie

0:09	Kyrie eleison	Lord have mercy.
0:53	Christe eleison	Christ have mercy.
2:10	Kyrie eleison	Lord have mercy.

Gloria   The four remaining sections of the Mass—the Gloria, Credo, Sanctus, and Agnus Dei—introduce countless new points of imitation, which are interspersed with occasional text phrases set in homophony.

In the second subsection of the Gloria, beginning with the words *Qui tollis,* polyphony and homophony are contrasted in a highly expressive way. At the beginning, we can almost envisage one or two persons timidly invoking Him "who takes away the sins of the world" (polyphony), and then the whole congregation—or, symbolically, the whole of Christendom—urgently responding together with a plea for mercy and relief: "have mercy" (homophony). This music gives a dramatic sense of communal worship.

The "Qui tollis" as a whole includes eight points of imitation and four homophonic or nearly homophonic phrases. (The point for "Tu solus Dominus" is illustrated on page 81.) Even in the imitative phrases, the vocal lines fit together smoothly into chords, and while the sequence of these chords seems hard to predict, at least for modern ears, it does not seem arbitrary. The remarkable mood of Josquin's music—at once sober, quietly energetic, and reverential—owes much to its Phrygian (E) mode. Like the hymn "Pange lingua," the *Pange lingua* Mass is in this mode.

> " Throughout the motet ["Planxit autem David," by Josquin] there is preserved what befits the mourner, who at first is inclined to cry out constantly, then murmur to himself, then quiet down or—as passion breaks out anew—raise his voice again in a loud cry. All these things we see most beautifully observed in this composition."
>
> *An admirer of Josquin, writing a quarter century after his death*

LISTEN   Josquin, *Pange lingua* Mass, from the Gloria

(Capital letters indicate phrases sung in homophony.)

1
9

0:00	Qui tollis peccata mundi,
	    MISERERE NOBIS.
		You who take away the sins of the world,
		    have mercy upon us.

0:34	Qui tollis peccata mundi,
	    SUSCIPE DEPRECATIONEM NOSTRAM.
	Qui sedes ad dexteram Patris,
	
	    miserere nobis.
		You who take away the sins of the world,
		    hear our prayer.
		You who sit at the right hand of the
		    Father,
		have mercy upon us.

1:18	Quoniam tu solus sanctus,
	    tu solus Dominus,
	    tu solus altissimus,
	    Jesu Christe,
	cum sancto spiritu,
	    in gloria Dei Patris.
	AMEN.
		For you alone are holy,
		    you alone are the Lord,
		    you alone are the most high,
		    Jesus Christ,
		With the Holy Spirit,
		    in the glory of God the Father.
		Amen.

3 Music as Expression

In parts of Josquin's *Pange lingua* Mass, as we have just seen, the music does not merely enhance the service in a general way, but seems to address specific phrases of the Mass text and the sentiments behind them. Music can be said to "illustrate" certain words and to "express" certain feelings. The exploration of music's power to express human feelings was a precious contribution by musicians to the Renaissance "discovery of the world and of man."

Renaissance composers derived inspiration for their exploration of music's expressive powers from reports of the music of ancient Greece, just as artists, architects, and writers of the time were also looking to ancient Greece and Rome for inspiration. Philosophers such as Plato had testified that music was capable of arousing emotions in a very powerful way. In the Bible, David cures Saul when he is troubled by an evil spirit by playing on his harp; there are similar stories in Greek myth and Greek history.

How modern music could recapture its ancient powers was much discussed by music theorists after the time of Josquin. They realized that both music and words could express emotions, and they sought to match up the means by which they did so. Composers shared this expressive aim of matching words and music; in fact, devotion to the ideal of musical expression, by way of a text, was one of the main guiding ideas for musicians of the later Renaissance. This led to two important new developments in the music of the time.

¶ First, composers wanted the words of their compositions to be clearly heard. They strove for accurate **declamation**—that is, they made sure that words were sung to rhythms and melodies that approximated normal speech.

This may seem elementary and obvious, but it is simply not true of most medieval organum and motets (or of many plainchants). The Renaissance was the first era when words were set to music naturally, clearly, and vividly.

¶ Second, composers began matching their music to the *meaning* of the words that were being set. The **word painting** is used for this musical illustration of the text. Words such as "fly" and "glitter" were set to rapid notes, "up" and "heaven" to high ones, and so on:

Fly,   Love, a - loft   to heav'n to seek out for - tune . . .

Sigh was typically set by a motive including a rest, as though the singers have been interrupted by sighing. *Grief, cruel, torment, harsh,* and exclamations such as *alas*—words found all the time in the language of Renaissance love poetry—prompted composers to write dissonant or chromatic harmony. First used extensively in the sixteenth century, word painting has remained an important expressive resource of all later vocal music. For examples from the Baroque period, when it was especially important, see pages 104, 107, 162, and 166.

For examples from the Baroque period, when it was especially important, see pages 104, 107, 162, and 166.

JOSQUIN DESPREZ
Chanson, "Mille regrets"

Listen now to another work by Josquin, the polyphonic chanson, or song, "Mille regrets," a lover's lament at leaving his or her beloved. Though the words are little more than a string of clichés, their sorrowful tone seems to be perfectly captured in Josquin's music: in its somber harmonies, its drooping melodies, its slow-moving rhythms. Particularly effective are two homophonic moments in this song. The first singles out the phrase "J'ai si grand deuil" ("I feel such great sorrow"); the second, after a short point of imitation on "Qu'on me verra," ends the song with repeated affirmations of "brief mes jours déffiner" ("my days are numbered").

It is revealing to compare "Mille regrets" with Guillaume de Machaut's isorhythmic motet "Quant en moi," an earlier polyphonic song concerned with the pains of love (see page 70). There we have the sense of an exuberant play of musical structure rather than an expression of the poetry's sentiments; in Josquin's chanson, we experience instead a straightforward musical depiction of the generalized grief of the words.

" My Lord, if in our century there is any more excellent music than that of Orlande Lassus, I leave that judgment to masters of that art. I will say only this: that Plato, who liked so much to teach political harmony through musical proportions, would have taken his examples from Orlande had they lived at the same time.**"**

Publisher's promotion of an edition of music by Lassus, 1575

1

10

Mille regrets de vous abandonner
Et d'élonger votre face amoureuse.
J'ai si grand deuil et peine douloureuse
Qu'on me verra bref mes jours déffiner.

A thousand regrets at leaving you
and departing from your loving look.
I feel such great sorrow and grievous pain
that all will see my days are numbered.

4 Late Renaissance Music

As we noted above, the High Renaissance style established by the generation of Josquin Desprez proved remarkably stable. Yet it was also flexible enough that composers were able to do new things with it all the way to the end of the sixteenth century. While its use was clearest in the church music of the time, important new secular genres also made use of this style, in a modified form.

The universality of the style is symbolized by the geographical spread of its four most famous masters, Palestrina, Lassus, Victoria, and Byrd. *Giovanni Pierluigi da Palestrina* (c. 1525–1594) was born just outside Rome and worked in the Holy City all his life. *Roland de Lassus* (c. 1532–1594), also

Music at court: singers of the Bavarian Court Chapel in 1565, under Roland de Lassus. Each man and boy is carefully and solemnly depicted. With this imposing picture (and another, of an equally large group of court instrumentalists), the duke showed off the size and distinction of his retinue—a reflection, of course, of his own glory.

known as Orlando di Lasso, was a worldly and much-traveled Netherlander who settled at the court of Munich. His output was enormous. *Tomás Luis de Victoria* (c. 1548–1611), a Spanish priest, spent many years in Rome working for the Jesuits but ended up in Madrid. *William Byrd* (1540–1623) was organist of England's Chapel Royal under Queen Elizabeth I but also a member of the English dissident Catholic minority, who wrote Masses for illegal and highly dangerous services held in secret in barns and attics.

GIOVANNI PIERLUIGI DA PALESTRINA (c. 1525–1594)
Pope Marcellus Mass (1557)

Palestrina was a singer in, or choirmaster of, many of Rome's most famous churches and chapels, including the Sistine (Papal) Chapel. He lived in the repressive atmosphere of the Counter-Reformation movement, which was launched by the pope in 1545 to combat a growing revolt in northern Europe against Catholicism as then practiced (this revolt was the Protestant Reformation). Palestrina wrote secular compositions in his youth, some of which were widely popular, but later he recanted and apologized for them. He wrote over a hundred Masses and published his first examples with a highly symbolic frontispiece, which shows the kneeling composer presenting the pope with a special papal Mass.

Because singing is so powerful a force in religion, as we noted on page 58, societies have felt a need to control it carefully. Christianity has witnessed periodic reforms to prune church services of musical features that came to be seen as extravagant abuses. The Counter-Reformation staged just such a reform. Palestrina's most famous composition, the *Pope Marcellus* Mass, was supposed to have convinced the pope and his council that composers of complicated polyphonic church music could still set the sacred words clearly, with clear enough declamation so that the congregation could hear them. Partly because of this legend, and partly because of the particular calmness and purity of his musical style, Palestrina became the most revered Renaissance composer for later centuries. His works are still treasured by Catholic choir directors today.

Gloria   A part of the Gloria of the *Pope Marcellus* Mass, the "Qui tollis," shows how the High Renaissance *a cappella* style changed after the time of Josquin. Compared with Josquin's setting of these same words in his *Pange lingua* Mass (see page 84), Palestrina's setting employs much more homophony. Apart from some fuzziness on a few individual words, only the last and longest line of Palestrina's composition uses polyphony; as such it makes a fine climax.

Beyond this, we notice at once that vocal sonority is of major importance in Palestrina's setting. He uses a larger and richer choir than Josquin — six vocal parts, rather than four — and keeps alternating between one and another choral group, or semichoir, drawn from the total choir. Thus the first phrase, in high voices, is answered by the second, in low voices, and so on. The whole choir does not sing all together until the word *suscipe*.

What matters most to Palestrina are the rich, shifting tone colors and harmonies, which he uses to produce a generalized spiritual aura, sometimes ethereal, sometimes ecstatic. And with the dictates of the Counter-Reformation in mind, he is certainly careful to declaim the words very clearly.

The frontispiece of Palestrina's *First Book of Masses*, 1554, announces to all the world that this music has the pope's blessing. The book in Palestrina's hands is open to the papal Mass *Ecce Sacerdos magnus* ("Behold the great priest").

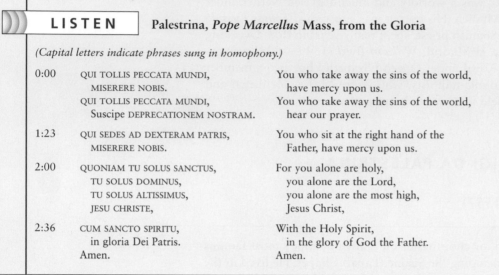

LISTEN   Palestrina, *Pope Marcellus* Mass, from the Gloria

(Capital letters indicate phrases sung in homophony.)

0:00	QUI TOLLIS PECCATA MUNDI, MISERERE NOBIS.	You who take away the sins of the world, have mercy upon us.
	QUI TOLLIS PECCATA MUNDI, Suscipe DEPRECATIONEM NOSTRAM.	You who take away the sins of the world, hear our prayer.
1:23	QUI SEDES AD DEXTERAM PATRIS, MISERERE NOBIS.	You who sit at the right hand of the Father, have mercy upon us.
2:00	QUONIAM TU SOLUS SANCTUS, TU SOLUS DOMINUS, TU SOLUS ALTISSIMUS, JESU CHRISTE,	For you alone are holy, you alone are the Lord, you alone are the most high, Jesus Christ,
2:36	CUM SANCTO SPIRITU, in gloria Dei Patris. Amen.	With the Holy Spirit, in the glory of God the Father. Amen.

The Motet

The term *motet* has been applied to very different kinds of music over the ages; thus motets by Palestrina or Byrd have little in common with motets by Machaut or even Dufay. The sixteenth-century **motet** is a relatively short composition to Latin words made up of short sections in the homophony and imitative polyphony that were the staples of the High Renaissance style. The words are nearly always religious, taken from a variety of sources—sometimes directly from the Bible. Thus, as compared with the Mass of the same time, the motet is basically similar in *musical style,* but different in *scope* and, of course, in text.

It was the variety of the text possibilities in the motet, as contrasted to the invariable Mass, that recommended it to sixteenth-century composers. By providing them with new words to express, motets allowed church composers to convey religious messages in their music with more verve and power than ever before.

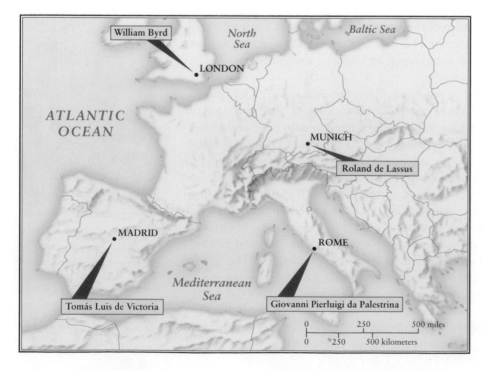

The dispersion of the High Renaissance style across Europe.

The Italian Madrigal

It was in the secular field, however, that the Renaissance ideal of music as expression made the greatest inroads. This took place principally in an important new Italian genre, after around 1530, called the **madrigal**.

The madrigal is a short composition set to a one-stanza poem—typically a love poem, with a rapid turnover of ideas and images. Ideally it is sung by one singer per part, in an intimate setting. The music consists of a sometimes equally rapid turnover of sections in imitative polyphony or homophony. Essentially, then, the plan is the same as that in High Renaissance sacred works such as Masses and motets.

But with secular words came a decisive change of emphasis. The points of imitation were shorter, and the imitation itself less strict; there was generally much more homophony; and the words assumed more and more importance. Both declamation and word painting were developed with great subtlety. For three generations a line of Italian madrigal composers, or *madrigalists*, pioneered an amazing variety of techniques to make words more vivid and to illustrate and illuminate them by musical means.

> **"** If therefore you will compose madrigals, you must possess yourself of an amorous humor, so that you must be wavering like the wind, sometimes wanton, sometimes drooping, sometimes grave and staid, otherwise effeminate; and show the very uttermost of your variety, and the more variety you show the better shall you please."
>
> *From a music textbook by madrigal composer Thomas Morley, 1597*

The English Madrigal

A genre like the madrigal, tied so closely to its words—Italian words—would seem difficult to transplant. All the same, Italian madrigals became all the rage in Elizabethan England and led to the composition of madrigals in English. This popularity may well have reflected the taste and interests of Queen Elizabeth I herself. The Virgin Queen not only maintained a splendid musical establishment, like all other ambitious monarchs and princes of the time, but she was also an accomplished musician in her own right.

In 1601, twenty-three English composers contributed madrigals to a patriotic anthology in her honor, called *The Triumphs of Oriana*. All the poems end with the same refrain: "Then sang the shepherds and nymphs of Diana: Long live fair Oriana!" Oriana was a pseudonym for Elizabeth, and the nymphs and shepherds of Diana—the goddess of virginity—were her subjects. The *Triumphs* was obviously a court-inspired project, and as such it reminds us vividly of one of the main functions of court music of all times: flattery.

Queen Elizabeth I playing the lute. This miniature portrait is reproduced close to its original size.

THOMAS WEELKES (c. 1575–1623)
Madrigal, "As Vesta Was from Latmos Hill Descending" (1601)

Thomas Weelkes never rose beyond the position of provincial cathedral organist-choirmaster; in fact, he had trouble keeping even that post in later life, when the cathedral records assert that he became "noted and found for a common drunckard and notorious swearer and blasphemer." Although he is not a major figure, as are the other composers treated in this unit, he is one of the best composers of madrigals in English.

Written in better days, Weelkes's contribution to *The Triumphs of Oriana* is a fine example of a madrigal of the lighter kind. (Weelkes also wrote serious and melancholy madrigals.) After listening to the music of Josquin and Palestrina, our first impression of "Vesta" is of the sheer exuberant brightness of the musical style. Simple rhythms, clear harmonies, crisp melodic motives — all look forward to music of the Baroque era and beyond. This music has a modern feel about it.

The next thing likely to impress the listener is the elegance and liveliness with which the words are declaimed. We have already stressed the importance of declamation in Renaissance composers' program of attention to verbal texts. Weelkes nearly always has his words sung in rhythms that would seem quite natural if the words were spoken, as shown at the right (where – stands for a long syllable, ˘ for a short one). The declamation is never less than accurate, and it is sometimes expressive: The rhythms make the words seem imposing in the second phrase shown, dainty in the third.

Leav-ing their God-dess all
a-lone

Then sang the shep-herds
and nymphs of Di-a-na

To whom Di-a-na's dar-lings

As for the word painting, that can be shown in a tabular form:

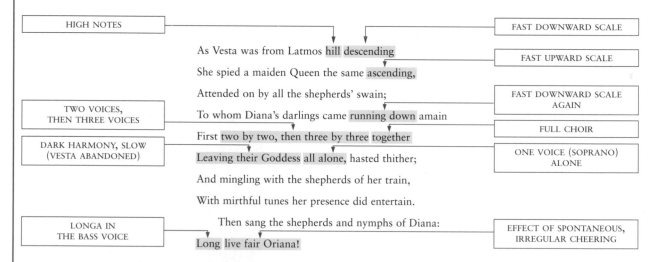

(The "maiden Queen" is Elizabeth, and "Diana's darlings" are the Vestal Virgins, priestesses of Vesta, the Roman goddess of hearth and home. The archaic word *amain* means "at full speed.")

This brilliant six-part madrigal uses two sopranos, alto, two tenors, and bass. Weelkes makes particularly good use of this group in his extended imitative setting of the poem's last line. Here we can easily imagine six loyal voices (or many more) endlessly cheering their Queen in a spontaneous, irregular way, one after another. Shakespeare and his contemporaries, Weelkes among them, were very fond of puns. Weelkes has the word "long" sung by the bass voice on a note four times the duration of a whole note—a note whose Latin name was *longa*. So this madrigal has its esoteric, in-joke side for musicians, as well as its public, political side for Elizabeth's subjects.

5 Instrumental Music: Early Developments

The best sixteenth-century composers concentrated almost entirely on vocal genres, on music with words. Except for the English master William Byrd, none of them devoted much attention to music for instruments alone. We have spoken above of the Renaissance preoccupation with expression in music, expression through the association of music with words.

Nevertheless, instruments and music for instruments developed significantly during this period. The first violins and harpsichords date from the sixteenth century; many other instruments such as the lute (see page 46) were perfected during this time. Originally from the Near East, the lute was as popular then as the guitar is today. Instrumental music was to become one of the great glories of the Baroque era, and the basis for this was laid in the Renaissance.

Around 1500, hardly any music was written specifically for instruments. Instrumentalists would either play along with singers in vocal music, or else play motets, chansons, and other vocal genres by themselves, without words. The principal vocal genre after 1550, however, the madrigal, would not have made much sense performed without its words. By this time, in any case, new genres had been developed for instrumental performance.

Renaissance Dances

The most widespread of Renaissance instrumental genres was the dance, a reflection of the great popularity of dancing at the time.

Many dance types are described in detail in sixteenth-century instruction books—the steps themselves, and also their order or sequence. (In this regard, old dances were closer to square dances than to some modern social dancing, where there is no fixed order for steps or movements.) One of the most popular was the **pavan** (paván), a solemn dance in duple meter, with the participants stepping and stopping formally. The pavan was usually paired with the **galliard**, a faster dance in triple meter.

Simpler, less formal Renaissance dance types include the Italian *saltarello*, the Irish *jig*, known also in Scotland and the north of England, and the French *bransle*—whose name is related to our word *brawl*. The Renaissance also saw elaborately choreographed ballets, court dances in which kings and nobles could participate.

Conforming to the dance steps, dance music was written in easy-to-follow phrases, almost always four to eight bars long. Ending with especially clear cadences, the phrases were each played twice in succession to produce forms such as **a a b b** or **a a b b c c**.

ANONYMOUS (sixteenth century)
Galliard, "Daphne"

The title of this melodious Elizabethan dance suggests that originally it may have been a song. But if so, at some point the song was pressed into galliard form, **a a b b c c,** and this is the only way it has survived.

Played in our recording by an early violin ensemble, "Daphne" is mainly homophonic. The meter is kept very clear, and the distinct quality of the phrases ending **a, b,** and **c** makes it easy for the dancers to remember the place in the dance step sequence. The first violin provides ornamentations at the second playing—an instrumental practice as old as the estampie (see page 66) and as new as jazz (page 396).

ANONYMOUS (sixteenth century)
"Kemp's Jig"

Will Kemp was an Elizabethan actor, comedian, and song-and-dance man, immortalized for having created comic roles in Shakespeare, such as Dogberry, the addle-headed constable in *Much Ado About Nothing*. Kemp specialized in a type of popular dance number, called a jig, that was regularly presented in Elizabethan theaters after the main play. He accompanied himself with pipe and tabor—a type of simple flute, blown like a recorder, and a snare drum.

"Kemp's Jig" is a lively—perhaps "perky" is the right word—and seemingly simple dance tune in **a a b** form. It is played several times on our recording, first by a recorder and then by a viol, an early stringed instrument in the cello range; ornaments are piled on, first to the repeated phrase **a** and then to all the repetitions. A lute accompanies.

bedfordstmartins.com/listen
▶ Quizzes and Flashcards

Dance Stylization

"Kemp's Jig" can lead us to an important topic that extends past the Renaissance. An oddity of this particular dance is that in phrase **a,** the cadence—a stopping place (see page 26)—comes in the fourth bar, whereas in phrase **b,** a cadence comes in the fifth. Though the motion does not stop, the tonic is reached in a very solid way at this point (bar 9). Another cadence comes three bars later, in measure 12. A dancer might be confused, even thrown off by this.

A listener, on the other hand, might enjoy the interesting effect caused by this irregularity in the cadences. If we like to think that this little dance puts us in touch with true folk music, we must also suspect that a musician of some sophistication has been tinkering with it.

"Kemp's Jig" is not as simple as it seems, then. It illustrates a tendency that will gain more and more importance later: the tendency to make dance music more and more elaborate and "artistic." Composers (and performers making it up on the spot) provided dance music with elements of a more strictly musical interest over and above the dancers' basic needs. Such elements are irregular cadences, as in "Kemp's Jig," subtle phrase lengths, unusual harmonies, and even counterpoint.

This was the first stage of a process that we can call the *stylization* of dance music. Already well established in the sixteenth century, dance stylization was to attain new heights in the dance suites by Bach and the symphony minuets of Haydn and Mozart. In the twentieth century,

Not Will Kemp of "Kemp's Jig," but another famous comic of Shakespeare's time: Richard Tarleton, with the traditional tools of his trade, the pipe and tabor.

fox-trot tunes were (and sometimes still are) stylized into jazz numbers. Louis Armstrong and Charlie Parker did not expect that people who came to listen to them were going to dance to such stylized versions.

Global Perspectives   2

Music and Early European Colonialism

In introducing the Renaissance, on page 76, we echoed the words of a historian who saw in it "the discovery of the world and of man." But we have not yet said much about the *world* part of this formulation.

The period from 1480 to 1620 marks the first great phase of European expansion into other parts of the world. The most famous European voyages of exploration, by Bartolomeu Dias, Vasco da Gama, Columbus, and Magellan, were followed by countless others. Trade routes to Africa and the New World were quickly established—so quickly that from 1492 on, only one year passed without European journeys to the Americas.

The voyages of exploration were more than sheer adventurism or innocent trading ventures. They were also expeditions of military conquest and territorial expansion. They marked the beginning of aggressive European colonization of large portions of the rest of the globe that would last almost half a millennium, well into the 1900s, and would profoundly shape the modern world.

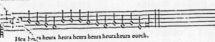

A European depiction from the 1590s of the song and dance of the Tupi Indians of Brazil. At the bottom you can see an attempt to render Tupi singing in European music notation.

Cultural Conquest and Music

The European attempt to conquer was cultural as well as military. In the immediate wake of European soldiers and *conquistadors* came missionaries aiming to convert the native peoples to Christian beliefs—whether by persuasion or coercion. And wherever they went, soldiers, missionaries, and merchants reported the novelties they found back to a fascinated Europe.

These reports—some precise and evidently accurate, others very fanciful—often made room for descriptions of music. They inform us of musical traditions that today are at least much changed and, in many cases, simply extinct. From the 1590s comes a description of African music in the Congo (for discussion of West African drumming, see page 404). English mariners report on Native North American song and dance (see page 75), and Dutch explorers tell about the elaborate gong orchestras, or *gamelans*, still played today in Indonesia (see page 220). The Jesuit Father Matteo Ricci, the first European allowed to reside in the imperial capital of Beijing, was scandalized by Chinese opera, "a curse," in his view, "more prone to vice" than any other activity (for more on Chinese opera, see page 316).

Music of the Aztecs and Incas

The Aztec and Inca empires were the greatest civilizations Europeans came upon in the New World. They amazed their conquerors with their cultural achievements and complexity, their riches, and their astonishing capitals: Tenochtitlán, in the middle of a Mexican lake that has long since disappeared, and Cuzco, built so high up in the Andes that the Spaniards had to establish Lima, a low-lying city on the coast, for themselves.

Since they had elaborate religious institutions of their own, the Mexicans and Andeans presented the European missionaries with their first great challenges for religious conversion in the New World. The missionaries systematically studied Aztec and Incan culture to determine how best to achieve their goal, and they taught the natives all the elements of a Christian life as they

A church procession in seventeenth-century Cuzco, with the Virgin Mary atop a wagon carrying musicians (not painted to scale). The aristocrat at the far left wears traditional Inca garb.

saw it. Prominent among their studies was native music; central to their teachings was European music.

Inevitably, the two musics were thrust into confrontation. A Mexican church council of the sixteenth century ruled that native musicians "shall sing polyphonic music only when their singing conforms to standards we consider acceptable . . . and they shall not be permitted to sing songs that remind people of their old idolatrous customs." A church council at Lima tried to abolish singing and dancing at native harvest festivals and to destroy the instruments and costumes used. Yet at the same time, the missionaries *encouraged* native song and dance in *Christian* festivals, hoping that they would hasten the Andeans' acceptance of the new, foreign religion.

These efforts could not succeed completely. We know that native singers preserved their traditional songs, often singing them secretly, away from the eyes and ears of the authorities. At the same time they easily learned and adopted the European music the missionaries pressed on them. (They sometimes had incentives: In Mexico the quickest learners had their taxes waived.) By the mid-seventeenth century Native Latin Americans were composing European-style church music in more than one newly built cathedral.

Inca Processional Music

The song "Hanaq pachap kusikuynin" is a fascinating case of the musical merging of two cultures. Published in 1631 by a Franciscan friar named Bocanegra, it is the first piece of elaborate music to be published anywhere in the New World. The words of the song are in the native Andean language Quechua (*ket*-chwa). Was it the work of Bocanegra himself, or one of the new Indian composers?

The song is a hymn to the Virgin Mary. Bocanegra says that it was sung during religious processions honoring her. Imagine the scene in 1630 in front of the still unfinished cathedral of Cuzco, built on the sturdy foundations of an Inca palace: Native singers march in procession across the plaza, wearing the traditional garb still permitted for Christian festivals, singing Quechua words set to European-style music, and accompanying themselves on Andean flutes and drums. As they enter the church, they regroup as a choir for services including Gregorian chant, now with Latin words—perhaps "Ave maris stella," the widely used hymn to the Virgin that we have already studied. Next comes newly composed polyphonic music. Such are the cultural mixes that arise in colonial situations.

Our performance of "Hanaq pachap kusikuynin" is tamer than this—no instruments are used. The music is simple but moving. It sets the phrases of the Quechua text one by one, in the straightforward homophonic texture we have heard in Dufay's harmonization of "Ave maris stella" and Palestrina's *Pope Marcellus* Mass (see pages 78 and 87).

))) **LISTEN**   "Hanaq pachap kusikuynin"

Hanaq pachap kusikuynin	Bliss of heaven,
Waranqakta much'asqayki	A thousand times
	I adore you.
Yupay ruru puquq mallki	Tree of myriad fruits,
Runakunap suyakuynin	Hope of peoples,
Kallpannaqpa q'imikuynin	Pillar of the weak:
Waqyasqayta	Hear my cry.

(one more stanza)

CHAPTER 7

The Early Baroque Period

A t the end of the sixteenth century, music was undergoing rapid changes at the sophisticated courts and churches of northern Italy. Composers began to write motets, madrigals, and other pieces more directly for effect—with a new simplicity, in some respects, but also with the use of exciting new resources. A new style, the style of the early Baroque period, took hold rapidly all over Italy and in most of the rest of Europe.

1 From Renaissance to Baroque

As we have seen, the madrigal was the most "advanced" form in late Renaissance music. Toward the end of the sixteenth century, the search for expression led madrigal composers to increasingly extreme—even weird—kinds of word painting. Previously taboo dissonances and rhythmic contrasts were explored to illustrate emotional texts in a more and more exaggerated fashion.

At the same time, a reaction set in *against* the madrigal. In Florence, an influential group of intellectuals mounted an attack on the madrigalists' favorite technique, word painting. Word painting was artificial and childish, they said, and the many voices of a madrigal ensemble could not focus feeling or express it strongly. Whatever the madrigalists thought, a choir singing counterpoint could only dilute strong emotions, not concentrate them.

True emotionality could be projected only by a single human agent, an individual, a singer who would learn from great actors and orators how to move an audience to laughter, anger, or tears. A new style of solo singing was developed, *recitative,* that was half music, half recitation. This led inevitably to the stage and, as we shall see, to opera. Invented in Florence around 1600, opera became one of the greatest and most characteristic products of the Baroque imagination.

Music in Venice

Meanwhile, there were important developments in Venice, the city of canals. The "Most Serene Republic," as Venice called itself, cultivated especially brilliant styles in all the arts—matched, it seems, to the city's dazzling physical appearance.

> " Why cause words to be sung by four or five voice so that they cannot be distinguished, when the ancient Greeks aroused the strongest passions by means of a single voice supported by a lyre? We must renounce counterpoint and the use of different kinds of instruments and return to simplicity!"
>
> *A Florentine critic, 1581*

Venice, the most colorful of European cities, and one of the most musical. Several major painters made a speciality of Venetian scenes, which were very popular; this one, of an aquatic fete across from the central square, the Piazza San Marco, is by Canaletto (1697–1768).

Wealthy and cosmopolitan, Venice produced architects whose flamboyant, varied buildings were built of multicolored materials, and painters—the Bellinis, Titian, Tintoretto—who specialized in warm, rich hues. Perhaps, then, it is more than a play on words to describe Venetian music as "colorful."

From the time of Palestrina's *Pope Marcellus* Mass, sixteenth-century composers had often subdivided their choirs into low and high semichoirs of three or four voice parts each. The semichoirs would alternate and answer or echo each other. Expanding this technique, Venetian composers would now alternate two, three, or more whole choirs. Homophony crowded out polyphony as full choirs answered one another stereophonically, seeming to compete with one another throughout entire motets and Masses, then joining together for climactic sections of glorious massed sound.

The resources of sonority were exploited even further when the choirs were designated for singers on some parts and instruments on others. Or else whole choirs would be made up of instruments. As the sonorous combinations of Venetian music grew more and more colorful, the stately decorum of the High Renaissance style was forgotten (or left to musical conservatives). Magnificence and extravagance became the new ideals, well suited to the pomp and ceremony for which Venice was famous. And as Venice became the tourist center of Europe, its distinctive music proved to be one of its big attractions.

Extravagance and Control

Wherever they looked, knowledgeable travelers to Italy around 1600 would have seen music bursting out of its traditional forms, styles, and genres. Freedom was the order of the day. But they might have been puzzled to notice an opposite tendency as well: In some ways musical form was becoming more rigorously controlled and systematic. As composers sought to make music more untrammeled in one respect, it seems they found they had to organize it more strictly in another. Listeners could not be allowed to lose track of what was happening.

The control composers exercised over Baroque form, in other words, was an appropriate response to Baroque extravagance, exaggeration, and emotionality. We shall see similar forces and counterforces at other points in musical history later in this book.

GIOVANNI GABRIELI (c. 1555–1612)
Motet, "O magnum mysterium"

15

The most important composers in Venice were two Gabrielis, Andrea and his nephew Giovanni. (Andrea's dates are c. 1510–1586.) As organists of St. Mark's Basilica, both of them exploited the special acoustics of that extraordinary building, which still impress tourists today. By placing choirs of singers and instrumentalists in some of the cathedral's many different choir lofts, they obtained brilliant echo effects that even modern audio equipment cannot duplicate.

Giovanni's "O magnum mysterium," the second part of a longer motet, was written for the Christmas season. The text marvels that lowly animals — the ox and the ass — were the first to see the newborn Jesus. This naive, touching text made "O magnum mysterium" a favorite for motet settings at the time; there are lovely versions by Victoria and William Byrd.

And the music marvels along with the text. Quite in the manner of a madrigal, the exclamation "O" is repeated like a gasp of astonishment. Then lush chord progressions positively make the head spin, as the words *O magnum mysterium* are repeated to the same music, but pitched higher (that is to say, in sequence: see page 26). A momentary change in the meter, which slips from duple (**2/2**) into triple (**3/2**), provides a new feeling of majesty, as much as astonishment:

Gabrieli uses two choirs, each with three voice parts and four instrumental parts, plus organ, though at first all we hear is a sumptuous blend of brass instruments and voices. Solo voices emerge at the word *sacramentum*. First solo tenors, then boy sopranos echo one another during the line *iacentem in presepio*, where a new rapid motive bounces back and forth from tenors to sopranos to brass.

Gabrieli unleashes his musical resources in a big way at the choral *alleluia* section. The music moves in quick triple meter, matching the jubilation of repeated *alleluias,* and the choirs echo back and forth across the sound space:

	FAST—triple meter									SLOW—duple meter	
	1 2 3	1 2 3	1 2 3	1 2 3	1 2 3	1 2 3	1 2 3	1 2 3	1 2 3	1 2 3 4	1 2 3 4	1

CHOIR 1   Al-le- |lu-ia, al-le-lu-|ia;   al-le-lu-|ia,   al-le-lu-|ia: [Al - - le-| lu------|ia

CHOIR 2   Al-le-|lu-ia, al-le-lu-|ia,   al-le-lu-|ia,   [Al - - le-| lu------|ia

To make a grand conclusion, the two choirs come together again. There is another wash of voice-and-brass sonority as the tempo slows and the meter changes to duple for a climactic *alleluia.* For yet another *alleluia,* the music adds a solemn extra beat, the meter changing once again:

Al - le - lu   -   ia,   Al - le - lu   -   ia

And for still more emphasis, Gabrieli repeats the entire *alleluia* section, comprising the fast triple-time alternations and the massive slow ending.

Notice that there are certain parallels between the beginning and the end of "O magnum mysterium." These include the tempo and meter (slow, changing from **2/2** to **3/2**), the texture (massed choirs), and the musical technique (sequence). Gabrieli has imposed a kind of organization and control on the flamboyant chords and the solo rhapsodies. This is an example of the combination of extravagance and control in early Baroque music that we discussed above.

LISTEN   Gabrieli, "O magnum mysterium"

1

15

0:00	O magnum mysterium,	O, what a great mystery,
0:30	et admirabile sacramentum	and what a wonderful sacrament—
0:53	ut animalia viderunt Dominum natum	that animals should see the Lord new born
1:23	iacentem in presepio:	lying in the manger.
1:56	Alleluia, alleluia.	Hallelujah, hallelujah.

2 Style Features of Early Baroque Music

Music from the period of approximately 1600 to 1750 is usually referred to as *baroque,* a term that captures its excess and extravagance. (It was originally a jeweler's term for large pearls of irregular shape.) A number of broad stylistic features unify the music of this long period.

Rhythm and Meter

Rhythms become more definite, regular, and insistent in Baroque music; a single rhythm or similar rhythms can be heard throughout a piece or a major segment of a piece. Compare the subtle, floating rhythms of Renaissance music, changing section by section as the motives for the imitative polyphony change.

(Renaissance dance music is an exception, and in the area of dance music there is a direct line from the Renaissance to the Baroque.)

Related to this new regularity of rhythm is a new acceptance of meter. One technical feature tells the story: Bar lines begin to be used for the first time in music history. This means that music's meter is systematically in evidence, rather than being downplayed as it was in the Renaissance. (Full disclosure: For ease of reading, we have added bar lines to our examples in Chapters 5 and 6, but there are no bar lines in the original music.) The strong beats are often also emphasized by certain instruments, playing in a clear, decisive way. All this is conspicuous enough in Gabrieli's motet "O magnum mysterium."

Texture: Basso Continuo

Some early Baroque music is homophonic and some is polyphonic, but both textures are enriched by a feature unique to the period, the **basso continuo.**

As in a Renaissance score, in a Baroque score the bass line is performed by bass voices or low instruments such as cellos or bassoons. But the bass part in Baroque music is also played by an organ, harpsichord, or other chord instrument. This instrument not only reinforces the bass line, it also adds chords continuously (hence the term *continuo*) to go with it. The basso continuo — or just continuo — has the double effect of clarifying the harmony and of making the texture bind or jell.

One can see how this device responds to the growing reliance of Baroque music on harmony (already clear from Gabrieli's motet). In the early days, the continuo was simply the bass line of the polyphony reinforced by chords; but later the continuo with its chords was mapped out first, and the polyphony adjusted to it. Baroque polyphony, in other words, has systematic harmonic underpinnings.

This fact is dramatized by a musical form that is characteristically Baroque, the **ground bass.** This is music constructed from the bottom up. In ground-bass form, the bass instruments play a single short figure many times, generating the same set of repeated harmonies (played by the continuo chord instruments). Above this ground bass, upper instruments or voices play (or improvise) different melodies or virtuoso passages, all adjusted to the harmonies determined by the bass.

Baroque ground-bass compositions discussed in this book are "Dido's Lament" from the opera *Dido and Aeneas* by Henry Purcell (page 106), a passacaglia by Girolamo Frescobaldi (page 110), and Vivaldi's Violin Concerto in G, Op. 4, No. 12 (page 138).

Another name for the ground bass comes from Baroque Italian musicians: **basso ostinato,** meaning "persistent" or "obstinate" bass. By extension, the term *ostinato* is also used to refer to any short musical gesture repeated over and over again, in the bass or anywhere else, especially one used as a building block for a piece of music. Ostinatos are found in most of the world's musical traditions (see page 112). This is not surprising, since the formal principle they embody is so very fundamental: Set up a repeating pattern and then pit contrasting musical elements against it.

Functional Harmony

Inevitably, in view of these new techniques, the art of harmony evolved rapidly at this time. Whereas Renaissance music had still used the medieval modes, although with important modifications, Baroque musicians developed the modern major/minor system which we discussed on pages 32–36. Chords

A ground bass
(the Pachelbel Canon)

= repeated
many times

66 Music is a roaring-meg against melancholy, to rear and revive the languishing soul; affecting not only the ears, but the very arteries, the vital and animal spirits, it erects the mind and makes it nimble."

Oxford scholar Robert Burton, 1621

A torchlight concert in a German town square. The harpsichord continuo is at the center of the action. Notice the big music stands or racks, and the two timpani sunk in a panel, like a double sink.

became standardized, and the sense of tonality—the feeling of centrality around a tonic or home pitch—grew much stronger.

Composers also developed a new way of handling the chords so that their interrelation was felt to be more logical, or at least more coherent. Each chord now assumed a special role, or function, in relation to the tonic chord (the chord on the home pitch). Thus when one chord follows another in Baroque music, it does so in a newly predictable and purposeful way. **Functional harmony,** in this sense, could also be used as a way of organizing large-scale pieces of music, as we will see later.

In a Baroque composition, as compared with one from the Renaissance, the chords seem to be going where we expect them to—and we feel they are determining the sense or the direction of the piece as a whole. Harmonies no longer seem to wander, detour, hesitate, or evaporate. With the introduction of the important resource of functional harmony, Baroque music brings us firmly to the familiar, to the threshold of modern music.

3 Opera

Opera—drama presented in music, with the characters singing instead of speaking—is often called the most characteristic art form of the Baroque period. For Baroque opera combined many different arts: not only music, drama, and poetry, but also dancing, highly elaborate scene design, and spectacular special effects. Incredibly ingenious machines were contrived to portray gods descending to earth, shipwrecks, volcanos, and all kinds of natural and supernatural phenomena. Scene designers often received top billing, ahead of the composers.

Opera began in Florence, as we have mentioned; the early operas were court entertainments put on to celebrate royal weddings and the like. But an important step was taken in 1637 with the opening of the first public opera theater. First in Venice and then in the whole of Italy, opera soon became the leading form of entertainment. By the end of the century, seven opera houses in Venice fulfilled much the same function as movie theaters in a comparable modern city (around 145,000 people).

Opera was a perfect answer to the general desire in the early Baroque era for individual emotionalism. Opera provided a stage on which the single individual could step forward to express his or her feelings in the most direct and powerful fashion. Indeed, composers felt a need to relieve the constant emotional pressure exerted on their characters by the ever-changing dramatic action. They had to contrive moments of relaxation, moments when the characters could stop and reflect. This led to a standard dualism that has been with opera ever since: *recitative* and *aria*. This dualism between action and reflection on that action is related to that other Baroque dualism, between freedom and strictness, extravagance and control.

Recitative

<u>Recitative</u> (re-si-ta-téev), from the Italian word for "recitation," is the technique of declaiming words musically in a heightened, theatrical manner. It is descended from the careful declamation practiced by late-Renaissance composers (page 85).

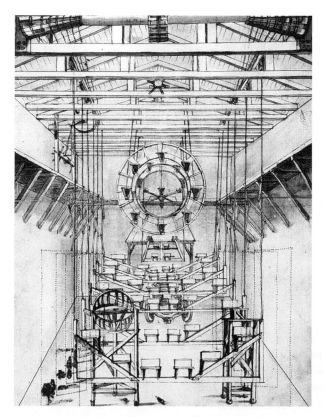

Stage designers of Baroque opera specialized in rapidly moving scenery for their most dazzling effects. Shown here is the machinery for one such set and a drawing of the intended realization.

The singing voice closely follows the free rhythm of highly emotional speech; it mirrors and exaggerates the natural ups and downs that occur as an actor raises his or her voice at a question, lowers it in an aside, or cries out in distress. The accompaniment is usually kept to a minimum, ensuring that all the words can be heard clearly.

Recitative—the "free" side of the operatic dualism—is used for plot action, dialogue, and other situations in the drama where it is particularly important for the words to be brought out. On the other hand, where spoken drama would call for soliloquies or meditations, opera uses arias.

Aria

An **aria** is an extended piece for solo singer that has much more musical elaboration and coherence than a passage of recitative. The vocal part is more melodic, the rhythm is more consistent, and typically the accompaniment includes the entire orchestra. Here the singer-actor mulls over his or her feelings at some leisure, instead of reacting moment by moment, as in recitative. Emotion is controlled and frozen into a tableau. Paradoxically, when the music gets more elaborate, the emotion stands still.

Recitative required great singing actors, and arias required artists who could convert the notes of a score into these tableaus of furious, sensuous, or tragic emotion. Opera houses in the seventeenth century became showcases of vocal virtuosity—as they still are today. Ever since the Baroque era, dramatic expression and vocal display have vied with one another as the driving force of opera.

Claudio Monteverdi (1567–1643)

One figure stood out above all others in music around 1600, just as Josquin Desprez had around 1500. Claudio Monteverdi, an enormously imaginative and innovative composer, also has the dubious distinction of being the first great composer whose music was attacked publicly for being too radical. Radical it was. Monteverdi has aptly been called "the last great madrigalist and the first great opera composer"; indeed, while his earliest madrigals are close enough in style to those of Thomas Weelkes, some of his later ones are more like small opera scenes.

Monteverdi first worked at the music-loving court of Mantua, in northern Italy. There he wrote his first stage work, *Orfeo* (Orpheus, 1607), famous in music history as the first masterpiece of opera. He was then appointed choirmaster of St. Mark's Cathedral in Venice, the most prestigious musical position in Europe, where the Gabrielis had held forth. At the end of his life, in the 1640s, he helped inaugurate public opera, Venice's greatest contribution to the history of music.

CLAUDIO MONTEVERDI
The Coronation of Poppea (1642)

16–17

After his first opera, *Orfeo,* none of Monteverdi's operas were printed, and some have been completely lost—a grievous loss indeed. All we have left of his *Arianna* is the heroine's big lament, one of the greatest hits of the day, which Monteverdi published by itself in several different arrangements. Fortunately, two late masterpieces have survived: *The Return of Ulysses* and *The Coronation of Poppea.*

Monteverdi as a young man, and as pictured on a commemorative edition of poems honoring him, published in Venice ("in VENETIA") just after his death. The design shows a fine collection of old instruments, including four lutes, shown in front and back views.

Background Even today, the story of *The Coronation of Poppea* can shock by its startling and cynical dramatic realism. Poppea, mistress of the notorious Roman Emperor Nero, schemes to get his wife, Ottavia, deposed and his eminent adviser, Seneca, put to death. She succeeds in both. In a counterplot, Ottavia blackmails Ottone, Poppea's rejected lover, into an attempt on Poppea's life. He tries but fails. The counterplotters are all exiled. As an added cynical touch, Poppea's ruthless maneuvering to be crowned empress of Rome is shown to be aided by the God of Love and the Goddess of Fortune.

After a prologue sung by the mythological characters, Act I begins with Ottone arriving at Poppea's house at daybreak, and retreating in dismay after he sees Nero's guards outside it. In an ironic alba (see page 66), the guards curse military life and exchange scurrilous gossip about Poppea's scheming. This is a vivid prelude to the first of the opera's several steamy love scenes.

Recitative Enter Nero and Poppea, who tries to wheedle Nero into staying with her. Delaying his departure as long as possible, she makes him promise to return. Accompanied by a lute as continuo instrument — a voluptuous sound, in this context — she repeats the question *"Tornerai?"* ("Won't you return?") in increasingly seductive accents until Nero stops evading the issue and agrees: *"Tornerò"* ("Yes, I will return"). Notice how the vocal line does not form itself into real melodies, but goes up or down or speeds or slows, following the words in speechlike fragments.

Nero's most extended evasion is a short arialike fragment, called an **arioso**. Then the recitative resumes. On the final *addios* — some of them melting, others breathless — the singers say good-bye, improvising delicate vocal ornaments.

LISTEN | Monteverdi, *The Coronation of Poppea,* from Act I

(Italics indicate repeated words and lines. For a word about singing Italian, see page 105.)

1

16–17

16

RECITATIVE

0:00	**Poppea:**	Tornerai?	Won't you return?
	Nero:	Se ben io vò,	Though I am leaving you,
		Pur teco io stò, *pur teco stò* . . .	I am in truth still here . . .
	Poppea:	Tornerai?	Won't you return?
	Nero:	Il cor dalle tue stelle	My heart can never, never be torn away
		Mai mai non si disvelle . . .	from your fair eyes . . .
	Poppea:	Tornerai?	Won't you return?

ARIOSO

0:24	**Nero:**	Io non posso da te, *non posso*	I cannot live apart from you
		da te, da te viver disgiunto	
		Se non si smembra l'unità	Unless unity itself can be divided . . .
		del punto . . .	

RECITATIVE

0:56	**Poppea:**	Tornerai?	Won't you return?
	Nero:	Tornerò.	I will return.
	Poppea:	Quando?	When?
	Nero:	Ben tosto.	Soon.
	Poppea:	Ben tosto, me'l prometti?	Very soon—you promise?
	Nero:	Te'l giuro.	I swear it!
	Poppea:	*E me l'osserverai?*	And will you keep your promise?
	Nero:	*E s'a te non verrò,*	If I do not come, you'll come to me!
		tu a me verrai!	
1:23	**Poppea:**	Addio . . .	Farewell . . .
	Nero:	Addio . . .	
	Poppea:	Nerone, Nerone, addio . . .	
	Nero:	Poppea, Poppea, addio . . .	
	Poppea:	Addio, Nerone, addio!	Farewell, Nero, farewell!
	Nero:	Addio, Poppea, ben mio.	Farewell, Poppea, my love.

Many men's roles in early opera were written for castrati, male soprano singers (see page 157). On our recording, Nero is sung by a female mezzo-soprano, Della Jones, whose lower, more focused voice contrasts with that of the soprano singing Poppea.

17 2:25 **ARIA** (Section 1)

0:10	2:35	**Poppea:**	Speranza, tu mi vai	O hope, you
			Il core accarezzando;	Caress my heart;
			Speranza, tu mi vai	O hope, you entice my mind;
			il genio lusingando;	
			E mi circondi intanto	As you cloak me
			Di regio si, ma immaginario	In a mantle that is royal, yes, but illusory.
			manto.	

(Section 2)

0:46	3:12	No no, non temo, no, *no no,*	No, no! I fear no adversity:
		non temo, no di noia alcuna:	

(Section 3)

1:03	3:28	Per me guerreggia, *guerreggia,*	I have fighting for me,
		Per me guerreggia Amor,	I have fighting for me Love and Fortune.
		guerreggia Amor e la Fortuna,	
		e la Fortuna.	

Aria As soon as Nero leaves, Poppea shows her true colors in a jubilant aria, a sort of victory dance. Accompanied by a small orchestra, it contains three short sections. The first is an orchestral tune (strings and recorder) to which Poppea sings her first two lines of text:

Allegro

POPPEA (with strings, recorder)

Speran - za _____ tu mi va - i   il core ac - ca - rez - zando _____

Note that a moment of uncertainty ("a mantle that is . . . illusory") is marked by a momentary lapse into recitative. Her mood becomes harder and more determined in the aria's second section. Finally, in section 3, she sings lighthearted, fast military fanfares—this is word painting in the madrigal tradition—as she crows that the gods are fighting on her behalf.

Mercurial, manipulative, fearless, dangerously sensual: Poppea has been characterized unforgettably by Monteverdi's music in this scene.

Singing Italian

The Coronation of Poppea is the first of many Italian texts printed in this book. To follow the recordings, it will help to know a few simple rules about Italian pronunciation and singing conventions.

❧ The consonants *c* and *g* are soft (pronounced "ch" and "j") when followed by *e* or *i* (cello, Genoa, cappuccino, DiMaggio). They are hard when followed by other letters, including *h* (Galileo, spaghetti con Chianti).

❧ In poems, when an Italian word *ending* with a vowel is followed by another word *beginning* with a vowel, the two vowels are elided, run together as one.

❧ In Italian (and German) *z* is pronounced *dz* or *tz* (pizza, Mozart).

Lines from our selection from *The Coronation of Poppea* are sung as indicated below:

3	Pur teco io stò	= Pur téc'yo stó
18	tu a me verrai	= tw'a méh verráh-ee
26	Il core accarezzando	= Il cór' accar-etzándo
28	E mi circondi intanto	= E mi chircond' intánto
33	Per me guerreggia Amor	= Per méh gwerréj' Amór

Henry Purcell (1659–1695)

Italy was the undisputed leader in music throughout the seventeenth century. However, music also flourished in France, Germany (or what is now Germany), and other countries, always under Italian influence.

The greatest English composer of the Baroque era, Henry Purcell, was the organist at Wetminster Abbey and a member of the Chapel Royal, like several other members of his family. In his short lifetime he wrote sacred, instrumental, and theater music, as well as twenty-nine "Welcome Songs" for his royal masters. Purcell combined a respect for native traditions, represented by the music of William Byrd, Thomas Weelkes, and others, with a lively interest in the more adventurous French and Italian music of his own time. He wrote the first English examples of a new Italian instrumental genre, the sonata.

Henry Purcell

HENRY PURCELL
Dido and Aeneas (1689)

Though Purcell composed a good deal of music for the London theater, his one true opera, *Dido and Aeneas,* was performed at a girls' school (though there may have been an earlier performance at court). The whole thing lasts little more than an hour and contains no virtuoso singing roles at all. *Dido and Aeneas* is an exceptional work, then, and a miniature. But it is also a work of rare beauty and dramatic power—and rarer still, it is a great opera in English, perhaps the only great opera in English prior to the twentieth century.

Background   Purcell's source was the *Aeneid,* the noblest of all Latin epic poems, written by Virgil to celebrate the glory of Rome and the Roman Empire. It tells the story of the city's foundation by the Trojan prince Aeneas, who escapes from Troy when the Greeks capture it with their wooden horse. After many adventures and travels, Aeneas finally reaches Italy, guided by the firm hand of Jove, king of the gods.

In one of the *Aeneid's* most famous episodes, Aeneas and the widowed Queen Dido of Carthage fall deeply in love. But Jove tells the prince to stop dallying and get on with his important journey. Regretfully he leaves, and Dido kills herself—an agonizing suicide, as Virgil describes it.

In Acts I and II of the opera, Dido expresses apprehension about her feelings for Aeneas, even though her courtiers keep encouraging the match in chorus after chorus. Next we see the plotting of some witches—a highly un-Virgilian touch, but ever since Shakespeare's *Macbeth,* witches had been popular with English theatergoers, perhaps especially with school-age ones. For malicious reasons of their own, these witches make Aeneas believe that Jove is ordering his departure.

In Act III, Aeneas tries feebly to excuse himself. Dido spurns him in a furious recitative. As he leaves, deserting her, she prepares for her suicide.

Recitative   Dido addresses this regal, somber recitative to her confidante, Belinda. Notice the imperious tone as she tells Belinda to take her hand, and the ominous word painting on *darkness.* Purcell even contrives to suggest a kind of tragic irony when Dido's melodic line turns to the major mode on the word *welcome* in "Death is now a welcome guest."

Aria   The opera's final aria, usually known as "Dido's Lament," is built over a slow ground bass or ostinato (see page 99), a descending bass line with chromatic semitones repeated a dozen times. The bass line sounds mournful even without accompaniment, as in measures 1–4. Violins in the string orchestra imitate this line while Dido is singing, and especially after she has stopped.

As often happens in arias, the words are repeated a number of times; Dido has little to say but much to feel, and the music needs time to convey the emotional message. We experience an extended emotional tableau. Whereas recitative makes little sense unless the listener understands the exact words, with arias a general impression of them may be enough. Indeed, even that is unnecessary when the song is as poignant as Purcell's is here.

The most heartbreaking place comes (twice) on the exclamation "ah," where the bass note D, harmonized with a major-mode chord during the first six appearances of the ground bass, is shadowed by a new minor chord:

Our Songs and our Musick
Let's still dedicate
To *Purcell,* to *Purcell,*
The Son of *Apollo,*
'Till another, another,
Another as Great
In the Heav'nly Science
Of Musick shall follow.

—*Poet Thomas d'Urfey,
seventeenth century (Apollo
was the Greek god of music.)*

**" *Dec. 6, 1665.* Here the best company for musique I ever was in, in my life, and I wish I could live and die in it, both for the musique and the face of Mrs. Pierce, and my wife, and Mrs. Knipp, who is pretty enough and sings the noblest that ever I heard in my life."

London civil servant Samuel Pepys, from his diary (first published in 1825)

Chorus The last notes of this great aria run into a wonderful final chorus. We are to imagine a slow dance, as groups of sorrowful cupids (first-graders, perhaps) file past the bier. Now Dido's personal grief and agony are transmuted into a sense of communal mourning. In the context of the whole opera, this chorus seems even more meaningful, because the courtiers who sing it have matured so much since the time when they thoughtlessly and cheerfully urged Dido to give in to her love.

The general style of the music is that of the madrigal—imitative polyphony and homophony, with some word painting. (The first three lines are mostly imitative, the last one homophonic.) But Purcell's style clearly shows the inroads of functional harmony and of the definite, unified rhythms that had been developing in the seventeenth century. There is no mistaking this touching chorus for an actual Renaissance madrigal.

Like "Dido's Lament," "With drooping wings" is another emotional tableau, and this time the emotion spills over to the opera audience. As the courtiers grieve for Dido, we join them in responding to Dido's tragedy.

		LISTEN	Purcell, *Dido and Aeneas*, Act III, final scene	

(Italics indicate repeated words and lines.)

		RECITATIVE		
18	0.00	**Dido:**	Thy hand, Belinda! Darkness shades me; On thy bosom let me rest. More I would—but death invades me: Death is now a welcome guest.	
		ARIA		
	0:58	**Dido:**	When I am laid, *am laid* in earth May my wrongs create No trouble, *no trouble* in thy breast; (*repeated*)	
	2:17		Remember me . . . *remember me*, but ah, forget my fate; *Remember me, but ah, forget my fate.* (*stabs herself*)	
		CHORUS		
19	4:01	**Courtiers:**	With drooping wings, ye cupids come (*words repeated*) And scatter roses, *scatter, scatter roses* on her tomb. Soft, soft and gentle as her heart.	Colored type indicates words treated with word painting.
1:30	5:31		Keep here, *here* your watch; *Keep here, here, keep here your watch,* and never, *never, never,* part.	

4 The Rise of Instrumental Music

The development of instrumental music—music without words, music that does not depend on words—counts as one of the most far-reaching contributions of composers in the early Baroque period. Broadly speaking, we can trace instrumental music to three main sources.

¶ *Dance,* the first of these sources, is one we have already discussed (p. 00) In the Baroque period dance received a special impetus from opera, the genre that most fascinated people at the time. This is because opera was firmly linked to ballet, as we have seen in *Dido and Aeneas.* Musicians, especially in France, the center of ballet at the time, would put together sets of dances selected from operas or ballets. These dance **suites,** as they were called—groups of dances—could then be played by an orchestra and enjoyed apart from an actual stage performance.

   Composers also wrote many dances and suites for harpsichord. These are *stylized* dances (see page 92), pieces written in the style or the form of dance music but intended for listening rather than dancing, for mental rather than physical pleasure.

¶ *Virtuosity* was the second source from which composers of instrumental music drew. As long as instruments have existed there have surely been virtuoso players ready to show them off—and audiences ready to applaud the show. But the art of early virtuosos was improvised and scarcely ever written down; only in the sixteenth and seventeenth centuries was some of their art incorporated systematically into written-out compositions. Even then, not all the virtuosity on which the compositions depended for their effect was notated. Much was left to be improvised, and so modern performers often have to play a good deal more than what appears in the old scores.

¶ *Vocal music* was the third source for instrumental music. More specifically, the principal technique of vocal music, imitative polyphony (imitation), was transferred to the instrumental medium. In fact, this had happened already in the Renaissance, which developed several instrumental genres modeled on vocal music in this way. Each genre consists of a series of points of imitation (see pages 81, 83) built on different motives, like a motet or a madrigal.

   From these genres developed the characteristic polyphonic genre of the Baroque era, the **fugue.** A typical fugue uses only one theme throughout—like a single extended point of imitation—and often treats that theme with a good dead of contrapuntal ingenuity and learning. The art of improvising and writing fugues was practiced especially by keyboard players: organists and harpsichordists. We will discuss fugue more fully in Chapter 9.

   Vocal music influenced instrumental music in another way as well. It gave instrumentalists a fund of materials they could use as the basis for sets of **variations**—that is, sectional pieces in which each section repeats certain musical elements while others change around them.

Girolamo Frescobaldi (1583–1643)

The three main sources of instrumental music are all evident in the keyboard works of Girolamo Frescobaldi. Frescobaldi was the foremost organ virtuoso of the early seventeenth century, famed through much of Europe for his expressive and even extravagant improvising and composition. Organist of St.

> ❝ Even that vulgar and tavern music, which makes one man merry, another mad, strikes in me a deep fit of devotion, and a profound contemplation of the first Composer; there is something in it of divinity more than the ear discovers.
>
> *Physician-author Sir Thomas Browne, 1642*

Peter's in Rome, he was an influential teacher, and his influence reached far beyond his own pupils. A century later Johann Sebastian Bach—keyboard virtuoso in his own right and composer of an immense body of organ and harpsichord works—carefully studied Frescobaldi's music. We will hear Frescobaldi's music on an organ specially modeled on an instrument of his own time. The player employs four different *registrations,* that is, different combinations of the organ's many sets of pipes: See page 46.

Frescobaldi composed organ works in several distinct genres:

❧ **Toccatas,** free-formed pieces meant to capture the spirit of Frescobaldi's own improvisation (*toccata* means "touched" in Italian, as in the touching of keys);

❧ **Canzonas,** more rigorously organized works emphasizing imitative texture—the ancestors of later fugues;

Girolamo Frescobaldi

❧ Stylized dances, formed of two phrases each, one or both of them repeated to yield the pattern **a a b** or **a a b b** (for similar Renaissance patterns, see page 91); these dances are sometimes grouped together in small suites; and

❧ Sets of variations on melodic or harmonic patterns borrowed from contemporary vocal music.

GIROLAMO FRESCOBALDI
Suite (Canzona, Balletto, Corrente, and Passacaglia) (1627–1637)

20–23

Frescobaldi's Balletto, Corrente, and Passacaglia is a miniature suite made up of two short dance movements followed by a set of variations. We introduce it, as Frescobaldi himself might have done, with the opening section of one of his canzonas.

20 *Canzona* This piece opens with a point of imitation (see page 83) using a theme that begins with long leaps followed by running sixteenth notes:

After four entries of this theme the music comes to a cadence. Then a new theme enters at the top of the texture, this one marked by three repeated notes at its start (see the example to the right). Frescobaldi immediately combines the second theme in counterpoint with the first, pitting the two against each other until he brings the music to a solid cadence.

21, 22   *Balletto and Corrente*   Each of these dance movements consists of two phrases, both of which are repeated: **a a b b.** Careful listening reveals that the two dances are related, especially by their bass lines:

While sharing a bass line, however, the dances also contrast strongly in their meters, the first duple, the second triple. Such metrical contrast from one dance to the next was a basic principle of suites from the late Renaissance on. (Compare the pavan and galliard on page 91.)

23   *Passacaglia*   This mellifluous term (pronounced *pas-sa-cáhl-ya*) refers to a set of variations on a brief series of chords and also the bass line associated with the chords. Both the harmonies and the bass line first arose in vocal music. Because of the repeating bass lines, the **passacaglia** bears a close kinship to slower ostinato pieces like "Dido's Lament." But usually the bass line of a passacaglia is repeated less strictly than is the ostinato of Purcell's work; it can even disappear entirely, leaving only the general chord progression to mark the variations. New at the time of Frescobaldi, the genre remained popular a century later in the age of Bach and Handel.

Violins are varnished and sun-dried in Cremona, a little town in northern Italy famous for its violin makers since the 1600s. Violinist-composers such as Vivaldi (see page 136) wrote for instruments by Antonio Stradivarius and other master craftsmen. See page 132.

The bass line of this passacaglia (and many others) runs in its simplest form something like the example to the right. Its length determines the length of each variation: four measures of fairly quick triple meter. (Get used to the main beat of the piece and then count **1** 2 3|**2** 2 3|**3** 2 3|**4** 2 3.) You can hear the bass line in its original, descending form in the first four measures, the theme, and many times more thereafter. Already in the second variation, however, and several times later, Frescobaldi plays a trick on the listener, composing an *ascending* bass line instead of the descending one while maintaining essentially the same progression of harmonies.

Frescobaldi seems able to milk endless variety from this simple material; this facility is the essence of skillful composing of variations. He is especially fond of coloring his music with piquant flashes of unexpected half steps, or **chromaticism** (especially piquant on this historical organ). At the same time he devises many different rhythmic patterns, some with fast running notes, others slower, some even and flowing, some dotted and jaunty.

Listen also for one more clever twist near the end of the movement: Frescobaldi changes key, or modulates, and at the same time shifts from major to minor mode. There are eighteen quick variations in all; the last five of them, starting at 1:37 of our recording, take place in this new key.

The instrumental music of the early seventeenth century was the precursor to an explosion of new instrumental styles and genres in the late Baroque era. We go on to discuss this in Unit III, after an introductory Prelude chapter dealing with the history and culture of the time.

bedfordstmartins.com/listen
▶ Quizzes and Flashcards

LISTEN

FRESCOBALDI
Suite

0:00	Canzona	
0:27	new theme	
0:00	**Balletto**	a
0:08		a
0:16 (0:30)		b b
0:00	**Corrente**	a
0:10		a
0:21 (0:36)		b b
0:00	**Passacaglia**	
0:14	Variation 2	
1:37	Variation 14	

Global Perspectives   3

Ostinato Forms

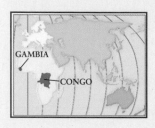

Though we borrow the term *ostinato* from Italian Baroque music, the technique is much older than the seventeenth century and is dispersed around the globe. The organizational principle at stake is, indeed, basic: Set up a brief repeating musical unit and use it as the foundation for other more varied melodies and harmonies.

Musical forms built according to this principle come in a wide variety of shapes and patterns. We have already begun to appreciate this variety in comparing "Dido's Lament" by Purcell with Frescobaldi's Passacaglia: The first presents a free-flowing melody over an unchanging bass line, while the second rings changes on an underlying harmonic pattern.

African Ostinatos

Nowhere in the world is ostinato form more prominent, or practiced with a richer array of techniques, genres, and instruments, than in Africa. Up and down the continent, ostinato forms multiply in fascinating variety: from North and West African nations, with ancient traditions of troubadour-like singers accompanying themselves on a single instrument, all the way to South Africa, with its electrified, rock'n'roll–derived Township Jive. (Rock itself is a great repository of ostinato forms.)

On our CD we hear two examples of African ostinato forms, one from the Gambia, a small nation lying along the West African coast, and the other from the Mbuti pygmies of the rainforests of Congo in central Africa.

A Minstrel's Song

In the first, Gambian excerpt, a singer-reciter named Foday Musa Suso accompanies himself on a plucked-string instrument called a *kora*. This is a complicated affair, a cross between a lute and a harp, with two sets of strings, twenty-one in all. The player, as our picture shows, holds it facing himself, plucking the strings with the thumbs and index fingers of both hands. Traditions of a singer accompanying himself on an instrument like

the kora or harp or lyre are very ancient around the Mediterranean Sea, whether in Europe, the Middle East, or Africa—think of the Biblical David with his harp or of Homer singing the *Iliad* and *Odyssey* to the lyre.

In West Africa, singers to the kora often belong to guilds, with musical expertise passed down in families from generation to generation. Foday Musa Suso comes from such a family and guild. For centuries these singers have fulfilled a wide variety of social roles, singing the praises of patrons and rulers, narrating in song historical or legendary events, contributing to weddings and other celebrations, and—especially in recent times— simply providing informal entertainment. Their styles have also fed into recent developments in African pop music. In fact, Foday Musa Suso himself emigrated from Gambia to Chicago in the 1970s, where he made a name for himself playing music that fuses jazz, pop, and traditional African styles. He has also performed with classical crossover musicians like the Kronos String Quartet (see p. 209).

Our recording is an early one, from before Foday's move, and offers a brief example of the kind of praise-song a West African minstrel might sing for a wealthy patron. But our main point in introducing it is to sample an African ostinato form. After a short introductory flourish on the kora, Foday lays down an ostinato pattern, plucked mainly on the low-pitched strings with his thumbs. He overlays this here and there with quick, cascading melodies, played on the higher strings with

Foday Musa Suso, with kora, crossing over to jazz performance.

the index fingers. Enriching the texture further is his singing, a freely repeated melodic phrase that starts high and drifts languidly down (first heard at 0:23). In between these phrases, Foday seems to be absorbed in his kora playing, singing quietly along with the fast melodies he plucks above the ever-present ostinato (listen especially from 1:01). To bring the performance to a close, he reserves a special effect: two strings, dissonant with each other, plucked in syncopated rhythms high above the ostinato (starting at 2:11).

Pygmy Polyphony

Since it was first recorded in the 1950s, singing in Mbuti pygmy communities has become famous for its delicate and complex polyphony. You may recognize the style, even if you have not heard recordings of pygmies before, since it has often been imitated by pop and world-beat singers such as Madonna and the group Zap Mama.

Pygmy polyphony is created in improvised group singing, sometimes in rituals central to the society, sometimes to accompany work, sometimes for simple pleasure and relaxation. It involves a technique common to many kinds of African music: *interlocking ostinatos*. In a pygmy chorus, various voices form an intricate, repetitive texture by singing over and over again their own short melodic lines — often only one or two notes — in quick alternation. (This technique may remind us of the *hocket* we encountered in the isorhythmic motet of the Middle Ages; see page 72.) The overall effect is of a multistranded, hypnotically recycling ostinato. This choral ostinato can be savored

on its own or else, as in our example, used as the foundation for freer melodies of lead singers.

A Hunting Song for Chorus

Two exclamations for the whole chorus announce the beginning of a song describing the bravery and daring of an elephant hunt. At first, we hear no clear ostinato. Instead, the two lead singers alternate prominent melodic phrases while, underneath them, the chorus softly sings — almost murmuring — an indistinct, ostinato-like melody.

Then something marvelous happens. At about 0:47 on track 32 the individual melodic motives of a polyphonic ostinato begin to crystallize in the chorus. We hear the polyphony taking shape. (How many distinct components of the ostinato can you make out?) By 1:30 the choral ostinato is fully formed and clearly articulated; it continues through to the end of the song (not heard here) underneath the soloists.

The singing is underlaid throughout by the simplest of instrumental accompaniments: two sticks struck together to mark the beat. The Mbuti rarely employ more elaborate instruments in their choral singing, though in other contexts they regularly play on drums, flutes, musical bows, and other instruments.

This song was recorded in the mid-1950s by Colin Turnbull, a British anthropologist who was among the first to study the pygmies. He described their society poetically and lovingly in a book still read today, *The Forest People,* but he didn't give the names of the singers of this song.

Mbuti villagers, singing and dancing to tall drums

The Eighteenth Century

The first body of music this book takes up in some detail is the music of the eighteenth century, the earliest music we hear regularly in concerts and on the radio. The eighteenth century in music covers two very different style periods: the late Baroque era and the era of Viennese Classicism. In the following pages we will try to clarify the differences between these periods and their music.

In spite of these differences, the music of the eighteenth century can be thought of as a unit. The reason is not a matter of musical style, at least not directly, important as style may be. Rather, it has to do with a certain quality of musical expression, a certain objectivity in the feelings this music seems to express or depict. Even when it is powerful and moving, it keeps its distance from the listener. Music of the nineteenth century is more demonstrative, more personal, more obviously intense; this music is called "romantic." In drawing the broadest distinctions, then, it is fair to put Baroque and Classical music on one side, Romantic music on the other. Romantic music often seems to want to share—even impose—feelings. Eighteenth-century music seems rather to demonstrate feelings.

Radio stations that play classical music play a lot of eighteenth-century music—Mozart is a favorite—often under the banner "music to relax by." Musicians cringe at this, but they cannot deny that music of the eighteenth century as a whole admits casual listening more easily than that of the nineteenth (let alone the twentieth and the twenty-first). It's possible to be expressive and relaxed at the same time, and not a bad thing.

The social and economic conditions under which the music was originally produced are behind this broad distinction in expressive quality. In our "Prelude" chapters, Chapters 8 and 11, we look at the cultural background and the social setting of eighteenth-century music, and suggest how these factors influenced musical style and expression. The other chapters in this unit look into specific works by the leading late Baroque composers Bach, Handel, and Vivaldi, and the Classical composers Haydn and Mozart.

CHAPTER **8**

Prelude
The Late Baroque Period

Music from the period of approximately 1600 to 1750 is usually referred to as "baroque," a term borrowed from art history. Art historians themselves borrowed the term from seventeenth-century jewelers, who applied it to large pearls of irregular shape. At one time, then, Baroque art was considered imperfect, bizarre, or at least erratic. With changing taste over the centuries, however, what was originally a negative implication has turned positive.

And over the last fifty years, with the help of recordings, Baroque music has grown more and more popular. Instruments of the period have been revived to play it, among them the harpsichord, the recorder, and a special high-pitched trumpet without valves. (Some of these instruments were discussed on pages 37–47.) Most of the Baroque music heard today dates from the eighteenth century—from around 1700 to 1750, a subperiod sometimes classified as the "late Baroque." Johann Sebastian Bach and George Frideric Handel were the greatest composers of this period, and among their most important contemporaries were Alessandro Scarlatti and Antonio Vivaldi in Italy, François Couperin and Jean-Philippe Rameau in France, Domenico Scarlatti (the son of Alessandro) in Spain, and Georg Philipp Telemann in Germany.

1 Absolutism and the Age of Science

Baroque is a period term used by art historians and musicologists. Historians are more likely to speak of the period from 1600 to 1750 as the Age of Absolutism. This was the time of belief in the divine right of kings, the idea that the right of kings to rule was absolute because they were chosen by God. Louis XIV of France became the most powerful monarch in all of European history, and also one of the most ruthless. The pomp and splendor of his court were emulated by a host of lesser kings and nobles.

Students of the history of ideas, on the other hand, speak of this as the Age of Science. In this era, the telescope and the microscope revealed their first secrets; Newton and Leibniz invented calculus; Newton developed his laws of mechanics and the theory of gravity. These discoveries stimulated both technology and philosophy—not only the formal philosophy of the great empiricist thinkers Descartes, Locke, and Hume, but also philosophy in a more informal sense. People began to think about ordinary matters in a new way, affected by the newly acquired habits of scientific experimentation and proof.

Louis XIV's palace of Versailles, with a procession of carriages arriving in the great courtyard. Note the formal gardens and canal.

The mental climate stimulated by science significantly affected the music and the art we call Baroque.

Absolutism and science were two of the most vital currents that defined life in the seventeenth and early eighteenth centuries. The result was an interesting dualism that can be traced throughout Baroque art: pomp and extravagance on the one hand, system and calculation on the other. The same dualism can be traced in Baroque music.

Art and Absolutism

As far back as ancient times, rulers in Europe sponsored the arts. Before the Baroque era, the artistic glories of the Renaissance were supported by powerful merchant-princes, such as the Medici family in Florence, who were determined to add luster to the city-states they ruled. But sponsorship of the arts rose to new heights in the seventeenth century, and one state loomed larger than any other in the scope and grandeur of its projects: France under Louis XIV (1638–1715), the so-called Sun King.

All of French life orbited around the royal court, like planets, comets, and cosmic dust in the solar system. Pomp and ceremony were carried to extreme lengths: The king's *levée*—his getting-up-in-the-morning rite—involved dozens of functionaries and routines lasting two hours. Artists of all kinds were supported lavishly, so long as their work symbolized the majesty of the state (and the state, in Louis's famous remark, "is me"—*"l'état, c'est moi"*).

Art in the service of royalty: a *very* idealized portrait of Louis XIV by the greatest sculptor of the day, Gianlorenzo Bernini (1598–1680).

The influence of this monarch and his image extended far beyond France, for other European princes and dukes envied his absolute rule and did everything they could to match it. Especially in Germany — which was not a united country, like France, but a patchwork of several hundred political units — rulers vied with one another in supporting artists who built, painted, and sang to their glory. Artistic life in Europe was kept alive for many generations by this sort of patronage. The brilliance and grandeur of much Baroque art derives from its political function.

Art was to impress, even to stupefy. Thus Louis XIV built the most enormous palace in history, Versailles, with over three hundred rooms, including an eighty-yard-long Hall of Mirrors, and great formal gardens extending for miles around. Many nobles and high-ranking churchmen built little imitation-Versailles palaces, among them the archbishop of Würzburg in Germany, whose magnificent residence was built in Bach's lifetime. The rooms were decorated by the Venetian artist Giovanni Battista Tiepolo (1696–1770), a master of Baroque ceiling painting.

Looking up at the ceiling shown on page 120, and trying to imagine its true dimensions, we are dazzled by figures in excited motion, caught up in great gusts of wind that whirl them out of the architectural space. Ceiling painting provides a vivid example of the extravagant side of the Baroque dualism.

The Music of Absolutism

Just as painting and architecture could glorify rulers through color and designs in space, music could glorify through sound. The nobility demanded horn players for their ceremonial hunts, trumpeters for their battles, and orchestras for balls and entertainments. They required smaller groups of musicians for *Tafelmusik* ("table music"), background music for their lengthy banquets. A special "celebratory" or "festive" orchestra featuring military instruments — trumpets and drums — was used to pay homage to kings and princes; by

Design for an opera stage set by G. G. Bibiena. This astonishing scene was intended for an opera at the court of Dresden in Germany.

extension, it also glorified God, the "King of Kings," as he is called in Handel's "Hallelujah" Chorus. The words sung by the chorus in this famous work praise God, but the accompanying orchestra with its trumpets also pays splendid homage to King George II of England (see pages 162–63).

The main musical vehicle of Baroque absolutism was opera. Opera today is an expensive entertainment in which a drama is presented with music and stage spectacle. So it was in the Baroque era. The stage set shown above was created by a member of the Bibiena family, the foremost set designers of the time. It conveys the majestic heights and distances of an ideal Baroque palace by means of perspective, though the stage was actually quite shallow. The figures gesture grandly, but they are dwarfed by pasteboard architecture that seems to whirl as dizzily as does the painted architecture on Tiepolo's ceiling (see page 120).

One aspect of Baroque opera is unlike opera today: The stories were allegorical tributes to the glory and supposed virtue of those who paid for them. For example, one favorite Baroque opera story tells of the Roman Emperor Titus, who survives a complicated plot on his life and then magnanimously forgives the plotters. This story was set to music in operas by dozens of court composers. It told courtiers that if they opposed their king, he might well excuse them out of the godlike goodness of his heart (for he claimed to rule by divine right). But it also reminded them that he was an absolute ruler—a modern Roman tyrant—who could do exactly the reverse if he pleased. Operas flattered princes while at the same time stressing their power and, not incidentally, their wealth.

Art and Theatricality

Opera was invented in Italy around the year 1600. Indeed, opera counts as Italy's great contribution to the seventeenth century's golden age of the theater. This century saw Shakespeare and his followers in England, Corneille and Racine in France, and Lope de Vega and Calderón in Spain.

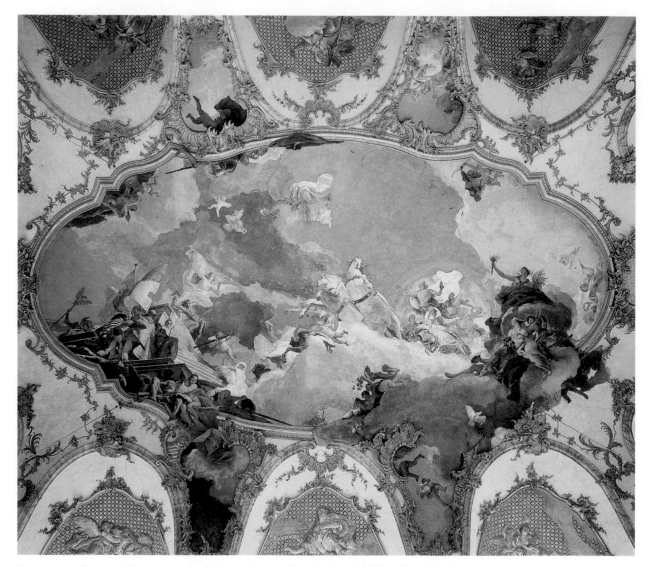

Baroque grandeur: a ceiling painting by Giovanni Battista Tiepolo (1696–1770). The oval measures 30 feet by 60 feet.

The very term *theatrical* suggests some of the extravagance and exaggeration we associate with the Baroque. But the theater is first and foremost a place where strong emotion is on display, and it was this more than anything else that fueled the Baroque fascination with the theater. The emotionality that we generally sense in Baroque art has a theatrical quality; this is true even of much Baroque painting. Compare Raphael's calm Renaissance Madonna on page 49 with the early Baroque Madonna by Guercino. Jesus seems to be falling out of the picture as he twists toward his mother; she gestures in theatrical fashion, clenching with one hand while pointing delicately with the other; and the stagey lighting contrasts bright patches of flesh with dark shadows.

Science and the Arts

All this may seem some distance away from the observatories of Galileo and Kepler and the laboratories where Harvey discovered the circulation of the blood and Leeuwenhoek first viewed microorganisms through a microscope. And indeed, the scientific spirit of the time had its most obvious effect on artists who were out-

Madonna and Child with the Young St. John the Baptist, by Giovanni Francesco Barbieri (1591–1666), known as Il Guercino.

side the realm of absolutism. The Dutch were citizens of free cities, not subjects of despotic kings. In Jan Vermeer's painting of his own city, Delft, the incredibly precise depiction of detail reflects the new interest in scientific observation. The painter's analysis of light is worthy of Huygens and Newton, fathers of the science of optics. There is something scientific, too, in the serene objectivity of this scene.

View of Delft, by Jan Vermeer (1632–1675)

The Age of Absolutism and the Age of Science converge in this painting of Louis XIV founding the Academy of Sciences.

Human control over nature is also symbolized by Baroque formal gardens. Today, landscape architecture is not usually regarded as one of the major arts, but it was very important in the age of the Baroque palace. Baroque gardens regulate nature strictly according to geometrical plans. Bushes are clipped, lawns tailored, and streams channeled, all under the watchful eye of big statues of Venus, Apollo, Hercules, and the rest, lined up in rows. Such gardens spell out the new vision of nature brought to heel by human reason and calculation.

Below the surface, furthermore, science is at work in even the most grandiose and dazzling of Baroque artistic efforts. The perspective of Tiepolo's ceiling painting or Bibiena's stage set depends on the use of very sophisticated geometry. (Bibiena published a manual detailing the mathematics behind his scene designs.) In Baroque music too, the influence of new scientific ideas can be found at the heart of extravagant, emotional expression.

Science and Music

Various aspects of Baroque music reflect the new scientific attitudes that developed in the seventeenth century. Scales were tuned, or *tempered*, more exactly than ever before, so that for the first time all the twenty-four major and minor keys were available to composers. Their interest in exploring this resource is evident from collections such as Bach's *The Well-Tempered Clavier*, containing preludes and fugues in every key. Harmony was systematized so that chords followed one another in a logical and functional way.

Regularity became the ideal in rhythm, and in musical form—the distribution of sections of music in time—we find a tendency toward clearly ordered, even schematic plans. Whether consciously or not, composers seem to have viewed musical time in a quasi-scientific way. They divided it up and filled it systematically, almost in the spirit of the landscape architects who devised Baroque formal gardens.

In the important matter of musical expression, too, science was a powerful influence. Starting with the French philosopher-mathematician René Descartes, thinkers sought to apply the new rational methods to the analysis and classification of human emotions. It had always been felt that music has a special power to express and arouse emotions. Now it seemed that there was a basis for systematizing—and hence maximizing—this power.

Thus scientifically inclined music theorists compiled checklists of musical devices and techniques corresponding to each of the emotions. Grief, for example, was projected with a specific kind of melodic motive and a specific kind of rhythm—even with a specific key. By working steadily with these devices and saturating their pieces with them, composers believed they could achieve the maximum musical expressivity.

The emotions of Hope and Fear, as represented in a Baroque scientific treatise. Like composers of the time, the artist felt that feelings could be isolated and depicted in the abstract.

2 Musical Life in the Early Eighteenth Century

The eighteenth century was a great age for the crafts—the age of Chippendale in furniture, Paul Revere in silver, Stradivarius in violin making, to name just a few. Though attitudes were changing, composing music was also regarded as a craft. The Romantic idea of the composer—the lonely genius working over each masterpiece as a long labor of love expressing an individual personality—was still far in the future. Baroque composers were more likely to think of themselves as servants with masters to satisfy. They were artisans with jobs, rather than artists with a calling, and they produced music on demand to fill a particular requirement.

This is why many Baroque pieces do not seem especially individualized in their expression. They are not so much unique masterpieces as satisfactory examples of their style and genre, of which there are many other equally satisfactory examples.

There were three main institutions where composers could make a living by practicing their craft. In order of increasing glamour, these were the church, the court, and the opera house.

¶ *The church.* In the cathedrals, monasteries, and town churches of the Baroque era, the general assumption was that the organists or choirmasters would compose their own music, then play and conduct it. Organists had to improvise or write out music to accompany certain parts of the church services. They played long pieces to see the congregation out when the service was over.

At large institutions, important occasions called for elaborate music scored for chorus, soloists, and instruments: a Catholic Mass for the installation of an archbishop, for example, or a Lutheran Church cantata for the anniversary of the Reformation. Church musicians were also responsible for training the boys who sang in their choirs, often in special choir schools.

¶ *The court.* Under the patronage of kings or members of the nobility, a musician was employed on the same terms as a court painter, a master of the hunt, or a head chef. To be sure, musicians had to work entirely at the whim of their masters. They could nevertheless count on a fairly secure existence, a steady demand for their services, and a pension.

Naturally, conditions varied from court to court, depending on the ruler's taste. For some, music was a good deal less interesting than hunting or

A Baroque opera performance (Turin, 1740). The stage set represents a great palace hall; the characters are striking various extravagant attitudes. Note the orchestra, a boy selling oranges, and a security guard.

banqueting. Others could not have enough of it. Frederick the Great of Prussia was a very keen flutist, so at his court concertos and sonatas for flute were composed at an especially healthy rate (see page xv). He wrote many himself.

Court musicians kept in better touch with musical developments than church musicians, since they were required to travel with their employers. They made extended trips to major cities, where diplomacy was eased along by music composed for the occasion.

¶   *The opera house.* Although many opera houses were attached to courts, others were maintained by entrepreneurs in major cities. (The public opera house existed before the public concert hall; in the Baroque era, public concerts were not a regular feature of musical life.) Audiences were alert to the most exciting new singers, and it was part of the composer's job to keep the singers well supplied with music that showed off their talents. Composers traditionally conducted their own operas, sitting at the harpsichord.

The revival of an older opera — usually because a favorite singer liked his or her part in it — was nearly always the occasion for massive recomposition, because another singer might want *her* part redone, too. If the opera's original composer had moved to the next town, other musicians would have no hesitation about rewriting (or replacing) some of the music. It was an exciting, unpredictable life, promising great rewards as well as daunting reverses.

The life stories of the two greatest composers of the late Baroque period show a good deal about the interaction between musicians, the patrons who supported them, and the institutions that required music. Johann Sebastian Bach labored as a church organist, a court musician, and then a major composer-administrator for the Lutheran Church. George Frideric Handel, who also had a court position, became an independent opera composer and opera promoter. Their biographies are given on pages 143 and 160.

3   Style Features of Late Baroque Music

If any one characteristic can be singled out as central to the music of the late Baroque period, it would be its thorough, methodical quality. After listening to a short Baroque piece, or to one section of a longer piece, we may be surprised to realize, first, how soon all the basic material is set forth, and second, how much of the music after that consists of inspired repetition and variation. It is as though the composers had set out to draw their material out to the maximum extent and wring it dry, as it were.

Indeed, the shorter pieces we will be examining in Chapters 9 and 10 — pieces like Contrapunctus 4 from Bach's *The Art of Fugue* and the aria "La giustizia" from Handel's opera *Julius Caesar* — contain little if any notable contrast in rhythm, dynamics, melody, texture, or tone color (see pages 146 and 158). Baroque composers preferred thoroughness and homogeneity.

With longer pieces, Baroque composers tended to break them up into blocks of music that contrast with one another in obvious ways, but are still homogeneous in themselves. This is the case with Bach's *Brandenburg* Concerto No. 5, for example, where the orchestral and solo sections contrast clearly enough. Within each orchestral or solo section, however, things are usually quite regular (page 140).

Rhythm

Baroque music is brimming with energy, and this energy is channeled into a highly regular, determined sort of motion. Like today's popular music, Baroque music gets its rhythmic vitality by playing off distinctive rhythms against a very steady beat. The meter nearly always stands out, emphasized by certain instruments in the ensemble. Most characteristic of these "marking-time" instruments is the busy, crisp harpsichord.

Another common feature that hammers home the beat is the so-called **walking bass,** a bass part that moves in absolutely even notes, usually eighths or quarters. In the Air from Bach's Suite No. 3 in D (see page 151), the bass keeps going for 138 "walking" eighth notes, plus 8 sixteenth notes and one half note (at the final cadence). Rhythmic variety in the upper instruments is heard in reference to absolute regularity below.

Attentive listening will also reveal another aspect of regularity in the steady *harmonic rhythm*—that is, a Baroque piece tends to change chords at every measure or at some other set interval. (Do not expect to hear this happening all the time, but it happens often enough so that we can speak of a tendency.)

Dynamics

Another steady feature of Baroque music is dynamics. Composers rarely used loud and soft indications (*f* and *p*) in their scores, and once a dynamic was chosen or set, it remained at about the same level for the whole section—sometimes even for the whole composition.

Neither in the Baroque period nor in any other, however, have performers played or sung music at an absolutely even level of dynamics. Instrumentalists made expressive changes in dynamics to bring out rhythmic accents, and singers certainly sang high notes louder than low ones. But composers did not go much beyond natural variations of these kinds. Gradual buildups from soft to loud, and the like, were rarely used.

Abrupt dynamic contrasts were preferred—again, between fairly large sections of a longer piece, or whole movements. A clear *forte/piano* contrast is built into the concerto genre, with its alternating blocks of music for the full orchestra and for one or more quieter solo instruments. When, exceptionally, a Baroque composer changed dynamics in the middle of a section or a phrase of music, he could count on the great surprise—even the amazement—of his listeners. A famous sudden *forte* in Handel's "Hallelujah" Chorus has been known to electrify the audience, to bring them to their feet (page 163).

We spoke earlier of a characteristic dualism between extravagance and order that can be detected in various aspects of Baroque culture (page 117). The methodical, regular quality of Baroque musical style that we are tracing here reflects the orderly, quasi-scientific side of this dualism. But Baroque music can also be highly dramatic, bizarre, or stupendous—a reflection of the other side of the dualism. Indeed, the magnificent momentary effects that occur occasionally in Handel and Bach are all the stronger because of the regular music around them.

Tone Color

Tone color in Baroque music presents something of a contradiction. On the one hand, the early part of the period evinced a new interest in sonority, and the end of it echoed with some very sophisticated sounds: Handel's imaginative orchestration in his operas, Bach's notably sensitive writing for the flute, and the refined harpsichord textures developed by several generations of composers in France. There are distinctive and attractive Baroque sounds that we do not hear in other periods: the harpsichord, the bright Baroque organ, the virtuoso recorder, and what we will call the festive Baroque orchestra, featuring high trumpets and drums.

On the other hand, a significant amount of music was written to allow for multiple or alternative performing forces. Thus it was a regular practice to designate music for harpsichord *or* organ, for violin *or* oboe *or* flute. Bach wrote a sonata for two flutes and rewrote it as a sonata for viola da gamba (a cello-like instrument) and harpsichord. Handel took solo arias and duets and rewrote them as choruses for his oratorio *Messiah*. In the last analysis, then, it seems the original tone color was often not critical in Baroque music.

The Baroque Orchestra

The core of the Baroque orchestra was a group of instruments of the violin family. The famous orchestra maintained by Louis XIV of France in the late seventeenth century was called "The Twenty-Four Violins of the King"; it consisted of six violins, twelve violas, and six cellos. A great deal of Baroque music was written for such an orchestra or a similar one—what would today be called a "string orchestra": violins, violas, cellos, and one or two bass viols.

Eighteenth-century instruments: recorder, violin, lute (back view), and *cornetto*—a wooden instrument played with a trumpet-like mouthpiece, with the pitch controlled by finger holes, as in a flute.

To this was added a keyboard instrument as continuo (see page 129)—usually a harpsichord in secular music and an organ in church music.

Woodwinds and brass instruments were sometimes added to the string orchestra, too, but there was no fixed complement, as was to be the case later. For special occasions of a festive nature—music celebrating a military victory, for example, or Christmas music ordered for a great cathedral—composers augmented the basic Baroque orchestra with trumpets or French horns, timpani, bassoons, and oboes and/or flutes. This festive orchestra has a particularly grand, open, and brilliant sound.

THE BASIC BAROQUE ORCHESTRA as in Vivaldi's Concerto in G (page 134)	
STRINGS	KEYBOARD
Violins (divided into two groups, called violins 1 and violins 2) Violas Cellos Bass viol (playing the same music as the cellos an octave lower)	Harpsichord or organ

THE FESTIVE BAROQUE ORCHESTRA as in Bach's Orchestral Suite in D (page 150)				
STRINGS	WOODWINDS	BRASS	PERCUSSION	KEYBOARD
Violins 1 Violins 2 Violas Cellos Bass viol	2 Oboes 1 Bassoon	3 Trumpets	2 Timpani (kettledrums)	Harpsichord or organ

Melody

Baroque melody tends toward complexity. Composers liked to push melodies to the very limits of ornateness and luxuriance. As a rule, the range of Baroque melodies is extended; they use many different rhythmic note values; they twist and turn in an intricate way as they reach high and low. It can be maintained that in the European classical tradition, the art of melody reached a high point in the late Baroque era, a point that has never been equaled since.

These long, intricate melodies, with their wealth of decorations added to the main direction of the line, are not easy to sing, however. They hardly ever fall into any simple pattern resembling a tune; even their appearance on the page seems to tell the story:

One easily recognized feature of Baroque melodies is their frequent use of sequence (see page 26; a sequence is shaded on the melody above). Baroque melodies repeatedly catch hold of a motive or some longer section of music and play it again and again at several pitch levels. Sequences provide Baroque music with one of its most effective means of forward motion.

Ornamentation

Not all melodies of the time are as ornate as the one shown above, however, and some, such as the simpler Baroque dances, are exceptions to the rule. On the other hand, the most highly prized skill of the elite musicians of the era, opera singers, was improvising melodic extras in the arias they sang night after night in the theater. This practice is called **ornamentation.**

Before the present era of sound amplification, when volume does much of the work, audiences thrilled to brilliant, fast, very high (or very low) music played and especially improvised by singers and instrumentalists. This is still very much the case with jazz. In the Baroque era, enough improvisations were written down, as guides for lesser musicians, to give us some idea of the art of the greatest virtuosos—such as the singers Bordoni and Cuzzoni (page 164) and the violinist-composer Vivaldi (page 136). They would spontaneously add all kinds of ornaments (jazz players would call them "riffs" or "licks") to whatever scores composers placed before them. Artists today have re-created Baroque ornamentation, or something like it; for a superb example, listen to Handel's aria "La giustizia," page 158.

Texture

The standard texture of Baroque music is polyphonic (or contrapuntal). Even many Baroque pieces that consist of just melody and bass count as contrapuntal because of the independent melodic quality of the bass. And large-scale pieces spin a web of contrapuntal lines filling every nook and cranny of musical spacetime. While cellos, bass viols, bassoons, and organ pedals play the lowest line, the other string instruments stake out their places in the middle, with oboes and flutes above them and the trumpets piercing their way up into the very highest reaches of the sound universe. The density achieved in this way is doubly impressive because the sounds feel alive—alive because they are all in motion, because they are all parts of moving contrapuntal lines.

Again, some exceptions should be noted to the standard polyphonic texture of Baroque music. Such are the homophonic orchestra sections (the *ritornellos*) in the concerto, and Bach's highly expressive harmonizations of old German hymns (chorales: see page 165).

There is nothing uniquely Baroque about musical ornamentation. If you heard the soul legend Aretha Franklin at Super Bowl XL, you heard "The Star-Spangled Banner" sung with ornaments added, not absolutely "straight."

But it is no accident that these textures appear *within pieces that feature polyphony elsewhere.* The ritornello in Bach's *Brandenburg* Concerto No. 5 alternates with polyphony played by the solo flute, violin, and harpsichord (see page 140). The harmonized hymn in his Cantata No. 4 comes at the very end, where it has the effect of calming or settling the complex polyphony of all the preceding music (see page 166).

The Continuo

Yet all this polyphony is supported by a solid scaffold of harmony. The central importance of harmony in Baroque music appears in the universal practice of the *basso continuo,* or just **continuo.**

The continuo is a bass part (the lowest part in polyphonic music) that is always linked to a series of chords. These chords are played by a harpsichord, organ, or lute as support or accompaniment for the important melodies in the other instruments. Indeed, we might say "mere accompaniment," for composers did not bother to write the chords out in detail, but only notated them in an abstract way by a numerical shorthand below the bass part. (Another name for continuo, **figured bass,** derives from this numerical shorthand.)

This left continuo players with a good deal to do, even though their role was considered subsidiary. By reading the basso continuo part, the harpsichordist or organist would play along with the cellos or bassoons—this with the left hand, which doubles the bass line. But the right-hand chords could be played in many ways: high or low, widely or closely spaced, smoothly connected or not. A certain amount of quick, on-the-spot improvisation was (and still is) required to "realize" a continuo, that is, to derive actual chords from abstract numbers.

Continuo part, as written: cello and harpsichord, left hand

Simple realization of chords: harpsichord

More ornate realization: harpsichord

Continuo chords provide the basic harmonic framework against which the contrapuntal lines of Baroque music trace their airy patterns. Under the influence of the continuo, Baroque texture may be described as *polarized*—a polarity of voices between a strong bass and a clear, high (soprano) range, the domain of the melody. Less clearly defined is a middle space containing the improvised chords. In Baroque works on the largest scale, this space is also filled in by polyphonic lines drawn from the median range of the orchestra and chorus, such as violas, tenors, and altos. In more modest works a characteristic texture is a hollow one: one or two high instruments (violins, flutes) or voices, a bass instrument, and subsidiary chord improvisation in the middle.

Baroque music is usually easily identified by the presence of the continuo—by the continuous but discreet sound of the harpsichord or organ playing continuo chords in the background. Indeed, the Baroque era in music was once called the basso continuo era, not a bad name for it.

Musical Form

Musical forms are clearer and more regular in the Baroque period than in most other historical periods. Two factors that appear to have contributed to this, one of them social, the other intellectual, were mentioned earlier.

The social factor is the patronage system, whereby the court and the church demanded a large amount of music and expected it to be produced in a hurry, almost as soon as it was ordered. Therefore composers needed to rely on formulas that could be applied quickly and efficiently. What is amazing about the church cantatas that Bach wrote at Leipzig, one a week, is how imaginatively he varied the standard forms for the various components of a cantata. But it was very helpful—in fact, it was absolutely necessary—for him to have those standard forms in place as a point of departure.

The other factor is the scientific spirit of the age, which affected composers only indirectly, but affected them nonetheless. One can detect the composer's ambition to map the whole range of a piece of music and to fill it in systematically in an orderly, logical, quasi-scientific way. This ambition seems to have been based on the conviction that musical time could be encompassed and controlled at will, an attitude similar to that of scientists, philosophers, and craftsmen of the time.

The music of Bach, in particular, shows this tendency on various levels. Look, for example, at the symmetrical arrangement of the seven sections of his Cantata No. 4, diagrammed on page 166. The last fugue in his *Art of Fugue* (he died before finishing it) is a more famous example. An ordinary fugue, as we shall see, is a polyphonic composition that deals exclusively with a single theme. This fugue deals with *four* themes, one after another, in four sections; then in the last section all four themes combine in four-part counterpoint. Theme No. 4 spells "Bach" in a musical code (!). A simpler Bach fugue may still have a ground-plan that is highly symmetrical (see page 146).

4 The Emotional World of Baroque Music

All music, it seems safe to say, is deeply involved with emotion. But in the music of different cultures, and also in the music of different historical eras within a single culture, the nature of that involvement can be very different. The emotional effect of Baroque music strikes the modern listener as very powerful and yet, in a curious way, also impersonal. Baroque composers believed firmly that music could and should mirror a wide range of human feelings, or *affects,* such as had been analyzed and classified by the scientifically oriented psychology of the day. But these composers did not believe, however, that it was their task to mirror feelings of their own. Rather, they tried to isolate and analyze emotions in general—at a distance—and then depict them consistently.

The exhaustiveness of their musical technique made for a similar exhaustiveness of emotional effect. A single movement or aria was usually restricted to depicting one specific emotion, feeling, or mood. As the rhythms and themes are repeated, the music intensifies a single strong feeling. Sadness in Baroque music is presented as the deepest gloom, calmness as profound quiet, brightness as pomp and splendor, happiness as loud rejoicing.

These are extreme sentiments; the people who can be imagined to experience them would have to be almost larger than life. All this fits perfectly into

In a typical Baroque texture, singers and violins in the upper register are supported by the *continuo*, played by three musicians in this performance. A cello plays the bass, and the middle range is filled in by two chord-playing instruments (harpsichord and lute).

place with the Baroque fascination with the theater. The Baroque theater concentrated on grand gestures and high passion, on ideal emotions expressed by ideal human beings. Kings and queens were shown performing noble actions or vile ones, experiencing intense feelings, delivering thunderous speeches, and taking part in lavish stage displays. How these personages looked and postured can be seen in the picture on page 124.

Theatrical emotion has the virtues of intensity, clarity, and focus; it has to have, if it is to get past the footlights and reach its audience. Actors analyze the emotion they are asked to depict, shape it and probably exaggerate it, and then methodically project it by means of their acting technique. It is not their personal emotion, though for the moment they *make* it their own. We may come to feel that Baroque composers worked in a similar way, not only in their operas—actual stage works set to music—but also in their oratorios and church cantatas, and even in their instrumental concertos and sonatas.

bedfordstmartins.com/listen
▶ Quizzes and Flashcards

CHAPTER 9

Baroque
Instrumental Music

In most societies, music with words is the norm; strictly instrumental music is less common or less important. So it is with popular music today, and so it was with the early music of Europe. In the Middle Ages, words for the church services were sung by monks and nurs as Gregorian chant, and later some of these same words were set to new polyphonic music for cathedral choirs and royal chapels. Troubadours set their love poems as solo songs. In the Renaissance, love poetry was set to music as madrigals, intricate part-music for a small group of solo singers. Vocal music was still very important in the late Baroque era, as we shall see in Chapter 10.

But part of the importance of the Baroque era was that for the first time, listeners and musicians began to take instrumental music much more seriously. A momentous change was set in motion, and the reasons for it are not entirely clear. It can hardly be a coincidence, however, that the rise of instrumental music took place at the same time as a similar development in the technology of instrument making. The name of Antonio Stradivarius (1644–1737) is known to many because of auctions where prices soar into the millions for one of his violins, unmatched after three hundred years. (They rarely come on the market. "Strad" cellos are even rarer.) Instruments by other master builders of the era, less well known, can still sound glorious: the organs of Gottfried Silbermann, the harpsichords of François Étienne Blanchet, the viols of Barak Norman (a viola da gamba or viol is pictured on page 137 and also to the right).

An early instrument that has now been revived, the viola da gamba is like a cello, with a quieter but also a rather husky sound. The beautiful viols by the Baroque maker Barak Norman have elaborately carved pegboards.

In any case, the rise of instrumental music meant that there had to be a basic understanding between composers and audiences about instrumental forms and genres. To pose the most basic question: When the music starts, how long should the composer keep going, and what should the listener expect? With vocal music, the answer was (roughly speaking): until the words end — when the sense of the sentence, paragraph, or total text is completed with a punctuation mark, a summing-up, or a concluding passage. For instrumental music, there was no such sense. Conventional forms and genres had to supply it.

In this chapter we look at the most important instrumental forms and genres established in the Baroque era. Baroque vocal music will be treated in Chapter 10.

1 Concerto and Concerto Grosso

The **concerto** and the **concerto grosso** (plural: concerti grossi) are the most important orchestral genres of the Baroque era. The basic idea underlying these genres is contrast between an orchestra and a soloist (in the concerto) or a small group of soloists (in the concerto grosso). Indeed, the word *concerto* comes from the Latin word *concertare*, to contend — an origin that accurately indicates a sort of contest between solo and orchestra.

This contest pits the brilliance of the soloist or soloists — and brilliance often involves improvisation — against the relative power and stability of the orchestra. Contrast comes to these genres naturally, then; a good deal of Baroque music is more uniform, as we shall see. But people soon tire of music that stays more or less the same. Composers who wanted to develop large-scale forms had to find ways of bringing contrast into their music; they wanted large-scale forms because audiences, then as now, were more impressed by extended compositions than by short ones.

Movements

One way to extend a composition was and is to lay it out in several movements (or, to put it another way, join together several movements as a single composite work). A **movement** is a self-contained section of music that is part of a larger work; movements can be compared to chapters in a book. Movements in a multimovement work will always show some variety in tempo, meter, key, mood, and musical form.

The typical late Baroque concerto has three movements. The *first* movement is a bright, extroverted piece in a fast tempo. After this, the *second* movement strikes an obvious contrast: It is quieter, slower, and more emotional. The *third* movement is fast again — if anything, faster than the first. In the first concerto we study, Vivaldi's Violin Concerto in G, the three movements exploit two conventional forms of the Baroque era. The first and last movements are in ritornello form, the second movement in ground bass form.

Ritornello Form

Many concerto movements are in *ritornello form,* from **ritornello,** the name for the orchestral music that typically starts the movement off. Contrast is basic to the concerto, and ritornello form focuses on contrast between two

> **" If the first movement [of a concerto] takes five minutes, the Adagio five to six, and the last movement three to four, the whole is of the proper length. And it is in general better if listeners find a piece too short rather than too long."**
>
> *J. J. Quantz (1697–1773), court composer to Frederick the Great, 1752*

musical ideas, or groups of ideas—one belonging to the orchestra and the other to the soloist. The orchestral material (the ritornello) tends to be solid and forceful, the solo material faster and more brilliant.

Ritorno, the Italian word for "return," tells us that the function of the ritornello in ritornello form is to return many times as a stable element of the form. Usually it returns only in part, and usually it is played in different keys as the movement proceeds. As for the musical ideas for the solo, sometimes these are virtuoso passages, sometimes themes, sometimes larger sections including themes and other material. To end the movement, the orchestral ritornello returns in the tonic key and, often, at full length.

Ritornello form can be diagrammed as shown below, where RIT stands for the entire ritornello, [RIT] for any part of the ritornello, and Solo 1, 2, 3, etc. for the solo sections.

RIT		[RIT]		[RIT]		[RIT]		[RIT]
	Solo 1		Solo 2		Solo 3		Solo 4	

Tonic key ——————————————— Other keys ——————————————— Tonic key

We need not worry too much about the exact number of ritornello fragments, the keys, and other details shown in such form diagrams. More important is the general impression that the form gives: the sense of a sturdy, reliable support in the orchestra for rapid and sometimes fantastic flights by the solo or solo group. Alongside the quasi-improvisational freedom of the solo instruments, the ritornello is always there, ready to bring them back down to earth and remind us of the original point of departure.

ANTONIO VIVALDI
Violin Concerto in G, *La stravaganza,* Op. 4, No. 12 (1712–1713)

24–26   3–4

The undisputed champion of the concerto was the Venetian composer Antonio Vivaldi. Vivaldi wrote hundreds of concertos, but published relatively few of them, in sets of six or twelve; each set was given a work number (*opus* is Latin for "work"). To some opuses he gave titles which evoke the extravagant side of the Baroque dualism (see page 117), such as "Harmonic Whims" (*L'estro armonico,* Opus 3) and "Extravagance" (*La stravaganza,* Opus 4). This Concerto in G is the last and one of the best of his Opus 4.

It is a concerto for solo violin and the basic Baroque orchestra of strings and continuo (see page 127); on our recording the continuo chords are played by a large lute (an *archlute*). The orchestra is quite small. In the age of Antonio Stradivarius, violin maker

Archlute, heard in the Vivaldi slow movement

LISTENING CHART 3

Vivaldi, Violin Concerto in G, first movement

Ritornello form, 2 min., 46 sec.

0:00	**Ritornello**	a
0:11		b
0:18		c
0:26	**Solo 1**	Contrasting solo violin music
0:41	**Ritornello 2**	c
0:49	**Solo 2**	Virtuoso solo violin music; several different sections
		Continuo drops out for a short time.
1:17	**Ritornello 3**	Part of this is derived from **a** and **c**; the rest is free.
		CADENCE in a minor key
1:33	**Solo 3**	More expressive
1:52	**Ritornello 4**	Even freer than Ritornello 3
2:10	**Solo 4**	Very fast
2:24	**Ritornello 5**	b c

bedfordstmartins.com/listen
▶Interactive Listening Chart 3

supreme, a great deal of music was composed at least partly to show off this favorite instrument. The violin's brilliance was especially prized, as was its ability to play expressively.

The Concerto in G begins and ends with movements in ritornello form.

First Movement (Spiritoso e non presto) "Spirited, not too fast" writes Vivaldi at the start of this triple-meter movement. The first and second violins of the orchestra echo one another brightly. Read the following material about the first movement, checking the various points with the entries in Listening Chart 3 on this page. Then listen, following along with the Listening Chart—see page xvii if anything about the chart (or the icons) is not clear. Read again, listen again.

The opening ritornello—with its typical loud, extroverted sound, marked *f*—consists of three parts. The first begins with a couple of loud chords to catch the audience's attention and set the tempo (**a**); then comes a central section with a distinct sequence (**b**), and then a cadential section where the dynamic changes to *p* for a moment (**c**):

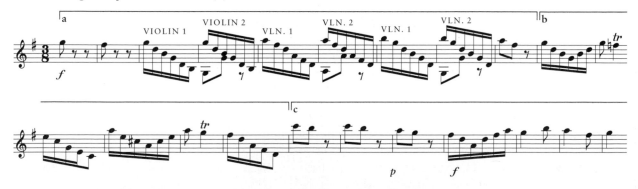

Once the ritornello ends with a very solid cadence (another typical feature of Baroque ritornellos), the solo violin enters, first with music moving at about the same speed as the ritornello, but soon speeding up. Virtuosity for the

Antonio Vivaldi (1678–1741)

The son of a Venetian violinist, Antonio Vivaldi was destined to follow in his father's footsteps. He entered the priesthood—where his bright red hair earned him the nickname of the "Red Priest"—and in 1703 became a music teacher at the Seminario Musicale dell'Ospedale della Pietà, a Venetian orphanage for girls. The Ospedale was one of several such institutions in Venice that were famous for the attention they paid to the musical training of their students. A large proportion of Vivaldi's works were composed for the school, whose concerts were a great tourist attraction.

The Ospedale allowed him frequent leaves of absence, so Vivaldi toured a good deal, but the composer's contract specified that he should write two concertos a month for the pupils and rehearse them if he was in town. Near the end of his life, Vivaldi left Venice permanently to settle in Vienna.

Internationally renowned as a virtuoso violinist, Vivaldi is remembered today chiefly for his brilliant concertos. He wrote more than four hundred of these, including concertos for harp, mandolin, bassoon, and various instrumental combinations; we know of more than 250 solo violin concertos, including our Concerto in G from *La stravaganza*. Critics of the day complained that Vivaldi's music was thin and flashy and that the composer was always playing for cheap effects. But the young Bach, before writing his *Brandenburg* Concertos, carefully copied out pieces by Vivaldi as a way of learning how to write concertos himself.

Vivaldi's most famous work—it has been recorded over a hundred times—is also one of his most unusual: *The Four Seasons,* a set of four violin concertos that illustrate, in one way or another, spring (bird songs, gentle breezes, and so on), summer (a nap in the sun), fall (a tipsy peasant dance at a harvest festival), and winter ("the horrible wind," says the score). Baroque composers were fond of musical illustration, especially with the words of vocal music, as we shall see; but they seldom pursued it this far.

Since no reliable portrait seems to exist of Vivaldi, we show a contemporary caricature.

Chief Works: Solo concertos for many different instruments, including the very famous *Four Seasons* • Concerti grossi for various instruments • 21 extant operas; oratorios; cantatas

Encore: After the Violin Concerto in G, listen to *The Four Seasons;* Concerto for Two Violins in A Minor, Op. 3, No. 8.

Baroque violinist meant jumping from the high strings to the low, executing fast scales, in fact any and all kinds of fast playing.

Ritornello 2 is an exact repetition of **c** from the first ritornello. The second solo has several subsections, which makes it much longer than any of the others; in one section the continuo drops out entirely. Ritornello 3 begins with derivatives of **a** and **c** but then wanders off freely and ends in a minor key. This provides a springboard for some expressive playing in the next solo. Ritornello 4 is freer still; it takes just enough from the original ritornello (especially part **b**) so that it seems to fit in with it and, indeed, to grow out of it spontaneously.

Vivaldi seems to have wanted his first four ritornellos to feel freer and freer, before he finally pulls the piece back in line. After the last solo (following Ritornello 4) cuts in very energetically, he ends the movement with a literal statement of **b** and **c**. (Absent is **a**, perhaps because its attention-getting function is no longer needed.) Compare the inner form of this movement with the standard outer form shown in the previous diagram.

RIT a b c		[RIT 2] c		[RIT 3] (a c)	[RIT 4] free		[RIT 5] b c
	Solo 1		Solo 2	Solo 3		Solo 4	

As this child appears to be finding out, music lessons can often serve as a cover for lessons in something else — a fact that helps explain the enduring popularity of music lesson pictures.

Baroque Variation Form: The Ground Bass

Variation forms are among the simplest and most characteristic of Baroque forms. Although they are not as common as other forms, they project the Baroque desire for systematic, thorough structures in a very direct way. This is because **variation form** entails the successive, uninterrupted repetition of one clearly defined melodic unit, with changes that rouse the listener's interest without ever losing touch with the original unit, or theme.

That theme may be a complete melody in the soprano range or a shorter melodic phrase in the bass. Given the emphasis in the Baroque era on the basso continuo (see p. 129), it is not surprising that Baroque variations tend to occur above stable bass patterns. A name for such patterns is **basso ostinato,** meaning "persistent" or "obstinate" bass. Sometimes the bass itself is slightly varied — though never in such a way as to hide its identity. Dynamics, tone color, and some harmonies are often changed in variations. Tempo, key, and mode are changed less often.

There are a number of names for compositions in variation form, which seem to have grown up independently all over Europe, first as improvisations and then as written-out compositions. Besides the French *chaconne* and the Italian *passacaglia (pas-sa-cáhl-ya)*, there was the English term *ground* (the repeating bass figure being called the **ground bass**). One seventeenth-century Italian composer, Girolamo Frescobaldi, left a passacaglia for organ with exactly a hundred variations. More compact examples of variation form sometimes appear as one movement in a larger Baroque genre, such as a concerto.*

Note that the term *ostinato* is also used to refer to any short musical unit repeated many times, in the bass or anywhere else, especially one used as a

---

*We examine earlier examples of variation (ground bass) form on page 106 and 110: "Dido's Lament" from *Dido and Aeneas* by Henry Purcell and a Passacaglia — with 18, not 100, variations — by Frescobaldi.

building block for a piece of music. Ostinatos are by no means unique to European music of the Baroque; in some form they are found in almost all musical traditions (see, for example, pages 112 and 223).

ANTONIO VIVALDI
Violin Concerto in G, *La stravaganza,* Op. 4, No. 12 (1712–1713)

24–26   3–4

Second Movement (Largo)   As is typical, Vivaldi's Concerto in G has three contrasting movements—the first vigorous and brilliant, the second gentle and slow. This slow movement is in variation (ground bass) form.

Our first impression of this music is probably of its texture—the gentle throbbing, the ingenious weaving in and out of the orchestral violins and the solo violin, and the delicate, subsidiary continuo sounds. There is, however, not much melody to listen to in the violin's music. There is less, in fact, as the movement goes along and the texture changes.

Sooner or later we notice that the only real melody is in the bass, where a solemn, quiet theme (the ground bass) is heard repeatedly in the cellos and bass viol. The theme sinks down and down, ending with a strong cadence:

We develop a sort of double listening for music like this, listening simultaneously to the unchanging theme and to the changing material presented above that theme. (This is no harder to do than taking in a distant view while also watching someone in the foreground.) After the theme's initial statement, four more statements with violin variations follow, during which the solo

LISTENING CHART 4

Vivaldi, Violin Concerto in G, second movement
Variation (ground bass) form. 2 min., 59 sec.

25   4

0:00	Theme	**Orchestra and Solo:** descending bass	
0:22	Var. 1	Solo:	Flowing material
0:41	Var. 2		Faster flowing material
1:03	Var. 3		Even faster music, though now in spurts
1:23	Var. 4		Faster yet: rapid figuration
		CADENCE	Brief stop at the cadence ending Variation 4
1:44	Var. 5		Thin texture (organ and lute drop out), with expressive violin material over a varied bass: in the minor mode
2:04	Var. 6		Like Variation 5, but the violin is a little faster and more expressive.
2:26	Theme	**Orchestra and Solo:** as at the beginning (i.e., back to the major mode, and the continuo returns)	

bedfordstmartins.com/listen
▶Interactive Listening Chart 4

violin plays faster and faster material above the unvaried ground bass. In its quiet way, this movement is showing off the violinist's ability to play music that is fast and sleek.

After Variation 4, however, there is a marked stop. Variation 5 makes a grand contrast of the kind relished by Baroque composers and audiences. The continuo stops, and since the texture is now thin and ethereal, the bass (played by the orchestra violins) can be heard more clearly—and what we hear is that the theme itself has been varied. It is now in the minor mode.

The mood becomes muted and melancholy; the violin is now showing off not its speed, but its expressive capabilities. The mood deepens in Variation 6. Rather abruptly, after this, the original theme returns in the full orchestra and continuo, played just as it was at the beginning, to end the movement.

The construction of this movement as a set of variations over a ground bass exemplifies the thorough, methodical quality of so much Baroque music. The effect of the contrast that Vivaldi has added with Variations 5 and 6 is not diminished by the steadily repeating, even obsessive bass. On the contrary, double listening can make the contrast seem richer and more interesting.

Third Movement (Allegro) Like the first movement, the third movement of the Concerto in G is a fast one in ritornello form. This time ritornello form is treated much more freely—or, as Vivaldi might have said, "extravagantly." More even than the first movement, this movement demonstrates that the outer ritornello form could accommodate a free and wide-ranging inner form.

Vivaldi begins with a long solo passage for the violin—and when the orchestra finally breaks in, all it can offer by way of a ritornello is a sort of hasty fanfare, interrupted by a short solo. The second ritornello is a much longer, very spirited passage of new music. Extravagant features of this movement would include the eviction of the orchestra from its customary place at the beginning; the fact that the lively second ritornello has nothing whatsoever to do with the official ritornello, namely the fanfare; and the way the solo violin keeps darting around and changing the kind of virtuoso material it plays throughout the movement.

However, order is asserted when the third ritornello takes the original fanfare as its point of departure (in the minor mode). And the final ritornello returns to its origins almost literally, as in the first movement.

))) LISTEN

VIVALDI
**Violin Concerto
in G,** third
movement

1
26

0:00	**Introduction** solo
0:16	**Ritornello 1** interrupted by solo
0:30	**Solo**
1:15	**Ritornello 2**
2:08	**Ritornello 3**
2:53	**Ritornello 4**
3:46	**Ritornello 5**

JOHANN SEBASTIAN BACH
Brandenburg Concerto No. 5, for Flute, Violin, Harpsichord, and Orchestra (before 1721)

2
1–5

1
5–9

A concerto grosso is a concerto for a group of several solo instruments (rather than just a single one) and orchestra. In 1721 Johann Sebastian Bach sent a beautiful manuscript containing six of these works to the margrave of Brandenburg, a minor nobleman with a paper title—the Duchy of Brandenburg had recently been merged into the kingdom of Prussia, Europe's fastest-growing state. We do not know why this music was sent (if Bach was job-hunting, he was unsuccessful) or if it was ever performed in Brandenburg.

To impress the margrave, presumably, Bach sent pieces with six different combinations of instruments, combinations that in some cases were never used before or after. Taken as a group, the *Brandenburg* Concertos present an unsurpassed anthology of dazzling tone colors and imaginative treatments of the Baroque concerto contrast between soloists and orchestra.

Brandenburg Concerto No. 5 features as its solo group a flute, violin, and harpsichord. The orchestra is the basic Baroque string orchestra (see page 127). The harpsichordist of the solo group doubles as the player of the orchestra's continuo chords, and the solo violin leads the orchestra during the ritornellos.

First Movement (Allegro)   In ritornello form, the first movement of *Brandenburg* Concerto No. 5 opens with a loud, bright, solid-sounding orchestral ritornello. The melody is attractive and easily recognized but, like so many Baroque melodies, becomes more complicated as it proceeds:

(For simplicity's sake, the music example above omits the note-repetitions on the eighth notes.) You could probably learn to sing phrase **a** easily enough, but **b** and **c** are much harder. There is no clear stop between them, and the melody begins to wind around itself in an intricate way. Yet it is undoubtedly just these features that give the ritornello its strength and its flair and keep it fresh when fragments of it return later in the movement.

Once the ritornello ends with a solid cadence, the three solo instruments enter with rapid imitative polyphony. They dominate the rest of the movement. They introduce new motives and new patterns of figuration, take over some motives from the ritornello, and toss all these musical ideas back and forth between them. Every so often, the orchestra breaks in again, always with clear fragments of the ritornello, in various keys. All this makes an effect very, very different from Vivaldi's Violin Concerto in G, not only because of the sheer length of the movement but because of the richness of the counterpoint and the harmony.

During a particularly striking solo section in the minor mode (the first red-shaded section on Listening Chart 5), the soloists abandon their motivic style and play music with even richer harmonies and intriguing, special textures. After this, you may be able to hear that all the remaining solos are closely related to solos heard before the minor-mode section—all, that is, except the very last. Here (the second red-shaded section on the Listening Chart) the harpsichord gradually outpaces the violin and the flute, until finally it seizes the stage and plays a lengthy virtuoso passage, while the other instruments wait silently.

An improvised or improvisatory solo passage of this kind within a larger piece is called a <u>cadenza</u>. Cadenzas are a feature of concertos in all eras; the biggest cadenza always comes near the end of the first movement, as in *Brandenburg* Concerto No. 5.

In this cadenza, the harpsichord breaks out of the regular eighth-note rhythms that have dominated this long movement. Its swirling, unexpectedly powerful patterns prepare inexorably for the final entrance of the orchestra. The whole ritornello is played, exactly as at the beginning; after nine minutes of rich and complex music, we hear it again as a complete and solid entity, not in fragments.

I Shall
1. set the boys a shining example of an honest, retiring manner of life, serve the School industriously, and instruct the boys conscientiously
2. Bring the music in both the principal Churches of this town [Leipzig] into a good state, to the best of my ability
3. Show to the Honorable and Most Wise Town Council all proper respect and obedience . . .

Bach's contract at Leipzig, 1723—the first three of fourteen stipulations

FLUTE

VIOLIN

LISTENING CHART 5

Bach, *Brandenburg* Concerto No. 5, first movement

Ritornello form. 9 min., 37 sec.

1 **5**	0:00	**Ritornello**	Complete ritornello is played by the orchestra, **forte**: bright and emphatic.
	0:20	**Solo**	Harpsichord, flute, and violin in a contrapuntal texture (often in trio style). Includes faster rhythms; the soloists play new themes and also play some of the motives from the ritornello.
	0:44	**Ritornello** (first phrase)	Orchestra, *f*
	0:50	**Solo**	Similar material to that of the first solo
	1:09	**Ritornello** (middle phrase)	Orchestra, *f*
	1:15	**Solo**	Similar solo material
	1:35	**Ritornello** (middle phrase)	Orchestra, *f;* minor mode
	1:41	**Solo**	Similar solo material at first, then fast harpsichord runs are introduced.
2 **6**	2:23	**Ritornello** (middle phrase)	Orchestra, *f*
0:06	2:29	**Solo**	This solo leads directly into the central solo.
0:32	2:54	Central solo	Quiet flute and violin dialogue (accompanied by the orchestra, *p*) is largely in the minor mode. The music is less motivic, and the harmonies change less rapidly than before.
0:58	3:19		Detached notes in cello, flute, and violin; sequence
1:35	3:52		Long high notes prepare for the return of the ritornello.
3 **7**	4:06	**Ritornello** (first phrase)	Orchestra, *f*
0:04	4:10	**Solo**	
0:48	4:54	**Ritornello** (first and second phrases)	Orchestra, *f;* this ritornello section feels especially solid because it is longer than the others and in the tonic key.
1:00	5:05	**Solo**	
1:28	5:34	**Ritornello** (middle phrase)	Orchestra, *f*
1:34	5:40	**Solo**	Fast harpsichord run leads into the cadenza.
4 **8**	6:18	Harpsichord cadenza	*Section 1:* a lengthy passage developing motives from the solo sections
1:46	8:04		*Section 2:* very fast and brilliant
2:12	8:31		*Section 3:* long preparation for the anticipated return of the ritornello
5 **9**	9:14	**Ritornello**	Orchestra, *f,* plays the complete ritornello.

bedfordstmartins.com/listen
▶Interactive Listening Chart 5

This painting is thought to depict a viol da gamba player of Bach's time named C. F. Abel and his musician sons. It is a symbolic picture: The kindly, soberly dressed father is holding his continuo instrument (the viol) as a support for the upper lines of the boys, who wear the frothy costumes of a later era. One of them would become a major composer.

Second Movement (Affettuoso)   After the forceful first movement, a change is needed: something quieter, slower, and more emotional (*affettuoso* means just that, emotional). As often in concertos, this slow movement is in the minor mode, contrasting with the first and last, which are in the major.

Baroque composers had a simple way of reducing volume: They could omit many or even all of the orchestra instruments. So here Bach employs only the three solo instruments—flute, violin, and harpsichord—plus the orchestra cello playing the continuo bass.

Third Movement (Allegro)   The full orchestra returns in the last movement, which, however, begins with a lengthy passage for the three soloists in fugal style (see "Fugues, Free and Learned," page 145). The lively compound meter with its triple component—one two three *four* five six—provides a welcome contrast to the duple meter of the two earlier movements.

2 Fugue

Fugue is one of the most impressive and characteristic achievements of Baroque music, indeed of Baroque culture altogether. In broad, general terms, fugue can be thought of as systematized imitative polyphony (see page 30). Composers of the Middle Ages first glimpsed imitative polyphony, and Renaissance composers developed it; Baroque composers, living in an age of science, systematized it. The thorough, methodical quality that we pointed to in Baroque music is nowhere more evident than in fugue.

A **fugue** is a polyphonic composition for a fixed number of instrumental lines or voices—usually three or four—built on a single principal theme. This theme, called the fugue **subject,** appears again and again in each of the instrumental or vocal lines.

Johann Sebastian Bach (1685–1750)

During the Baroque era, crafts were handed down in family clans, and in music the Bach clan was one of the biggest, providing the region of Thuringia in central Germany with musicians for many generations. Most of the Bachs were lowly town musicians or Lutheran Church organists; only a few of them gained court positions. Johann Sebastian, who was himself taught by several of his relatives, trained four sons who became leading composers of the next generation.

Before he was twenty, Bach took his first position as a church organist in a little town called Arnstadt, then moved to a bigger town called Mühlhausen. Then he worked his way up to a court position with the duke of Weimar. As a church organist, Bach had to compose organ music and sacred choral pieces, and at Weimar he was still required to write church music for the ducal chapel, as well as sonatas and concertos for performance in the palace.

The way his Weimar position terminated tells us something about the working conditions of court musicians. When Bach tried to leave Weimar for another court, Cöthen, the duke balked and threw him in jail for several weeks before letting him go. At Cöthen the prince happened to be a keen amateur musician who was not in favor of elaborate church music, so Bach concentrated on instrumental music.

In 1723 Bach was appointed cantor of St. Thomas's Church in Leipzig, a center of Lutheran church music in Germany. He not only had to compose and perform, but also organize music for all four churches in town. Teaching in the choir school was another of his responsibilities. Almost every week, in his first years at Leipzig, Bach composed, had copied, rehearsed, and performed a new cantata—a religious work for soloists, choir, and orchestra containing several movements and lasting from fifteen to thirty minutes.

Bach chafed under bureaucratic restrictions and political decisions by town and church authorities. The truth is he was never appreciated in Leipzig. Furthermore, at the end of his life he was regarded as old-fashioned by modern musicians, and one critic pained Bach by saying so in print. Indeed, after his death Bach's music was neglected by the musical public at large, though it was admired by composers such as Mozart and Beethoven.

Bach had twenty children—seven with his first wife, a cousin, and thirteen with his second, a singer, for whom he prepared a little home-music anthology, *The Note-Book of Anna Magdalena Bach*. The children were taught music as a matter of course, and also taught how to copy music; the performance parts of many of the weekly cantatas that Bach composed are written in their hands. From his musical response to the sacred words of these cantatas, and other works, it is clear that Bach thought deeply about religious matters. Works such as his Passions and his Mass in B Minor emanate a spirituality that many listeners find unmatched by any other composer.

Bach seldom traveled, except to consult on organ construction contracts (for which the fee was often a cord of wood or a barrel of wine). Blind in his last years, he continued to compose by dictation. He had already begun to assemble his compositions in orderly sets: organ chorale preludes, organ fugues, preludes and fugues for harpsichord. He also clearly set out to produce works that would summarize his final thoughts about Baroque forms and genres; such works are the Mass in B Minor, the thirty-three *Goldberg* Variations for harpsichord, and *The Art of Fugue,* an exemplary collection of fugues all on the same subject, left unfinished at his death.

Bach was writing for himself, for his small devoted circle of students, perhaps for posterity. It is a concept that would have greatly surprised the craftsmen musicians who were his forebears.

Chief Works: More than 200 sacred and secular cantatas; two Passions, with words from the gospels of St. Matthew and St. John; Mass in B Minor • *The Well-Tempered Clavier,* consisting of 48 preludes and fugues in all major and minor keys for harpsichord or clavichord • Three sets of suites (six each) for harpsichord—the French and English Suites and the Partitas; solo cello suites; violin sonatas; *Goldberg* Variations • Organ fugues and chorale preludes • *Brandenburg* Concertos, other concertos, orchestral suites, sonatas • Late composite works: *A Musical Offering* and *The Art of Fugue* • Chorale (hymn) harmonizations

Encore: After *Brandenburg* Concerto No. 5, listen to the Concerto for Two Violins; Mass in B Minor (Gloria section).

Bach's musical handwriting—the most beautiful and intricate of any composer's.

Fugue by Josef Albers. One can almost see the exposition and the subsequent subject entries, as in Bach's Contrapunctus 4.

The term *fugue* itself comes from the Latin word *fuga,* which means "running away"; imagine the fugue subject being chased from one instrument to another. Listening to a fugue, we follow that chase. The subject stays the same, but it takes on endless new shadings as it turns corners and surrounds itself with different melodic and rhythmic ideas.

Fugal Exposition

A fugue begins with an **exposition** in which all the voices present the subject in an orderly, standardized way. (The contrapuntal lines in fugues are referred to as *voices,* even when the fugue is written for instruments. We shall be speaking of the lines in a Bach fugue for strings as the *soprano, alto, tenor,* and *bass.*)

First of all, the subject is announced in the most prominent fashion possible: It enters in a single voice without any accompaniment (usually), while the other voices wait. Any voice can begin; in the diagram below, we follow the regular order of the example on our CD (soprano, alto, tenor, bass), but any order is possible. After leading off, voice 1 continues with new material of its own while the subject enters in voice 2. Next, the subject arrives in voice 3 — with 1 and 2 continuing in counterpoint with it (and with each other), using more new material, and so on. This section of a fugue, the exposition, is over when all the voices have stated the subject.

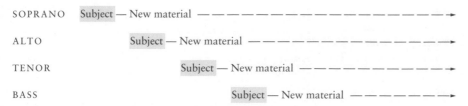

After the exposition, the subject enters at intervals, spaced out by passages of other music. It may come at the top of the texture (in the soprano), the bottom (bass), or half hidden away in the middle; see the diagram on page 146. Some of these later **subject entries** come in different keys. Although the modulations to these other keys may not be very obvious — less so than in music of the Classical era, for example — without them the music would be dull and stodgy.

Fugues, Free and Learned

Fugue is a somewhat complicated concept. We need to think of fugue not always as a genre ("*a* fugue"), but also as a style or a procedure (just "fugue," or fugal style), which is not always used strictly over the full length of a composition.

For in fact, full-scale fugues were very seldom written for public performance, at concerts (of which there were few in the Baroque era, anyway) or courts. Fugues occur as parts of French overtures—curtain-raisers for operas—but such fugues are invariably free, in that the individual voice lines are not maintained all the way through, as they are in virtually all of Bach's freestanding fugues. Since Bach is unquestionably the greatest master of fugue, there is a tendency to think of strict fugues as the main kind.

Nonetheless, free fugues are the more common and important. They can be free in the sense that they take up only part of a composition, not the whole of it (sometimes called *fugato*). They can be free by constantly slipping out of polyphony—the true texture of fugue—into homophony and then back again.

As for Bach, his greatest fugues are keyboard works written for study purposes, not for public performance: Such are *The Well-Tempered Clavier,* his very famous collection of preludes and fugues in each of the twelve major and twelve minor keys, and *The Art of Fugue.*

And in the study context, fugues developed technical refinements, showing off the composers' contrapuntal skill and treating the subject in various learned, seemingly intellectual ways. Some of these *fugal devices* are:

❧ *countersubject* The name given to the "new material" in the diagram on page 144 when it sticks with the subject, accompanying it one way or another throughout the fugue (i.e., the countersubject is the melodic line in voice 1 that is heard while the subject enters in voice 2).

❧ *stretto* One subject entry overlaps another entry in time, with the second jumping in before the first is complete.

❧ *augmentation, diminution* All note lengths in the subject are multiplied or divided (usually by two): A half note becomes a whole note, etc.

❧ *inversion* All intervals in the subject are reversed: Steps up become steps down, and so on.

Sometimes these fugal devices sound as academic and dry as their descriptions, but the Baroque masters of fugue could make wonderful music out of such technical procedures. *The Well-Tempered Clavier* includes learned fugues that are moving and serene, airy and even comical. Some sound very much like dance music.

Contrapunctus 4 from *The Art of Fugue,* from the first edition of 1751. The fugue subject can be seen entering from high to low on lines 5, 6, 7, and 12.

The passages of music separating the later subject entries are called **episodes.** They provide a contrast to the subject entries. This is true even though their motives are often derived from the subject; in such cases, the episodes do not present the subject in full, and so stand apart from subject entries. A regular feature of fugal episodes is the use of sequences (see page 26).

After the exposition, the form of a fugue falls into an alternating pattern: Episodes of various lengths come between subject entries in various voices and in various keys. Here is a diagram of a typical short fugue:

Exposition	Episode	Entry	Episode	Entry	Longer Episode	Entry
Subject						Subject
Subject		Subject				
Subject				Subject		
Subject						

| TONIC KEY | | ANOTHER KEY | | ANOTHER KEY | | TONIC KEY |

JOHANN SEBASTIAN BACH
The Art of Fugue, **Contrapunctus 4 (published 1751)**

Bach wrote *The Art of Fugue* at the end of his life, as a testament to his astonishing skill in writing fugues of all kinds, and with all shades of feeling. This huge work consists of twenty different canons and fugues — Bach uses the archaic and slightly pompous term *contrapunctus* — all on the same fugue subject. The number is not quite certain; Bach did not finish *The Art of Fugue,* and the heirs made something of a muddle when they published whatever they could find, soon after his death.

As a demonstration of his "art of fugue," Bach showed off the fugal devices mentioned in the box on page 145 in most of the fugues. But in Contrapunctus 4, one of the most melodious, he seems more interested in the long, smooth, and attractive episodes that come between the subject entries. These episodes are derived mainly from two sources, one from art — the rapid ending of the fugue subject, marked *x* on the music below — and the other from nature, it seems: a cuckoo figure, used repeatedly yet never sounding silly.

By comparison, the subject itself sounds restrained and serious, and it is presented in a very orderly way. The exposition brings the voices in a regular order from high to low (soprano, alto, tenor, bass). After an episode, four more entries follow the same order, modulating to a major key. After another episode, another four entries arrive in the reverse order — which is more climactic, since the highest entry comes last — and meanwhile the over all pitch range of the subject is expanded, as shown below:

This change automatically makes the subject sound more intense, and also lets the music modulate naturally, increasing the intensity even more. This climax is recalled later, in the fugue's imposing conclusion.

66 The bearer, *Monsieur* J. C. Dorn, student of music, has requested the undersigned to give him a testimonial to his knowledge *in musicis . . .* As his years increase it may well be expected that with his good native talent he will develop into a quite able musician."

Joh. Seb. Bach (a tough grader)

The Art of Fugue was written for harpsichord, but it is sometimes played by an instrumental group of some kind, which allows the individual voices to be heard more clearly. Mozart and Beethoven both arranged Bach fugues for string ensembles. We use an arrangement for string quartet by the English composer Robert Simpson (1921–1997).

))) LISTENING CHART 6

Bach, *The Art of Fugue*, Contrapunctus 4

Fugue form. 3 min., 30 sec.

	Exposition	*Fugue subject in:*
0:00		S (soprano; violin 1)
0:06		A (alto; violin 2)
0:15		T (tenor; viola)
0:21		B (bass; cello)
0:28	**Episode**	Uses a cuckoo figure, in sequence, then motive *x*, going up and down
0:39	**Subject Entries**	S Major mode
0:45		A Major
0:51		T Minor mode
0:56		B Minor
1:03	**Long Episode**	Similar material, plus lead-up to the cadence →
		☐CADENCE☐ minor mode
		Similar material
1:29	**Entries**	B ⎫
1:35		T ⎪
1:46		A ⎬ Climactic: expanded form of the fugue subject, modulating
1:57		S ⎭
1:58	**Long Episode**	
2:05		☐CADENCE☐ major mode (different key)
		Similar material, plus lead-up to the cadence →
2:29		☐CADENCE☐ minor mode (different key)
		Similar material
2:36	**Entries**	T
2:42		A (with a very close *stretto* in the S)
2:48	**Episode**	Episode material becomes more and more fluid.
3:09	**Final Entries**	T Expanded form of subject
3:15		A

cuckoo

x

bedfordstmartins.com/listen
►Interactive Listening Chart 6

3 The Dance Suite

Dance music was popular in the Baroque era, as has been true in every era, including of course our own. Dance music also inspired the greatest composers of the time to some of their best efforts.

The custom was to group a collection of miscellaneous dances together in a genre called the **suite**. Composers usually wrote "stylized" dances, that is, their music was intended for listening rather than dancing. Compared with music written for the actual dance floor, stylized dances naturally allowed for more musical elaboration and refinement, while still retaining some of the special features of the various dances.

Suites were written for orchestra, for chamber music combinations, or even for solo instruments such as the harpsichord or lute. Harpsichord suites are some of the very finest. Which dances occurred in a suite was not subject to any general rule, nor was there any specified order. All the dances in a suite were kept in the same key, and the last of them was always fast—frequently a **gigue**, a dance in compound meter that may have been derived from the Irish jig. Otherwise there was no standard overall structure to a suite.

Baroque Dances

Many different dances existed in the Baroque era. What distinguished them were features originally associated with the dance steps—a certain meter, a distinctive tempo, and some rhythmic attributes. The dance called the *gavotte*, for example, always begins with a double *upbeat*, two weak beats preceding the first strong beat (the *downbeat*) of a measure.

These are the main Baroque dances and their distinguishing features:

DANCE	USUAL METER	TEMPO	SOME RHYTHMIC CHARACTERISTICS
Allemande	4/4	Moderate	Upbeat sixteenth note; flowing motion
Courante	3/2	Moderate	Occasional substitution of **6/4** measures
Sarabande	3/4	Slow	Often a secondary accent on beat 2 (no upbeat)
Minuet	3/4	Moderate	Rather plain in rhythm (upbeat optional)
Gavotte	4/4	Moderate	Double upbeat of two quarter notes
Bourrée	2/2	Rather fast	Short upbeat
Siciliana	12/8	Moderate	Gently moving uneven rhythms; minor mode
Gigue	6/8	Fast	Short upbeat; uneven rhythms; lively movement

Baroque Dance Form

Although the number, type, and arrangement of dances in a suite varied widely, the *form* of individual dances was standardized. The same simple form was applied to all types, and it is an easily recognized feature of all Baroque dance music.

A Baroque dance has two sections, **a** and **b.** Each ends with a strong cadence coming to a complete stop, after which the section is immediately repeated. Both sections tend to include the same motives, cadences, and other such musical details, and this makes for a sense of symmetry between them, even though **b** is nearly always longer than **a**.

Hence Baroque dance form is diagrammed

a a b b *abbreviated as:* |: a :||: b :|

where the signs |: and :| indicate that everything between them is to be repeated. This form is also called **binary form.**

Trio   With shorter dances, composers tended to group them in pairs of the same type, with the first coming back after the second. The result was a large-scale **A B A** form. The **B** dance in such a pair was called the **trio,** because in seventeenth-century orchestral music it had often been scored for only three instruments.

This made for a simple, agreeable contrast with the full orchestration of the **A** dance. Even when the trio is scored for full orchestra, the idea of con-

Royals perform a Baroque
court dance.

trast between the two dances was always kept; the second is quieter than the
first, or it changes mode. (As for the term *trio,* to indicate a contrasting, subsidiary section, that was still used in the waltzes of Johann Strauss and the
marches of John Philip Sousa.)

Thus a Baroque minuet and trio, to choose this dance as an example, consists of one minuet followed by a second, quieter minuet, after which the first
is heard again. This time, however, the repeats in the binary form are normally
omitted:

	MINUET	TRIO	MINUET
	A	**B**	**A**
	a a b b	c c d d	a b
abbreviated as:	|: a :||: b :|	|: c :||: d :|	a b

The French Overture

A dance suite begins not with the first dance but with a special preparatory
number called a <u>French overture</u>. *Overture* is of course a general term for any
substantial piece of music introducing a play, opera, or ballet. The French
overture was a special type developed by the court orchestra of Louis XIV, designed to symbolize the pomp and majesty of his court. Even after the French
overture style had become antiquated, it was kept alive for the benefit of lesser
rulers outside of France who aped everything associated with the Sun King.

The French overture consists of two sharply contrasted sections, an **A** section and a faster **B** section. They are typically arranged in an **A B A′** pattern,
where **A′** stands for a variant—often a shortened version—of **A**.

The slow **A** section is the one that is distinctively "French"; dotted rhythms
(see page 21), sweeping scales and heavy accents, and other such features give

Concerts began late in the Baroque era. They were sometimes given in parks, where music accompanied gossip, flirtation, and food.

it a majestic, pompous gravity that is easily recognized (and was easily imitated). This section was often labeled with the French word *Grave* (*grahv*).

The fast **B** section is in imitative polyphony. In some overtures this section amounts to a full-scale fugue.

JOHANN SEBASTIAN BACH
Orchestral Suite No. 3 in D (c. 1730)

2   1
7–8   11

It is thought that Bach wrote this suite for the Collegium Musicum of the University of Leipzig, a student music organization that seems to have provided a congenial outlet for his later work. The Suite in D is scored for the festive Baroque orchestra diagrammed on page 127: strings, two oboes, three trumpets, two timpani, and harpsichord. Bach carefully varied the orchestration from number to number.

This suite, like others written all over Europe, uses French titles as an acknowledgment of French leadership in ballet and the dance. After the overture, its movements are cast in the Baroque dance form described above.

Ouverture   The French overture that starts the suite is scored for all the instruments, and in fact it is the only movement in which the oboes have (slightly) independent parts that do not always double the violins. What is more, a solo violin emerges unexpectedly to dominate two passages during the **B** part of the overture, which is a full-scale fugue.

The form of this overture is **A B A′**. Shown below are the beginning of the **A** section, the "Grave," with its arresting drum roll and the obligatory "French" dotted rhythms, and part of the fugal exposition in **B**:

Grave FULL ORCHESTRA, with TRUMPETS, TIMPANI

Viste [fast]

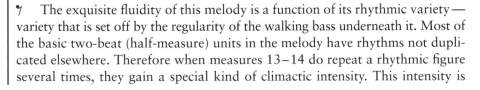

The episodes in this fugue are played by the solo violin. Indeed, this **B** part of the movement can be understood in two ways: as a fugue with solo violin episodes, or as a Baroque concerto with a fugal ritornello.

Following the overture come four pieces in dance form. In all of them the individual dances follow the Baroque pattern |: **a** :||: **b** :|. Notice the "full stop" effect after each playing of all the **a**'s and **b**'s. Only the gavotte, the second of the dances, has a trio and so falls into **A B A** (gavotte and trio) form.

Air *Air* is the French word for "aria," or song—and Bach composed this "instrumental song" in dance form, since it has to take its place in a dance suite. It is perhaps Bach's most famous and beloved melody. Only the strings and continuo play, as the quiet melody in the first violins is accompanied by a regular, downward-moving, soothing bass line in the cellos and bass viols (a **walking bass:** See page 126). And there are subsidiary but highly expressive counterpoints in the second violins and violas.

The exquisite fluidity of this melody is a function of its rhythmic variety—variety that is set off by the regularity of the walking bass underneath it. Most of the basic two-beat (half-measure) units in the melody have rhythms not duplicated elsewhere. Therefore when measures 13–14 do repeat a rhythmic figure several times, they gain a special kind of climactic intensity. This intensity is

Eighteenth-century debates on the merits of French and Italian music could become catty. In this French cartoon, Italy's greatest composers—each playing the instrument he was famous for—join "Le chat de Caffarelli" in an aria (Caffarelli was a leading castrato).

underpinned by quiet *upward* motion in the bass, which had generally been moving downward. The second violin part picks up energy here.

❦   Anticipated by some melodic figures in **a**, the figures in **b** keep reaching ever upward, in a wonderfully spontaneous way. This sense of aspiration is balanced by the graceful falling cadences ending **a** and **b**.

❦   To counteract all the rhythmic and melodic variety, Bach puts in several beautiful sequences, whose repetitive quality ensures a sense of organization: See measures 3–4, 13–14, and 15–16.

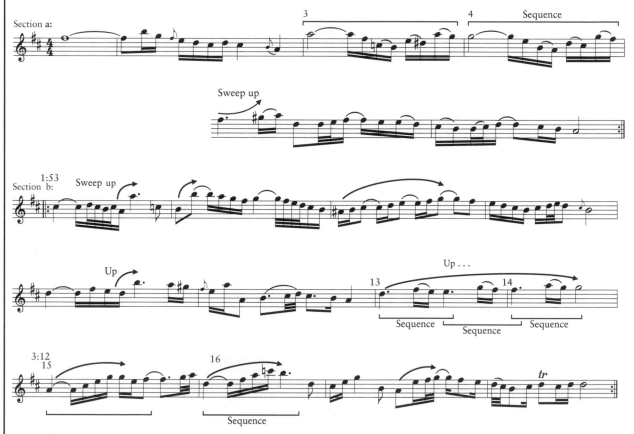

Gavotte   The wind instruments and timpani return in this number; the trumpets make this dance sound more like a march, as the festive orchestra evokes the military conquests that formed the basis of Baroque princely power. Trumpets deliver the strong two-quarter-note upbeat that characterizes the gavotte. Then Bach inverts the bold opening melody of **a** to obtain the opening of **b**. This inversion may *look* academic — a technical trick to be appreciated by the Collegium Musicum connoisseurs — but it *sounds* fresh and natural, another product of Bach's endlessly fertile melodic imagination:

LISTEN

BACH
Suite No. 3 in D, Gavotte

0:00	Gavotte (**A**): **a**
0:14	**a** *repeated*
0:27	**b**
0:49	**b** *repeated*
1:11	Trio (**B**): **c c**
1:54	**d d**
2:38	**A** (**a b**)

The trio, or second gavotte, also fully orchestrated, sounds even more military than the first. Strings and oboes play fanfares to begin both **c** and **d**.

Bourrée   The lightest dance in this suite, a bourrée, is scored for full orchestra; the wind instruments and timpani are used mainly to underscore the sharp, exhilarating rhythms.

Gigue   Another drum roll (as in the French overture) launches this vigorous gigue, the most common dance for the last movement in a suite. The violins, doubled by the oboes, play almost continuous eighth notes in 6/8 time.

bedfordstmartins.com/listen
▶Quizzes and Flashcards

CHAPTER 10

Baroque Vocal Music

Vocal music — music for solo voices, choruses, or both — formed a major part of the output of most Baroque composers. We have seen that composers were supported by three main institutions: the church, the opera house, and the court. Each of these demanded vocal music. Indeed, of the three, only the court was a major source of instrumental music — and every court had its chapel, for which the court composers were also required to provide vocal music. Courts had their own opera theaters, too.

Words and Music

Theories of musical expression in the Baroque era were touched on in Chapter 8 (page 130). It was believed at the time that emotions could be isolated, categorized, and listed in a fairly simple way, and that music could enhance or even arouse each emotion by means of certain musical devices applied consistently, even single-mindedly, throughout a piece. Theorists developed checklists of musical devices corresponding to each of the "affects," as they called emotions conceived in this way.

It was particularly in vocal music — where the words that are sung define or suggest a specific emotion — that this musical vocabulary of the emotions was applied most consistently. If a text refers to "rejoicing," for example, a Baroque composer would match this with fast, lively runs; a mention of "victory" would probably require trumpets and drums to evoke battle music. "Sorrow" would call forth sighing melodic gestures and intense, dissonant harmonies, and so on.

1 Opera

The principal genre of secular vocal music of the Baroque era was opera. Introduced around the year 1600, opera soon flourished mightily all over Europe, and became the most glamorous and probably the most adventurous and influential artistic genre of the Baroque era.

In characterizing the emotional world of Baroque art (see page 131), we stressed its theatrical quality. The Baroque was fascinated by the theater, and especially by opera — the ultimate multimedia experience of its day, combining poetry, drama, music, vocal virtuosity, scenic splendor, dance, and more. Spec-

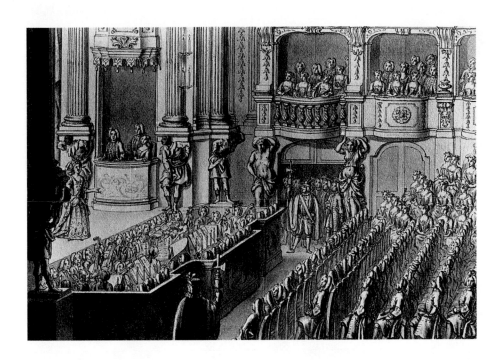

A German opera house of the Baroque era. Notice that the best seats were actually on the stage.

tacular singing was of the essence in Baroque opera, and so was spectacular stage architecture, featuring amazing transformation scenes and the like. Systems of pulleys and counterweights could rapidly change the set from a palace to a magic garden, with gods and goddesses descending from the heavens in a fiery chariot. Opera offered a wealth of satisfactions, then—most obviously, no doubt, for the vocal connoisseurs of the day, the fans of great singers. They are said to have gossiped, gambled, and flirted in the boxes while waiting for their favorites to sing their special arias.

But opera's ability to project emotion was the real basis of its appeal. First and foremost, opera erected a stage on which individual singers could step forward to express feelings in the most direct and powerful fashion. Since the singers were portraying characters in a drama, they were repeatedly thrown into situations which made it seem natural for them to experience (and express) intense emotions.

Such emotions were intensified, of course, by music. Emotion could be intensified by great vocal virtuosity, too. The most obvious kind of vocal virtuosity is *coloratura* singing—fast brilliant runs, scales, high notes, vocal cadenzas, and so on, stressing technique for its own sake. But the legendary singers of old moved their audiences not only by singing faster than anyone else, but by singing more beautifully, more delicately, and more emotionally.

Italian Opera Seria

The principal type of Italian Baroque opera was **opera seria,** or serious opera. The plots—mostly derived from ancient history, with all kinds of alterations and additions—were designed to stir up powerful emotions, such as passion, rage, grief, and triumph. Such plots gave the singers many opportunities to excel in one kind of expression or another. Opera seria consisted mainly of solo singing by sopranos and mezzo-sopranos, including castrati (see page 157). Tenors and basses played subordinate roles; there were few duets or choruses.

The words of an opera are called the *libretto* ("little book"), and their author is the *librettist*. Librettists had to build up the drama as a whole from a series of brief texts, alternating with one another, for *recitatives* and *arias*.

A much more informal picture of a Baroque opera performance—evidently during a recitative, to judge from the interaction of the characters on stage and the inattention of the audience. (The painting is perhaps by Antonio Longhi, 1702–1785.)

Recitative

Recitative (re-si-ta-téev), from the Italian word for "recite," is a technique of declaiming words musically in a heightened, theatrical manner. There is always an instrumental accompaniment. The singing voice closely follows the free rhythm of emotional speech; it mirrors and indeed exaggerates the natural ups and downs that occur as an actor raises his or her voice at a question, lowers it in "asides," or cries out angrily. The composer makes no effort to organize these speechlike utterances into real melodies.

Recitative was used for plot action, dialogue, and other places in the drama where it is particularly important for the words to be brought out. Text phrases and individual words are not ordinarily repeated, of course, any more than they would be in speech.

Most of the time, recitative accompaniment was kept to a minimum—basso continuo (cello and harpsichord) alone—so that the singer could interpret the dialogue or the action as spontaneously as possible. A name for recitative with continuo accompaniment is secco recitative, from the Italian word secco, meaning "dry" (think of the sound of the harpsichord).

In every opera seria, however, one or two of the most excited, emotion-filled recitatives were provided with orchestral accompaniment of one kind or another. This type is called **accompanied recitative.**

Aria

An **aria** is a set piece for solo singer that has much more musical elaboration and coherence than a passage of recitative. The vocal part is more melodic, and ordinarily the accompaniment includes the orchestra, not just the continuo, as in secco recitative. Here the singer-actor is mulling over his or her emotions at some leisure, "getting his feelings out," instead of reacting moment by moment, as in recitative. Consequently in arias the repetition of poetic phrases or words is common and, in principle, appropriate.

The standard form for the Baroque Italian opera aria is **da capo** form, **A B A** (less usual is free da capo form, **A B A′**). Both the words and music of **A** are repeated after **B**; *da capo* ("from the head") is a direction on scores meaning repeat from the beginning. The composer wrote the music for **A** and **B** only, leaving the performers to do the rest. Indeed, the singer would do more than just repeat **A**. He or she would also ornament the music with improvised runs, cadenzas, and so on, so as to create an exciting enhanced effect the second time around.

For connoisseurs of the day, a great deal depended on the **A** repeats, since it was there that the star singers really dazzled their audiences. Many modern singers have relearned the lost improvisational art of the Baroque era, and we can recapture some of the original excitement on recordings.

> **"** If we can neither get [the famous castrato] Senesino, nor Carestini, then Mr. Handel desires to have a man soprano and a woman contralto, and the price (for both) must not exceed 1100 guineas, and that the persons must set out for London the latter end of August, and that no engagement must be made with one without a certainty of getting the other."
>
> *Letter from one of Handel's agents, 1730*

The Castrato

Intimately tied up with Italian opera seria was the castrato singer (plural: *castrati*). The starring male roles in opera were hardly ever sung by tenors or basses but rather by men who had submitted to castration as young boys in order to preserve their voices in the soprano or alto range. At its best, the castrato voice was a prized virtuoso instrument, more powerful and brilliant than a woman's soprano.

This practice seems an outrage to us today, as it did to everybody outside Italy at the time (and to many in Italy itself). Nevertheless, in Italy and all over Europe—though France was a notable exception—castrati were gladly accepted because of their wonderful singing and given top billing, along with women prima donnas. But the presence of frankly unnatural men in the main opera roles, which were of course usually romantic roles, made it hard to believe in the ideal of opera as serious drama in music. Contributing to the side-show quality, it was common in opera seria plots for male characters to disguise themselves as women (and vice versa). Then the male soprano voice was used for female impersonation.

The most famous castrati were international stage figures. Some were pampered stars and objects of ridicule at the same time, such as Caffarelli (see page 151), who was

Farinelli

once jailed for indecent gestures during a performance. Others were serious artists. Carlo Broschi, whose stage name was Farinelli, the most famous of all, was also a composer and later in life an influential figure at the court of Spain.

Most castrati, however, worked out of the limelight, in Italian churches. The last known castrato, a member of the Sistine Choir in Rome who was born as late as 1852, made a recording in 1902; the voice has been described as "penetrating and curiously disembodied."

You can rent the 1994 film *Farinelli*, for which a virtual castrato voice was invented by digital wizardry.

GEORGE FRIDERIC HANDEL
Julius Caesar (Giulio Cesare in Egitto) (1724)

As a young man, Handel wrote a few German operas for the Hamburg opera company (most of the music is lost) and a few Italian operas for theaters in Florence and Venice; in his maturity he wrote as many as forty Italian operas for London. Probably the most famous of them is *Julius Caesar,* one of a trio of Handel masterpieces written in the years 1724–25, the others being *Rodelinda* and *Tamerlano.*

Background   Like most opera seria plots of the late Baroque era, *Julius Caesar* draws on Roman history. Cleopatra, the famous Queen of Egypt, applied her formidable charms to Julius Caesar and then, after Caesar's assassination, also to his successor Mark Antony. Shakespeare deals with the second of these famous affairs in his play *Antony and Cleopatra;* Handel tackles the first.

But Handel's librettist added a great deal of nonhistorical plot material that Shakespeare would have shaken his head at. History tells that Pompey — who comes into the story because he waged war on Caesar and lost and fled to Egypt — was murdered by one of his soldiers, but in the opera the murderer is Cleopatra's brother Ptolemy. Pompey's widow Cornelia is thrown into Ptolemy's harem and has to resist his advances (among others'). Her son Sextus rattles around the opera swearing vengeance on Ptolemy and finally kills him. The historical Cleopatra poisoned Ptolemy, but her character in the opera is whitewashed, and she gets to sing some of the most ravishing music, seductive indeed, while she is disguised as her own maid.

Although the role of Sextus, for mezzo-soprano, was presumably meant for a castrato, at the first performance it was sung by a woman singer who was one of Handel's regulars.

Aria, "La giustizia"   Sextus promises revenge on Ptolemy, not for the first time, in the aria "La giustizia" (Justice). This aria is preceded or, rather, set up by a recitative (as usual). Since it makes more sense to study recitative when the words are in English, we leave that discussion until we get to Handel's *Messiah.*

The aria starts with a ritornello (see page 133) played by the string orchestra, establishing the mood right away:

The "affect" Handel means to covey by this strenuous, vigorous music is anger, and Sextus starts up with the same music. We will hear this ritornello three more times, once in a shortened form, prior to the second **A** section.

Apart from this abbreviated ritornello, "La giustizia" is in strict **A B A** (da capo) form. In the **A** section Handel goes through the words three times, with short ritornellos in between to allow the singer to catch her breath. (These short spacers are not marked on the Listening Chart.) Notice how the music tends to explode angrily on certain key words, principally by the use of *coloratura* (fast scales and turns), as on "ven-*det*-ta" (vengeance) and "tradi-*tor*" (traitor). Even more vivid are the sudden high notes on "pu-*ni*-re" (punish) and a suspense-making long note on "tradi-*tor.*"

There is a flamboyant effect typical of the Baroque near the end of **A**, where Sextus pauses dramatically for effect. After a breathless fermata (see page 16), he moves on to make a very forceful final cadence. Revenge is nigh!

The aria's **B** section introduces some new keys for contrast; otherwise it is brief and seems rather subdued — the strings drop out, leaving only the continuo as accompaniment. What the audience is waiting for is the da capo of **A**, where we can forget about Sextus and get to admire a display of vocal virtuosity. Lorraine Hunt Lieberson, the singer on our recording, adds brilliant improvised flourishes to the high notes on "pu-*ni*-re" and the long note on "tradi-*tor.*" When she gets to the fermata in **A** she fills it in with a cadenza (page 140), and her (ornamented) final cadence sweeps us away. Anyone who can carry off a feat like this, the aria seems to say, will be more than a match for Ptolemy.

Vocal cadenzas at the time were short, because they were supposed to be sung in a single breath — thus showing off virtuoso breath control as well as vocal technique and inventiveness.

Lorraine Hunt Lieberson in another Handel opera role

LISTEN		Handel, *Julius Caesar,* Aria "La giustizia"		
0:00	**A**	RITORNELLO		
0:16		*St. 1:* first time	La giustizia ha già sull' arco	Justice now has in its bow
			Pronto strale alla vendetta	The arrow primed for vengeance
			Per punire un traditor	To castigate a traitor!
0:50		*St. 1:* second time	*La giustizia . . . etc.*	
1:10		*St. 1:* third time	*La giustizia . . . etc.*	
1:31		RITORNELLO		
1:47	**B**	*St. 2:*	Quanto è tarda la saetta	The later the arrow is shot
			Tanto più crudele aspetta	The crueler is the pain suffered
			La sua pena un empio cor.	By a dastardly heart!
2:15	**A**	RITORNELLO		
2:22		(abbreviated)	*La giustizia . . . etc.*	Justice . . . etc.

For a note on Italian pronunciation, see page 105: "La joostidzia (ah) jah sool arco."

---

2 Oratorio

Sacred, or religious, vocal music of the Baroque era exhibits much diversity in style and form. Most of it was written directly for church services, and so its style and form depend first of all on whether those services were of the Roman Catholic, Lutheran, or Anglican rite. Every service has places where music is appropriate, or even actually specified by the liturgy. In principle, each place gives rise to a different musical genre.

There are, however, two general factors that are important for all Baroque sacred-music genres — oratorio and passion, cantata, Mass, and motet. One of these factors is traditional in origin; the other is specific to the Baroque era.

The traditional factor is the participation of the choir. A simple point, perhaps; choral music has had a functional place in the religious music of virtually all rites and ages. For when one person utters a religious text, he or she speaks as an

George Frideric Handel (1685–1759)

Georg Friedrich Händel—he anglicized his name to George Frideric Handel after settling in England—was one of the few composers of early days who did not come from a family of musicians. His father was a barber-surgeon and a valet at a court near Leipzig. He disapproved of music, and the boy is said to have studied music secretly at night, by candlelight. In deference to his father's wishes, Handel studied law for a year at Halle, one of Germany's major universities, before finally joining the orchestra at Hamburg, Germany's leading center of opera.

From then on, it was an exciting, glamorous life. Still in his teens, Handel fought a duel with another Hamburg musician about which of them was to get top billing. In 1706 he journeyed to the homeland of opera and scored big successes in Venice, Florence, and Rome. Though he became a court musician for the elector of Hanover, in northern Germany, he kept requesting (and extending) leaves to pursue his career in London, a city that was then beginning to rival Paris as the world capital.

Here Handel continued to produce Italian operas, again with great success. He also wrote a flattering birthday ode for Queen Anne and some big pieces to celebrate a major peace treaty; for this he was awarded an annuity. In 1717, after the elector of Hanover had become George I of England, Handel got back into his good graces by composing music to be played in a royal celebration on barges on the River Thames. This famous *Water Music* consists of two suites for the Baroque festive orchestra.

As an opera composer, Handel had learned to gauge the taste of the public and also to flatter singers, writing music for them that showed off their voices to the best advantage. He now became an opera impresario—today we would call him a promoter—recruiting singers and negotiating their contracts, planning whole seasons of opera, and all the while composing the main attractions himself: an opera every year, on average, in the 1720s and 1730s. He also had to deal with backers—English

aristocrats and wealthy merchants who supported his opera companies, and persuaded their friends to take out subscriptions for boxes.

Handel made and lost several fortunes, but he always landed on his feet, even when Italian opera went out of style in Britain, for he never lost a feel for his audience. After opera had failed, he popularized oratorios—retellings of Bible stories (mostly from the Old Testament) in a half operatic, half choral form. Opera audiences had always been ready to identify opera's virtuous Roman emperors with local princes. Now they were delighted to identify oratorio's virtuous People of Israel with the British nation.

Handel was a big, vigorous man, hot-tempered but quick to forgive, humorous and resourceful. When a particularly temperamental prima donna had a tantrum, he calmed her down by threatening to throw her out the window. At the end of his life he became blind—the same surgeon operated (unsuccessfully) on both him and Bach—but he continued to play the organ brilliantly and composed by dictating to a secretary.

Chief Works: 40 Italian operas, including *Giulio Cesare* (Julius Caesar) ▪ Near-operatic works in English: *Semele* and *Acis and Galatea* ▪ Oratorios, including *Messiah, Israel in Egypt, Samson,* and *Saul* ▪ Concerti grossi and organ concertos ▪ *Water Music,* written for an aquatic fete on the River Thames, and *Royal Fireworks Music,* celebrating the end of the War of the Austrian Succession, in 1747 ▪ Sonatas for various instruments

Encore: After *Messiah,* listen to the *Royal Fireworks Music;* Concerto Grosso in B-flat, Op. 6, No. 7.

---

individual, but when a choir does so, it speaks as a united community. A church choir can be said to speak for the whole church, even for the whole of Christianity.

¶ The other important fact about Baroque sacred vocal music is its strong tendency to borrow from secular vocal music—which is to say, from opera. In an era fascinated by the theater, the church grew more and more theatrical. Arias inspired by Italian opera seria appear even in Baroque settings of the Catholic Mass. Solo singers could display their vocal prowess at the same time as they were presenting parts of the divine service.

The most operatic of all religious genres was oratorio, which existed in Catholic and Protestant countries alike. An **oratorio** is basically an opera on a religious subject, such as an Old Testament story or the life of a saint. It has a narrative plot in several acts, real characters, and implied action—even though oratorios were not staged, but presented in concert form, that is, without scenery, costumes, or gestures. Oratorio takes over such operatic features as recitatives and arias. On the other hand, it also makes much use of the chorus—a major difference from Italian opera of the time, where the chorus played little role.

Unlike most other religious genres, an oratorio was not actually part of a church service. Indeed, in opera-crazed Italy, the oratorio was prized as an entertainment substituting for opera during Lent, a somber season of abstinence from opera as well as other worldly diversions.

In England, the oratorio was also a substitute for opera, though in a different sense. Thanks largely to Handel, Italian opera became very popular in London for a quarter of a century, but finally audiences tired of it. At that point, Handel, already in his mid-fifties, began composing oratorios, and these turned out to be even more popular yet, the pinnacle of his long career.

> **❝** On Tuesday the 2nd day of May will be performed, the Sacred Story of Esther, an Oratorio in English. Formerly composed by Mr. Handel, and now revised by him, with several Additions . . . *N.B.* There will be no Action on the Stage . . ."
>
> *London newspaper announcement, 1731*

GEORGE FRIDERIC HANDEL
Messiah (1742)

10–11 12–13

Handel's oratorio *Messiah,* his most famous work, is also one of the most famous in the whole of Western music. It is the only composition of its time that has been performed continuously—and frequently—since its first appearance. Today it is sung at Christmas and Easter in hundreds of churches around the world, as well as at symphony concerts and "*Messiah* sings," where people get together just to sing along with the Hallelujah Chorus and the other well-known choral numbers, and listen to the well-loved arias.

Unlike most oratorios, *Messiah* does not have actual characters acting out a biblical story in recitative and arias, although its text is taken from the Bible. In a more typical Handel oratorio, such as *Samson,* for example, Samson sings an aria about his blindness and argues with Delilah in recitative, while choruses represent the People of Israel and the Philistines. Instead, *Messiah* works with a group of anonymous narrators, relating episodes from the life of Jesus in recitative. The narration is interrupted by anonymous commentators who react to each of the episodes by singing recitatives and arias.

All this is similar in many ways to opera in concert form (that is, not staged); but in addition, the chorus has a large and varied role to play. On one occasion, it speaks for a group of angels that actually speaks in the Bible. Sometimes it comments on the story, like the soloists. And often the choristers raise their voices to praise the Lord in Handel's uniquely magnificent manner.

We shall first examine two numbers in *Messiah* covering the favorite Christmas story about the announcement of Christ's birth to the shepherds in the fields. Included are a recitative in four brief sections and a chorus.

Recitative Part 1 (secco) Sung by a boy soprano narrator accompanied by continuo (cello and organ), this recitative has the natural, proselike flow typical of all recitatives. Words that would be naturally stressed in ordinary speech are brought out by longer durations, higher pitches, and pauses: "*shep*herds," "*field*," "*flock*," and "*night*." As is typical in recitative, but unlike aria, no words are repeated.

Part 2 (accompanied) Accompanied recitative is used for special effects in operas and oratorios—here the miraculous appearance of angels. The slowly pulsing high-string background furnishes the angel with a sort of musical halo.

It is also a signal for more vigorous declamation: The words *lo, Lord,* and *glory* are brought out with increasing emphasis. The end of this brief accompanied recitative is heavily punctuated by a standard cadence formula, played by the continuo. This formula is an easily recognized feature of recitatives.

Part 3 (secco)   Notice that the angel speaks in a more urgent style than the narrator. And in *Part 4 (accompanied),* the excited, faster pulsations in the high strings depict the beating wings, perhaps, of the great crowd of angels. When Handel gets to what they will be saying, he brings the music to a triumphant high point, once again over the standard recitative cadence.

Chorus, "Glory to God"   "Glory to God! Glory to God in the *highest!*" sing the angels—the *high* voices of the choir, in a bright marchlike rhythm. They are accompanied by the orchestra, with the trumpets prominent. The *low* voices alone add "and peace on *earth,*" much more slowly. Fast string runs following "Glory to God" and slower reiterated chords following "and peace on earth" recall the fast and slow string passages in the two preceding accompanied recitatives.

good will to-ward men

After these phrases are sung and played again, leading to another key, the full chorus sings the phrase "good will toward men" in a fugal style. The important words are *good will,* and their two-note motive is happily sung (in imitation) again and again by all the voices of the angel choir. To conclude, the "good will" motive is singled out in an enthusiastic ascending sequence.

sequence

good will . . .

The whole chorus is quite concise, even dramatic; the angels do not stay long. At the very end, the orchestra gets quieter and quieter—a rare effect in Baroque music, here indicating the disappearance of the shepherds' vision.

Hallelujah Chorus   This famous chorus brings Act II of *Messiah* to a resounding close. Like "Glory to God," "Hallelujah" makes marvelous use of monophony ("King of Kings"), homophony (the opening "Hallelujah"), and

---

LISTEN   Handel, *Messiah,* Recitative
"There were shepherds" and Chorus, "Glory to God"

2   1

10   12

(Bold italic type indicates accented words or syllables. Italics indicate phrases of text that are repeated.)

RECITATIVE PART 1 (secco)

0:01   There were *shep*herds abiding in the *field,* keeping *watch* over
their *flock* by *night.*

PART 2 (accompanied)

0:13   And *lo!* the angel of the *Lord* came upon them, and the *glory*
of the Lord shone round about them; and they were sore afraid.   Standard cadence

PART 3 (secco)

0:34   And the angel said unto *them: Fear* not, for be*hold,* I bring
you good *ti*dings of great *joy,* which shall *be to all peo*ple.   Standard cadence
For unto you is born this *day* in the city of *Da*vid a *Sa*viour,
which is *Christ* the *Lord.*   Standard cadence

PART 4 (accompanied)

1:08   And *sud*denly there was with the *an*gel a *mul*titude of the
heavenly *host,* praising *God, and saying:*   Standard cadence

CHORUS

1:20   Glory to God, *glory to God,* in the highest, and peace on earth,
2:02   good will toward men *good will*
2:21   *Glory to God*

An oratorio performance,
caught by the satirical pen of
Handel's contemporary William
Hogarth (1697–1764). Note the words.
Is nothing sacred?

polyphony ("And he shall reign for ever and ever"); it is almost a textbook example of musical textures. Compare "And peace on earth," "Glory to God," and "Good will toward men" in the earlier chorus.

Hallelujah,   Hallelujah,   Hallelujah,   Hallelujah, Halle - lujah.

and he shall reign for ever and ev-er

In a passage beloved by chorus singers, Handel sets "The Kingdom of this world is become" on a low descending scale, **piano**, swelling suddenly into a similar scale in a higher register, **forte**, for "the Kingdom of our Lord, and of his Christ"—a perfect representation of one thing becoming another thing, similar but newly radiant. Later the sopranos (cheered on by the trumpets) solemnly utter the words "King of Kings" on higher and higher long notes as the other voices keep repeating their answer, "for ever, Hallelujah!"

George II of England, attending the first London performance of *Messiah*, was so moved by this chorus that he stood up in his box—prompting everyone else to stand in honor of the King of Kings, no doubt, but also reminding everyone of his own majesty, which was being acclaimed by the typical Baroque festive orchestra. Audiences still sometimes stand during the "Hallelujah" Chorus.

LISTEN   **Handel, *Messiah*, Hallelujah Chorus**

2 1
11 13

(Italics indicate phrases of text that are repeated.)

0:07 Hallelujah, *Hallelujah!*

0:26 For the Lord God omnipotent reigneth. *Hallelujah!*
      For the Lord God omnipotent reigneth.

1:17 The Kingdom of this world is become the kingdom
      of our Lord and *of his Christ.*

1:35 And He shall reign for ever and ever, *and he shall reign for ever and ever.*

1:58 KING OF KINGS *for ever and ever, Hallelujah!*
      AND LORD OF LORDS *for ever and ever, Hallelujah!*

Women in Music

Before the twentieth century, opportunities for women were limited. Though some women worked as teachers, nurses, and laborers, society viewed women's primary role as that of wife and mother. Occasionally accidents of royal succession placed a woman in a position of great power, and the eighteenth century saw two amazingly long-lasting cases: Catherine the Great, empress of Russia, who ruled from 1762 to 1796, and Maria Theresa, de facto empress of the Austrian Empire from 1740 to 1780. But what we now think of as careers were simply not open to women, with few exceptions.

Music provided one of those exceptions. It did so by way of the theater, because an opera singer, like an actress or a ballet dancer, could attain fame and fortune and the opportunity to develop her talents in the same way as men in those same fields. Indeed, opera depended on female singers; without them the genre could never have developed or survived.

The names—although not, alas, the voices—of opera's legendary prima donnas have come down to us, along with those of opera's great composers: from **Anna Renzi** (c. 1620–c. 1660), who sang in Monteverdi's *Poppea* (see page 102), to the notorious rival sopranos **Faustina Bordoni** (1700–1781) and **Francesca Cuzzoni** (1698–1770) in the age of Handel, and beyond. Cuzzoni

Bordoni

Cuzzoni

sang in the star-studded premiere of Handel's *Julius Caesar* (see page 158).

Women of the theater paid a price for their career opportunities, of course. They were displaying themselves—their legs or their voices—for the enjoyment of, mainly, men, who paid for the privilege. There was always a question about the respectability and marriageability of opera singers.

While female opera singers were a fixture in the musical workplace of the Baroque, female instrumentalists were much rarer. Women composers were simply flukes. Remember that composers, such as Bach and Handel (and Farinelli—see page 157), were also always performers; a notable harpsichordist-composer of the Baroque era was **Elizabeth-Claude Jacquet** (1667–1729), a Mozart-style prodigy who was sponsored by Louis XIV himself. Famous as a harpsichordist, she composed music of all kinds, including an opera that was put on at the forerunner of the Paris Opéra—then as now the grandest venue for opera in Europe.

There was no respectability problem with Jacquet; by the time she was seventeen she was married to an organist, one Marin de la Guerre, whose name is usually hyphenated with hers. **Francesca Lebrun** (1756–1791), a prima donna of a later generation, was also a composer; we will come to her in Chapter 13 (page 203).

3 The Church Cantata

Second in importance to oratorio among Baroque sacred-music genres is the **church cantata**. *Cantata* is a general name for a piece of moderate length for voices and instruments. Many Baroque cantatas are not sacred music, but in Germany church cantatas were written to be performed during Lutheran church services. Lutheran churches had (and still have today) fixed readings and hymns specified for every Sunday of the year, as well as for special occasions such as Easter and Christmas. The words of cantatas addressed the religious content of the day in question. Sung before the sermon, the cantata was in effect a second, musical sermon.

As cantor, or music director, of Leipzig's biggest church (the Thomaskirche), Bach was required to produce cantatas for the entire year—a stupendous task that kept him very busy indeed for years after he was appointed. Over two hundred cantatas by Bach have survived, each of them with several movements, including some secular cantatas written for court or civic celebrations. Some were written for the University of Leipzig.

The Lutheran Chorale

The content and structure of the church cantata were quite various. One kind, for example, has singers who represent Hope, Fear, the Soul, and so on, discussing Christian issues in operatic arias and recitatives, like a short scene from an oratorio. (Most nonsacred cantatas, likewise, resemble a short scene from an opera.) A special feature of nearly all Lutheran cantatas is their use of traditional congregational hymns. Lutheran hymns are called **chorales** (co-ráhls), from the German word for hymn (*Choral*).

Martin Luther, the father of the Protestant Reformation, placed special emphasis on hymn singing by the congregation when he decided on the format of Lutheran services. Two hundred years later, in Bach's time, a large body of chorales served as the foundation for Lutheran worship, both in church services and also at informal pious devotions in the home. Everybody knew the words and music of these chorales. You learned them as a small child and sang them in church all your life. Consequently when composers introduced chorale tunes into cantatas (and other sacred-music genres), they were drawing on a rich source of association.

Just how were tunes introduced? There were many ways. The last movement of a Bach cantata is usually a single hymn stanza sung straight through, in much the same simple way as the congregation would sing it, but with the orchestra playing.

Longer cantata movements present the individual lines or phrases of the chorale one by one, with gaps in between them, while other music runs on continuously, both during the chorale phrases (that is, in counterpoint with them) and during the gaps. In a **gapped chorale,** the chorale melody is delivered in spurts. It can be sung, or it can be played by one prominent instrument—an oboe, say, or a trumpet—while the continuous music goes along in the other instruments and/or voices.

> **❝** I have always been very fond of music. Whoever is proficient in this art is a good man, fit for all other things. Hence it is absolutely necessary to have it taught in the schools. A schoolmaster must know how to sing or I shan't tolerate him."
>
> *Martin Luther, 1538*

Chorale, sung simply (phrases):

Gapped chorale movement:

JOHANN SEBASTIAN BACH (1685–1750)
Cantata No. 4, "Christ lag in Todesbanden" (Christ Lay in Death's Dark Prison) (1707)

12–14

In his posts as an organist and cantor, Bach made multiple settings of many hymns, both in cantatas and also as chorale preludes for organ (see page 167). We will study just a few of his settings of the Easter chorale "Christ lag in Todesbanden" (Christ Lay in Death's Dark Prison).

This rugged old tune, given below in its entirety, had been fitted with even more rugged words by Martin Luther himself, in 1524. The seven stanzas of the chorale, each ending with "Hallelujah!," tell in vivid language of mankind's struggle with Death and the victory achieved through Christ's sacrifice. The fact that this hymn is in the minor mode throws a tough, sober shadow over all the rejoicing; the mood is unforgettable.

There - fore   let   us __   thank - ful   be   And   praise   our   Sa - viour   joy - ful - ly,
All' __   sein   Recht   und __   sein'   Ge - walt,   Da   blei - bet   nichts   denn   Tod's   Ge - stalt,

So   sing   we, __   Hal - le - lu - jah,   Hal - le - lu - jah!
Den   Stach'l   hat __   er   ver - lo - ren.   Hal - le - lu - jah!

The cantata based on "Christ lag in Todesbanden," one of Bach's earliest, employs simple forces: voices and a string orchestra, with continuo.* The words of the seven movements are Martin Luther's words of the seven stanzas of the famous Easter chorale.

Bach set these seven stanzas with a sharp eye (or ear) for symmetry. Not all of the voices sing in all of the stanzas; the diagram below tallies the voices that sing in each one:

SINFONIA	STANZA 1	2	3	4	5	6	7	
Orchestra	Soprano	S		S		S	S	*Color shading indicates which voice sings the chorale melody.*
	Alto		A		A		A	*(In stanza 6, it is*
	Tenor			T	T		T	T	*divided between*
	Bass				B	B		B	*two voices.)*

After a short orchestral prelude—Bach calls it "sinfonia," or symphony—all the stanzas except the last are set as gapped chorales of some sort.

Stanza 3   The tenor sings the gapped chorale tune; follow him along with the music, above. Accompanied by the continuo (played on the organ), a violin plays an urgent melody at both ends of the piece and in the gaps between the lines. At the word *nichts* ("nothing") the music comes to a wrenching stop and a slowdown, a quite astonishing effect. Then the violin starts up again as though nothing had happened. The sudden absence of music tells us what is left of Death's power: *nichts,* zilch!

Stanza 4   Here it is the alto (doubled by an organ stop) that sings the gapped chorale tune, more slowly than the tenor of stanza 3. The continuous music is assigned to other voices singing faster imitative polyphony to the same words, always using fragments of the same chorale melody. (Compare the music to the right with the chorale melody.) Perhaps all this busy imitative polyphony makes a good illustration of the warfare described with such gusto in this stanza. Perhaps, too, the jaunty rhythm at *ein Spott* can indeed be heard as mocking Death who has lost his sting.

Stanza 7   No longer gapped, this is a straightforward presentation of the hymn as it might be sung by the congregation. Bach's rich harmonies below the soprano melody are sung by the lower voices, doubled by the instruments. The cantata comes to a restful conclusion at last, as the text turns from battles to the confidence of faith. Even "hallelujah" can now be uttered simply.

STANZA 4

line 1 Es war ein wunder . . .

line 5 Die Schrift hat . . .

line 6 Wie ein Tod . . .

line 7 Ein Spott . . .

*When Bach wrote Cantata No. 4 he was a young small-town organist, and probably could not count on more than one singer to a part, as on our recording—which compensates, however, by adding reverberation to suggest an echoing church.

LISTEN | Bach, "Christ lag in Todesbanden"

2
12–14

12 | *Stanza 3:* Jesus Christus, Gottes Sohn,
An unser Statt ist kommen,
Und hat die Sünde weggetan,
Damit den Tod genommen
All' sein Recht und sein' Gewalt;
Da bleibet *nichts*—denn Tod's Gestalt;
Den Stach'l hat er verloren.
Hallelujah!

Jesus Christ, the Son of God,
Has come on our behalf,
And has done away with our sins,
Thereby robbing Death
Of all his power and might;
There remains nothing but Death's image;
He has lost his sting.
Hallelujah!

13 | *Stanza 4:* Es war ein wunderlicher Krieg,
Da Tod und Leben rungen;
Das Leben da behielt das Sieg,
Es hat den Tod verschlungen.
Die Schrift hat verkündiget das
Wie ein Tod den andern frass;
Ein Spott aus dem Tod ist worden.
Hallelujah!

It was a marvelous war
Where Death and Life battled.
Life gained the victory;
It swallowed up Death.
Scripture has proclaimed
How one Death gobbled up the other;
Death became a mockery.
Hallelujah!

14 | *Stanza 7:* Wir essen und leben wohl
Im rechten Osterfladen.
Der alter Sauerteig nicht soll
Sein bei dem Wort der Gnaden.
Christus will die Koste sein
Und speisen die Seel' allein,
Der Glaub' will keins andern leben.
Hallelujah!

We eat and live fitly
On the true unleavened bread of Passover;
The old yeast shall not
Contaminate the word of grace.
Christ alone will be the food
To feed the soul:
Faith will live on nothing else.
Hallelujah!

4 The Organ Chorale

German churches took special pride in their organs, both in their appearance and their acoustic quality. Organ technology developed prodigiously in the Baroque era. The **chorale prelude,** or *organ chorale,* an important genre of keyboard music at the time, is an organ composition incorporating a hymn (chorale) tune.

Like cantatas, organ chorales incorporated hymn tunes in many ways. The gapped method (see page 165) was common. Played on the organ, the tune could also be ornamented with scales, trills, and so on, for expressive purposes—much the same technique as was applied to opera melodies.

In religious terms, the effect of an organ chorale was probably not very different from a sung one. Lutherans knew their hymns by heart, so the tune on the organ would automatically bring to mind the hymn text and its message or lesson.

JOHANN SEBASTIAN BACH
Chorale Prelude, "Christ lag in Todesbanden"
(Christ Lay in Death's Dark Prison) (1715)

2
15

At certain points in a Lutheran service, the organist would play chorale preludes based on seasonal hymns. On Easter Sunday, Bach might well have played this organ prelude on "Christ lag in Todesbanden."

The music is powerful and triumphant—a wordless hallelujah for the miracle of Easter. The chorale tune can be heard on the high organ pipes,

❝ When Bach seated himself at the organ, he used to choose some theme and treat it in all the various forms of organ composition. First, he used this theme for a prelude and fugue, with the full organ. Then he showed his art of using the stops for a trio, quartet, etc., on the same theme. After- wards followed a chorale, the melody of which was playfully surrounded by the same theme in three or four contrapuntal parts . . ."

From the first biography of Bach, 1802

Lavishly decorated in Baroque style, the splendid organ of St. John's Church in Lüneburg, northern Ger- many, would have been played by the young Bach, who studied with its organ- ist, Georg Böhm. Böhm was an important composer of organ music.

ORGAN PEDALS

played without any gaps, but with a vigorous faster motive accompanying it, a motive that clatters away splendidly in the organ pedals (that is, the large keys that the organist plays with his feet; see page 46). The rich harmonies are formed by dense counterpoint. Perhaps next in the service the hymn would have been sung by the congregation; thus a chorale prelude could serve as a prelude to the congregation's singing of the chorale it incorporated.

This piece comes from the *Orgelbüchlein*, a "Little Organ Book" of no fewer than 162 chorale preludes that Bach planned for use in different services throughout the entire church year. This not-so-little collection bears witness to both sides of Bach's temperament: encyclopedic on the one hand and on the other, strictly practical.

CHAPTER 11

Prelude
Music and
the Enlightenment

I n the second part of the eighteenth century, a new musical style emerged in
Europe. Called the Classical style, it had important pioneers in Italy and
northern Germany; one of the most important of all was Carl Philipp Emanuel
Bach, one of several composer sons of Johann Sebastian, working in Berlin.
But the Classical style was developed particularly by composers active in
Vienna, capital of Austria. Here conditions seem to have been ideal for music.
Geographically, Austria stands at the crossroads of four other musical
nations—Germany, Bohemia (now the Czech Republic), Hungary, and
Italy—and Vienna was also central in political terms. As the capital of the
powerful Hapsburg empire, Vienna was plunged into every European conflict
of the time and exposed to every new cultural and intellectual current.

Vienna's golden years were from 1780 to 1790, during the reign of Emperor Joseph II, the most enlightened of the long line of Hapsburg monarchs.
Joseph emancipated the peasantry, furthered education, and reduced the
power of the clergy; he supported music and literature with his patronage and
encouraged a free press. In a city of only 150,000 people, there were three
hundred newspapers and journals during Joseph's reign, representing every
shade of opinion.

In this liberal atmosphere, Franz Joseph Haydn of nearby Eisenstadt became recognized as the principal composer of Europe; his symphonies were
commissioned from far-off Paris and London. The young Wolfgang Amadeus
Mozart was drawn to the capital in 1781 from Salzburg, a hundred miles to
the west, to spend his brilliant last decade there. And in 1792 a young musician from the other end of Germany, who had composed a long cantata
mourning Emperor Joseph's death, decided to come to this great musical center to launch his career. His name was Ludwig van Beethoven.

1 The Enlightenment and Music

To describe Joseph II as an "enlightened" ruler is both to commend him and
also to locate him in European intellectual history. Like a number of other
rulers of the time, Joseph II derived his principles of governance from an
important intellectual movement of the eighteenth century known as the Enlightenment. This movement also helped to define the music that flourished
under Joseph's reign.

Emperor Joseph II

Centered in France, the Enlightenment had strong roots in English philosophy and strong offshoots in Germany and Austria. Its original source was the faith in reason that led to the great scientific discoveries of the Baroque period, from Galileo to Newton and Leibniz. Now, however, the emphasis veered away from the natural world toward the social sphere. People were less intent on controlling natural forces by science than on turning these forces to human benefit. People also began to apply the same intelligence that solved scientific problems to problems of public morality, education, and politics.

Social injustice came under especially strong fire in the eighteenth century; so did established religion. For the first time in European history, religion ceased to be an overriding force in many people's minds. There were currents of agnosticism and even outright atheism — to the outrage of the English poet and mystic William Blake:

> Mock on, mock on, Voltaire, Rousseau:
> Mock on, mock on, 'tis all in vain!
> You throw the sand against the wind,
> And the wind blows it back again.

The two French philosophers named by Blake are always mentioned in connection with the Enlightenment: François Marie Arouet, whose pen name was Voltaire (1694–1778), tireless satirist and campaigner for justice and reason, and the younger, more radical, more disturbing Jean-Jacques Rousseau (1712–1778). Rousseau is one of the few major figures of European philosophy who had a direct effect on the history of music, as we shall see.

Voltaire, by Jean-Antoine Houdon (1740–1828), master sculptor of the neo-Roman busts that were much favored at the time. (All the other portrait busts in this chapter are also by Houdon.)

The phrase "Viennese Classical style" brings to mind Haydn, Mozart, and Beethoven; each of them came to the capital city from other, smaller centers.

In the Classical era, lighter entertainments took over the stage, in place of the heavy drama characteristic of the Baroque. Compare this picture (a London ballet of 1791) with the opera seria shown on page 124.

"The Pursuit of Happiness"

The Enlightenment was also the occasion for the first great contribution to Western civilization from America. In colonial days, the austere Puritan spirit was hardly in step with the growing secularization of European society, but the Declaration of Independence and the Federalist Papers proved to be the finest flowers of Enlightenment idealism. The notion that a new state could be founded on rational principles, set down on a piece of paper, and agreed to by men of good will and intelligence — this could only have emerged under the influence of the political and philosophical writings of the eighteenth century.

"Life, liberty, and the pursuit of happiness": The last of these three famous rights, too, was very much of its time. One can imagine the medieval barons who forced King John to accept the Magna Carta insisting on life and liberty, of a sort, but it would never have occurred to them to demand happiness as a self-evident right for all. Voltaire and Rousseau fought passionately for social justice so that people might live good lives according to their own convictions.

The eighteenth century was an age of good living, then, an age that valued intelligence, wit, and sensitivity. The age cultivated elegant conversation, the social arts, and hedonism. One of its inventions was the salon — half party, half seminar: a regular gathering in a fashionable lady's home where notables would discuss books, music, art, and ideas. Another innovation of the time was the coffee house. Another was the public concert.

Art and Entertainment

Entertainment, for most people, contributes to the good life — though certainly Thomas Jefferson was thinking of more than entertainment when he wrote of "the pursuit of happiness." However, the pursuit of entertainment was not something that the eighteenth century looked down upon at all. Art was expected to *please* rather than to instruct, impress, or even express, as had been the case in the Baroque era. The result of this attitude is evident in the style of all the arts in the eighteenth century.

Thomas Jefferson

A French rococo
ceramic plaque

For a time at mid-century a light and often frothy style known as *Rococo* was fashionable in painting, decoration, furniture and jewelry design, and so on. Our illustration — a ceramic plaque — catches the spirit of this entertainment art with special charm. Wreathed in leaves that fit in with the border, two well-dressed court gentlemen cavort in an ideal countryside; one plays the flute while the other dances. The subject, the feathery designs on the frame, even the pretty rim itself, are all characteristic of the light art of the rococo.

Music of the mid-eighteenth century, just before the formation of the Viennese Classical style, was also very light — charming but often frivolous. A genre that was typical of the time was the **divertimento**, a piece designed to divert, amuse, and entertain. Elegant figurines of musicians and ornamented music boxes, playing little tunes, were extremely popular (see page 180).

The Viennese Classical music of Haydn and Mozart that we will study is far from this light style, yet these composers never put pen to paper without every expectation that their audiences were going to be "pleased." Every historical era, no doubt, has had its entertainment music. But only in the Classical era was great music of the highest quality put forth quite frankly and plainly as entertainment.

Jean-Jacques Rousseau and Opera

Rousseau is remembered today as Europe's first alienated intellectual. Whatever his subject, he always came around to blasting the social institutions of his day as stifling to the individual. Passionately devoted to nature and to personal feeling, he disseminated the very influential idea of "natural man," born good but corrupted by civilization. This interest, incidentally, caused Rousseau to think hard and sympathetically about the so-called primitive peoples in the Americas, peoples whom Europeans had colonized and enslaved for over two hundred years. If Rousseau had lived longer, we can be sure he would have joined those who denounced the double standard of the Founders in demanding liberty for whites but not for blacks.

To the great French *Encyclopédie* of 1751–65, the ancestor of all modern encyclopedias and the bible of Enlightenment thought, Rousseau contributed articles on two subjects: politics and music. For Rousseau was also a self-taught composer who made his living for years as a professional music copyist.

Both by means of his fiery writings and by example, Rousseau launched a devastating attack on the aristocratic opera of the late Baroque era. And to attack opera—the most important, extended, and glamorous musical genre of the time—was to throw Baroque music itself into question. For Rousseau, the complicated plots of Baroque operas were as impossibly artificial as their complicated music. He demanded a kind of opera that would portray real people in actual life—simple people, close to nature, singing "natural" music.

So Rousseau eagerly championed an Italian comic opera that was a hit at the time in Paris, G. B. Pergolesi's *La serva padrona* ("The Maid as Mistress," 1733). The music is lively and catchy, with simple harmonies and tunes and without elaborate coloratura singing or exaggerated emotional outpourings. And the story could scarcely be more down-to-earth or rudimentary: A servant girl uses a simple ruse to trick a rich old bachelor into marrying her.

Thanks to Pergolesi and Rousseau—and to Mozart—comic opera became the most progressive operatic form of the later part of the century. It dealt not with Roman emperors and their idealized noble sentiments, but with contemporary middle- and lower-class figures expressing everyday feelings in a relatively vivid and natural way. *Opera buffa*, as Italian comic opera was called, is discussed on pages 210–11.

Jean-Jacques Rousseau

The Novel

In its ideals, this new kind of opera can be compared to the most important new literary genre that grew up at the same time. This was the novel, which—together with the symphony—counts as the Enlightenment's greatest artistic legacy to the nineteenth and twentieth centuries.

Precursors of the novel go back to ancient Rome, but the genre did not really capture the European imagination until around 1750. Among the best-known early novels are Henry Fielding's *Tom Jones,* the tale of a rather ordinary young man and his adventures in town and country, and Samuel Richardson's *Pamela,* a domestic drama that manages to be sexually explicit, sentimental, and moralistic all at the same time. Rousseau wrote novels; Voltaire wrote *Candide.* Just before the end of the century, Jane Austen began her subtle explorations of the social forces at work on the hearts of her very sensitive (and sensible) characters in novels such as *Pride and Prejudice, Emma, Persuasion,* and others. These novels still provide plots for Hollywood films today.

Sharp, realistic observation of contemporary life and sensitive depiction of feeling—these are the ideals shared by late eighteenth-century opera and the novel. It is no accident that within a few years of their publication, both *Tom Jones* and *Pamela* were turned into major operas, one French, the other Italian.

In Mozart, opera buffa found a master comparable to Jane Austen in the sensitive response to feeling and action. In his opera *Don Giovanni,* for example, the three women romantically involved with the hero—the coquettish

Rousseau himself composed a very successful opera of the uncomplicated kind he recommended. Pictured are the shepherdess Colette, with sheep, and her lover Colin from Rousseau's *Le Devin du village (The Village Soothsayer),* 1752.

A late eighteenth-century court musician surrounded by the tools of his trade. However, he is depicted not in a palace of the era, but in a sober imitation classical temple—amusing testimony to the Neoclassical enthusiasms and aspirations of the time.

country girl, Zerlina; the steely aristocrat, Donna Anna; and the sentimental Donna Elvira—are depicted in music with the greatest human sympathy and psychological insight. One can come to feel that the same qualities are reflected in Mozart's symphonies and concertos.

Neoclassicism

It is from the standpoint of "the natural," that great rallying cry of the Enlightenment, that we should understand Neoclassicism, an important movement in the visual arts at this time influenced by the Greek and Roman classics.

The classics have meant many things to many eras. To the eighteenth century, they meant a return to simple, natural values. They meant a rejection of the complex solemnities of the Baroque on the one hand, and of the pleasant frivolities of the Rococo on the other. The busts by Jean-Antoine Houdon shown throughout this chapter are prime examples of eighteenth-century Neoclassical art. They were modeled on ancient Roman busts.

There was also a strong Neoclassic trend in music, due to Christoph Willibald von Gluck (1714–1787), a composer who made a stir in both Vienna and Paris. Gluck used austere classical subjects in a determined effort to reform (that is, simplify and ennoble) eighteenth-century opera. His *Orfeo ed Euridice* (1762) is based on the Greek myth of Orpheus, his *Alceste* (1767) on a classical Greek drama. When *Alceste* reached Paris, it was greeted enthusiastically by the aging Rousseau.

Apart from the operas of Gluck, however, Neoclassical art has little direct connection with music in what is traditionally called the Classical style. One can perhaps see that a taste inclined toward moderation, simplicity, and balance would also appreciate the order and clarity of late eighteenth-century music. But the traditional label "Classicism" was an afterthought to the music of Haydn and Mozart, coined in the nineteenth century to distinguish their music from the "Romanticism" that came later.

Christoph Willibald von Gluck

2 The Rise of Concerts

A far-reaching development in the sociology and economics of music was the rise of public concerts. Occasional concerts had been given before, in taverns, private homes, palaces, and theaters, but it was only in the middle of the eighteenth century that they became a significant force in musical life. Concert series, financed by subscription, were put on by the forerunners of today's promoters and presenters. Concerts for the benefit of charity were set up on a regular basis as major society events.

In 1748 Europe's first hall designed especially for concerts was built in a college town, Oxford. Still in use, the Holywell Music Room holds about 150 people.

Music of all kinds was presented at these new public concerts; one major series—the Parisian *Concert spirituel,* founded in 1725—originally concentrated on sacred vocal music. But orchestral music was the staple. The importance of concerts lay mainly in the impetus they gave to the composition of orchestral music—symphonies and concertos. For there were, after all, other public forums for church music (churches) and opera (opera houses). Now purely orchestral music, too, moved into the public domain, and its importance and prestige grew rapidly.

However, the livelihood of musicians still depended principally on court patronage, the opera house, and the church (see page 123). Concerts were certainly a factor in the careers of both of the masters of Classical style already mentioned: Haydn wrote his last symphonies, called the London symphonies, for concerts on two celebrity tours to that city, and Mozart wrote most of his piano concertos—among his greatest works—for concerts he himself put on in Vienna. But concerts were a resource that Haydn did not draw upon significantly until the end of his long life, and they were not an adequate resource, alas, to sustain Mozart.

For the Benefit of Mr. F L A G G.
This Evening,
A public CONCERT of
Vocal and Inftrumental MUSIC,
Will be performed at Concert Hall in Queen-ftreet.
The Vocal part to be performed by Four Voices, and to conclude with the BRITISH GRENADIERS.——N. B. *TICKETS* to be had at the Printers, or at the London Book-ftore, at *HALF a DOLLAR* each.—To begin precifely at half after feven.
⁂ The laft Concert this Seafon.

The rise of concerts: With only around 15,000 inhabitants, pre-revolutionary Boston already had a concert hall and a concert promoter (bandmaster Josiah Flagg). This advertisement is from the *Boston Chronicle* of 1769.

3 Style Features of Classical Music

In discussing the musical style of the late Baroque period, we started with a single guiding concept. There is a thorough, even rigorous quality in the ways early eighteenth-century composers treated almost all aspects of music, and this quality seems to underpin the expressive gestures of grandeur and overstatement that are characteristic of the Baroque.

Classical music cannot be discussed quite as easily as this. We have to keep two concepts in mind to understand it, concepts that were constantly on the lips of men and women of the time. One was "natural," and the other was "pleasing variety." In the late eighteenth century, it was taken for granted that these two artistic ideals went hand in hand and supported one another.

Today we can see that sometimes they pulled in opposite directions. For although "variety" was invoked as a guard against boredom, it was also an invitation to complexity, and complexity would seem to run counter to "natural" simplicity and clarity. In any case, in Classical music one or the other—and sometimes both—of these qualities can be traced in all the elements of musical technique: in rhythm, dynamics, tone color, melody, texture, and form. A new expressive quality developed in this music as a result of its new technique.

Rhythm

Perhaps the most striking change in music between the Baroque and the Classical periods came in rhythm. In this area the artistic ideal of "pleasing variety" reigned supreme. The unvarying rhythms of Baroque music came to be regarded as dreary, obvious, and boring.

Classical music is highly flexible in rhythm. Throughout a single movement, the tempo and meter remain constant, but the rhythms of the various themes tend to differ in both obvious and subtle ways. In the first movement of Mozart's Symphony in G Minor, for example, the first theme moves almost entirely in eighth notes and quarters, whereas the second theme is marked by longer notes and shorter ones—dotted half notes and sixteenths.

First theme

Second theme

Audiences wanted variety in music; composers responded by refining the rhythmic differences between themes and other musical sections, so that the differences sound like more than differences—they sound like real contrasts. The music may gradually increase or decrease its rhythmic energy, stop suddenly, press forward by fits and starts, or glide by smoothly. All this gives the sense that Classical music is moving in a less predictable, more interesting, and often more exciting way than Baroque music does.

Dynamics

Variety and flexibility were also introduced into dynamics. Passages were now conceived more specifically than before as loud, soft, very loud, and so on, and marked *f, p, ff, mf* by composers accordingly. Again, concern for variety went along with a new sensitivity to contrast. By insisting on the contrast between loud and soft, soft and very soft, composers made variety in dynamics clearly perceptible and, we must suppose, "pleasing."

Furthermore, instead of using the steady dynamics of the previous period, composers now worked extensively with gradations of volume. The words for growing louder (*crescendo*) and growing softer (*diminuendo*) first came into general use in the Classical period. Orchestras of the mid-eighteenth century were the first to practice long crescendos, which, we are told, caused audiences to rise up from their seats in excitement.

The clearest sign of the new flexibility in dynamics was the rise in popularity of the piano, at the expense of the ever-present harpsichord of the Baroque era. The older instrument could manage only one sound level, or at best a few sound levels, thanks to its two or three separate sets of strings. The new pianoforte could produce a continuous range of dynamics from soft to loud (the name, in fact, means "soft-loud" in Italian). It attracted composers because they wished their keyboard instruments to have the same flexibility in dynamics that they were teaching to their orchestras.

Tone Color: The Orchestra

Classical composers also devoted increasing attention to tone color. The clearest sign of this was the emergence of the Classical orchestra. The orchestra standardized in this period formed the basis of the symphony orchestra of later times.

Domestic music making in the eighteenth century: a group portrait by Johann Zoffany (1733–1810), one of many fashionable painters in Britain (and British India). It was not uncommon for members of the gentry—including, here, an earl—to order pictures showing off their musical accomplishments.

The heart of the Classical orchestra was still (as in the Baroque orchestra) a group of stringed instruments: violins, divided into two groups, first violins and second violins; violas; and cellos, with a few basses playing the same music as the cellos an octave lower. As we saw on page 127, there was a basic Baroque orchestra consisting of just these instruments, plus the continuo, and various other possibilities, including the festive Baroque orchestra:

THE BASIC BAROQUE ORCHESTRA

STRINGS	KEYBOARD
Violins (divided into two groups, called violins 1 and violins 2) Violas Cellos Bass viol (playing the same music as the cellos, an octave lower)	Harpsichord or organ

THE FESTIVE BAROQUE ORCHESTRA

STRINGS	WOODWINDS	BRASS	PERCUSSION	KEYBOARD
Violins 1 Violins 2 Violas Cellos Bass viol	2 Oboes 1 Bassoon	3 Trumpets	2 Timpani (kettledrums)	Harpsichord or organ

In the Classical orchestra, however, the woodwind and brass instruments were given clearly defined, regular roles. With the strings as a framework, woodwind instruments were added: in the high range, pairs of flutes, oboes, and (a bit later) clarinets; in the low, bassoons. These instruments provided "pleasing variety" by playing certain melodies and other passages; each of the woodwinds contributed its own intriguing tone color or timbre. They also strengthened the strings in loud sections.

THE CLASSICAL ORCHESTRA

STRINGS	WOODWINDS	BRASS	PERCUSSION
Violins 1 Violins 2 Violas Cellos Bass viols	2 Flutes 2 Oboes 2 Clarinets* 2 Bassoons *Optional	2 French horns 2 Trumpets* *Optional	2 Timpani

Brass instruments were added in the middle range. The function of French horns and trumpets was mainly to provide solid support for the main harmonies, especially at points such as cadences when the harmonies needed to be made particularly clear. But sometimes they played short solos, which always stood out. The only regular percussion instruments used were two timpani, which generally played along with the brass.

The great advance in the orchestra from the Baroque to the Classical era was in flexibility — flexibility in tone color and also in rhythm and dynamics. The orchestra now became the most subtle and versatile musical resource that composers could employ, as well as the grandest.

Melody: Tunes

In the case of Classical melody, the Enlightenment ideal of "pleasing variety" was a secondary issue. Rather the demand was for simplicity and clarity, for relief from the complex, richly ornamented lines of the Baroque period. When people at the time demanded "natural" melodies, what they meant were tunes: uncomplicated, singable melodies with clear phrases (and not too many of them), melodies with easily grasped parallelisms and balances.

Confronted with a Baroque work such as Bach's Suite No. 3 in D (see page 150), a late eighteenth-century audience might have tolerated the fairly straightforward Gavotte, but would have been unmoved by the beautiful Air. Its elegant winding lines and the mere fact of its great length would have struck them as completely "unnatural":

In their move toward melodic simplicity, composers of the Classical period moved much closer to popular music, and some varieties of folk music, than their Baroque predecessors had. There is an unmistakable popular lilt in Haydn's music that people have traced to the Croatian folk melodies he heard in childhood. Short tunes — or, more often, attractive little phrases that sound as though they might easily grow into tunes — are heard again and again in Classical symphonies, quartets, and other pieces. Tunes are not the only melodic material to be heard in these works, as we shall see in a moment. Nonetheless, by comparison with a Baroque concerto, a Classical symphony leaves listeners with a good deal more to hum or whistle as they leave the concert.

Often entire tunes were worked into larger compositions. For example, variation form (theme and variations) grew popular both for separate pieces improvised by virtuosos and for movements in multimovement genres. Haydn wrote variations on the Austrian national anthem (he also wrote the tune), and Mozart wrote variations on "Twinkle, Twinkle, Little Star," in its original French version, "Ah vous dirai-je, maman" ("Oh mama, I must tell you"). Occasionally, popular songs were even introduced into symphonies. There is a contemporary opera tune in Mozart's "Jupiter" Symphony, the last he composed.

Texture: Homophony

The predominant texture of Classical music is homophonic. In Classical compositions, melodies are regularly heard with a straightforward harmonic accompaniment in chords, without counterpoint and without even a melodic-sounding bass line. Again, this was thought (with some reason) to be a more "natural," clearer way of presenting a melody than polyphony.

All this made, and still makes, for easy listening. The opening of Mozart's famous Symphony No. 40 in G Minor proclaims the new sonorous world of the late eighteenth century:

A single quiet chord regrouped and repeated by the violas, the plainest sort of bass support below, and above them all a plaintive melody in the violins — this simple, sharply polarized texture becomes typical of the new style.

Homophony or melody with harmony was not, however, merely a negative reaction to what people of the time saw as the heavy, pedantic complexities of Baroque counterpoint. It was also a positive move in the direction of sensitivity. When composers found that they were not always occupied in fitting contrapuntal parts to their melodies, they also discovered that they could handle other elements of music with more "pleasing variety." In particular, a new sensitivity developed to harmony for its own sake.

One aspect of this development was a desire to specify harmonies more precisely than in the Baroque era. The first thing to go was the continuo, which had spread its unspecified (because improvised) chord patterns over nearly all Baroque music. Classical composers, newly alert to the sonorous quality of a particular chord, wanted it spaced and distributed among various instruments just so. They refused to allow a continuo player to obscure the chord with unpredictable extra notes and rhythms.

It may seem paradoxical, then, but the thrust toward simplicity in texture and melody led through the back door to increased subtlety in other areas, notably in rhythm and in harmony.

Classical Counterpoint

The rise of homophony in the Classical period represents a major turnaround in musical technique, for although Baroque composers did write some homophonic pieces, as we have seen, the predominant texture of music at that time was polyphonic.

Yet it is not the way of history to abandon important resources of the past completely, even when the past is discredited. Classical composers rejected Baroque music, but they cautiously retained the basic principle of counterpoint. They were able to do this by refining it into a more delicate, unobtrusive kind of counterpoint than that of the Baroque era. And there was a sharper awareness now of counterpoint's expressive possibilities. In a texture that was mostly simple and homophonic, counterpoint attracted special attention; this texture could be used to create the impression of tension, of one line rubbing against another. The more intense, artificial texture of polyphony stood out against natural homophonic texture.

Hence, as we shall see in the next chapter, the section in Classical sonata form called the development section, whose basic function is to build up tension, typically involves contrapuntal textures. Sonata form was the most important musical form of the time, and so counterpoint was often heard.

4 Form in Classical Music

How can a piece of music be extended through a considerable span of time when listeners expect everything to be natural, simple, and easily understood? This was the problem of musical form that composers of the Viennese Classical era faced. They arrived at a solution of considerable elegance and power, involving several elements.

Repetitions and Cadences

First, themes in Classical music tend to be *repeated* immediately after their first appearance, so that listeners can easily get to know them. (In earlier music, this happened only in dance music, as a general rule.) Later in the piece, those same themes are repeated again.

Second, themes are *led into* in a very distinctive manner. The music features prominent transitional passages that do not have much melodic profile, only a sense of urgency about arriving someplace—the place where the real theme will be presented (and probably presented twice).

Third, after themes have been played, they are typically *closed off* just as distinctively. Often there are quite long passages consisting of cadences repeated two, three, or more times, as though to make it clear that one musical idea is over and another, presumably, is coming up. Composers would devise little cadential phrases, often with minimal melodic interest, that could be repeated and thus allow for such multiple cadences.

Multiple cadences are a characteristic and easily recognizable feature of Classical music, particularly, of course, at the very ends of movements. Two clear examples come from our CD set.

Haydn, Symphony No. 95 in C Minor, second movement: This is rather formal-sounding, deliberate music, so the repeated cadences at the end sound even a little pompous. It is as though each of the instruments of the Classical

Porcelain musicians, c. 1770

orchestra wants to make sure the movement ends properly: first the violins, playing ornamented cadences (thirty-second notes) with bassoons in the background; then the French horns alone; then the rest of the orchestra. For the dynamics at the very end (*pp* and *ff*), see page 193.

¶ *Aria "Ho capito" from* Don Giovanni: Near the end of this aria (1:11), the singer sings much the same cadence over and over again. (A few seconds later, the orchestra has its own cadence, and the whole piece is over.) The situation is explained on page 213. Sputtering with rage at Zerlina, Masetto keeps reiterating his sarcastic taunts until he is finally chased away. This cadence, then, is even more solid than it needed to be—for Mozart, a comical effect:

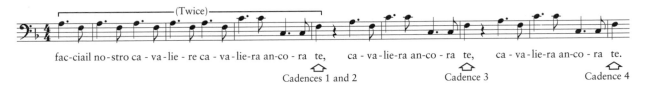

Classical Forms

A third feature designed to cope with the problem of musical form in Classical music is perhaps the most far-reaching. Composers and their audiences came to rely on a limited number of *forms*, or standard formal patterns, the most important of which are *sonata form, minuet form, rondo,* and *theme and variations form.*

These provided a commonly understood frame of reference for composing music and appreciating it. Broadly speaking, after listening for just a short time to some new piece, an eighteenth-century music lover could always tell what sort of themes and keys it would include, when they would return, and about how long the piece would last. This frame of reference is not so obvious today, so the four Classical forms just mentioned will be taken up in some detail in Chapter 12.

The repetitions, self-conscious transitions, and emphatic cadences that are so characteristic of the Classical style all help clarify the forms. And the forms themselves were a special necessity at a time when composers were filling their compositions with contrasts of all kinds. It is a mark of the aesthetic success of Classical music that the contrasts don't sound too drastic, because the forms control and, in effect, tame them. The seemingly inexhaustible emotional range of Classical music is directly proportional to the extent of those contrasts, on the one hand, and, on the other, to the elegance of their control by musical form.

Houdon's most unclassical portrait bust—of his wife

CHAPTER 12

The Symphony

The genres of music that arose in the Classical period, replacing those of the Baroque era, continued to hold their own in the nineteenth century, and all the way through the first half of the twentieth. Indeed, they are still in use today, at least in the sense that their names are still encountered. Not surprisingly, the style, the number of movements, and the forms employed today bear little relation to norms from two hundred and more years ago. But it is still true that if you compose a large, impressive concert piece for orchestra, the best way to convey that fact to conductors, musicians, and audiences is to name it a **symphony**.

One reason for the prominence of the symphony in the Classical era is its close association with a crucial development in the sociology of music, discussed in Chapter 11: the growth of public concerts. As concerts became more and more frequent, people felt a need for some genre that would make an effective, substantial focus for these occasions. Symphonies filled the bill — and in turn required more variety and flexibility of sound than anything orchestras of the early eighteenth century could provide. The symphony spurred a major technical development within music, the evolution of the Classical orchestra (see page 177).

The symphony, then, is rightly viewed as the crowning achievement of Viennese Classical music — but when any musician acknowledges this, he or she wants to add a plea in the same breath: Please don't forget the other genres that grew up alongside the symphony, for in these genres you will find music just as beautiful, music that has become for us just as precious. In Chapter 13 we study the sonata, the Classical concerto, the string quartet, and — in the field of opera — Italian *opera buffa* (comic opera).

Movements of the Symphony

Opening Movement
   tempo: fast/moderate
   form: sonata form
     (sometimes preceded by
     a slow **Introduction**)

Slow Movement
   tempo: slow/very slow
   form: sonata form
     variations, rondo, other

Minuet (with Trio)
   tempo: moderate
   form: minuet form

Closing Movement
   tempo: fast/very fast
   form: sonata form or
     rondo form

1 The Movements of the Symphony

As with Baroque genres, works in the Classical period consist of several movements, which contrast in tempo and are composed in different musical forms. The outline in the margin of this page gives the particulars for the four movements of a typical symphony. Compare the following brief description with the description given on page 133 for the Baroque concerto:

¶ The *first* movement of a symphony is a substantial piece in fast or moderate tempo, written in the most important new form of the time: sonata form (which we will study in the next section). Sometimes this fast music is preceded by a short but solemn *introduction* in a slower tempo.

¶   The *second* movement strikes an obvious contrast with the first by its slow tempo and its quiet mood.

¶   The *third* movement contrasts in another way, by its persistent dance rhythms: It is always a minuet and trio. A minuet is a moderately paced dance in triple meter: See page 148.

¶   The *fourth,* closing movement is fast again—if anything, faster than the first. It may be in sonata form, like the first movement, though rondo is also a common choice.

If we compare the symphony table shown on the previous page with a parallel table for the Baroque concerto, on the right, we see many differences, but also certain similarities. The forms used for the movements are entirely different, and there is the extra minuet. However, in the broadest terms, the sequence from *fast/complex* to *slow/quiet* to *fast/brilliant* is the same.

A word of caution: The symphony table on page 182 represents the norm, but there are always exceptions. Some famous ones are Mozart's *Prague* Symphony, lacking a minuet, and Haydn's *Farewell* Symphony with an extra slow movement—five movements in all. (There were exceptions also to the Baroque scheme: Bach's *Brandenburg* Concerto No. 1 has two dance movements added to the usual three for the concerto.)

*Movements of
the Baroque Concerto*

Opening Movement
  tempo: fast/moderate
  form: ritornello form

Slow Movement
  tempo: slow/very slow
  form: no standard form

Closing Movement
  tempo: fast/very fast
  form: ritornello form

2 Sonata Form

A new form developed at this time, called **sonata form**, is closely associated with the symphony—even though it turns up in much other music of the time. The opening movement of every symphony is in sonata form, and this movement counts as the intellectual and emotional core of the whole work. Many Classical works have two or even three movements in this same form.

The reason for this wide use, perhaps, was that more than any other form, sonata form exploited what was the overriding interest of Classical composers. Their interest was in contrasts of every kind—especially contrast of thematic material and contrast of key, or tonality. Composers found sonata form particularly rich and flexible in its expressive application. It was something they could use for forceful, brilliant, pathetic, even tragic opening movements, gentle or dreamy slow movements, and lively, often humorous closing movements.

Viewed on the highest level, sonata form is simple enough—a very large-scale example of **A B A′** form, usually with repetitions: |: **A** :||: **B A′** :| or |: **A** :|| **B A′**. What is less simple, and what makes sonata form different from other **A B A** forms, is the nature and the function of the musical material in each letter section. This is implied by the special terms used for them: **A** is called the *exposition,* **B** the *development,* and **A′** the *recapitulation.* What do these terms signify?

Exposition (A)

The **exposition** of a sonata-form movement is a large, diverse section of music in which the basic material of the movement is presented (or "exposed"). The material always consists of the following elements:

❦   To begin, a main theme is presented in the first key, the tonic key (see page 31; this key is the key of the piece as a whole — in Mozart's Symphony in G Minor, the tonic is G minor). This **first theme** may be a tune, a group of small phrases that sound as though they might grow into a tune, or just a motive or two (see page 27) with a memorable rhythmic character.

❦   After the first theme is firmly established, often with the help of a repetition, there is a change in key, or *modulation*. The subsection of the exposition that accomplishes this change is called the **bridge,** or the *transition*.

The modulation in the bridge is an essential feature (even *the* essential feature) that gives sonata form its sense of dynamic forward movement. With a little experience, it is not hard to hear the contrast of key and sense the dynamism, for the idea is not to make the crucial modulation sound too smooth. There has to be a sense of tension in the way the new themes, now to be introduced, "sit" in the new key.

❦   Next comes a group of themes or other musical ideas in the new key, called the **second group.** At least some of these new themes contrast with the first theme in melody, rhythm, dynamics, and so on, as well as in key. Usually one new theme stands out by its melodious quality; this is called the **second theme.**

❦   The last theme in the second group, the **cadence theme,** or *closing theme,* is constructed to make a solid ending prior to a full stop and the big repeat. The very end of the exposition is marked by a loud series of repeated cadences, as though the composer wanted listeners to know exactly where they are in the form. This **A** (exposition) section is usually repeated.

Development (B)

The following section, the **development,** heightens the tonal-thematic tension set up by the contrasting themes and keys of the exposition. The themes are "developed" by being broken up, recombined, reorchestrated, extended, and in general shown in unexpected and often exciting new contexts.

Eighteenth-century English spinet, a type of small harpsichord. Especially away from the main musical centers, the harpsichord continued in use along with the piano.

Most development sections use counterpoint to create a sense of breakup and turmoil. This section moves around restlessly from key to key; there are frequent modulations that can easily be heard. In all these ways the music sounds unstable.

After considerable tension has been built up, the last modulation of the development section returns to the first key. The passage that accomplishes this, called the <u>retransition,</u> has the function of discharging (calming down) the tension and preparing for the recapitulation to come. Classical composers were amazingly inventive in finding ways to make this crucial juncture of the form seem fresh, logical, and inevitable.

Recapitulation (A′)

With a real sense of relief or resolution, we now hear the first theme again, followed by all the other themes and other elements of the exposition. There may be minor changes, but in principle everything comes back in its original order. Hence the name for this section—the **recapitulation** (meaning a step-by-step review).

But there is an important difference: The music now remains in the same key, the tonic key. (In practical terms, this means that the whole second group is relocated in the tonic. To allow for this, the bridge has to be rewritten—often in an imaginative way.) Stability of key in the recapitulation is especially welcome after the instability of the development section. Basically, as we have said, sonata form depends on a strong feeling of balance between exposition and recapitulation (**A B A′**). But it is a weighted balance, because **A′** has achieved a new solidity.

The entire **B A′** sequence may be repeated. Whether this happens or not, another section in the tonic is often added at the end, a post mortem or wrap-up for the main action. This optional section is called the <u>coda</u> (in fact, coda is a general term for a concluding section in any musical form).

In the following schematic diagram for sonata form, changes of key (tonality) are shown on a continuous band. Notice the tonal stability of the recapitulation, where the steady horizontal band contrasts dramatically with the fluctuations of the exposition and development sections.

> **❝** I compare a symphony with a novel in which the themes are the characters. We follow their evolution, the unfolding of their psychology. . . . Some of these characters arouse feelings of sympathy, others repel us. They are set off against one another or they join hands; they make love; they marry or they fight."
>
> *Swiss composer Arthur Honegger, 1951*

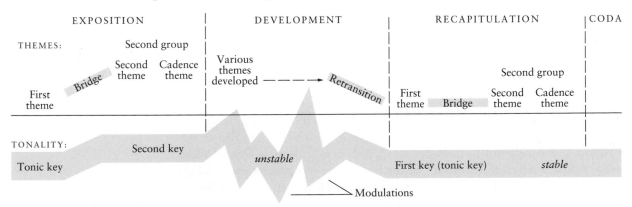

It may not be accidental that the terms used in discussing sonata form resemble those used in discussions of drama. We speak of the "exposition" of a play, where the initial situation is set forth, and of the "development" of the plot. Indeed, sonata form has a dramatic quality compared with the more architectural quality of Baroque music such as a fugue. In a Classical symphony, the themes seem almost like characters in a play or a novel to whom things are happening. They seem to change, take part in various actions, and react to other themes and musical processes.

WOLFGANG AMADEUS MOZART
Symphony No. 40 in G Minor, K. 550* (1788)

16–21   14–19

Mozart's Symphony in G Minor is one of the most famous and admired of all his works. The opening movement, with its sharp contrasts and clear demarcations, makes an arresting introduction to sonata form.

Not many Classical compositions convey as dark and uneasy a mood as does this symphony. (Not many Classical symphonies are in the minor mode.) It suggests some kind of muted struggle against inescapable restraints. Mozart's themes alone would not have created this effect; expressive as they are in themselves, they only attain their full effect in their setting. Mozart needed sonata form to manage these expressive themes—in a sense, to give them something to struggle against.

First movement (Molto allegro)   We have already cited this movement's open-ing texture—melody with a strictly homophonic accompaniment—as char-acteristic of the Viennese Classical style (see pages 178–79). So also are the delicate dynamic changes toward the end of the theme and the loud repeated cadences that terminate it. The unique nervous energy of this theme, a blend of refinement and subdued agitation, stamps the first movement unforgettably.

Exposition   The first theme is played twice. The second playing already be-gins the modulation to the exposition's second key, and a forceful bridge pas-sage completes this process, after which the music comes to an abrupt stop. Such stops will come again and again in this movement.

The second theme, in the major mode, is divided up, measure by measure or phrase by phrase, between the strings and the woodwinds:

Then it is repeated with the role of the instruments reversed, the strings taking the notes originally played by the winds, and vice versa. These instrumental al-terations contribute something absolutely essential to the character of the theme, and show Mozart's fine ear for tone color, or timbre.

The second appearance of the second theme does not come to a cadence, but runs into a series of new ideas that make up the rest of the second group. Since all of them are so brief, and leave so little impression on the rest of the movement, it is best not to consider these ideas actual themes. One of these ideas begins to develop the motive of the first theme—a premature develop-ment process, one might think; but once again, it goes by so fast that we do not take it for the real development section.

A short cadence theme, *forte,* and a very insistent series of repeated ca-dences bring the exposition to a complete stop. (We still hear the rhythm of theme 1.) After one dramatic chord, wrenching us back from major to the original minor key, the whole exposition is repeated.

Original

Fragmented

*Mozart's works are identified by *K numbers,* after the chronological catalog of his works com-piled by Ludwig von Köchel. The first edition (1862) listed 626 works composed by Mozart in his short lifetime; later editions add many more that have come to light since then.

Freemasonry in the eighteenth century was a high-minded society of intellectuals and aristocrats, promulgating ideas that were often radical. "Enlightened" Emperor Joseph II tolerated them, barely. Mozart joined the group and wrote a good deal of music for their secret meetings; this extraordinary painting shows him seated at the far right.

Development   Two more dramatic chords—different chords—and then the development section starts quietly. The first theme is accompanied as before. It modulates at once, and seems to be losing itself in grief, until the rest of the orchestra bursts in with a furious contrapuntal treatment of that tender, nervous melody.

The music seems to exhaust itself. It comes to another stop. But in the following *piano* passage, the modulations continue, with orchestral echoes based on smaller and smaller portions of the first theme, as shown at the bottom of page 186. Breaking up a theme in this way is called *fragmentation*.

Passion breaks out anew in another *forte* passage; but the modulations, we notice, have finally ceased. The fragmentation reaches its final stage, as shown. At last the harmony seems to be waiting or preparing for something, rather than shifting all the time. This passage is the *retransition*.

Recapitulation   After its fragmentation in the development section, the first theme somehow conveys new pathos when it returns in its original form, and in the original tonic key. The bassoon has a beautiful new descending line.

And pathos deepens when the second theme and all the other ideas in the second group—originally heard in a major-mode key—are now re-capitulated in the tonic key, which is a minor key. The result is a great many small alterations of the exposition material—small, but they change the mood decisively. The recapitulation is more stable than the exposition—for one thing, both the first and the second groups are now in the same mode (minor), as well as in the same key. The bridge theme, much expanded, also hammers away at the minor mode, recalling the contrapuntal outburst of the development section. It is a passage of great power.

Coda   In a very short coda, Mozart refers one last time to the first theme. It sounds utterly disheartened, and then battered by the usual repeated cadences.

For a comment on the third movement of the Symphony in G Minor, a minuet in form but not in spirit, see page 198.

The Mozart children as prodigies. Both seem to have been great talents, but—inevitably for that time—it was the boy who went ahead. Nannerl grew up to be a rather straitlaced woman, married, and took care of her father in his old age.

bedfordstmartins.com/listen
▶ Interactive Listening Chart 7

LISTENING CHART 7

Mozart, Symphony No. 40 in G Minor, first movement

Sonata form. 8 min., 16 sec.

16–21   14–19

16 14	**EXPOSITION**		
	0:01 **Theme 1** **(main theme)**	Theme 1, *p*, minor key (G minor); repeated cadences *f*	 *p*
	0:25	Theme 1 repeats and begins the modulation to a new key.	
	0:34 **Bridge**	Bridge theme, *f*, confirms the modulation.	*f*
		CADENCE Abrupt stop	
	Second Group		
17 15	0:53 **Theme 2**	Theme 2, *p*, in major key; phrases divided between woodwinds and strings	*p*
0:11	1:04	Theme 2 again, division of phrases is reversed.	
0:29	1:22	Other shorter ideas, *f*, and *p*: echoes of theme 1 motive	
0:55	1:48 **Cadence theme**	Cadence theme, *f*, downward scales followed by repeated cadences	*f*
		CADENCE Abrupt stop	
1:12	2:04 *Exposition repeated*		
	DEVELOPMENT		
18 16	4:10 **Theme 1** **developed**	Theme 1, *p*, modulating	
0:16	4:26 **Contrapuntal** **passage**	Sudden *f*: contrapuntal treatment by the full orchestra of theme 1	
0:44	4:54 **Fragmentation**	Sudden *p*: beginning of theme 1 echoes between strings and woodwinds; theme fragmented from ♫♩ ♫♫♩ ♩♩ to ♫♩ ♫♩ ♩♩ and finally to ♫♩.	
1:01	5:11	Retransition *f* (full orchestra), *p* (woodwinds), which leads into the recapitulation	
19 17	**RECAPITULATION**		
	5:26 **Theme 1**	Theme 1, *p*, G minor, as before	
0:24	5:50	Theme 1, modulating differently than before	
0:33	5:59 **Bridge**	Bridge, *f*, longer than before	
		CADENCE Abrupt stop	
	Second Group		
20 18	6:41 **Theme 2**	Theme 2, *p*, this time in the minor mode (G minor)	
		All the other second-group themes are in the tonic key (minor mode); otherwise much the same as before	
1:00	7:41 **Cadence theme**	Scale part of the cadence theme, *f*	
21 19	**CODA**		
	7:54	New imitative passage, *p*, strings; based on theme 1 motive	
0:10	8:03	Repeated cadences, *f*	 *p*
		Stop, this time confirmed by three solid chords	

Wolfgang Amadeus Mozart (1756–1791)

Mozart was born in Salzburg, a picturesque town in central Austria, which today is famous for its music festivals. His father, Leopold, was a court musician and composer who also wrote an important book on violin playing. Mozart showed extraordinary talent at a very early age. He and his older sister, Nannerl, were trotted all over Europe as child prodigies; between the ages of six and seventeen, Wolfgang never spent more than ten successive months at home. His first symphony was played at a London concert when he was only eight years old.

But mostly Wolfgang was displayed at courts and salons, and in a somewhat depressing way this whole period of his career symbolizes the frivolous love of entertainment that reigned at midcentury. The future Queen Marie Antoinette of France was one of those for whose amusement the six-year-old prodigy would name the keys of compositions played to him, and sight-read music at the piano with a cloth over his hands.

It was much harder for Mozart to make his way as a young adult musician. As usual in those days, he followed in his father's footsteps as a musician at the court of Salzburg, which was ruled by an archbishop. (Incidentally, one of their colleagues was Joseph Haydn's brother Michael.) But the archbishop was a disagreeable autocrat with no patience for independent-minded underlings. Mozart hated working for him. In 1781, he extricated himself from his court position, not without an ugly scene, and set himself up as a freelance musician in Vienna.

It seems clear that another reason for Mozart's move was to get away from his father, who had masterminded the boy's career and now seemed to grow more and more possessive as the young man sought his independence. Leopold disapproved of Wolfgang's marriage around this time to Constanze Weber, a singer. (Mozart had been in love with her older sister, Aloysia—a more famous singer—but she rejected him.)

Mozart wrote his greatest operas in Vienna, but only the last of them, *The Magic Flute*, had the success it deserved. Everyone sensed that he was a genius, but his music seemed too difficult—and he was a somewhat difficult personality, too. He relied for his living on teaching and on the relatively new institution of concerts. Every year he set up a concert at which he introduced one of his piano concertos. In addition, the program might contain arias, a solo improvisation, and an overture by somebody else.

But as happens with popular musicians today, Mozart seems (for some unknown reason) to have suddenly dropped out of fashion. After 1787, his life was a struggle, though he did receive a minor court appointment and the promise of a church position, and finally scored a really solid hit with *The Magic Flute*. When it seemed that financially he was finally getting out of the woods, he died suddenly at the age of thirty-five.

He died under somewhat macabre circumstances. He was composing a Requiem Mass, that is, a Mass for the Dead, commissioned by a patron who insisted on remaining anonymous. Mozart became ill and began to think he was writing for his own demise. When he died, the Requiem still unfinished, a rumor started that he had been poisoned by the composer Antonio Salieri.

Unlike Haydn, the other great master of the Viennese Classical style, Mozart allowed a note of disquiet, even passion, to emerge in some of his compositions (such as the Symphony in G Minor). The Romantics correctly perceived this as a forecast of their own work. Once we recognize this, it is hard not to sense something enigmatic beneath the intelligence, wit, and sheer beauty of all Mozart's music.

Chief Works: The comic operas *The Marriage of Figaro, Don Giovanni, Così fan tutte* (That's What They All Do), and *The Magic Flute* ▪ *Idomeneo*, an *opera seria* ▪ Church music: many Masses, and a Requiem (Mass for the Dead) left unfinished at his death ▪ Symphonies, including the *Prague*, the G minor, and the *Jupiter* ▪ String quartets and quintets ▪ Concertos for various instruments, including nearly twenty much-loved piano concertos ▪ Piano sonatas; violin sonatas ▪ Lighter pieces (such as divertimentos, etc.), including the famous *Eine kleine Nachtmusik*

Encore: After Symphony No. 40, listen to the Clarinet Quintet and *The Marriage of Figaro* (Act I).

Mozart's musical handwriting

3 Classical Variation Form

Variation form, as we saw on page 137, entails the repetition of a clearly defined melodic unit, the *theme,* with various changes at each repetition. In the Baroque era, the theme was usually a bass pattern (sometimes called a ground bass). The same basic principle is at work in Classical variation form, but now the theme is a tune in the upper register.

We can understand why the Baroque era, which developed the idea of the basso continuo supporting harmonies from below, would have cultivated variations on a bass pattern, whereas the Classical era, with its emphasis on simple melody, preferred variations on short tunes in the upper register.

Variations in the visual arts: Claude Monet (1840–1926) painted dozens of pictures of Rouen Cathedral at different times of the day and in different lights. Variations in music could also be said to show their theme in "different lights."

The point of variations is to create many contrasting moods with the same theme, which is transformed but always somehow discernible under the transformations. Nothing distracts from this process, at least until the end, where composers usually add a coda. There are no contrasting themes, modulations, transitions, cadence sections, or development sections, as there are in sonata form movements (and in many rondos).

A Classical <u>theme and variations</u> movement begins with a theme that is typically in |: **a** :||: **b** :| or |: **a** :||: **ba** :| form. This miniform nests within the larger variation form:

Theme	Variation 1	Variation 2 . . .	Coda
|: **a** :||: **b** :|	|: **a**^{1} :||: **b**^{1} :|	|: **a**^{2} :||: **b**^{2} :|	(free)

Variations were part of the stock-in-trade of virtuosos of the Classical era. At a musical soiree, someone might suggest a popular opera tune, and the pianist would improvise variations on the spot, for as long as his or her imagination held out. <u>Twelve was a common number for these variations</u> when they were published; virtuosos piled them up for maximum effect.

In symphonies and concertos, theme and variations movements are less extended, since they have to fit into a time scale with all the other movements. For our example we turn to Joseph Haydn, since tuneful, witty variations movements in symphonies were a specialty of his.

FRANZ JOSEPH HAYDN
Symphony No. 95 in C Minor (1791)

2 22–36   **1** 20–31

Over the last twenty years of his active career, from around 1780 to 1800, Joseph Haydn averaged better than one symphony a year, nearly all of them masterpieces.

The most famous of them are the last twelve, written for concerts in London, where Haydn enjoyed enormous success on two tours after his retirement from the court of the Esterházy princes. Symphony No. 95 is one of these *London* symphonies, composed on the first tour in 1791.

First movement (Allegro moderato)   Symphonies always begin with movements in sonata form, and since we have already worked on this form with Mozart's Symphony in G Minor, we will not go through Haydn's movement in the same detail. (Follow the mini–Listening Chart at the right.) The music starts in the minor mode, in a rather somber mood, but this all clears up when **22** in the recapitulation it turns cheerfully to the major and stays there. Compare Mozart's first movement, which ends in the minor. In lighter moods, Haydn is every bit the equal of Mozart, but in his late years, at least, he avoids the beautiful shadows that occasionally—and unforgettably—darken Mozart's music, **23** as in the G-minor Symphony.

Coming out of a long, eventful development section, Haydn slips into the expanded recapitulation before we even notice. Where Mozart's recapitulation mostly mirrors the exposition, Haydn's is more like an imaginative rewrite, **24** treating the exposition material quite freely.

Second movement (Andante)   The second movement of a symphony is the slow movement—a restful episode to contrast with the vigorous first movement.

Haydn, Movements of Symphony No. 95

Opening Movement
   tempo: fast
   form: sonata form

Slow Movement
   tempo: slow
   form: variations

Minuet (with Trio)
   tempo: moderate
   form: minuet form

Closing Movement
   tempo: fast
   form: rondo

LISTEN

HAYDN
Symphony No. 95, first movement
2 22–24

EXPOSITION
0:00 Theme 1: minor
0:49 Theme 2, etc.: major
1:45 *Repeated*

DEVELOPMENT
0:00 Uses theme 1
0:42 Uses theme 2
0:59 Back to theme 1

RECAPITULATION
0:00 Theme 1: minor
0:43 Theme 2, etc. major
End expanded: major

Esterháza, near Vienna, where Haydn spent most of his life—a huge palace built by Esterházy princes in imitation of Versailles. It cannot compare with the real item, however: See page 117.

There is no standardized form for slow movements (either in symphonies or in other genres, such as sonatas or concertos). Mozart, in his late symphonies, preferred sonata form or some derivative of sonata form. Haydn favored his own version of variation form.

In Symphony No. 95 the variation theme is a graceful tune in |: **a** :||: **b** :| form. Whereas **a** is rather simple, the melody of **b** melts into counterpoint for a time, before ending peacefully in the low register.

Now the variations start; the music example on page 194 shows the key melody notes that each of them preserves, while much else is varied. The normal expectation would be the basic scheme shown in the margin, as discussed on page 191. Haydn wrote dozens of variation movements like this—though not, interestingly, in symphonies. He seems to have felt it would be boring for a concert audience, and he needed to do something freer and more interesting. For example, instead of repeating the **a** and **b** phrases in the variations exactly, he sometimes writes variations within variations, as indicated by prime marks on the following diagram:

THEME	|: a :||: b :|
Variation 1	|: a_1 :||: b_1 :|
Variation 2	|: a_2 :||: b_2 :|
Variation 3	|: a_3 :||: b_3 :|

LISTENING CHART 8

Haydn, Symphony No. 95, second movement (Andante cantabile)

Variation form. 4 min., 17 sec.

2 25–29   **1** 20–24

THEME			Strings only
25 / 20	0:00 **a** 		
	0:14 **a**		
	0:27 **b**		
	0:47 **b**		
VARIATION 1			
26 / 21	1:07 **a**	Cello solo—begins with the melody of **a**	
0:13	1:20 **a₁'**	Triplet sixteenth notes 	
0:24	1:31 **b₁**	Cello—now in triplets, then violins	
0:41	1:49 **b₁**		
VARIATION 2	Minor mode		
27 / 22	2:06 **a₂**		
0:12	2:19 **b₂**		Winds: *f*
0:32	2:38 **b₂'**	Ends with a transition to variation 3	Winds: *f*
VARIATION 3	Back to the major mode		
28 / 23	2:58 **a₃**	(= **a**; unvaried)	Strings
0:13	3:11 **a₃'**	Thirty-second notes, *f* 	More use of winds
0:24	3:23 **b₃**		Still more
CODA			
29 / 24	3:40 **a₄**	New, expressive harmony	Strings
		Continuation: extra cadences	Wind solos
0:30	4:11	*Surprise!* **ff**	

Haydn's musical handwriting

	"NORMAL" VARIATIONS	HAYDN, SYMPHONY NO. 95
THEME	a a b b	a a b b
Variation 1	a₁ a₁ b₁ b₁	a₁ a₁' b₁ b₁
Variation 2	a₂ a₂ b₂ b₂	a₂ b₂ b₂' —— transition —→
Variation 3	a₃ a₃ b₃ b₃	a₃ a₃' b₃

(Diagrams such as this one can sometimes make simple things look complicated. Don't worry about a couple of gaps in Haydn's treatment of the form, or the added transition from Variation 2 to Variation 3. The music flows naturally and clearly until the very end.)

Variation 1 starts with a cello solo that stays very close to the theme itself, with new material in the other strings above. It is as though the composer wants to remind us of the original **a**, one more time, before varying it further in $\mathbf{a_1}'$. In $\mathbf{a_1}'$ and the two $\mathbf{b_1}$ phrases, the variation is supplied by fast-moving violins that effectively swamp the melody. Still, the melody's phrases and its harmonic pattern are clear.

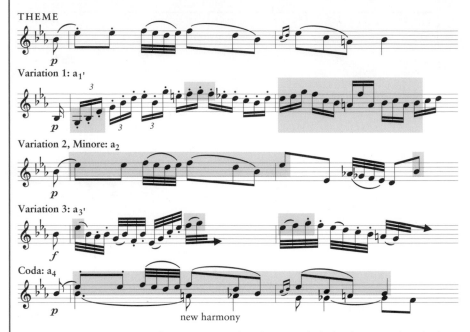

Variation 2 goes to the minor mode; the mood shifts from melancholy (in $\mathbf{a_2}$) to blustering (in $\mathbf{b_2}$) and then apprehensive. Perhaps we need a moment to recover from all this, before returning to the major mode and the original feeling. Haydn provided a short transition passage to ease the way.

Variation 3 begins with $\mathbf{a_3}$, equivalent to **a** in its original, unvaried form—another reminder of the fundamental source of all the variations. Then $\mathbf{a_3}'$ and $\mathbf{b_3}$ sound like a more intense version of Variation 1, with the violins moving faster. There is a hush, and a lovely new harmonization of **a** suggests the arrival of another variation. But instead of continuing with the theme, repeated cadences marked *p* and *pp* begin guiding the music to its close. It is an utter surprise, then, when the very last chords are jolted by a sudden *ff*.

Haydn used this kind of effect on more than one occasion. Is he making fun of the repeated cadences, which do sound a bit heavy-handed, or is the joke on this whole elegant movement—or even on the whole Classical style itself? Haydn can write serious, profound music, yet there are times when he seems to make a point of not taking himself too seriously.

Notice that at first this slow movement is scored for strings alone, and that the wind instruments play a larger and larger role, until they play alone in the coda.

bedfordstmartins.com/listen
▶ Interactive Listening Chart 8

4 Minuet Form (Classical Dance Form)

Stylized dances—music in the style and form of dances, but intended for listening rather than dancing—reached a state of high development in the Baroque era. In Chapter 9 we saw how various dance types such as the gavotte and the bourrée were assembled into suites. Unlike the Baroque era, which

Franz Joseph Haydn (1732–1809)

Unlike so many other composers, Haydn did not come from a family of professional musicians. But his father, an Austrian village wheelwright, was a keen amateur musician. As a boy Joseph had a beautiful voice, and at the age of eight he was sent to Vienna to be a choirboy in St. Stephen's Cathedral. After his voice broke, he spent several difficult years as a freelance musician in Vienna before obtaining the position of Kapellmeister with Prince Paul Anton Esterházy, one of the most lavish patrons of music at the time.

After this, Haydn's career reflects the changing social situation in the later eighteenth century, when the old system of court patronage coexisted with an early form of the modern concert system. Indeed, there is no finer tribute to the system of court patronage than Haydn's thirty-year career with the Esterházys. The post of Kapellmeister involved managing and writing music not only for the prince's chapel (the *Kapell*), but also for his private opera house, his marionette theater, and for palace chamber music and orchestral performances. Haydn had a good head for administration. Hiring his own musicians, he was able over many years to experiment with the symphony and other genres and develop his style under ideal conditions.

Haydn's output was staggering. He composed 104 symphonies, 83 string quartets, numerous divertimentos, trios, and sonatas, and over 20 operas. He also had to write a great deal of music for baryton—a bizarre archaic instrument fancied by the next Esterházy prince, Nikolaus, which was something like a cello with extra strings that could be plucked, like guitar strings.

The Esterházys had a splendid estate some miles outside of Vienna, but Haydn's duties there did not prevent him from spending a good deal of time in the capital. In the 1770s his string quartets made a particularly strong impression in the metropolis. In the 1780s he befriended Mozart, and the two actually played together in an amateur string quartet.

Meanwhile the spread of Haydn's international fame accelerated with the growth of public concerts. At first his symphonies were picked up by French concert organizers (who paid Haydn nothing). Then in the 1780s his six *Paris* symphonies were commissioned for concerts in that city, and in the 1790s twelve *London* symphonies were written for two highly successful tours to Britain.

Toward the end of his life Haydn turned to choral music: six impressive Latin Masses for soloists, chorus, and orchestra, and two German oratorios inspired by Handel, *The Creation* and *The Seasons*, admired by his contemporaries as the apex of an exemplary career in music.

Haydn's most famous composition is a simple Austrian patriotic song:

It appears with variations in his *Emperor* Quartet, Op. 76 No. 3 (1797). The tune was adopted for the German national anthem, "Deutschland über Alles," and for the hymn, "Glorious Things of Thee Are Spoken."

One of the most attractive personalities in the gallery of the great composers, Haydn was shrewd but generous-minded, humorous, always honorable, and though fully aware of his own worth, quite ready to praise his young, difficult colleague, Mozart. "Friends often flatter me that I have some genius," he once said—without contradicting them—"but he stood far above me."

Haydn's music combines good-humored simplicity of melody with a very sophisticated delight in the manipulations of musical form and technique. No composer has ever enjoyed a (musical) joke more. In his reasonableness, his wit, and his conviction that his art should serve humanity (a conviction he both expressed and acted upon), Haydn is the true musical representative of the Enlightenment.

Chief Works: 104 symphonies; the last twelve, composed for London in 1791–95, include the *Surprise*, *Clock*, and *Drum Roll* symphonies ▪ A cello concerto and a delightful trumpet concerto ▪ Over 80 string quartets; piano trios and piano sonatas ▪ Choral music in his late years: six Masses and the oratorios *The Creation* and *The Seasons*

Encore: After Symphony No. 95, listen to Symphony No. 102; Trumpet Concerto.

Baryton

developed a single genre made up of different dances, the Classical era focused on a single stylized dance and introduced it into many different genres.

The sole dance type from the Baroque suite to survive in the multimovement genres of the Classical period was the **minuet**. One reason for its endurance was simply the dance itself: originally popularized at the court of Louis XIV in the seventeenth century, it continued as one of the major fashionable social dances in the eighteenth. However much the minuet movement of a symphony differed from a simple dance tune, it was always a reminder of the aristocratic courts that had originally established orchestras.

Another reason was more technical. As a moderately paced piece in triple meter, the minuet makes an excellent contrast to the quick duple meter that was by far the most common meter in the opening and closing movements of Classical symphonies, quartets, and the like.

Works with four movements—symphonies and string quartets—always included a minuet, usually as a light contrast after the slow movement. Mozart even managed to fit a minuet into some of his piano concertos, though traditionally the concerto, as a three-movement genre, did not leave room for one.

Baroque and Classical Dance Form

A Baroque minuet consists of two sections; each comes to a complete stop and is immediately repeated (|: **a** :|: **b** :|). See page 149. Minuets tend to come in pairs, alternating in an **A B A** pattern. The second dance, **B**, is called the **trio**, because in early days it was often played by only three instruments.

An eighteenth-century minuet, with music and notation for the dance steps.

> **"** The admirable and matchless HAYDN! From whose productions I have received more pleasure late in my life, when tired of most Music, than I ever received in the ignorant and rapturous part of my youth."
>
> *English music historian Charles Burney, 1776*

> **"** Be assured, my D. H., that among all your numerous admirers NO ONE has listened with more PROFOUND attention, and no one can have such veneration for your MOST BRILLIANT TALENTS as I have. Indeed, my D. H., no tongue CAN EXPRESS the gratitude I FEEL for the infinite pleasure your Music has given me . . ."
>
> *Letter to Haydn from another, more intimate English admirer, 1792*

A Baroque minuet movement can be diagrammed as follows. (Remember that |: :| means repeat, and that in the second **A** the parts are not repeated.)

MINUET	TRIO	MINUET
A	**B**	**A**
|: a :||: b :|	|: c :||: d :|	a b

Classical composers extended the internal form of minuets (and trios) by developing internal **a b a** structures according to one of the following schemes:

MINUET	TRIO	MINUET		MINUET	TRIO	MINUET
A	**B**	**A**	or	**A**	**B**	**A**
|: a :||: b a :|	|: c :||: d c :|	a b a	(more often)	|: a :||: b a' :|	|: c :||: d c' :|	a b a'

Prime marks (a' and c') indicate significant changes or extensions to the original **a** and **c** sections. It is easy to see why Classical dance form is sometimes called **ternary form**.

FRANZ JOSEPH HAYDN
Symphony No. 95 in C Minor, third movement (Menuetto)

30–32   25–27

The minuet movement of Symphony No. 95 takes a small mental journey from the ballroom to the countryside, and then back again. Perhaps it is not a real countryside but a stylized one, like the one shown on the Rococo plaque on page 172.

Minuet Although the minuet starts with a quiet and weakly accented theme, it soon switches into the easy, energetic swing of a real ballroom dance, as **a** switches from the original minor to the major mode.

Informal pencil drawing of Haydn, which he once singled out as the best likeness he had ever seen: not the choice of a vain man. Compare page 195.

If you count the triple-meter bars, you will find almost all of them fit into the four- and eight-bar phrases that are necessary for the dance floor, if the dancers are to keep going. However, this is a stylized minuet, ripe for one of Haydn's jokes, and in phrase **a'** he suddenly puts in a long rest, with a fermata. The music starts up again coolly, with a mysterious harmony, and goes on to a solid conclusion, but any in-the-flesh dancers would be thrown off completely.

Trio As happens quite often in Haydn, this trio sounds less like a court dance, even of a muscular kind, than like some sort of country dance, with a suggestion of none-too-competent peasant musicians. The tempo slows, the mode changes from minor to major, and a somewhat awkward tune, all in even eighth notes, is played by a solo cello (who also starred, we remember, in the slow movement). Haydn knew that London audiences liked solo turns in symphonies.

Phrase **c'** is another joke: The cello player seems to forget how to go on, and has to be given a cue by the violins. Then, doesn't the cellist play for time by repeating the cue over and over again, before finding a way to the cadence?

LISTENING CHART 9

Haydn, Symphony No. 95, third movement (Menuetto)

Minuet form. 4 min., 56 sec.

30–32   25–27

30 **25**	**MINUET (A)**		
	0:00 a	Theme	
	0:09	Theme again, moving to the major mode	
	0:26 a	*Repetition*	
	0:51 b	(Picks up a motive introduced for the previous cadence)	
	1:00 a'	Theme (back in the minor)	
	1:13	Unexpected pause, with fermata ⌒	
	1:20	Strong return to the minor	
	1:30 b a'	*Repetition*	
31 **26**	**TRIO (B)**		
	2:12 c	Slower tempo, major mode: cello solo	
0:13	2:25 c	*Repetition*	
0:26	2:38 d		
0:40	2:52 c'		
0:46	2:58	Violins	
0:59	3:11 d c'	*Repetition*	
32 **27**	**MINUET (A)**		
	3:46	*Repetition of* a b a'	

CELLO   *p*

bedfordstmartins.com/listen
▶ Interactive Listening Chart 9

Minuet   The minuet returns unchanged, except for omission of the repeats. But coming after the quiet trio, there is an interesting new feel to the minuet's quiet opening.

Unlike a recapitulation in a sonata-form movement, the return of **A** after the trio in minuet form does not give the impression of emerging out of previous musical events and completing them. Minuet returns are more formal, less organic. We probably listen to them less reflectively than to recapitulations, re-membering their origin in the ballroom, where dances are played as many times as the dancers need them and are always gratefully received.

The minuet movement of Mozart's Symphony in G Minor is not on our CD set, but it is easy to find and fascinating to compare with the minuet from Haydn's Symphony No. 95. There are no jokes in Mozart, and if there is any-thing rustic about his trio, the quality is laced with nostalgia, even romanti-cism. The minuet itself is even more highly stylized than Haydn's. Full of raging music in three-bar phrases with grating counterpoint—both features guaranteed to confuse ballroom dancers—it hardly ever modulates so as to depart from the gloom of the minor mode. In this extraordinary minuet, the mood of Mozart's symphony intensifies, from nervous agitation and distress in the first movement to near-tragedy in the third.

5 Rondo Form

The <u>rondo</u> is a relatively simple form with popular leanings. In the symphonies and other multimovement genres of the Classical era, it was used mainly for closing movements, which tend to be relatively light.

Actually, the rondo (or *rondeau,* in French) is a form dating back to the Baroque era; to hear a typically simple, non-symphonic rondo of the Classic era, go to the sonata by Francesca LeBrun on page 203. How different this is from the enormously expanded rondo we are about to encounter in Haydn's symphony! Yet the formal principle is the same: both introduce a full-fledged tune (**A**) and come back to it after episodes (**B, C,** etc.) serving as spacers between its appearances. The longer rondo tunes may return abbreviated. If **A** is in the favorite |: **a** :|: **b a′** :| pattern of the time, for example, the recurrence of **A** throughout the rondo may present **a b a′** or **b a′**, or even **a** alone. There is always enough of the tune for one to recognize.

In simple rondos, the episodes feature little tunes much like **A,** as in the LeBrun sonata. In symphonies, the episodes may contain transitions to new themes, cadence formulas, and even sonata-form style developments. (Rondos of these kinds are sometimes called *sonata rondos.*) Various schemes are possible; often a coda is added. Whatever the specific structure, the regular return of the main tune **A** is the critical feature of rondo form.*

Rondo schemes:

A B A C A coda
A B A C A B A
A B A C A D A
—and others

Symphony No 95:
A B A B C A coda

FRANZ JOSEPH HAYDN
Symphony No. 95 in C Minor, fourth movement (Finale. Vivace)

The rondo theme, **A,** starts out as a rather delicate, airy tune. The form could be diagrammed |: **a** :|: **b** :|, but |: **a** :|: **b c** :| better represents what we actually hear. Phrases **a, a,** and **b** are played by the strings alone. Then, when **b** seems to have answered **a** and rounded it off with a full cadence, the wind instruments enter much less delicately, adding **c** as a lively appendage lasting as long as **a** and **b** together. Notice a three-note figure ♩♩♩𝄾 that appears *in* **a** and **c** and *under* **b**.

The first episode, **B,** starts with a bang right on the last note of **A.** It is a fugue on a subject derived from **A** (the beginning of **a** played in sequence):

*In some ways, rondo form resembles ritornello form (see page 133), but the differences are worth noting. <u>Ritornello form</u> usually brings back its ritornello in fragments and in different keys; rondo form usually brings back its theme complete and in the same key.

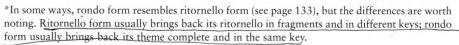

LISTENING CHART 10

Haydn, Symphony No. 95, fourth movement (Finale. Vivace)

Rondo. 3 min., 41 sec.

33 28	0:00	A (Tune)	a		Dynamic is *p*
	0:08		a		
	0:15		b		
	0:22		c		Long extension (winds)
	0:37		b c		
34 29	0:58	B (Episode 1)	Fugal exposition, *f*:		First subject entry
0:06	1:04				Second entry (rapid counterpoint in the bassoons)
0:10	1:08				Third entry (stretto)
0:14	1:12		Further material: many new, nonfugal ideas		
0:19	1:17		Seems to head for a big cadence; trumpets		
0:40	1:38		Fugue resumes:		Subject entry
0:48	1:46				Final entry — in the bass
1:04	2:02		Expectant STOP		
35 30	2:05	A	a b c ⌒		*p*
0:28	2:33	B (Episode 2)	Fugue starts up again, *f*: seems to almost *reach* a cadence		
0:41	2:46	C	***Surprise! sudden stormy section in the minor mode, ff***		
1:00	3:05		Transition (in several short stages)		
36 31	3:14	A	a	New, expressive harmony	*p*
0:12	3:27	Coda		Brass fanfares	*f*

We spoke earlier of free and learned fugues (page 145), and this one is free, very free. Once the exposition of only three (instrumental) voices is over, the polyphonic texture changes to homophony and even monophony, in sweeping downward scales.

Theme **A** returns, this time without the repeats, and the next episode starts much like **B**, that is, with the same fugue — which turns out to be a trick. After a few bars the mode changes suddenly from major to minor and the dynamic rises from *f* to *ff* for a passage of furious, stormy music that would have jolted — and also delighted — the London audience during Haydn's first triumphant tour.

They would have been delighted because they would have recognized it as another of Haydn's jokes, similar in spirit to the sudden fortissimo ending of this symphony's slow movement (see page 194). For the music here is not just noisy and furious, it is disproportionately noisy and furious, a manic explosion that rattles the orderly Classical style of the rest of the finale.

The harmony soon returns to the major mode and the storm subsides (the audience knew this would happen, too). We touch base on **A** one more time, with its **a** phrase in a newly harmonized version, and the piece comes quickly to a close.

Thinking back on Haydn's Symphony No. 95, we might ask if there is any aesthetic quality that derives from the combination of the particular four movements we have heard. Is the whole greater than the sum of the parts?

If so, this is not something that musicians or musicologists have been able to explain with any consistency. It seems, rather, that Classical composers wrote symphony movements to fit together only in a general way, without thinking very much about connections between them, or any greater whole. This is as true of Mozart's agitated G-minor Symphony as of Haydn's more cheerful Symphony No. 95.

Indeed, the question only comes up because later, nineteenth-century symphonies often *do* make such connections. Symphony No. 5 by Ludwig van Beethoven seems to trace a psychological process from turmoil to triumph. The *Fantastic* Symphony by Hector Berlioz traces a story line written by the composer himself. See pages 231 and 270.

bedfordstmartins.com/listen
  ▶ Quizzes and Flashcards

CHAPTER 13

Other Classical Genres

I n Chapter 12 we examined the symphony as exemplified by Haydn's Symphony No. 95 in C Minor and Mozart's Symphony No. 40 in G Minor. We go on in this chapter to examine the other main genres of music in the Viennese Classical era: the sonata, the Classical concerto, the string quartet, and opera buffa, the name for Italian comic opera of the time.

It would be impractical to spend the same amount of detail on each of these genres as on the symphony, and also somewhat redundant, for many features of the symphony are duplicated in these other genres. Indeed, for Classical instrumental music, the symphony can be used as a sort of prototype. Bear in mind the symphony outline from Chapter 12; we reprint it on this page.

In the following pages we select a sonata, a concerto, and a string quartet and then discuss a single movement from each (using recordings and Listening Charts, as usual). The discussions emphasize generic specificity — that is, the specific features that differentiate the genre of music in question from the symphony. In the case of opera buffa, two numbers serve as samples of the whole.

Movements of the Symphony

Opening Movement
  tempo: fast/moderate
  form: sonata form
    (sometimes preceded
    by a slow **Introduction**)

Slow Movement
  tempo: slow/very slow
  form: sonata form,
    variations, rondo, other

Minuet (with Trio)
  tempo: moderate
  form: minuet form

Closing Movement
  tempo: fast/very fast
  form: sonata form
    or rondo form

1 The Sonata

The term <u>sonata</u> has multiple meanings. We know it as an adjective in the term *sonata form,* the scheme employed in the first movements of symphonies, but as a noun the term goes back before the Classical period and simply meant a piece for a small number of instruments or a single one. (In Italian, *sonata* means, simply, "sounded.") In the Baroque period there were trio sonatas and solo sonatas — solo plus continuo, usually — but in the Classical period the term was restricted to compositions for one or two instruments only.

Sonatas were not designed for concerts, which in any case were still rare at this time, but for private performances, often by amateurs. The symphony is a public genre, the sonata a domestic one — and increasingly the domestic clientele was made up of women (see the next page). Although professional female musicians were still rare, more and more women played music in the home. Given their amateur audience, some (not all!) sonatas are easy to play and may be limited in expressive range.

Piano sonatas were composed for solo piano, the favorite new instrument of the time, and *violin sonatas* were composed for violin and piano. (The early

> 66 The sonata was said by a German critic to be intended by its earliest writers to show in the first movement what they could do, in the second what they could feel, and in the last how glad they were to have finished."
>
> *Philadelphia musician
> P. H. Goepp, 1897*

From the late eighteenth century on, musical accomplishment was regarded as a highly desirable social asset for women worldwide: for a French princess (painted by Elizabeth Vigée-Lebrun, a fashionable court painter, 1755–1842) or an American First Lady — Louise C. (Mrs. John Quincy) Adams — at a later period.

piano was called *fortepiano;* see page 208). In Classical sonatas with violin, the piano is not a mere accompaniment but an equal partner; it holds its own in such combinations in a way that the earlier harpsichord usually did not.

Compare the three-movement plan for the sonata, shown at the right, with the four-movement symphony prototype on the previous page; they are similar except for the omission of the minuet movement in the sonata. But also note that sonatas are much less uniform than symphonies, concertos, or quartets. In Mozart's sonatas, for example, only about two-thirds follow the plan, leaving many exceptions. None of them has more than three movements, however, and the movements are always shorter than those of a symphony. Some sonatas have only two movements — including two ever-popular ones by the youthful Beethoven.

Movements of the Sonata

Opening Movement
tempo: fast/moderate
form: sonata form

Slow Movement
tempo: slow/very slow
form: sonata form, variations, rondo, other

Closing Movement
tempo: fast/very fast
form: often rondo

FRANCESCA LEBRUN (1756–1791)
Sonata in F, Op. 1, No. 3 (c. 1783)

Since sonatas were increasingly composed for and played by women, we will for once take our example not from a well-known male but from an almost forgotten female composer, Francesca LeBrun. Franziska, as she was originally known, was born into a musical family from Mannheim, one of Germany's most musical cities. Her father, Innozenz Danzi, a prominent cellist, brought up his daughter to be a soprano, and she created roles in famous operas of the time that are no longer remembered. Her brother Franz was a composer of some importance. But Francesca, too, found time to compose, and her sonatas were published in several countries and much praised at the time. Married to an oboe virtuoso named LeBrun, Francesca had the reputation as one of the best — and best-paid — divas of her time.

No doubt one reason Francesca LeBrun is forgotten is that she died so young, while her career was still on the way up. She lived exactly as long as

❝ We lunched with Herr LeBrun, his wife, Cannabich, and a priest. A pheasant as an additional dish was served in cabbage, and the rest was fit for a prince. Finally, we had oysters . . .❞

From a letter by Mozart, 1785. J. C. Cannabich (1731–1798) was a composer from LeBrun's hometown, Mannheim.

Francesca LeBrun sits for England's leading painter of the time, Thomas Gainsborough (1727–1788). She had herself depicted as a great lady, not as a musician.

LISTEN

LEBRUN
Sonata in F,
Rondeau

0:00	A	a a′
0:18	B	b b′
0:36	A	
0:54	C	c c′
1:16	D	
1:34	C	c c″
1:55	transition	
2:10	A B A	(a a″)
3:03	coda	

Mozart, whom she knew: thirty-six years. Her dates are exactly the same as his: 1756–1791.

The Sonata in F has two movements, the first in sonata form, as usual. The second is a straightforward rondo.

Second Movement (Rondeau: Allegretto)   The first theme **A** of this rondo has real sparkle, which means that the whole piece can keep us interested and amused.

Rondeau: Allegretto

B uses some of the same motives as **A**, and **C** turns to the minor mode (and to quite different rhythms) for a contrast. After **C**, a rather stormy episode leads back to the tonic key, and there is a deft coda after the last return of **A**, introducing syncopations (see page 14) for the first time — just a few of them, but very effective.

2 The Classical Concerto

On page 133 we discussed the Baroque concerto and concerto grosso at the time of Bach and Vivaldi in terms of the basic concerto idea — the contest between soloist and orchestra. This basic idea was refined and sharpened by the Viennese Classical composers.

Instrumental virtuosity remained a central feature of the Classical concerto. At the same time, the orchestra was growing. With its well-coordinated string, woodwind, and brass groups, the Classical orchestra was much more flexible than the Baroque concerto orchestra could ever be.

So the balance between the two contesting forces — solo instrument and orchestra — presented a real problem, a problem that Mozart worked out in a series of seventeen superb piano concertos written during his years in Vienna, mostly for his own concert use. He pitted the soloist's greater agility, brilliance, and expressive capability against the orchestra's increased power and variety of tone color. The contestants are perfectly matched; neither one ever emerges as the definite winner.

Compare the movement plan for the Classical concerto with the symphony prototype in the margin of page 202. Concertos have long opening movements — see below — and no minuet movements.

Movements of the Classical Concerto

Opening Movement
   tempo: fast/moderate
   form: double-exposition sonata form
   cadenza near the end

Slow Movement
   tempo: slow/very slow
   form: sonata form, variations, rondo, other

Closing Movement
   tempo: fast/very fast
   form: rondo form (occasionally variation form)

Double-Exposition Form

For the first movements of concertos, Mozart developed a special form to capitalize on the contest that is basic to the genre. Though the diagram for **double-exposition form** may look rather cluttered, it is in fact simply an extended variant of sonata form. Compare the sonata-form diagram on page 185:

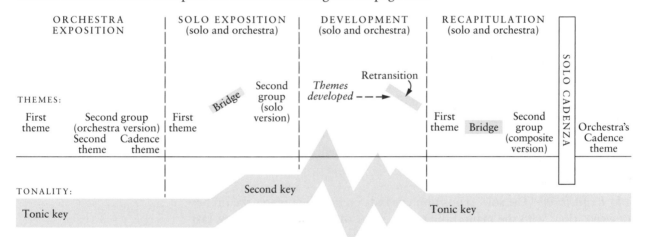

In sonata form, the exposition presenting all the basic material is repeated; here each of the competing forces presents the thematic material in its own somewhat different version. Note that unlike the exposition in a symphony, in a concerto the **orchestra exposition** does not modulate — an important difference. The point is to save the change of key (which counts for so much in all sonata-form compositions) until the **solo exposition**. The listener senses that the orchestra can't modulate and the soloist can — evidence of the soloist's superior range and mobility. This is demonstrated spectacularly by the soloist playing scales, arpeggios, and other brilliant material, making the solo exposition longer than the orchestral one.

The recapitulation in double-exposition form amounts to a composite of the orchestral and solo versions of the exposition. Typically the orchestra's cadence theme, which has been crowded out of the solo exposition to make room for virtuoso activity, returns at the end to make a very satisfactory final cadence.* Shortly before the end, there is a big, formal pause for the soloist's **cadenza** (see page 140). The soloist would improvise at this point — to show his or her skill and flair by working out new thematic developments on the spot, and also by carrying off brilliant feats of virtuosity.

---

*Double-exposition form, like sonata form, may also have a coda — a feature exploited by Beethoven more than Mozart and Haydn.

WOLFGANG AMADEUS MOZART (1756–1791)
Piano Concerto No. 23 in A, K. 488 (1786)

This favorite Mozart concerto proceeds from one of his most gentle and songful first movements to a second movement that is almost tragic, followed by an exuberant, sunny finale. The first movement might almost have been intended as a demonstration piece for double-exposition form, except for one unique feature: a new theme introduced halfway through.

First Movement (Allegro)   No fewer than four themes in this movement could be described as gentle and songful—though always alert. For a work of this character, Mozart uses a reduced orchestra, keeping the mellow clarinets but omitting the sharper-sounding oboes as well as trumpets and timpani.

Orchestra Exposition   Theme 1, played *piano* by the strings and repeated by the woodwinds, is answered by a vigorous *forte* passage in the full orchestra.

This "response" idea returns many times, balancing the quiet themes, and often leading to something new—here, theme 2, another quiet melody, full of feeling. An agitated passage interrupts, suddenly emotional, touching on two different minor keys, but only briefly. This whole section remains in the major tonic key, without any actual modulation. The cadence theme that ends the section maintains the gentle mood.

Solo Exposition   The solo exposition expands on and illuminates the orchestra exposition, with the piano taking over some of it, while also adding fast-moving scales or other figuration of its own. The main difference comes at the bridge; the modulation, needed to give the music a lift, is engineered by the piano. The orchestral second theme sounds especially intimate and lovely when played on the piano—as Mozart planned. And at the end, instead of the gentle cadence theme, the piano has a moment of brilliant passage work, culminating in a drawn-out, triumphal cadence with a long trill.

Showy cadences of this kind are a regular feature of Classical concertos; the orchestra always answers with loud music of its own, like a cheer. Here it is the orchestra's response passage again. But this time it stops in mid-course, as though the orchestra has suddenly remembered something intimate and a little serious. A new theme (yet another quiet, gentle melody, this time with a thoughtful character) appears out of nowhere:

After the orchestra plays the new theme, the solo repeats it in an elaborated version, and we slip into the development section.

Development   The basic idea behind concertos, the contest between orchestra and soloist, is brought out wonderfully here. Mozart sets up a rapid-fire dialogue between the two contestants; fragments of the new theme in the

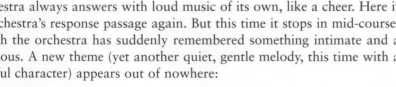

> " These piano concertos are a happy medium between too easy and too difficult; they are very brilliant, pleasing to the ear, and natural, without being simple-minded. There are passages here and there which only connoisseurs will be able to appreciate, but less learned listeners will like them too, without knowing why."
>
> *Letter from Mozart to his father, 1782*

Mozart, Piano Concerto in A, K. 488, first movement

Double-exposition form. 11 min., 16 sec.

2

37–41

On this chart, the column arrangement distinguishes the main orchestra and solo sections.

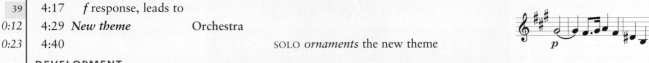

37	**ORCHESTRA EXPOSITION**				
	0:00 Theme 1, *p*	Orchestra	Strings; woodwinds for the second playing		
	0:33 *f* response				
	0:56 Theme 2, *p*				
	1:26 "Deflection" passage		Two minor-mode keys are suggested.		
	1:57 Cadence theme, *p*				

Cadence theme

38	**SOLO EXPOSITION**			
	2:06 Theme 1		SOLO: melody is increasingly ornamented.	
0:29	2:35 *f* response	Orchestra, with SOLO cutting in		
0:37	2:43 Bridge—modulates			
0:59	3:05 Theme 2			
1:28	3:34 "Deflection" passage			
1:57	4:03 Solo virtuoso passage			
39	4:17 *f* response, leads to			
0:12	4:29 *New theme*	Orchestra		
0:23	4:40		SOLO *ornaments* the new theme	

	DEVELOPMENT		
0:36	4:54	Orchestra and SOLO: *dialogue* around the new theme; modulations	
1:18	5:35 Retransition		
1:38	5:56 Short cadenza		in free time; ends with a fermata

40	**RECAPITULATION**		
	6:12 Theme 1, *p*	Orchestra, with SOLO cutting in for the second playing	
0:29	6:41 *f* response	Orchestra, with SOLO cutting in again	
0:37	6:49 Bridge		
0:57	7:09 Theme 2		
1:27	7:39 "Deflection" passage		
41	8:12 *New theme* (longer virtuoso passage)	(the first time the SOLO plays it without ornaments)	
0:42	8:54 *f* response, leads to		
0:54	9:06 *New theme*		
1:11	9:23 Main CADENZA	SOLO free, improvised passage	
2:31	10:43 *f* response	Orchestra	
2:45	10:57 Cadence theme, *p*		
2:52	11:04 Brief ending *f* ⟶ *p*		

Doodle on a Mozart concerto score

Mozart's fortepiano, the early version of today's piano; compare the sound in our recording of LeBrun's sonata (page 203) with the piano in Mozart's A-Major Concerto. In the smaller fortepiano, the strings were strung less tightly because the frame was wood, not iron; hence the volume was lower. The fortepiano makes up for this by its responsive touch and delicacy of tone.

woodwinds seem to discuss or argue with the piano, as the music modulates to minor-mode keys and the material is developed.

The new theme turns unexpectedly anxious in the retransition (see the music in the margin, to the right). Finally, with a brief cadenza, the piano pulls out of the dialogue and steers the way to the recapitulation.

STRINGS

Recapitulation At the start of the movement, the songful first theme was claimed in turn by the orchestra and the solo in their respective expositions. In the recapitulation, a composite of the two expositions, they share it.

Otherwise, the recapitulation resembles the solo exposition, though the bridge is altered so that the whole remains in the tonic key. There is a beautiful extension at the end, and when the response passage comes again, it leads to a heavy stop, with a fermata—the standard way for the orchestra to bow out, after preparing for the soloist's grand re-entrance for the main cadenza. Compared to the cadenza in Bach's *Brandenburg* Concerto—see page 140—this one is much more varied. Written out by Mozart himself, it includes mild improvisatory moments as well as brilliant ones.

The solo's showy cadence after the cadenza is cheered along once again by the orchestra's response passage, which we have heard so many times before. This time it leads to something we have *not* heard many times—only once, nine minutes back: the quiet cadence theme of the orchestra exposition. Do you remember it? It makes a perfect ending for the whole movement, with an extra twist: a little flare-up to *forte* that subsides almost at once.

bedfordstmartins.com/listen
▶ Interactive Listening Chart 11

String quartets, then and now (left and below). Nineteenth-century quartets were often led by celebrated violin soloists; shown here is a group led by a virtuosa of the time, Wilma Norman-Néruda (1838–1911). From left to right: two violins, viola (slightly larger), and cello.

3 The String Quartet

Developed in the Classical era, the **string quartet** is a genre for four instruments: two violins, a viola, and a cello. ("String quartet" is also the name for a group of four musicians who work together playing quartets.) The plan for a string quartet, with its four movements, is close to that of the symphony; compare page 202. Indeed, next to the symphony the quartet counts as the most important genre of Classical music.

The quartet may have as many movements as the symphony, but of course it doesn't have as many instruments, and it cannot match the symphony's range of volume and tone color. This can disappoint listeners today. For the eighteenth century, however, volume was no issue, because quartets were never intended for concert listening. They were intended primarily for the performers, with small, informal audiences—or none at all. History tells of a quartet session with

Movements of the String Quartet

Opening Movement
  tempo: fast/moderate
  form: sonata form

Slow Movement
  tempo: slow/very slow
  form: sonata form, variations, rondo, other

Minuet (with Trio)
  tempo: moderate
  form: minuet form

Closing Movement
  tempo: fast/very fast
  form: sonata form or rondo form

The Kronos Quartet, based in San Francisco, plays almost exclusively contemporary music, including jazz arrangements and other crossover items. They have commissioned more than 400 new works in their 33-year history. Two violins, viola, and cello.

Haydn and Mozart playing along with two other well-known musicians of the time, the only audience being Mozart's family and their two servants.

As for range of tone color, the quartet compensates for this by its own special qualities: nuance, delicacy, and subtlety. Without any conductor, the quartet players are partners responding to one another as only old, close friends can. As developed by Haydn, the four instruments of the quartet grow more and more similar in their actual musical material, and more and more interdependent. There is a fine interplay as they each react to musical gestures by the others, sometimes supporting them, sometimes countering.

This interplay has been aptly compared to the art of cultivated conversation — witty, sensitive, always ready with a perfectly turned phrase — that was especially prized in eighteenth-century salons (page 171).

There are dozens of wonderful string quartets by Haydn and ten, equally wonderful, by Mozart. We could have chosen any one of these for the example on our CD set. However, since Haydn and Mozart are already well represented in this book, we will use an example by one of their younger contemporaries. If you like, jump ahead to page 237 for Ludwig van Beethoven's String Quartet in F, Op. 135. Or go back to Listening Exercise 6 (p. 36) and listen to a string quartet movement by the still younger Franz Schubert.

Chamber Music

The string quartet was the main but not the only genre developed at this time for small forces in relatively intimate circumstances. **Chamber music** is a term for music designed to be played in a room (a chamber) — in a palace drawing room or in a small hall. Chamber music can be taken as encompassing compositions for from two to nine players. Other types are the piano trio (violin, cello, piano: a favorite of Haydn) and string quintets (string quartet plus another low instrument; Mozart wrote four superb quintets with two violas, and one of Schubert's great masterpieces is a quintet with two cellos).

Broadly speaking, what has been said above about the intimate character of the quartet applies to all chamber music, though it's probably clear enough that a string octet must be less subtle and more orchestral than a string trio.

> ❝ Chamber music never sounds as well as when one is close to it. Probably the ideal place is directly in the middle of the players. Retreat forty feet, and at once the thing begins to be thin and wheezy. Go back sixty feet, and one may as well leave the place altogether."
>
> *H. L. Mencken, famously skeptical American critic, 1930*

4 Opera Buffa

In the late eighteenth century, comic opera grew to equal in importance the serious opera that was a hallmark of the Baroque era (see page 155). Roman emperors and their courtly confidants gave way to contemporary peasant girls and soldiers; castratos were edged aside by basses specializing in comical rants and exasperations, the so-called *buffo* basses (*buffone* is Italian for "buffoon"). Happy endings were the result of tricks and schemes rather than the decrees of magnanimous princes.

Comic opera stars had to be funny; they had to act, not just sing. The new flexibility of the Classical style was perfectly suited to the casual and swift effects that are the essence of comedy. As much as its humor, it was this "natural," life-like quality of comedy that appealed to audiences of the Enlightenment. Enlightened monarch Joseph II of Austria actively promoted comic opera.

Italian comic opera was the most important, though there were also parallel developments in Germany, France, and England. Serious Italian opera was called *opera seria;* comic Italian opera was called **opera buffa.** Just as Italian opera seria was very popular in London in Handel's time, so was Italian

Opera buffa showed contemporary people in comic situations—compare the attitudes struck by people in opera seria on page 124. In Mozart's comedy *The Marriage of Figaro*, a frightened page hiding in a chair (Cherubino) sees the Count trying to kiss the Countess's maid (Susanna).

Thank
end is mix
bravery, a
even if thi
bivalent fe

Act I, scei
and Zerlir
diately sp
to leave—

Aria, "He
vividly (ar
entirely in
he will lea
Then he r
He sings a
is going to

ORCHE

Towai
music he
ous words
as he sing
tion of the

opera buffa in Vienna at the time of Haydn and Mozart. Thus Haydn, whose court duties with the Esterházys included running their opera house, wrote twelve comic operas—all in Italian. Mozart in his mature years wrote six, three in German and three in Italian.

The Ensemble

Baroque opera seria, as we have seen (page 155), employs two elements in alternation: recitatives for the dialogue and the action, and numbers that are fully musical—almost always arias—for static meditation and "tableaus" of emotional expression. Classical opera buffa works with the same elements, except that the fully musical numbers include *ensembles* as well as solo arias.

An **ensemble** is a number sung by two or more people. And given the Classical composers' skill in incorporating contrast into their music, they were able to make their ensembles depict the different sentiments of the participating characters simultaneously. This meant that sentiments could be presented much more swiftly and vividly: swiftly, because we don't have to wait for the characters to sing whole arias to find out what they are feeling, and vividly, because the sentiments stand out in sharp relief one against the other.

The music also depicts these sentiments in flux. For in the course of an ensemble, the action proceeds and the situation changes. And changing sentiments are usually projected by means of new musical sections with different tempos, keys, and themes. A Classical opera ensemble, then, is a sectional number for several characters in which the later sections represent new plot action and the characters' new reactions to it.

Think back to the da capo aria of the Baroque opera seria (see page 157). There the return of the opening music—**A** in the **A B A** form—told us that the dramatic situation was just where it had been when the aria started. But at the end of a Classical ensemble, the drama has moved ahead by one notch or more. The music, too, has moved on to something different. The aria was essentially a static number, the ensemble a dynamic one. The ensemble transformed opera into a much more dramatic genre than had been possible within the Baroque aesthetic.

WOLFG

Don Gio

M ozar
of t
spurt in p
Giovanni
what enig
comedy —
comical ar
pigeonhol

Backgroun
endary Spa
is meant to
Certainly a
  But in
Giovanni i
ous undert
only agains
the Comm
  This a
from his p
proached b
tomb. (Yes.
The statue
to *its* hom
planted ahc
before the

The total effect is of a simple man (judging from the music he sings) who nonetheless feels deeply and is ready to express his anger. There is also a clear undercurrent of class conflict: Masetto the peasant versus Don Giovanni the aristocrat. Mozart was no political radical, but he had indeed rebelled against court authority; and the previous opera he had written, *The Marriage of Figaro,* was based on a notorious French play that had been banned because of its anti-aristocratic sentiments. Two years after *Don Giovanni* was composed, the French Revolution broke out in Paris.

Recitative   Next comes an amusing secco recitative, sung with just continuo accompaniment, as in Baroque opera (see page 156). Giovanni invites Zerlina up to his villa, promising to marry her and make her into a fine lady, just as Masetto had ironically predicted.

Duet, "Là ci darem la mano"   Operas depend on memorable tunes, as well as on musical drama. The best opera composers write melodies that are not only beautiful in themselves, but also further the drama at the same time. Such a one is the most famous tune in *Don Giovanni,* in the following <u>duet</u> (an ensemble for two singers) between Don Giovanni and Zerlina.

Section 1 (Andante)   Don Giovanni sings his first stanza to a simple, unforgettable tune that combines seductiveness with a delicate sense of banter.

Là   ci darem la   mano,   Là mi di-rai di   si;   Ve-di, non è lon-ta-no,   Par-tiam, ben mio, da   qui.
There you'll give me your hand, there you'll tell me yes;   You see, it isn't far—Let's go there, my dear!

When Zerlina sings the same tune to *her* first stanza, we know she is playing along, even though she hesitates (notice her tiny rhythmic changes, and her reluctance to finish the tune in eight measures—she delays for two more).

  In stanza 3, as Don Giovanni presses more and more ardently, yet always gently, Zerlina keeps drawing back. Her reiterated "non son più forte" ("I'm weakening") makes her sound very sorry for herself, but also coy. When the main tune comes back—section 1 of the ensemble falls into a **A A′ B A″ coda** form—Giovanni grows more insistent, Zerlina more coquettish. The words they sing (from stanzas 1–3) are closer together than before, and even simultaneous. The stage director will place them physically closer together, too.

Section 2 (Allegro)   Zerlina falls into Don Giovanni's arms, echoing his "andiam" ("let's go"). The "innocent love" they now mean to celebrate is depicted by a little rustic melody (Zerlina is a peasant girl, remember) in a faster tempo. But a not-so-innocent sensuous note is added by the orchestra after the singers' first phrase in this section.

  How neatly and charmingly an operatic ensemble can project dramatic action; this whole duet leads us step by step through Don Giovanni's successful line, or technique. By portraying people through characteristic action or behavior—Don Giovanni winning another woman, Zerlina playing her own coy game—Mozart exposes their personalities as convincingly as any novelist or playwright.

Don Giovanni and Zerlina, in an early engraving; page 216, a modern production.

" 17 MAY 1788. To the Opera. *Don Giovanni.* Mozart's music is agreeable and very varied."

Diary of a Viennese opera buff, Count Zinzendorf

LISTEN   Mozart, *Don Giovanni:* from Act I, scene iii

(Italics indicate phrases of the text that are repeated.)

2		**ARIA: "Ho capito"**		

	0:03	Masetto:
		(to Don Giovanni)
			Ho capito, *signor, si!*
			Chino il capo, e me ne vò
			Ghiacche piace a voi così
			Altre repliche *non fò.* . . .
			  Cavalier voi siete già,
			Dubitar non posso affè,
			Me lo dice la bontà,
			Che volete *aver per me.*
				I understand you, *yes sir!*
				I touch my cap and off I go;
				Since that's what you want
				I have nothing else to say.
				  After all, you're a lord,
				And I couldn't suspect you, oh no!
				You've told me of the favors
				You mean to do for me!

	0:30	*(aside, to Zerlina)*	(Briconaccia! malandrina! *Fosti ognor la mia ruina!)*	(You wretch! you witch! You have always been my ruin!)

		(to Leporello)
		(to Zerlina)
			Vengo, vengo!
			  (Resta, resta!
			È una cosa molto onesta;
				Yes, I'm coming—
				  (Stay, why don't you?
				A very innocent affair!

	0:45		Faccia il nostro cavaliere *cavaliera ancora te.)*	No doubt this fine lord Will make you his fine lady, too!)

(last seven lines repeated)

RECITATIVE (with continuo only)

3	1:32	Giovanni:	Alfin siam liberati, Zerlinetta gentil, da quel scioccone. Che ne dite, mio ben, so far pulito?	At last, we're free, My darling Zerlinetta, of that clown. Tell me, my dear, don't I manage things well?
		Zerlina:	Signore, è mio marito!	Sir, he's my fiancé!
		Giovanni:	Chi? colui? vi par che un onest' uomo un nobil Cavalier, qual io mi vanto, possa soffrir che qual visetto d'oro, qual viso inzuccerato, da un bifolcaccio vil sia strapazzato?	Who? him? you think an honorable man, a noble knight, which I consider myself, could suffer your pretty, glowing face, your sweet face, to be stolen away by a country bumpkin?
		Zerlina:	Ma signore, io gli diedi Parola di sposarlo.	But sir, I gave him My word that we would be married.
		Giovanni:	Tal parola Non vale un zero! voi non siete fata Per esser paesana. Un'altra sorte Vi procuran quegli occhi bricconcelli, Quei labretti sì belli, Quelle dituccie candide e odorose, Parmi toccar giuncata, e fiutar rose.	That word Is worth nothing! You were not made To be a peasant girl. A different fate Is called for by those roguish eyes, Those beautiful little lips, These slender white, perfumed fingers, So soft to the touch, scented with roses.

		Zerlina:
		Giovanni:
		Zerlina:
			Ah, non vorrei—
			  Che non voreste?
			  Alfine
			Ingannata restar! Io so che raro
			Colle donne voi altri cavalieri
			siete onesti e sinceri.
				Ah, I don't want to—
				  What don't you want?
				  To end up
				Deceived! I know it's not often
				That with women you great gentlemen
				Are honest and sincere.

		Giovanni:	È un' impostura Della gente plebea! La nobiltà Ha dipinta negli occhi l'onestà. Orsù non perdiam tempo; in quest'istante Io vi voglio sposar.	A slander Of the lower classes! The nobility Is honest to the tips of its toes. Let's lose no time; this very instant I wish to marry you.

		Zerlina:
		Giovanni:
			Voi?
			  Certo io.
			Quel casinetto è mio, soli saremo;
			E là, gioella mio, ci sposeremo.
				You?
				  Certainly, me;
				There's my little place; we'll be alone—
				And there, my precious, we'll be married.

DUET "Là ci darem la mano"

SECTION 1 Andante, **2/4** meter

4	3:17	Giovanni: A	Là ci darem la mano Là mi dirai di sì! Vedi, non è lontano; Partiam, ben mio, da qui!	There *[in the villa]* you'll give me your hand, There you'll tell me yes! You see, it isn't far— Let's go there, my dear!

		Zerlina:	A′	Vorrei, e non vorrei;	I want to, yet I don't want to;
				Mi tremo un poco il cor.	My heart is trembling a little;
				Felice, è ver, sarei,	It's true, I would be happy,
				Ma può burlarmi ancor.	But he could be joking with me.
0:40	3:58	Giovanni:	B	Vieni, mio bel diletto!	Come, my darling!
		Zerlina:		Mi fa pietà Masetto . . .	I'm sorry for Masetto . . .
		Giovanni:		Io cangierò tua sorte!	I shall change your lot!
		Zerlina:		Presto non son più forte . . .	All of a sudden I'm weakening . . .

(repetition of phrases [both verbal and musical] from stanzas 1–3)

1:01	4:19	Giovanni:	A″	Vieni, vieni! Là ci darem la mano
		Zerlina:		Vorrei, e non vorrei . . .
		Giovanni:		Là mi dirai di si!
		Zerlina:		Mi trema un poco il cor.
		Giovanni:		Partiam, ben mio, da qui!
		Zerlina:		Ma può burlarmi ancor.
1:28	4:46	Giovanni:	coda	Vieni, mio bel diletto!
		Zerlina:		Mi fa pietà Masetto . . .
		Giovanni:		Io cangierò tua sorte!
		Zerlina:		Presto *non son più forte* . . .
		Giovanni; *then* Zerlina:		Andiam!

		SECTION 2 Allegro, 6/8 meter			
1:57	5:14	Both:		Andiam, andiam, mio bene,	Let us go, my dear,
				A ristorar le pene	And relieve the pangs
				D'un innocente amor.	Of an innocent love

(words and music repeated)

Global Perspectives   4

Musical Form: Two Case Studies from Asia

As we have seen, musical forms in the Classical style become quite elaborate. It is certainly no accident that these intricate designs emerged across the eighteenth century, just when independent instrumental music was gaining unprecedented prestige in the European tradition. Instrumental music often seems to require such complexities. It is as if the removal of other determinants of form—a poem set to music, a specific religious ritual, or a pattern of dance steps—calls for a different, more abstract musical organization.

Taking the broadest view of these complex forms, however, we can see that they work changes through a simple process. Composers state a tune and then repeat it throughout a movement, joining with it contrasting elements that might be either more complex (sonata form, first-movement concerto form) or simpler (minuet and trio, most rondos and slow movements). Such a basic concept may be realized in many ways, according to the imagination and inclination of the composer, and result in an unlimited array of individual styles.

Other traditions of instrumental music around the world also start from this simple idea and elaborate it, building intricate forms. In this segment we offer a historical snapshot of two Asian instrumental traditions, from Japan and Indonesia, and we examine music from each.

1. *Japan*

The symphony orchestra as we know it emerged in the seventeenth century as a reflection of the power and splendor of European courts (see page 127). In Japan, a court orchestra had been established a thousand years

earlier. This was the period in Japanese history, from the sixth century C.E. to the eighth, when the first centralized control of the islands emerged. The new Japanese central government, many of its institutions, and even its newly constructed capital city of Nara were modeled on the greatest empire in Asia, China. In the process, many elements of Chinese culture were imported to Japan—most importantly Buddhism, which had in turn been imported to China from India centuries before.

The new Japanese court also imported various musical styles from continental Asia. These were altered and developed into an independent Japanese tradition, which came to play an important role in the court's ceremony and ritual. Altogether, these styles are known as **gagaku** (gáh-gáh-koo), from Chinese characters

The togaku orchestra: *kakko, biwa, sho,* and *hichiriki* (back left).

meaning "elegant music," though their sources are more than just Chinese.

The gagaku repertory is divided into two parts. One, known as *togaku* (tóh-gáh-koo), consists of music derived from Chinese styles (with ingredients from India and Southeast Asia as well). The other, *komagaku* (ko-máh-gáh-koo), is made up of works of Korean and Manchurian origin. Further distinctions are made when gagaku accompanies dance, which is often the case, just as with European Baroque orchestral music.

The Japanese Togaku Orchestra   The togaku orchestra is so distinctive, and so different from any European orchestra, that we should spend a moment getting to know the various instruments. While European orchestras are dominated by strings, all gagaku orchestras feature wind instruments. The instruments all have specific functions:

⁊   The sliding, wailing double-reed *hichiriki* (hée-chee-ree-kée) carries the main melody. Several are heard on our recording, playing together.

⁊   The side-blown flute called *ryuteki* (ree-óo-tay-kée) is the first instrument heard. It plays the melody along with the hichirikis, though in a slightly different version. Thus it produces a *heterophonic* texture with the hichirikis (see page 00); heterophony is an important feature in many non-Western musics.

Sho

⁊   The *sho*, a mouth reed-organ with seventeen pipes, plays chordal clusters of tones derived from the main melody. This unusual instrument contributes a haunting background of harmonic haze to the texture.

The togaku orchestra: *tsuridaiko* suspended on the large stand, back right, and, in the foreground, *gakuso*, *ryuteki*, and a small suspended gong not heard on our recording, called *shoko*.

❡ The *kakko*, a two-headed barrel drum played with sticks, is used for single strokes or short rolls. It is the first drum heard.

❡ A deep, larger barrel drum *tsuridaiko* (tzóo-ree-díe-koh; its first beat is heard at 0:13) marks off long phrases of the melody with two successive strokes, the first soft and the second louder.

❡ A *biwa*, or four-stringed lute (bée-wah, first plucked at 1:11), strums across several strings quickly, punctuating the melody.

❡ A *gakuso*, a zither with thirteen strings (gáh-kóo-so, first heard at 1:31), plays short motives, mainly of three notes related, again, to the melody. Both the biwa and the gakuso take a more active role as this performance proceeds, finally even playing some of the main melody.

Etenraku *Etenraku* is the most famous piece for the togaku orchestra. Its name means "music of divinity," and it emanates a deep, powerful calm associated with Buddhist contemplation. This is probably the oldest music on our CD set; its origins reach back almost to the origins of gagaku itself.

The musical form of this piece exhibits three characteristics of gagaku music. *First,* the piece as a whole is constructed from a single melody, according to a predetermined plan and without improvisation. In *Etenraku* the melody consists of three phrases, labeled **a, b,** and **c** in the musical example and Listening Chart on this page. Each phrase is 32 beats long. The beats move by slowly at first, so slowly that the phrases can be hard to discern; but as you get used to the melody you will be able to follow their repetitions.

Second, the instruments of the orchestra are introduced gradually and in a predetermined order as they fulfill their various functions. The melody is played through by some of the instruments and punctuated by others, as described above.

Third, the beat quickens, the meter is more clearly marked, and the general musical activity increases as the performance proceeds. At first, while the flute alone carries the melody, the beats are very slow and

		LISTENING CHART 12	
Etenraku	8 min., 4 sec.		
0:00	a	Ryuteki, kakko, tsuridaiko only	
0:51		Sho and hichirikis enter.	
1:11	a	Biwa enters.	
1:31		Gakuso enters, completing the orchestra.	
2:18	b		
3:15	b		
4:04	c	Paired beats of tsuridaiko every 8 beats	
4:46	c	Gakuso and biwa gradually play more and more fragments of main melody, joining in heterophony of hichirikis and ryuteki.	
5:25	a		
6:02	a		
6:37	b		
7:11	b	After the phrase is completed (at 7:55), biwa and gakuso end the piece with a brief coda.	

flexible—the music seems almost to have no meter at all. (Each pair of beats on the tsuridaiko drum, however, coming 16 very slow beats after the last, provides a certain sense of regularity and meter.) When the double-reed hichirikis enter, they play the melody along with the flute to a more prominent beat. Then, at the **c** phrases of the melody, the tsuridaiko doubles its pace, beating twice every 8 beats instead of every 16.

Meanwhile the tempo gradually quickens: At the outset the beats come every 2–3 seconds (*very* slow!), while at the close they move by at about one per second.

Phrase **a**

Phrase **b**

Phrase **c**

Even at this relatively quick tempo, the music never loses its sense of restraint. Virtuosic playing is strictly avoided. *Etenraku*'s aura of quiet, inward-looking Buddhist contemplation characterizes the gagaku repertory as a whole.

2. *Indonesia*

The Southeast Asian Republic of Indonesia consists of some six thousand islands in all, half of them inhabited. The central island is Java. Across Indonesia, ensembles playing traditional musics thrive — alongside, these days, many kinds of pop, rock, and world beat ensembles, especially in large urban centers such as Jakarta. A traditional musical ensemble in Indonesia is called a **gamelan**.

The Indonesian Orchestra: Gamelan   Gamelans assume a wide, even bewildering variety of shapes and sizes, as we might expect of musical traditions that extend back many centuries and that have served an array of religious, political, and social functions. Gamelans may involve three or four musicians or they may involve dozens. They sometimes include singers.

They frequently accompany drama or dance: sacred temple dances, danced dramas, or the famous Indonesian shadow-puppet plays enacting stories from Hindu epics. The music gamelans play may have been passed down over hundreds of years or it may be recently composed.

At the heart of gamelan music stands a great variety of gongs and **metallophones** (instruments like a xylophone, with metal keys). Indeed the word *gong* itself comes to us from Java, where it names (and also evokes the sound of) the largest gamelan instrument.

Balinese Gamelans   Nowhere in Indonesia are gamelans more prevalent than on Bali, a good-sized island to the east of Java. In 1980 it was estimated that there was a gamelan for every 350 inhabitants of the island — a staggering number, in a population of around two million!

Gamelans seem to have come to Bali in the sixteenth century, brought from Java by aristocratic refugees when their Hindu kingdom fell to Islamic invaders from the Asian mainland. Balinese gamelans, at least the elaborate ones with many instruments, were associated especially with temples and princely courts. When Bali came under colonial control of the Netherlands in 1906, the courts declined, but their traditions of gamelan music did not simply disappear.

Gamelan pelegongan, with floor gongs, drum, gangsas, and, in the rear, large suspended gongs.

Instead they were taken over more and more by village gamelan clubs, and these comprise the main venue in which Balinese gamelan music thrives today.

Gamelan Pelegongan   *Gamelan pelegongan,* heard on our recording, is a type of Balinese orchestra used primarily to accompany elaborate dance-dramas. It takes its name from this dance, called *legong.* The primary instruments in gamelan pelegongan are:

ɣ   two hand-beaten drums; the drummers direct the ensemble

ɣ   several gongs of varying sizes

ɣ   a large group of metallophones, some low-pitched, some high. Most of these have five metal keys each, with a range of a single octave, while some have thirteen keys and a wider range. The sounds, construction, and names of these metallophones vary, but all of them can be called by the umbrella term *gangsa,* "bronze."

ɣ   one or two bamboo flutes. What Western ears might hear as "out of tune-ness" in their playing is a quality cultivated and prized by Balinese musicians.

Form in Gamelan Music   A traditional piece for gamelan is usually organized around the repetition of a long, symmetrical melody. This melody is made up of smaller, equal phrases, generally 8 or 16 beats long, so that the whole melody will last a multiple of these numbers, especially 64 or 128 beats. A central group of instruments in the gamelan presents this nuclear melody. At the same time it may be played by other instruments in a simpler version, mainly in even note values, creating a heterophonic presentation.

At the end of each statement of the melody, the largest, deepest gong in the orchestra sounds. The unit between one gongstroke and the next, known as a *gongan,* is considered the basic structural unit for the piece. The gongan is divided into smaller units by other instruments in the gamelan: first into two units by a higher-sounding gong, then into four by other gongs, then into eight, and so forth. A 64-beat melody, for example, breaks down audibly into units of 32 beats, 16 beats, 8 beats, 4 beats, and so on.

This process of division continues right through the rhythmic level of the main melody, so that certain instruments elaborate upon its pitches twice as fast, four times as fast, perhaps even eight times as fast.

The whole texture, then, is an elaborately *stratified* polyphony, with rhythmic layers ranging from the gongan itself all the way down to subdivisions of individual beats. Each instrument or each instrumental group plays a single role, occupying one of these rhythmic strata. In the midst of it all is the nuclear

A *legong* dancer and part of the *gamelan pelegongan:* a drum, a small floor gong, and a thirteen-key gangsa are prominent.

A gamelan at a Balinese funeral. The large array of gongs in the foreground is not found in *gamelan pelegongan*.

melody, presented in one version or simultaneously in distinct versions.

Bopong   The piece on our recording, *Bopong*, is not a full dance piece but instead a sort of brief overture, played before the dancing begins. It was composed by I Lotring, a famous Balinese master musician born about 1900 and involved in many stylistic innovations of the 1920s and 1930s.

The 64-beat melody is played through three times; this is the traditional heart of the piece. Before it we hear introductory material, partly based on the main melody. After it comes a lengthy, separate section with an ostinato (see page 137), and then a new concluding melody played by the whole gamelan.

As you listen to the first statement of the nuclear melody itself, from 0:29 to 1:19, *count* the beats, counting slightly faster than one beat per second. The melody is 64 beats long and composed of four phrases of 16 beats each. The large gong sounds at the end of the 64-beat cycle.

The core melody, the most prominent melody you hear, is played by some of the gangsas and by two flutes, one high-pitched and one lower and less easy to hear. At the same time other gangsas play a simpler, unadorned version of this melody in slow notes. They are omitted from the beginning of the melody; listen for them starting at 0:42.

Around this melody is woven faster figuration, dividing each beat you count into four, played by brittle-sounding gangsas. They fall silent at the start of each statement of the melody. Then they enter, softly at first, finally asserting themselves with a clamorous outburst (listen for the first instance at 0:58). Such outbursts are a famous hallmark of the newer, post-court styles of Balinese gamelan music.

The third statement of the melody speeds up toward the end but does not quite finish. An entirely new melodic phrase breaks in to start a different section of

LISTENING CHART 13

I Lotring, *Bopong*   4 min., 33 sec.

0:00	Introduction: a few gangsas alone
0:04	Gong; introduction continues with fast gangsa figuration
0:29	Gong *first* statement of melody begins
1:19	Gong; *second* statement of melody
2:06	Gong; *third* statement of melody
2:38	Melody truncated
2:41	Ostinato begins (fourteen times through); gong every eight beats
4:04	Syncopated, unison closing melody
4:21	Final gongstroke

the piece. Beginning at 2:41, some of the gangsas play a single, eight-beat ostinato, repeated many times; other gangsas and the flutes play along with a slightly elaborated version. Meanwhile the brittle-sounding gangsas contribute spectacular figuration, moving eight times as fast as the main beat. The large gong, sounding at the end of every ostinato—hence every eight beats instead of every sixty-four—adds to the feeling of rhythmic climax.

Finally, all this energy is channeled into a single closing melody with striking syncopations (see page 14), played in unison by most of the gamelan.

The Nineteenth Century

*I*n Unit IV we take up music of the nineteenth century. Starting with the
towering figure of Beethoven in the first quarter of the century, famous
names now crowd the history of music: Schubert, Schumann, Chopin, Wagner,
Verdi, Brahms, Tchaikovsky, Mahler, and others. Nearly everyone, whether
conscious of it or not, knows a fair amount of music by these masters, or at
least some of their melodies. These tend to turn up as background music to
movies and television; some of them are metamorphosed into pop tunes and
advertising sound tracks.

*The appeal of this music today in the symphony hall and the opera house,
the classroom and the teaching studio, seems to rest on much the same grounds
as it did a hundred years ago and more. It is important to realize, first of all,
that nineteenth-century music was a great success story. For the first time in
European history, music was taken entirely seriously as an art on the highest
level. Composers were accorded a new, exalted role, to which they responded
magnificently, writing music that sounds important and impressive; and listeners
ever since have been thoroughly impressed.*

Music and Individual Emotion

*Music's prestige, in the Romantic scheme of things, derived first and foremost
from the belief that music more than any other art mirrors one's inner emotional life. Music, then, should have a unique power to convey individual
feeling. Again, composers rose to the challenge. Nineteenth-century music
is more direct and unrestrained in emotional quality than the music of any
earlier time. And for most audiences, full-blooded emotion in music—even
exaggerated emotion—seems never to lose its powerful attraction.*

*The individuality of all artists, including composers, was accorded spe-
cial value in the nineteenth century. Composers produced music with much
more pronounced personal attributes than in the late Baroque period or the
Classical period (when many pieces by Haydn and Mozart, for example,
sounded rather similar). It is therefore a natural tendency to think of the
history of nineteenth-century music in terms of great names, such as those
in the list given above. The prospect of getting to know all these distinct,
unusual, and probably fascinating characters—meeting them, as it were,
under the emotional conditions of Romantic music—surely contributes*

to the appeal of this particular body of music. And since the Romantic com-
posers have such strong, distinct personalities, it is not only natural but in-
evitable to find oneself drawn to certain of these individuals, and put off
by others. There are music lovers who recoil from Wagner. Others cherish
Schubert above even Beethoven and Bach.

Like eighteenth-century music, music of the nineteenth century is not stylisti-
cally homogeneous, yet it can still be regarded as a larger historical unit. We
shall take up the Romantic style, usually dated from the 1820s, after discussing
the music of Beethoven, who was born in 1770 and as a young man traveled
twice to Vienna, the city of Classicism — first to meet Mozart and then to
study with Haydn.

But while in technique Beethoven was clearly a child of the eighteenth
century, in his emotionalism, his artistic ambition, and his insistence on
individuality he was a true inhabitant of the nineteenth. Indeed, Beethoven
was the model, either direct or indirect, for many of the great nineteenth-
century composers who came after him. Understanding Beethoven is the
key to understanding Romantic music.

CHAPTER **14**

Beethoven

If any single composer deserves a special chapter in the history of music, that composer is Ludwig van Beethoven (1770–1827). Probably no other figure in the arts meets with such a strong universal response. People may pity van Gogh, respect Michelangelo and Shakespeare, and admire Leonardo da Vinci, but Beethoven instantly summons up a powerful, positive image: that of the tough, ugly, angry genius staring down adversity and delivering one deeply expressive masterpiece after another. Beethoven's music has enjoyed broad-based, uninterrupted popularity from his own day to the present. Today its place is equally secure with casual listeners and with the most learned musicians.

There is a sense, furthermore, in which music may be said to have come of age with Beethoven. For despite the great music that came before him—that of Bach, Mozart, and many other composers we know—the art of music was never taken so seriously until Beethoven's symphonies and sonatas struck listeners of his time as a revelation. They were almost equally impressed by the facts of his life, in particular his deafness, the affliction that caused him to retire from a career as a performing musician and become solely a composer.

A new concept of artistic genius was evolving at the time, and Beethoven crystallized this concept powerfully for his own age. He still exemplifies it today. No longer a mere craftsman, the artist suffers and creates; endowed not just with greater talent but with a greater soul than ordinary mortals, the artist suffers and creates for humanity. Music is no longer merely a product of bodily parts like the ear or the fingers. It emerges from the highest reaches of the artist's spirit.

> ❝ There is much to be done on earth, do it soon!
> I cannot carry on the everyday life I am living; art demands this sacrifice too. Rest, diversion, amusement— only so that I can function more powerfully in my art.❞
>
> *From Beethoven's journal, 1814*

1 Between Classicism and Romanticism

Beethoven is special in another sense, in the unique position he occupies between the eighteenth-century Viennese Classical style and nineteenth-century Romanticism. Beethoven's roots were firmly Classical. He was a student of Haydn when the latter was at the height of his fame. Beethoven remained committed to the principles of the Classical style until the end of his life.

Beethoven was committed to the *principles* of Classicism—but not to every one of its manifestations, and certainly not to the mood behind it. There is almost always a sense of excitement, urgency, and striving in Beethoven's music that makes it instantly distinguishable from Haydn's or Mozart's. It can be very violent; it can be solemn, severe, or exceptionally gentle. These qualities emerged in response to Romantic stirrings that are the subject of our next chapter.

The French Revolution

Romanticism, as we shall see, was originally a literary movement. Though well under way by the beginning of the nineteenth century, it was not yet influential in Vienna; and, in any case, Beethoven did not have a very literary sensibility. At the root of Romanticism, however, lay one great political upheaval that made an enormous impact on the composer's generation. This was the French Revolution. Beethoven was one of many artists who felt compelled to proclaim their sympathy with the ideal of freedom symbolized by that cataclysmic event.

When the Parisian crowd stormed the Bastille in 1789, Beethoven was a highly impressionable eighteen-year-old, already grounded in liberal and humanistic ideals. In 1803 his admiration for Napoleon Bonaparte as hero of the revolution led him to an extravagant and unprecedented gesture—writing a descriptive symphony called *Bonaparte*. Retitled the *Eroica* (Heroic) Symphony, it was the decisive breakthrough work of Beethoven's maturity, the first work to show his full individual freedom as an artist.

Before Beethoven could send the symphony to Paris, Napoleon crowned himself Emperor of France. Liberal Europe saw this as a betrayal of the revolution, and Beethoven scratched out the title in a fury. But idealism dies hard. To Beethoven, and to many of his contemporaries, the French Revolution still stood for an ideal of perfectibility—not so much of human society (as Beethoven himself acknowledged by deleting Napoleon's name) as of human aspiration. That ideal, too, is what Beethoven realized by his own triumph over his deafness. The point was not lost on those of his contemporaries who were swept away by his music.

And that is what listeners have responded to ever since. Listening to the *Eroica* Symphony, we sense that it has less to do with Napoleon than with the composer's own self-image. The quality of heroic striving and inner triumph is what emerges so magnificently in Beethoven's most famous compositions.

Storming the Bastille, a contemporary engraving of the most famous event of the French Revolution.

The revolution betrayed: Napoleon's coronation as Emperor of France in 1804, as portrayed by Jacques-Louis David (1748–1825), the greatest painter of Neoclassical art (see page 174). Today this huge (20 by 30 feet) and pompous painting repels some viewers almost as much as the actual event it depicts enraged Beethoven.

2 Beethoven and the Symphony

As we have said, what sets Beethoven instantly apart from Haydn or Mozart is his mood of excitement and urgency. This he achieved by maximizing virtually all musical elements. Higher and lower registers, sharper syncopations, stronger accents, harsher dissonances yielding to more profound resolutions—all of these are found in Beethoven's music. He made new demands on instruments, expanded the orchestra, and stretched Classical forms to their limits.

Given all this, it is not surprising that this composer should be especially associated with the symphony, the most public of Classical genres, with the greatest range of expression, variety, and sheer volume. In fact, Beethoven wrote fewer symphonies (nine) than piano sonatas (thirty-two) or string quartets (sixteen)—and no musician would rank these works any lower than the symphonies. But at the height of his career, from around 1800 to 1810, even many of his piano sonatas and string quartets sound like symphonies. The torrents of sound Beethoven summoned up in these works demanded whole new techniques of piano and string playing.

We can approach Beethoven's "symphonic ideal" through his Fifth Symphony, written in 1808. Three main features of this work have impressed generations of listeners: its rhythmic drive, its motivic consistency or unity, and the sense it gives of a definite psychological progression. The first feature can be apprehended at once, the second by the end of the opening movement, and the third only after we have experienced all four of the symphony's movements.

 His clothes were very ordinary and not in the least in the customary style of those days, especially in our circles. . . . [Beethoven] was very proud; I have seen Countess Thun on her knees before him begging him to play something— and he would not. But then, Countess Thun was a very eccentric woman."

An old lady remembers the young Beethoven (1867)

LISTENING CHART 15

Beethoven, Symphony No. 5 in C Minor (complete work)

31 min., 31 sec.

3 2
5–19 1–15

		FIRST MOVEMENT (Allegro con brio, 2/4; sonata form)	C minor, ff
		See Listening Chart 14.	

14 10		**SECOND MOVEMENT** (Andante, 3/8; variations)	A♭ major, p
	0:00	**Theme 1** Ends with repeated cadences	
	1:03	**Theme 2** Played by clarinets and bassoons	
	1:26	Trumpets enter (goes to C MAJOR, ff)	
	2:12	**Theme 1** Variation 1, played by strings	
	3:06	**Theme 2** Clarinets and bassoons	
	3:29	Trumpets enter (goes to C MAJOR, ff)	
	4:16	**Theme 1** Variations 2–4 (without repeated cadences), ending f; then a long, quiet transition: woodwinds	
	6:13	**Theme 2** Trumpets	C MAJOR, ff
15 11	6:59	**Theme 1** Variations 5 (minor; woodwinds) and 6 (full orchestra); cadences	
1:30	8:29	**Coda**	A♭ major

a CELLOS

		THIRD MOVEMENT (Allegro, 3/4; A B A′)	C minor, pp
16 12		**Scherzo (A)**	
	0:00	a b	
	0:41	a′b′	
	1:21	a″b″ Ends with a loud cadence built from b	

b FRENCH HORNS

17 13		**Trio (B)**	C MAJOR, ff
	1:52	‖: c :‖ Fugal	
0:33	2:25	d c′	
1:03	2:55	d c′ *Reorchestrated, p;* runs into scherzo (goes back to C minor, pp)	

c DOUBLE BASSES

fugue subject

		Scherzo (A′)	
1:38	3:30	Scherzo repeated, shorter and *reorchestrated, pp*	
2:54	4:46	**Transition** Timpani; leads directly into the fourth movement (goes to C MAJOR, ff)	

		FOURTH MOVEMENT (Allegro, 2/2; sonata form)	C MAJOR, ff
18 14		**Exposition**	with TROMBONES
	0:00	**Theme 1** March theme	
	0:34	**Bridge theme** Low horns and bassoons	
	1:00	**Theme 2**	
	1:27	**Cadence theme**	
		Development	
	1:57	Development begins; modulation	
	2:02	Theme 2 and its bass developed	bass:
19 15	3:31	**Retransition** Recall of the scherzo (A′, 3/4 meter) (recall of C minor, pp)	
		Recapitulation	C MAJOR ff
0:32	4:03	**Theme 1**	
1:07	4:38	**Bridge theme**	
1:36	5:07	**Theme 2**	
2:02	5:33	**Cadence theme**	
		Coda	
2:30	6:01	Coda; three sections, accelerating; uses parts of the bridge, cadence theme, and theme 1	C MAJOR, ff

The march proves to be the first theme of a sonata-form movement; the second theme includes a speeded-up version of the ♪ ♪ ♪ rhythm, with a slower, upward-stepping bass that will drive the development section. The bridge and the cadence theme are wonderfully gutsy. Then, at the end of the development, Beethoven offers another example of his inspired manipulation of musical form. The second theme (**b**) of the previous movement, the scherzo, comes back quietly once again, a complete surprise in these surroundings (there is even a change from the **4/4** meter of the march back to **3/4**). This theme now sounds neither forceful nor mysterious, as it did in the scherzo, but rather like a dim memory. Perhaps it has come back to remind us that the battle has been won.

All that remains is a great C-major celebration, in the recapitulation and then later in a huge accelerating coda. "There Fate knocks at the door" — but fate and terror alike yield to Beethoven's optimistic major-mode vision.

bedfordstmartins.com/listen
▶ Interactive Listening Charts 14 and 15

3 Beethoven's "Third Period"

Beethoven's output is traditionally divided into three style periods. The first period (until 1800, in round numbers) covers music building on the style of Haydn and Mozart. The middle period contains characteristically "heroic" works like the *Eroica* and Fifth Symphonies.

In the third period (from around 1818 to 1827) Beethoven's music loses much of its earlier tone of heroism. It becomes more abstract, introspective, and serene — yes, serene — and tends to come framed in more intimate genres than the symphony, such as the piano sonata and the string quartet. (However, Beethoven's mightiest symphony, the Ninth, also dates from this period.) His control of contrast and musical flow becomes more potent than ever, and a new freedom of form leads to a range of expression that can only be called miraculous. All the strength of his earlier music seems to be encompassed together with a new gentleness and spirituality.

While disruption was always a feature of Beethoven's music — think of the fermatas in the first movement of the Fifth Symphony, and the C-major trumpets in the second — now the breaks and breaches in the musical fabric can be almost frightening. At any rate, they proved incomprehensible in his own time and for many years thereafter. Today these features seem if anything to increase the power of Beethoven's late music.

LUDWIG VAN BEETHOVEN
String Quartet in F, Op. 135, second movement (Vivace) (1826)

3
20

Three blind mice, see how they run . . . the tiny and very quiet **a** phrase in this extraordinary movement skitters through the pitches A (three), G (blind), and F (mice) nearly thirty times before the piece is over.

Phrase **b**, consisting of just two pitches, is even simpler. Pitchwise, it contrasts with **a**, but resembles it in its constant use of syncopation (see the music example below). It is this rhythmic feature, syncopation, that makes the motion seem like a strange skittering, rather than just running fast.

Though Beethoven did not label this movement a scherzo (his heading was simply Vivace, meaning vivacious), that is what it is: a fast triple-meter movement, full of surprises and shocks, in **A B A** form. *Scherzo,* as we have seen, means "joke," and this scherzo is all smiles at first. Later, however, it taps into a level of ferocity that even this composer had scarcely touched before.

For he appears to have determined to carry the traditional contrast between minuet and trio to the breaking point. Whereas the scherzo **A** uses only a few adjacent pitches, as we have seen, at least up to the cadential **c** segment, the trio **B** takes off like a rocket. Scales shoot up through the octaves, starting—significantly!—first from F, then from G, then from A. In **B** the conventional form we might expect is thrown overboard—nothing like ‖: **c** :‖: **d c** :‖ happens here. After each of the upward scales has started with a *forte* jolt (Beethoven writes *fp,* meaning *f* followed directly by *p*), the dynamic swells up to an almost insane *ff* explosion, as the instruments get stuck sawing away at repeated figures. The beat is relentless, counteracting all the syncopation that came before.

This episode of turmoil, or terror, depending on how you react, could hardly make a greater contrast to **A**. As though to make the point, **A** now comes back without change—"vivacious," very quiet, smiling through its syncopations as though nothing has happened. But a brief coda ends with one final *f* jolt.

We have not said anything yet about the string quartet as a medium, and its special sounds and textures. The subtlety and variety of these are evident in Beethoven's Vivace movement. For example, take first of all the delicate counterpoint of the various instruments in **a**, which allows the original up-and-down bass line in the cello *below* "Three blind mice" to rise and shine later *above* it in the two violins (at the end of **a′**):

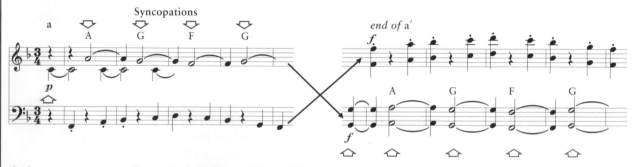

Only now are we really sure of the beat. In **c** and in the first of **B**'s scale passages, notice the interplay between high and low, the two violins answered back and forth by the cello and viola. The retching sound of the *ff* explosion passage in **B**—Beethoven's prediction of heavy metal—fades into ghostly syncopated octaves, with all four instruments playing the same pitches (which are A, G, and F, once again) in the unusual dynamic *ppp.*

))) LISTEN

BEETHOVEN
String Quartet in F,
Op. 135: Vivace

A (SCHERZO)
0:00 **a**(A G F G A)
0:08 ‖: **b a′ c** :‖

B (TRIO)
0:56 *fp* scales up from F
1:10 from G, then A
1:31 *ff* explosion
1:54 *ppp* A G F G A

A (SCHERZO)
1:58 *pp* **a** ‖: **b a′ c** :‖ coda

bedfordstmartins.com/listen
▶ Quizzes and Flashcards

CHAPTER 15

Prelude
Music after Beethoven: Romanticism

Baroque, as a designation for a historical style period in music, was adopted by musicologists from the field of art history many years after the period in question. The term *Romantic* was adopted from literature—and it was adopted by the literary Romantics themselves. When the first Romantic composers began their careers in the 1820s, their literary contemporaries were already excitedly talking about "Romantic" music.

This may seem like just one more footnote to history, but it tells us two important things about music after the time of Beethoven. One is that largely thanks to Beethoven, people had become highly aware of music as a major art. Music was treated with a new respect in cultivated circles; it was taken seriously in a way it never had been before.

The other is that it seemed quite natural for observers of the time to link up developments in music with parallel developments in literature. From Homer and Virgil to Shakespeare and Milton, literature had always been considered the most important and most convincing of the arts. The prestige and power of literature were now freely extended to music.

This fact is illustrated in a painting much admired at midcentury, showing a group of literary lions and lionesses at an imaginary soirée, listening to Franz Liszt at the piano (see page 240). Their expressions tell us how profoundly the music moves them; their aesthetic experience is very different, clearly, from the casual enjoyment of eighteenth-century listeners pictured on page 150. The painting tells us also how important Beethoven was taken to be in bringing about this change. Liszt gazes soulfully at Beethoven's larger-than-life bust. Does it rest on the books stacked on the piano, or loom outside the window, gigantic, against the turbulent sky?

1 Romanticism

Romantic literature and literary theory flourished particularly in and around the first two decades of the nineteenth century. In England, this was a great age of poetry: Wordsworth, Coleridge, Shelley, Keats, and Byron. There was also a brilliant outpouring of German Romantic literature during the same period,

The power of Romantic music: Liszt as the inspiration for novelists Alexandre Dumas, Victor Hugo, George Sand, Daniel Stern (on the floor), legendary violinist Niccolò Paganini, and opera composer Gioacchino Rossini. Daniel Stern was the pseudonym of the Countess d'Agoult (see page 268).

though the names of its writers are less familiar in the English-speaking world: Tieck, Novalis, Kleist, Hölderlin, and E. T. A. Hoffmann.

For us, the word *romantic* refers to love; this usage dates from the nineteenth century and derives from the literary movement. But the glorification of love was only one of the many themes of Romantic literature, themes that were also central to the music of the nineteenth century.

The Cult of Individual Feeling

Striving for a better, higher, ideal state of being was at the heart of the Romantic movement. Everyday life, to the Romantics, seemed dull and meaningless; it could be transcended only through the free exercise of individual will and passion. The rule of feeling, unconstrained by convention, religion, or social taboo (or anyone else's feelings, often enough)—this became the highest good. Emotional expression became the highest artistic goal. "Bohemians," as they were disparagingly called at the time, proclaimed romantic love, led irregular lives, and wore odd clothes. We have the Romantics to thank for one familiar image of the artist that is still around today.

These attitudes may be laid at the door of Jean-Jacques Rousseau—the same Enlightenment philosopher who had spoken up in the mid-eighteenth century for "natural" human feelings, as opposed to the artificial constraints imposed by society (see page 172). Hailed as the philosophical father of the French Revolution, Rousseau provided the Romantics with the ideal of individual, as well as political, freedom and fulfillment. We have also seen Rousseau as a proponent of a "natural" music, and indeed his own music was still being played at French revolutionary rallies and pageants.

But there was more than philosophy behind the new attitudes. The Industrial Revolution had already begun its inexorable course, and increasingly as the nineteenth century went on, people felt their helplessness in the face of the factories, slag heaps, and inhumane working conditions of developing capitalism. The smokestacks of what William Blake called "these dark, Satanic mills" now loomed over the European landscape. Understandably there was an element of escapism in Romantic striving.

Romanticism and Revolt

In the wake of the Industrial Revolution came actual revolution—the central fact in the politics of the age. It began with our own American Revolution. The French Revolution of 1789 rocked Europe as deeply in the nineteenth century as did the Russian Revolution of 1917 in the twentieth. It was followed by a whole set of aftershocks up to 1848, a year of major upheavals in France, Germany, Austria, and Italy.

The Romantics were inevitably cast in the role of rebels against the established order. Many musicians (like many poets and painters) associated themselves with libertarian politics, starting with Beethoven, who wrote a symphony named *Bonaparte* (which he renamed the *Eroica:* See page 228). In a later generation, Liszt briefly espoused a strange half-communistic, half-religious movement founded by a French priest, Father Felicité Lamennais. Giuseppe Verdi's name became an acronym for the Italian liberation movement. Richard Wagner was thrown out of Germany in 1849 for inflammatory speeches he made from the revolutionary barricades in the town of Dresden.

Along with political revolution went social revolution. The barriers of hereditary nobility were breached, and the lower and middle classes assumed more social mobility. Thus Liszt, who was the son of an estate foreman, could conduct glamorous liaisons—one stormy, the other stable—with a French countess and a Russian princess. The importance of this was not lost on Liszt's contemporaries; the countess is another of the celebrities included in the picture of Liszt at the piano (though the artist tactfully hid her face).

Music and the Supernatural

The supernatural—often linked to the macabre—loomed large in the Romantic firmament, as we might expect of a movement so intent on transcending the ordinary. In *Nightmare,* a weird picture by the early Romantic painter Henry Fuseli, dream is made concrete, visible, and public in the figure of a horrible incubus (see page 242). The magician Faust pledging his soul to the Devil for a single moment of transcendent happiness became the subject of the greatest poem of

La Marseillaise, the great rallying song of the French Revolution.

Nightmare, by Henry Fuseli (1741–1825), an eighteenth-century pre-Romantic painter, poet, and revolutionary who emigrated from Switzerland to England for political reasons.

the time, Goethe's *Faust.* Franz Schubert wrote "The Erlking," about a demon who claims a terrified child, in 1816 (see page 255); Mary Shelley wrote *Frankenstein* in 1818. The titles of some of the most famous operas of the time—*Robert the Devil, The Vampire, The Magic Bullet*—speak for themselves.

Composers cultivated strange harmonies and sinister orchestral sounds as their contribution to this aspect of Romanticism; the sounds they dreamed up can still be heard on video and movie soundtracks today. A famous scene of devilish conjuration in a deep forest, the Wolf's Glen scene in Carl Maria von Weber's opera *Der Freischütz* (*The Magic Bullet,* 1821), was an early monument to Romanticism in music. Spooky music was devised by Verdi for the witches in his Shakespeare opera *Macbeth,* and by Wagner for the ghost ship and its crew in *The Flying Dutchman.* And in his *Fantastic* Symphony, Hector Berlioz wrote a movement called "Dream of a Witches' Sabbath" that bears comparison with Fuseli's *Nightmare* (see page 273).

Artistic Barriers

The Romantics' search for higher experience and more intense expression provoked a reaction against the restraints of artistic form and genre. Artists resisted all rules and regulations. They distrusted abstract notions of "beauty" or "decorum" that they felt might hamper their spontaneity.

Eighteenth-century drama, for example, was hemmed in by such rules until the Romantics overturned them. Against the rules they cited the works of Shakespeare, where locations change scene by scene, tragedy clashes with farce, rich poetry mixes with bawdy prose, and noble characters share the stage with clowns. The lifelike turbulence and loose form of these plays made Shakespeare enormously popular in the nineteenth century. Dozens of composers wrote music associated with them, including Mendelssohn, Berlioz, Tchaikovsky, Wagner, and Verdi.

In music itself, composers worked to break down barriers of harmony and form. All the Romantic composers experimented with chords, or chord progressions, that had previously been forbidden. From the time of Schubert on, their music was enriched by imaginative new harmonies. And sonata form, the hallmark of Classicism, was treated so freely in Robert Schumann's piano sonatas, written in the 1830s, that he finally labeled the last (and greatest) of them "Fantasy"—a proclamation of his spontaneity on the one hand, and insurance against accusations of breaking the rules on the other.

Music and the Other Arts

Shakespearean, individualist in outlook, emotive, contemptuous of handed-down conventions—these are the general traits of Romantic art. In this climate new efforts were made to blend the arts together: poetry became more "musical," paintings and musical works were given "poetic" titles, and poetry, drama, music, and stagecraft merged in Wagner's unique and enormously influential "total artwork," or *Gesamtkunstwerk,* as we shall see. Within individual arts, blurred effects were cultivated—half-obscure verbal meanings, ambiguous shapes and color blends, and musical sounds that are imprecise but rich and evocative.

No one went further in this respect than the English landscape painter J. M. W. Turner. In one of his most famous pictures, *The "Fighting Téméraire,"* the grandeur of nature and the horrors of industrialization merge in dizzy, almost abstract swirls of color. Whereas Rousseau had admired nature for its

The "Fighting Téméraire" Tugged to Her Last Berth to Be Broken Up, 1838 by J. M. W. Turner (1775–1851).

Two Romantic depictions of nature: *Mountainous Landscape* by Caspar David Friedrich (left) and *The Bard* by John Martin (right). In each, man is dwarfed by nature—nature depicted as both menacing and thrilling.

simplicity, Turner captured what was called at the time its "sublime" quality: the majesty and mystery of nature, its boundlessness, even its menace. The great Romantic artists stared unblinkingly at the infinite, and tried to set it down in their art.

And it was exactly the boundless quality of music that gave it its special prestige and status. Music, people felt, could express inner experience more deeply than the other arts because the musician's imagination is not tied down to the meaning of words (like the poet's) or to the representation of things (like the painter's). This led philosophers of the time to incorporate music at the heart of their views. Here, too, Rousseau had pointed the way; he was followed by Arthur Schopenhauer (who influenced Wagner) and Friedrich Nietzsche (whom Wagner influenced) in Germany.

"All art aspires to the condition of music," wrote a famous Victorian critic, Walter Pater. All Romantic art tried to capture music's depth and freedom of emotional expression and its continuous, "infinite" quality.

2   Concert Life in the Nineteenth Century

So much for ideals. What about the marketplace?

Public concerts, first introduced in the Baroque era, during the age of aristocratic patronage of the arts, grew more important in the days of Haydn, Mozart, and Beethoven. As the nineteenth century progressed, the concert hall together with the opera house came to dominate the presentation of music. Every town of any size had its symphony association, organized by merchants, government officials, lawyers, and other members of the middle class. Concert halls built to accommodate symphony concerts were expressions of civic pride, as they still are today. In 1891 the New York Symphony, that city's second orchestra (the New York Philharmonic was founded in 1842), proudly presented a five-concert music festival led by Tchaikovsky in brand-new Carnegie Hall.

By the end of the century even intimate, domestic musical genres, designed for the drawing room or the studio, were presented on the concert stage. Concerts of *Lieder* (German songs) and string quartet concerts became established, though they were never as important as orchestral concerts. Concerts made more music available to more and more people.

Improved transportation, meanwhile, brought musicians on tour to remote areas, such as the American West. Italian Romantic opera in particular spread far and wide — to New York and Philadelphia, to San Francisco (where immigrant dockworkers were drafted to sing the choruses), to Buenos Aires, and even up the Amazon River.

However, the institutionalization of concert life also had its negative aspect, in that audiences gradually became more conservative in their musical tastes. The old aristocratic system had actually been more neutral in this respect. While many aristocratic patrons cared less about music than display,

Groundbreaking ceremony for Carnegie Hall in New York. The bearded man visible behind one of the vertical ropes is the famous railroad and steel baron Andrew Carnegie, the donor.

and some exercised the most whimsical of tastes, others actually encouraged composers to pursue new paths, or at least left them alone to do so. On the other hand, the concert public tended to conservatism. The mainly middle-class buyers of concert tickets naturally wanted value, as with anything else they bought. What counted as value was something already established as a masterpiece, something that they already knew and liked.

The Artist and the Public

For the reasons above, composers with an interest in innovation — and that includes every composer discussed in this unit — felt at one time or another that their work was being neglected by the concert world. A paradoxical situation developed. The composer's dependence on the public was tinged with resentment, and the public's admiration for composers was tinged with distrust, even hostility.

Thus the composer Robert Schumann started an important magazine to campaign for Romantic music in the face of public indifference to serious art and preference for what he regarded as flashy trivia. Editor Schumann invented a "League of David" to slay the "Goliath" of the concert audience. (Goliath was the champion of the Philistines; it was around this time that the adjective "philistine" came to mean "uncultured.") Later, the music of Liszt and Wagner was attacked by hostile critics as formless, dissonant, and overheated. Later still, the symphonies of Gustav Mahler were repeatedly rejected in Vienna, in spite of Mahler's important position as head of the Opera there.

The gap between innovative music and a conservative concert public, which opened up in the nineteenth century, widened in the twentieth, as we shall see. Here as elsewhere, the nineteenth century set the tone for modern musical life.

3 Style Features of Romantic Music

Since the main artistic value in the Romantic era was the integrity of personal feeling, every genuine artist was expected to have a personal style. Many artists cultivated styles that were highly personal and even eccentric. Furthermore, Romanticism's constant striving after ever-new states of consciousness put a premium on innovation; this could be seen as an exciting breaking down of artistic barriers on the one hand, and as a heroic personal breakthrough on the other. Consequently it is harder to define the Romantic style in general than to spot innovations, novelties, and individual peculiarities.

To be sure, nineteenth-century composers were united by some common interests, which will be discussed below: technical interests concerning melody, harmony, tone color, and, perhaps especially, musical form. But it is important to remember that one such common interest was to sound different from everybody else.

Rhythm: Rubato

The general Romantic tendency to blur all sharp edges found its musical counterpart in the rhythmic practice of *tempo rubato*, or just **rubato**. Rubato means that in musical performance the rhythm is handled flexibly; the meter itself may waver, or else the beat is maintained strictly in the accompaniment while the melody is played or sung slightly out of phase with it. (Literally *tempo rubato* means "robbed time" — that is, some time has been stolen from the beat — but the beat is likely to be slowed and the time given back a moment later.)

Rubato was practiced in the service of greater individual expressivity. Though seldom indicated in a score—indeed, no one has ever found an accurate way to indicate rubato in musical notation—its practice is documented by old recordings, made around 1900 by musicians who were close to the Romantic composers (or even by the composers themselves). Improvisation, in the sense of adding ornaments or other notes to a score, was all but abolished by the end of the nineteenth century. Let no mere performer tamper with notes which had been set down by a composer of transcendent genius! But performers of the time improvised *rhythmically,* in that they applied rubato freely to nearly every score they played.

Considered a sign of bad taste in Baroque or Classical music, at least when applied extensively, rubato is an essential expressive resource in the playing, singing, and conducting of Romantic music. A musician's sensitivity and "feeling" depends to a great extent on his or her artistic use of rubato.

Romantic Melody

The most instantly recognizable feature of Romantic music is its melodic style. Melody in the Romantic era is more emotional, effusive, and demonstrative than before. Often the melodic lines range more widely than the orderly, restrained tunes of the Classical era; often, too, they build up to more sustained climaxes. Melodies became more irregular in rhythm and phraseology, so as to make them sound more spontaneous.

A fine example is the so-called Love theme of Tchaikovsky's Overture-Fantasy *Romeo and Juliet* (page 295). It begins with a great outburst—a climax, at the very start—and then sinks down an octave and more, in melodic curves whose yearning quality grows more and more sensuous. Especially striking is the second part of the melody, where a rhythmic figure surges up, seven times in all, in preparation for a free return of the opening climax, now *ff*:

When one thinks of Romantic melody, what comes first to mind is the grand, exaggerated emotionality of Tchaikovsky or Mahler. Some Romantic melodies are more intimate, however—and they are no less emotional for sparing the handkerchief, as it were. Each in an individual way, Romantic composers learned to make their melodies dreamy, sensitive, passionate, ecstatic, or whatever shade of feeling they wished to express.

Romantic Harmony

Harmony was one of the areas in which Romantic music made the greatest technical advances. On the one hand, composers learned to use harmony to underpin melody in such a way as to bring out its emotionality. Romantic melody is, in fact, inseparable from harmony. In the *Romeo and Juliet* Love theme, for example, a rich new chord goes hand in glove with the warm upward scoop of the melodic line in measure 5.

On the other hand, harmony was savored for its own sake, and composers experimented freely with new chord forms and new juxtapositions of chords. These, it was found, could contribute potently to those mysterious, sinister, rapturous, ethereal, or sultry moods that Romantic composers sought to evoke.

Chromaticism is a term for a style that liberally employs all twelve notes of the chromatic scale (see page 18). Baroque and Classical style is not "chromatic" in this sense, but all Romantic composers pursued chromaticism to some extent, in order to expand the expressive range of both their melodies and their harmony. If you look closely at the *Romeo and Juliet* theme, you will find nearly all twelve notes of the chromatic scale included—something that seldom if ever happens in earlier music. Chromaticism was carried furthest in the nineteenth century by Richard Wagner, and further yet by the early twentieth-century modernists.

The Expansion of Tone Color

While tone color had been treated with considerable subtlety by the Viennese Classical composers, the Romantics seized on this aspect of music with particular enthusiasm. For the first time in Western music, the sheer sensuous quality of sound assumed major artistic importance on a level with rhythm, melody, and musical form.

So it is no accident that all instruments went through major technical developments during the nineteenth century—the piano not least. As orchestral instruments reached their present-day forms, the orchestra was expanded, soon reaching its present standard makeup. The chart below for a typical Romantic orchestra, when compared with the Classical orchestra chart on page 177, shows how the ranks of the brass, woodwind, and percussion sections were filled out:

The increased chromaticism of nineteenth-century music spawned this bizarre experimental harp, which is really two harps, crisscrossed, to accommodate all the notes of the chromatic scale.

A TYPICAL ROMANTIC ORCHESTRA

STRINGS	WOODWINDS	BRASS	PERCUSSION
First violins (12–16 players) Second violins (12–16) Violas (8–12) Cellos (8–12) Bass viols (6–10) *Note: Each string section is sometimes divided into two or more subsections, to obtain richer effects.* 2 Harps	2 Flutes 1 Piccolo 2 Oboes 1 English horn 2 Clarinets 1 High E♭ clarinet 1 Bass clarinet 2 Bassoons 1 Contrabassoon	4 French horns 2 Trumpets 3 Trombones 1 Bass tuba	3 Timpani Bass drum Snare drum Cymbals Triangle Tubular bells Piano

What such charts cannot show, however, are the ingenious new *combinations* of instruments that were now investigated. Composers learned to mix instrumental colors with something of the same freedom and virtuosity with which painters mix actual colors on a palette. The clear, sharply defined sonorities of the Classical era were replaced by multicolored shades of blended orchestral sound.

Romantic composers and audiences alike were fascinated by the symphony orchestra, and for the first time conductors came to the fore—conductors wielding batons. In earlier times, orchestras had simply followed the first violinist or the continuo player, but now they needed experts to control and balance out those special blended effects. The orchestra also became increasingly important in nineteenth-century opera. Major opera composers, such as

Weber, Meyerbeer, and Wagner, specialized in orchestral effects that sometimes even threatened to put the voices in the shade. If today, when one thinks of classical music, the symphony orchestra comes to mind almost automatically, that is a holdover from the Romantic nineteenth century.

4 Program Music

Program music is a term for nonvocal music written in association with a poem, a story, or some other literary source—or even just a highly suggestive word or two. While program music was certainly not new in the Romantic era, it gained new importance and prestige, for program music answered the general Romantic demand for transcending inter-art boundaries. Instrumental music could be made even more expressive, many felt, by linking it to poetry and ideas.

The term *program music* is sometimes restricted to music that tells or at least traces a story, the story being the "program." In 1829, at the premiere of his *Fantastic* Symphony, the composer Hector Berlioz actually handed out a pamphlet containing his own made-up program, and the music of the symphony behaves like a narrator a good deal of the time. From the weird shrieks and groans at the start of the symphony's last movement, through the riotous welcome of the heroine, to the final frenzied round dance, we are treated to musical events that follow the events of the story step by step (see page 269).

Another type of program music adopts a different strategy. Instead of telling a story, it attempts to capture the general flavor of a mood associated with some extramusical condition, concept, or personality. In short piano pieces, Schumann drew portraits of his friends (and even of himself), under coded names. The single word "nocturne," as the title for a whole genre of such compositions by Frédéric Chopin, is enough to set up expectations of night-time romance—and the music does the rest (see page 266).

Program music sparked a great debate in the nineteenth century, a debate that still goes on. Does the music *really* illustrate or represent the program? Suppose the music is played without listeners being given the program—could they tell it from the music? Shouldn't the music make complete sense on its own terms, even if we grant that the program provides an added dimension to it?

But the point is that the Romantics did not *want* to be without the program. They did not necessarily *want* the music to "make sense on its own terms." And it seems they were prepared to live with this apparent inconsistency: On the one hand they revered purely instrumental music as the highest form of art; on the other hand, they embraced music that is less "pure" because of its admixture with nonmusical elements, that is, program music.

5 Form in Romantic Music

Individual spontaneity was an important goal of the Romantic movement. And if there was any area in which the composer wanted to seem particularly free and spontaneous, it was the area of musical form. The music should bubble out moment by moment, irrepressible and untrammeled, like churning emotion itself. But composers faced a problem: how to control that spontaneity? They had to provide their music with enough sense of coherence so that listeners could follow it.

More and more complex orchestras required conductors, and conductors required batons. Before sticks came into use, the German opera composer Carl Maria von Weber (see page 277) seems to have used a tight scroll of paper (a score?).

In their use of standard forms or form-types, nineteenth-century composers broke with classical norms. To return to a distinction made earlier, on page 49, the Romantics wanted each work of art to express its own individual "inner form"; they distrusted "outer forms" as dry and conventional. Even when they followed forms such as sonata form, rondo, and so on, they tended to follow them so loosely that it gets to be a matter of opinion whether they are doing so at all. Themes tend to blend into one another, and there is much less of the neat, clear cadencing of Classical music.

Some Romantic compositions deliberately break down the boundary between music and nonmusical silence. Robert Schumann's song "Im wunderschönen Monat Mai" (page 259) begins hesitantly, as though already in the middle of a transition; we feel we have just begun hearing music that started long ago. Instead of ending with a decisive cadence, the song comes to a questioning dissonance, then—silence. The vague, atmospheric quality at the start and the suggestion of infinity at the end are typically Romantic.

Yet the music had to avoid real formlessness if it was to hold the attention of an audience. Once again, for romantic composers the problem was how to create the impression of spontaneous form while at the same time giving the listener some means of following the music. They developed a number of interesting and characteristic solutions.

Miniature Compositions

While many Romantic compositions last for about as long as works from the eighteenth century, special classes of music arose with quite different dimensions.

First of all, composers cultivated what we will call **miniatures,** pieces lasting only a few minutes. Mostly songs and short piano pieces, these were designed to convey a particularly pointed emotion, momentary and undeveloped. In this way the composer could commune with the listener intensely but intimately, as though giving him or her a single short, meaningful glance. The meaning might well be hinted at by a programmatic title.

Though short pieces were also written in earlier times, of course—think of minuet movements in classical symphonies—usually they were components of larger units, where their effect was balanced by other, longer movements.

The man has put down his violin to sit with the woman at the piano; we can imagine the four-hand music they are playing, perhaps, but we cannot see their faces. This picture catches both the intimacy and privacy of the Romantic miniature and also its characteristic location, the middle-class living room.

The grandiose compositions of the nineteenth century occasioned many cartoons — amusing enough, but not in the last analysis friendly to the advanced music of the time. Here it is Berlioz who is lampooned.

Romantic miniatures, though they were often published in sets, as we will see, nevertheless were composed so as to stand out as individuals in their own right, apart from their sets. Miniatures for piano were sometimes given general titles, such as Schubert's Impromptus (Improvisations) and Brahms's Capriccios (Whims). Sometimes they masqueraded as dances, like Chopin's Mazurkas (a Polish dance). Often they were given more suggestive, programmatic titles: *Years of Pilgrimage* by Franz Liszt, *Spring Song* by Felix Mendelssohn, *To a Wild Rose* by Edward MacDowell, America's leading late Romantic composer. Schumann was something of a specialist in such titles: *The Poet Speaks, Confession, The Bird as Prophet,* and — *Why?*

As for the problem of musical form, in such pieces this was not so much solved as bypassed. They are over before the listener begins to wonder where the music is going, what the next effect will be.

Grandiose Compositions

Another Romantic tendency was diametrically opposed to the miniatures. Many composers wrote what may be called grandiose compositions — larger and larger symphonies, cantatas, and so on, with more and more movements, increased performing forces, and a longer (sometimes much longer) total time span. For example, Hector Berlioz's symphony *Romeo and Juliet* of 1839 lasts for nearly an hour and a half. (Haydn's Symphony No. 95 lasts twenty minutes.) Starting with an augmented symphony orchestra, Berlioz added soloists and a chorus in certain of the movements and a narrator between them, and then threw in an off-stage chorus for still other movements.

In the field of opera, Richard Wagner's *The Nibelung's Ring* is a work that goes on for four evenings with a huge orchestra including specially invented instruments, a cast of thirty, and fifteen separate stage sets (see page 287). The total effect of these grandiose compositions was laced with poetry, philosophical or religious ideas, and (in operas) dramatic action. Listeners were impressed, even stupefied, by a combination of opulent sounds, great thoughts, powerful emotions, and sheer length.

These works met what we have called the problem of musical form in their own way. The bigger the work, the bigger the problem, but to help solve it composers could draw on extramusical factors—on the text of a vocal work, or the program of an instrumental one. Music could add emotional conviction to ideas or stories; in return these extramusical factors could supply a rhyme and reason for the sequence of musical events, that is, for the musical form.

The Principle of Thematic Unity

An important general principle developed by Romantic composers was that of thematic unity. There was an increasing tendency to maintain some of the same thematic material throughout whole works, even (or especially) when these works were in many movements.

In nineteenth-century symphonies and other such works, several different levels of thematic unity can be distinguished:

❧   Most obviously, themes from one movement may come back literally and quite clearly in other movements. We have already heard this happen in Beethoven's Fifth Symphony, when the scherzo theme returns in the last movement.

❧   In other compositions, new *versions* of a single theme are used at important new points in the music, either later in the same movement or in later movements. While these new versions are really nothing more than variations of the original theme, this procedure differs fundamentally from Classical theme-and-variations form (see page 190). In Classical variation form, the theme is an entire tune, and the variations follow one another directly. In the new Romantic procedure, the theme is (generally) much more fragmentary than a tune, and the new versions of the theme appear at irregular intervals.

The term **thematic transformation** is used for this variationlike procedure in Romantic music, whereby short themes are freely varied at relatively wide and unpredictable intervals of time. A precedent for it can be traced to works such as Beethoven's Fifth Symphony, where the ♪♪♪ motive of the first movement is evoked freely in each of the later ones. In Wagner's *The Valkyrie*, a storm theme from the orchestral Prelude is transformed into a theme associated with the exhausted and gloomy Siegmund.

❧   In still other nineteenth-century pieces, we hear themes with even looser relationships among them. Clearly different, they nonetheless seem to exhibit mysterious inner similarities—similarities that seem to help unify the music, though they are too shadowy to count as transformations in the Romantic definition, let alone as variations in the Classical style. Wagner's operas are famous for such themes.

Of all the levels of thematic unity employed by nineteenth-century composers, this last is the most typical of all. Vague similarity rather than clear likeness, suggestion rather than outright statement, atmosphere rather than discourse, feeling rather than form: All these go to the heart of Romanticism. We cannot appreciate Romantic music fully if we approach it in too literal a frame of mind. In much of this music, the inner form — the special spontaneous form of the individual piece, as distinct from standard outer forms such as sonata form and rondo — is tied to the principle of thematic unity. Listening to Romantic music requires ears that are not only attentive but also imaginative, exploratory, and more than a little fanciful.

bedfordstmartins.com/listen
▶ Quizzes and Flashcards

CHAPTER 16

The Early Romantics

Perhaps the most brilliant generation of composers in the entire history of music was that of the early Romantics. Franz Schubert was born in Vienna in 1797; then the ten-year period between 1803 and 1813 saw the births of Robert Schumann, Frédéric Chopin, Felix Mendelssohn, Franz Liszt, Hector Berlioz, Richard Wagner, and Giuseppe Verdi. It was a brilliant generation, but not a long-lived one. Only the last four of these composers survived to continue their major work into the second half of the century.

Two general points are worth making about this early Romantic galaxy. First, Beethoven's music had a profound effect on them, though this was naturally felt more strongly by German composers than by non-Germans. Schubert, who lived in Vienna under Beethoven's shadow, was influenced by the older master much more directly than Chopin, a Pole who lived in Paris.

The second important point is that these composers were deeply influenced by literary Romanticism, which had flourished since before they were born. Schubert wrote many songs to texts by Romantic poets such as Goethe, Novalis, and Friedrich Schlegel, and Schumann's enthusiasm for the German Romantic novelist Jean Paul Richter was reflected in his music, as well as in his own prose writings. We have mentioned that Shakespeare was particularly admired by the Romantics; nearly all the composers mentioned here wrote music associated with Shakespeare's plays.

1 The Lied

The ordinary German word for song is *Lied* (plural, *Lieder*—pronounced "leader"). The word also has a special application: the <u>lied</u> is a particular type of German song that evolved in the late eighteenth century and flourished in the nineteenth. As such, the lied is one of the most important "miniature" genres of the Romantic era.

Though one cannot generalize about the melodies of these songs—some consist of little more than a tune, others are melodically much more complex— they share some other characteristic features.

❧ *Accompaniment.* A lied is nearly always accompanied by piano alone, and the accompaniment contributes significantly to the artistic effect. Indeed, the pianist becomes more of a discreet partner to the singer than a mere accompanist.

Beethoven: a late Romantic view. The awesome, ideal figure—nude, and carved in marble, like a Greek statue—sits, kinglike, on a superb throne. He seems to be both reigning over and deploring the music that was written after his own time.

❧ *Poetry.* The text of a lied is usually a Romantic poem of some merit (at least in the composer's estimation). Hence, although we need to understand the words of almost any vocal music, with the lied we should also try to appreciate how the poem's words and meanings fit together as poetry. The art of the lied depends on the sensitivity of the composer's response to the poetic imagery and feeling.

❧ *Mood.* A third characteristic, harder to explain, is the intimacy of expression that is captured by these pieces. The singer and the pianist seem to be sharing an emotional insight with just you, rather than with an entire audience; words and music are uttered softly, inwardly. Composers intended lieder for the intimacy of a living room, not a formal concert hall, and that is where they are best heard.

> ❝ Is not music the mysterious language of a distant realm of spirits, whose lovely sounds re-echo in our soul and awaken a higher, more intensive life? All the passions, arrayed in shining armor, vie with each other, and ultimately merge in an indescribable longing that fills our breast.❞
>
> *Arch-Romantic novelist, critic, and composer E. T. A. Hoffmann, 1816*

FRANZ SCHUBERT
"Erlkönig" ("The Erlking") (1815)

The earliest and (for most musicians) greatest master of the lied is Franz Schubert. He wrote close to seven hundred songs in his short lifetime. In his eighteenth year, 1815, he averaged better than a song every two days! Many of these are quite short tunes with simple piano accompaniments, but Schubert's tunes are like nobody else's; he was a wonderfully spontaneous melodist. Later in life his melodies became richer but no less beautiful, and taken together with their poems, the songs often show remarkable psychological penetration.

Title page of the first edition of "The Erlking." Note the stunted tree; the literal meaning of "Erlkönig" is King of the Alders, or birches — in effect, a forest troll.

One of those songs from 1815 was an instant hit: "The Erlking," published as the composer's opus 1, and still today Schubert's best-known lied. In those early years, Schubert wrote a considerable number of long, narrative songs, though this one stands out from the others in its dramatic intensity.

The poem is by Johann Wolfgang von Goethe, the greatest literary figure of the day—by turns a Romantic and a Classic poet, novelist, playwright, naturalist, philosopher, and a favorite source of texts for many generations of lied composers. Cast in the old storytelling ballad form, which enjoyed a vogue in the Romantic era, and dealing with death and the supernatural, the poem is famous in its own right.

Though Goethe's poem consists of eight parallel stanzas, they are not set to the same music. Schubert provided the later stanzas with different or modified music; such a song is said to be **through-composed**. (A song that uses the same

Schubert playing at an evening with the Schubertians. To the left is Johann Vogel, an older singer, one of his main supporters. Their friend Moritz von Schwind started this picture but didn't quite finish it.

Franz Schubert (1797–1828)

Schubert was the son of a lower-middle-class Viennese schoolmaster. There was always music in the home, and the boy received a solid musical education in the training school for Viennese court singers. His talent amazed his teachers and also a number of his schoolmates, who remained devoted to him throughout his career. Schubert began by following in his father's footsteps as a schoolteacher, without much enthusiasm, but soon gave up teaching to devote all his time to music.

Schubert was an endearing but shy and unspectacular individual who led an unspectacular life. However, it was the sort of life that would have been impossible before the Romantic era. Schubert never married—it is believed he was gay—and never held a regular job. He was sustained by odd fees for teaching and publications and by contributions from a circle of friends who called themselves the Schubertians—young musicians, artists, writers, and music lovers. One of the Schubertians, Moritz von Schwind, who became an important painter, has left us many charming pictures of the group at parties, on trips to the country, and so on (see page 256).

It was an atmosphere especially conducive to an intimate musical genre such as the lied. Schubert wrote nearly seven hundred lieder and many choral songs. For a time he roomed with a poet, Johann Mayrhofer, who provided him with gloomy texts for about fifty of them.

But it's unfortunate that Schubert's wonderful songs have tended to overshadow his symphonies, sonatas, and chamber music. Starting out with Classical genres, Schubert in his very short lifetime transformed them under the influence of Romanticism. He never introduced himself to Beethoven, even though they lived in the same city; perhaps he instinctively felt he needed to keep his distance from the overpowering older master. It speaks much for Schubert that he was able to write such original and powerful works as the "Unfinished" Symphony, the so-called *Great* Symphony in C, and others, right under Beethoven's shadow.

A few of Schubert's instrumental works include melodies taken from his own songs: the popular *Trout* Quintet, the String Quartet in D Minor (*Death and the Maiden*), and the *Wanderer* Fantasy for piano.

Schubert died in a typhoid fever epidemic when he was only thirty-one. He never heard a performance of his late symphonies, and much of his music came to light only after his death.

Our portrait shows Schubert around the time he wrote *The Erlking*.

Chief Works: Lieder, including the song cycles *Die schöne Müllerin, Winterreise,* and *Schwanengesang,* "The Erlking," "Gretchen at the Spinning Wheel," "Hedgerose," "Death and the Maiden," "The Trout," and hundreds of others ▪ "Character" pieces for piano; waltzes ▪ Symphonies, including the "Unfinished"—Schubert completed only two movements and sketches for a scherzo—and the *Great* Symphony in C ▪ Piano sonatas; *Wanderer* Fantasy for piano ▪ Four mature string quartets; a string quintet; the genial *Trout* Quintet for piano and strings (including double bass)

Encore: After "The Erlking," listen to the "Unfinished" Symphony and songs from *Winterreise.*

music for all its stanzas is called **strophic:** See page 66.) In mood, the poem changes so much as it goes along that it certainly invites this kind of musical setting. A father rides furiously through the night with a child who is presumably running a high fever, for he claims to see and hear a murderous demon. The Erlking first beckons the child, then cajoles him, then threatens and assaults him. The father—uncomprehending, even impatient—tries to quiet the boy, but by the time they reach home the boy is—dead!

The opening piano introduction sets the mood of dark, tense excitement. The right hand hammers away at harsh repeated notes in triplets, representing the horse's hooves, while the left hand has an agitated motive:

Schubert invented different music for the poem's three characters (and also the narrator). Each "voice" characterizes the speaker in contrast to the others.

0:22	Wer reitet so spät, durch Nacht und Wind?	Who rides so late through the night and wind?
	Es ist der Vater mit seinem Kind;	It is the father with his child.
	Er hat den Knaben wohl in dem Arm,	He holds the youngster tight in his arm,
	Er fasst ihn sicher, er hält ihn warm.	Grasps him securely, keeps him warm.
0:55	"Mein Sohn, was birgst du so bang dein Gesicht?"	"My son, what makes you afraid to look?"
	"Siehst, Vater, du den Erlkönig nicht?	"Don't you see, Father, the Erlking there?
	Den Erlenkönig mit Kron' und Schweif?"	The King of the forest with his crown and train?"
	"Mein Sohn, est ist ein Nebelstreif."	"Son, it's only a streak of mist."
1:28	"Du liebes Kind, komm, geh mit mir!	"*Darling child, come away with me!*
	Gar schöne Spiele spiel' ich mit dir;	*I will play some lovely games with you;*
	Manch' bunte Blumen sind an dem Strand;	*Many bright flowers grow by the shore;*
	Meine Mutter hat manch' gülden Gewand."	*My mother has many golden robes."*
1:52	"Mein Vater, mein Vater, und hörest du nicht	"Father, Father, do you not hear
	Was Erlenkönig mir leise verspricht?"	What the Erlking is softly promising me?"
	"Sei ruhig, bleibe ruhig, mein Kind:	"Calm yourself, be calm, my son:
	In dürren Blättern säuselt der Wind."	The dry leaves are rustling in the wind."
2:14	"Willst, feiner Knabe, du mit mir gehn?	"*Well, you fine boy, won't you come with me?*
	Meine Töchter sollen dich warten schön;	*My daughters are ready to wait on you.*
	Meine Töchter führen den nächtlichen Reihn	*My daughters lead the nightly round,*
	Und wiegen und tanzen und singen dich ein."	*They will rock you, dance for you, sing you to sleep!"*
2:31	"Mein Vater, mein Vater, and siehst du nicht dort	"Father, Father, do you not see
	Erlkönigs Töchter am düstern Ort?"	The Erlking's daughters there in the dark?"
	"Mein Sohn, mein Sohn, ich seh es genau:	"My son, my son, I see only too well:
	Es scheinen die alten Weiden so grau."	It is the gray gleam in the old willow trees."
3:01	"Ich liebe dich, mich reizt deine schöne Gestalt,	"*I love you, your beauty allures me,*
	Und bist du nicht willig, so brauch' ich Gewalt."	*And if you're not willing, then I shall use force."*
	"Mein Vater, mein Vater, jetzt fasst er mich an!	"Father, Father, he is seizing me now!
	Erlkönig hat mit ein Leids getan!"	The Erlking has hurt me!"
3:27	Dem Vater grauset's, er reitet geschwind,	Fear grips the father, he rides like the wind,
	Er hält in Armen das ächzende Kind,	He holds in his arms the moaning child;
	Erreicht den Hof mit Müh and Not;	He reaches the house hard put, worn out;
	In seinen Armen das Kind war tot.	In his arms the child was—dead!

The father is low, stiff, and gruff, the boy high and frantic. Marked *ppp,* and inaudible to the father, the ominously quiet and sweet little tunes crooned by the Erlking, offering his "schöne Spiele," add a chilling note.

Two things help hold this long song together. First, the piano's triplet rhythm continues ceaselessly, until the very last line, where recitative style lets us know that the ride is over. (The triplets are muffled during the Erlking's speeches—because the child is hearing him in a feverish daze?) Second, there are some telling musical repetitions: the agitated riding motive (stanzas 1–2 and 8), and a desperately strained phrase sung higher and higher as the boy appeals to his father (stanzas 4, 6, and 7).

The Song Cycle

A **song cycle** is a group of songs with a common poetic theme or an actual story connecting all the poems. Composers would either find whole coherent groups of poems to set, or else make their own selections from a larger collection of a poet's work. Schubert, who wrote two great song cycles relatively late in his career, was able to use ready-made groups of poems published by a minor Romantic poet named Wilhelm Müller: *Die schöne Müllerin* ("The Fair Maid of the Mill") and *Winterreise* ("Winter Journey").

The advantage of the song cycle was that it extended the rather fragile expression of the lied into a larger, more comprehensive, and hence more impressive unit. It was, in a sense, an effort to get beyond "miniaturism," even while composing miniatures. The unity of such larger units, however, is always loose. The individual songs can often be sung separately, as well as in sequence with the rest of the cycle.

ROBERT SCHUMANN
Dichterliebe ("A Poet's Love") (1840)

22–23   33

"**S**chubert died. Cried all night," wrote the eighteen-year-old Robert Schumann in his diary under a date in 1828. Yet living in Zwickau, Germany, far from Schubert's Vienna, Schumann did not know many of the older composer's best-known works, his lieder. He loved Schubert's piano music, and indeed, for the first ten years of his own career as a composer, Schumann wrote only piano music.

Then in 1840, the year of his marriage, he suddenly started pouring out lieder. Given this history, it is not surprising that in Schumann's songs the piano is given a more complex role than in Schubert's. This is particularly true of his most famous song cycle, *Dichterliebe*, the first and last songs of which (nos. 1 and 16) we will examine here. *Dichterliebe* has no real story; its series of love poems traces a psychological progression from cautious optimism to disillusionment and despair. They are the work of another great German poet, Heinrich Heine, a man who reacted with bitter irony against Romanticism, while acknowledging his own hopeless commitment to its ideals.

"Im wunderschönen Monat Mai" ("In the wonderfully lovely month of May") The song begins with a piano introduction, halting and ruminative—which seems at first to be a curious response to the "wonderfully lovely" month of May. The piano part winds its way in and out of the vocal line, ebbing and flowing rhythmically and sometimes dwelling on quiet but piercing dissonant harmonies.

What Schumann noticed was the hint of unrequited longing in Heine's very last line, and he ended the song with the piano part hanging in midair, without a true cadence, as though in a state of reaching or yearning: a truly Romantic effect. Technically, the last sound is a dissonance that requires resolution into a consonance but does not get it (until the next song).

❝ To cast light into the depths of the human heart—the artist's mission!"

Robert Schumann

LISTEN   Schumann, "Im wunderschönen Monat Mai"

22   33

0:28	Im wunderschönen Monat Mai,	In the wonderfully lovely month of May,
	Als alle Knospen sprangen,	When all the buds were bursting,
	Da ist in meinem Herzen	Then it was that in my heart
	Die Liebe aufgegangen.	Love broke through.
1:05	Im wunderschönen Monat Mai,	In the wonderfully lovely month of May,
	Als alle Vögel sangen,	When all the birds were singing,
	Da hab' ich ihr gestanden	Then it was I confessed to her
	Mein Sehnen und Verlangen.	My longing and desire.

In this song, both stanzas of the poem are set to identical music. As mentioned earlier, such a song is called *strophic;* strophic setting is of course familiar from folk songs, hymns, popular songs, and many other kinds of music. For Schumann, this kind of setting had the advantage of underlining the similarity in the text of the song's two stanzas, both in meaning and in actual words. Certainly his music deepens the tentative, sensitive, hope-against-hope quality of Heine's understated confession of love.

The qualities of intimacy and spontaneity that are so important to Romantic miniatures can be inhibited by studio recording. Our recording of Schumann's song was made at a concert (you will hear applause as the artists enter).

"Die alten, bösen Lieder" ("The hateful songs of times past")   After many heart-wrenching episodes, the final song in the *Dichterliebe* cycle begins strongly. The insistent rhythm in the piano part sounds a little hectic and forced, like the black humor of Heine's poem. Although basically this is a through-composed song, there are musical parallels between many of the stanzas, and the music of stanza 1 comes back in stanza 5.

> **❝** During the night of October 17, 1833, I suddenly had the most frightful thought a human being can possibly have: 'What if you were no longer able to think?' Clara, anyone who has been crushed like that knows no worse suffering, or despair."
>
> *Letter from Robert Schumann, 1838*

Stanza 1

The hateful songs of times past,   The hateful, brutal dreams

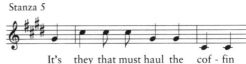

Stanza 5

It's   they that must haul the   cof - fin

LISTEN   Schumann, "Die alten, bösen Lieder"

0:05	Die alten, bösen Lieder, Die Träume bös' und arg, Die lasst uns jetzt begraben: Holt einen grossen Sarg.	The hateful songs of times past, The hateful, brutal dreams, Let's now have them buried; Fetch up a great coffin.
0:23	Hinein leg' ich gar Manches, Doch sag' ich noch nicht, was. Der Sarg muss sein noch grösser Wie's Heidelberger Fass.	I've a lot to put in it— Just what, I won't yet say; The coffin must be even bigger Than the Great Cask of Heidelberg.
0:41	Und holt eine Todtenbahre Und Bretter fest und dick, Auch muss sie sein noch länger Als wie zu Mainz die Brück'.	And fetch a bier, Boards that are strong and thick; They too must be longer Than the river bridge at Mainz.
0:59	Und holt mir auch zwölf Riesen, Die mussen noch stärker sein Als wie der starke Christoph Im Dom zu Köln am Rhein.	And fetch me, too, twelve giants Who must be stronger Than St. Christopher, the great statue At the Cathedral of Cologne on the Rhine.
1:18	Die sollen den Sarg forttragen Und senken in's Meer hinab, Denn solchem grossen Sarge Gebührt ein grosses Grab.	It's they that must haul the coffin And sink it in the sea, For a great coffin like that Deserves a great grave.
1:49	Wisst ihr, warum der Sarg wohl So gross und schwer mag sein? Ich senkt' auch meine Liebe Und meinen Schmerz hinein.	Do you know why the coffin really Has to be so huge and heavy? Because I sank all my love in it, And all of my great grief.

A rather amazing nineteenth-century score of Schumann lieder. The poem is given in ornate calligraphy and illustrated in the richest, most opulent Romantic style. The picture might well be for Clara Schumann's "The Moon Has Risen Softly" (page 263; actually, it is for Robert's similar song "Moonlit Night").

Robert Schumann (1810–1856)

Robert Schumann's father, a bookseller and writer, encouraged the boy's musical talent and started him studying the piano at the age of six. When his father died, his mother wanted him to go into law; he attended the University of Leipzig, but finally persuaded her to let him pursue the career of a piano virtuoso. He had to give this up, however, after an injury sustained when he tried to strengthen his fingers with a mechanical device.

Besides his musical talent, Schumann had a great flair for literature, no doubt inherited from his father. When he was only twenty-three, Schumann founded a magazine to campaign for a higher level of music, *Die Neue Zeitschrift für Musik* ("The New Music Journal" — it is still being published). For several years he wrote regular music criticism, often couched in a fanciful romantic prose style. For example, he signed some of his reviews with the names "Florestan" or "Eusebius," representing the opposite (but both thoroughly romantic) sides of his character — the impetuous side and the tender, dreamy side. He encouraged fledgling composers such as Chopin and (later) Brahms.

Schumann's piano works — among his most important music — are mostly "character pieces," often with imaginative titles, and occasionally signed "Eu." or "Fl." at the end. They are arranged in loosely organized sets, with titles such as *Butterflies, Scenes from Childhood,* and *Carnaval.*

Schumann fell in love with Clara Wieck, the daughter of his piano teacher; at the age of fifteen she was already a famous pianist. Thanks to her father's fanatical opposition — he did not think Robert was a very savory character — they had to wait until she was twenty-one (minus one day) before getting married, in 1840. A charming outcome of the marriage was that Robert, whose early compositions were almost all for piano, suddenly started to write love songs for Clara. Nearly one hundred and fifty songs were composed in this so-called song year.

A little later, he also turned to the composition of larger works: concertos, symphonies, chamber music, choral music, and one opera. Thereafter he worked as a teacher and conductor, but his withdrawn personality made him less than successful. Schumann suffered from mood swings and had experienced breakdowns in his youth, and now he began to show tragic signs of insanity. In 1854, tormented by voices, hallucinations, and loss of memory, he tried to drown himself in the river Rhine and was committed to an asylum. He died two years later.

Chief Works: Sets of miniatures for piano, among them *Scenes from Childhood, Album for the Young, Papillons* (Butterflies), and *Carnaval* ▪ Songs (lieder) and song cycles: *Woman's Life and Love, Dichterliebe* ▪ Piano Fantasy (a free sonata); Piano Concerto and the first important concerto for cello; four symphonies ▪ Chamber music: a quintet and a quartet for piano and strings ▪ An opera, *Genoveva*; incidental music to Byron's *Manfred* and Goethe's *Faust*; choral works

Encore: After *Dichterliebe* and *Carnaval*, listen to the Piano Concerto in A Minor.

But there is a sudden reversal of mood in stanza 6, as the poet suddenly offers to tell us what this morbid list of funeral arrangements is all about. In the music, first the accompaniment disintegrates and then the rhythm. All the poet's self-dramatization vanishes when he speaks of his grief in recitative-like rhythms; the end of the song would be a whimper if Schumann at the piano were not quietly and firmly in control. In a lovely meditative piano solo, music takes over from words. The composer comments on and comforts the poet.

Not only does the composer interpret the poet's words with great art, both in the hectic early stanzas and the self-pitying final one, but he adds something entirely his own in the final solo. The sixteen vignettes by Heine and Schumann in *Dichterliebe* add up to a memorable anthology of the endless pains and pleasures of love celebrated by the Romantics.

Clara Wieck (Clara Schumann) (1819–1896)

Clara Wieck was the eldest child (she had two younger brothers) of a highly ambitious music teacher named Friedrich Wieck (pronounced *Veek*). Wieck had his own piano method, and he determined to make Clara a leading pianist. By the age of fifteen she was widely known as a prodigy. Like most virtuosos of the time, she also composed music to play at her own concerts: variations on popular opera arias, waltzes, a piano concerto.

Robert and Clara Schumann figure in what must be music's greatest love story. Still, there seems to have been just a little friction between them because she was so much better a pianist; she, on her part, felt diffident about composing under his shadow, though he did encourage her to some extent, and they published one song cycle jointly, containing music by both of them. Clara often wrote songs to give Robert on his birthdays. The last of these is dated 1853, the year before he was committed to an insane asylum.

Even before that, Robert's depression and instability made life difficult for Clara. She continued her career as best she could, but more and more, she had to take care of the family. During the 1848 revolution in Leipzig, for example, it was up to her to get the five Schumann children out of town (three more were born later).

Things were difficult in another way when Robert died. At the age of thirty-seven, after losing the husband whom she loved and revered, Clara found herself more than half in love with his twenty-two-year-old protégé Johannes Brahms (see page 304). It is not known which of them withdrew from the relationship. They remained close friends; Brahms was a lifelong bachelor, and she did not remarry.

Today we tend to regret that Clara decided to give up composing, for she left enough good pieces to make us wish there were more. But she knew it would have been an uphill battle, given the all too common nineteenth-century view that great music couldn't be written by a woman. With children to support, she can hardly be blamed for concentrating instead on activities that had already earned her admiration and respect—and a good living: playing and teaching.

Clara Schumann went on to further establish herself as one of Europe's leading pianists and a much-sought-after pedagogue. She concertized and toured widely. Brahms (who always asked her to critique his new compositions) was just one in the eminent circle of her friends and associates. Outliving Robert by forty years, Clara became a major force in late nineteenth-century music.

Chief Works: Miniatures for piano, with names such as *Romances* and *Soirées musicales* ("Musical Evenings"); songs ▪ A piano concerto and a trio for piano, violin, and cello ▪ *Piano Variations on a Theme by Robert Schumann* (Brahms wrote a set of variations on the same theme)

Encore: After "Der Mond," listen to *Romances* for piano and the Piano Concerto.

CLARA SCHUMANN
"Der Mond kommt still gegangen" ("The moon has risen softly") (1843)

24   34

This lied is another perfect Romantic miniature, in spite of the cliché-filled poem, with its moonlight, its dreams of love, and its downhearted lover. Both melody and piano accompaniment are very plain, but the slightly unusual chords chosen by Schumann create a unique pensive mood. The form, too, is simple: modified strophic form, **A A A'**. Some modification, however slight, had to occur in stanza 3, where the poem's speaker, catching sight of the lit-up windows in the house, registers his excitement by crowding his poetic lines with extra words and extra syllables—which require extra notes.

There is an obvious, banal way of setting such crowded lines: See page 264, in the margin. But instead Schumann very skillfully pulls the words out of phase with the musical phrases, achieving beautiful rhythmic matches for some of the extra words: slower for *drunten* (down), livelier for *funkeln* (light—literally, sparkle), and very slow for *still* (silently):

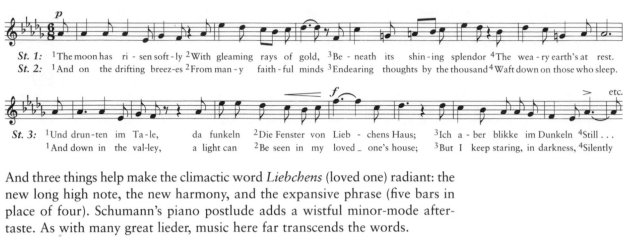

St. 1: ¹The moon has ri-sen soft-ly ²With gleaming rays of gold, ³Be-neath its shin-ing splendor ⁴The wea-ry earth's at rest.
St. 2: ¹And on the drifting breez-es ²From man-y faith-ful minds ³Endearing thoughts by the thousand ⁴Waft down on those who sleep.

St. 3: ¹Und drun-ten im Ta-le, da funkeln ²Die Fenster von Lieb-chens Haus; ³Ich a-ber blikke im Dunkeln ⁴Still . . .
¹And down in the val-ley, a light can ²Be seen in my loved _ one's house; ³But I keep staring, in darkness, ⁴Silently

And three things help make the climactic word *Liebchens* (loved one) radiant: the new long high note, the new harmony, and the expansive phrase (five bars in place of four). Schumann's piano postlude adds a wistful minor-mode aftertaste. As with many great lieder, music here far transcends the words.

LISTEN   Clara Schumann, "Der Mond kommt still gegangen"

0:03 *St. 1:* ¹Der Mond kommt still gegangen   The moon has risen softly
²Mit seinen goldn'en Schein,   With gleaming rays of gold,
³Da Schläft in holdem Prangen   Beneath its shining splendor
⁴Die müde Erde ein.   The weary earth's at rest.

0:30 *St. 2:* ¹Und auf den Lüften schwanken   And on the drifting breezes
²Aus manchem treuen Sinn   From many faithful minds
³Viel tausend Liebesgedanken   Endearing thoughts by the thousand
⁴Über die Schläfer hin.   Waft down on those who sleep.

0:58 *St. 3:* ¹Und drunten im Tale, da funkeln   And down in the valley, a light can
²Die Fenster von Liebchens Haus;   Be seen in my loved one's house;
³Ich aber blikke im Dunkeln   But I keep staring, in darkness,
⁴Still in die Welt hinaus.   Silently out to the world.

Obvious way she might have set stanza 3 (unmodified strophic setting)

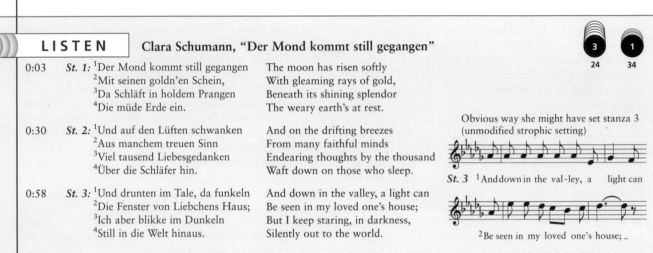

St. 3 ¹And down in the val-ley, a light can   ²Be seen in my loved one's house; _

2 The Character Piece for Piano

Besides the lied, the other chief type of Romantic miniature composition was the short piano piece. Such pieces were written in great profusion in the nineteenth century, and they appeared under many names. Frédéric Chopin preferred simple genre titles such as Nocturne, Waltz, Scherzo, or **Étude** (study). Robert Schumann preferred descriptive titles. Piano miniatures were composed at all levels of difficulty, ranging from virtuoso tours de force, which hardly anyone but their composers could manage, to unassuming pieces playable (and enjoyable) by beginning students.

A good general name for these short Romantic piano pieces (one sometimes used by the Romantics themselves) is **character pieces,** for the essential point about them is that each portrays some definite mood or character. In principle, at least, this is as true of the brilliant virtuoso works as of the simple ones. Each conveys an intense, distinct emotion—an emotion often hinted at by an imaginative title supplied by the composer.

This explains why the Romantic character piece can be thought of as analogous to the Romantic song, or lied, though without its poem. Indeed, six books of such piano pieces by Felix Mendelssohn—pieces that were very popular in Victorian times—are entitled *Songs Without Words.* Some of them have descriptive subtitles that stress still further their similarity to lieder: "Spinning Song," "Spring Song," "Venetian Boat Song."

FRANZ SCHUBERT
Moment Musical No. 2 in A-flat (1827?)

Creative publishers gave Franz Schubert's piano miniatures their titles: "Momens musicals" (spelled wrong!) and "Impromptus" (improvisations—Johannes Brahms would later call some of *his* miniatures "caprices").

In Moment Musical No. 2, the main idea, **A,** is a gentle rocking figure, with a nostalgic mood characteristic of Schubert. The mood deepens when **A'** is provided with a relatively long coda, which seems reluctant ever to let go. In between comes **B,** a sad melody in the minor mode; the piano texture changes from cloudy chords in **A** to plain melody with a steady moving accompaniment in **B.** As usual in piano miniatures, the form is simple, at least on the surface: **A B A' B' A".**

But in fact this is an excellent example of how much these impersonal form diagrams can hide. After **A B A'** with its coda, after four minutes, we think that the piece must be over—except, perhaps, for a hint when the piano moves to an unusually high register at the coda's final cadence. And indeed **B** returns—***fortissimo,*** in the high register, no longer sad but terribly anguished, a cry of pain. In the wake of this climax, there is a momentary switch from the minor mode to the major, a Schubert fingerprint we also noted in Listening Exercise 6 (page 36). Does this change heal the pain? By the end of **A"** the high register no longer hints at anything. It simply hovers at the border of hearing, a true Romantic effect, a Romantic evocation of the ineffable.

LISTEN
SCHUBERT
Moment Musical No. 2
A
0:00   a, *p*
0:35   a'
B
1:20   b: minor, *p*
A'
2:23   a" (longer)
3:17   coda
B'
3:58   b': minor, *ff*   Turns to the   major
A"
4:54   a''', *p*
5:36   coda

ROBERT SCHUMANN
Carnaval (1833–35)

25–27   35–36

Schumann's style of piano writing has a warmth and privacy that set it apart from the music of any of the other pianist-composers of his day. A favorite marking on his scores is the German word *innig,* meaning "inward," "intimate," or "heartfelt." Schumann typically assembled his piano pieces into collections with some general title and, often, some interesting musical means of connection among them. Just as the Romantic character piece for the piano is analogous to the Romantic lied, so these collections by Schumann are analogous to song cycles.

Such a collection is *Carnaval,* a set of twenty short character pieces that really *are* characters—musical portraits of masked guests at a Mardi Gras ball. After the band strikes up an introduction, the sad clown Pierrot arrives, followed by the pantomime figures Harlequin and Columbine, Schumann himself, two of his girlfriends masquerading under the names Estrella and Chiarina, a Coquette, and even the composers Paganini and Chopin. This diverse gallery provided Schumann with an outlet for his whimsy and humor, as well as all his Romantic melancholy and passion.

> " Eusebius: In sculpture, the actor's art becomes fixed. The actor transforms the sculptor's forms into living art. The painter turns a poem into a painting. The musician sets a picture to music. Florestan: The aesthetic principle is the same in every art; only the material differs."
>
> *Robert Schumann, 1833*

"Eusebius"   Eusebius was Schumann's pen name for his tender, dreamy self, and this little piece presents him at his most introspective. In the passage below, the yearning effect of the high notes (shaded) is compounded by the vague, languorous rhythm:

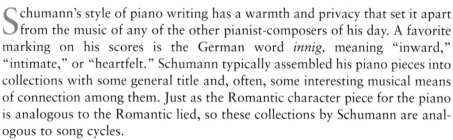

The right-hand triplets and quintuplets blur with the left-hand quarter notes, especially when played with Romantic rubato. The somewhat unusual form is **aa ba b'a' ba,** in which **b'a'** stands out although it differs from **ba** only in its much thicker chords and its use of the pedal.

26
35

"Florestan"   After "Eusebius" ends very tentatively, Schumann's impetuous other self makes his entrance. "Florestan" is built out of a single explosive motive; the piece moves in fits and starts. It gets faster and faster, almost madly, ending completely up in the air. This non-cadence is resolved only in the next number.

27

"Chiarina"   As we are probably meant to guess from the letters in the name, this is a musical portrait of then sixteen-year-old Clara Wieck. The heading is "Passionato," and by the end the dynamic has risen to *fortissimo*. Robert did not see his future wife as a shrinking violet.

FRÉDÉRIC CHOPIN
Nocturne in F-Sharp, Op. 15, No. 2 (1831)

28   37

Chopin's twenty-one **nocturnes,** meaning "night pieces," written throughout his career, are as different as twenty-one different nights. But each features a particularly striking tune—a languid serenade, for example, or a dark, secret lament. Something else is usually heard or overheard in the night, too, such as a distant procession, a passionate encounter, or even a fragment of a dance or a folk song.

The opening tune in Chopin's Nocturne in F-Sharp has an elegance unique to the composer—an elegance that stems partly from the wonderfully graceful rhythm, partly from the Romantic turns of harmony, and partly from the pianistic decorations of the melodic line. We have seen decorated melodies before, but Chopin's have an almost liquid quality, caused partly by chromaticism—by the free use of all the notes of the chromatic scale, as in this fragment:

> **LISTEN**
>
> **CHOPIN**
> **Nocturne in F-Sharp**
>
> 0:00 a
> 0:27 a' ornamented
> 0:58 b
> 1:28 c
> 2:13 a''
> 2:55 coda

Romantic form contributes to the Romantic effect. Chopin avoids sharp demarcations and literal returns; the music seems to grow spontaneously, in an almost improvisational way. The main tune, **A (a a' b),** does not really end, but gives way to plaintive sounds emerging out of nowhere, which surge up to a moment of real passion. Then the return of the tune (**a''**) is fragmentary—though in a way more intense—and the whole is capped by an unexpected and delicious little coda. Free rhythm in the performance (rubato) mirrors the freedom of form.

> **"** 'That's not your own fingering, is it?' he asked, in his melodious little voice. 'No, Liszt's' I said. 'Ah, that one has ideas, I tell you!' And Chopin began to try this fingering. 'But one could go down the whole keyboard this way like a crayfish scuttling back to his stream. It is perfect, your fingering! I shall use it!' "
>
> *Reminiscence by a student of Chopin, 1859*

Frédéric Chopin (1810–1849)

Chopin was born near Warsaw, where his father, a Frenchman who had emigrated to Poland and married a Polish lady, ran a private school for young gentlemen. In this atmosphere Fryderyk — later he adopted the French form Frédéric — acquired his lifelong taste for life in high society. Provided with the best teachers available, he became an extraordinary pianist. There are many reports of the exquisite delicacy of his playing, and his miraculous ability, as it seemed at the time, to draw romantic sounds out of the piano.

Furthermore, his set of variations on Mozart's "Là ci darem la mano" (see page 214), written when he was seventeen, was already an impressive enough composition to earn a rave review from Robert Schumann.

Chopin settled in Paris, where he found ready acceptance from society people and from other artists and intellectuals, such as the novelist Honoré de Balzac and the painter Eugène Delacroix, who produced a famous portrait of the composer. Chopin made his way as a fashionable piano teacher and by selling his music to publishers. The facts that he was Polish and that Poland was being overrun by Russia at that time seem to have made him even more glamorous to the French. Among Chopin's piano miniatures are over fifty Mazurkas and sixteen Polonaises, which are stylized Polish dances.

Chopin was a frail and fastidious personality. Though he sometimes played in public, he truly disliked the hurly-burly of concert life and preferred to perform for select audiences in great houses. More than any other of the great composers, he restricted his work to music for *his* instrument, the piano. Even his works for piano and orchestra — two concertos and a few other works — were all from his pre-Paris days.

The major event of his personal life was his ten-year romance with Aurore Dudevant, an early feminist and a famous novelist under the pen name George Sand. (They were introduced by Liszt, who wrote an admiring book about Chopin after his death.) The relationship was a rocky one; Sand sketched some unkind scenes from their life together in one of her novels. After the affair broke up in 1847, Chopin's health declined with his spirits. He toured England and Scotland unhappily in 1848 and died the next year, aged thirty-nine, of tuberculosis, a major killer in the nineteenth century.

Chief Works: Character pieces for piano: Preludes (including the "Raindrop" prelude), Nocturnes, Études, Ballades, Waltzes (including the "Minute" waltz), and Polish Mazurkas and Polonaises ▪ Three piano sonatas, including one with a famous funeral march as the slow movement ▪ Two piano concertos ▪ A cello sonata; a few Polish songs

Encore: Listen to some other Chopin Nocturnes, the Fantasy-Impromptu, and the Ballade in G Minor.

Was this striking painting, by a minor late nineteenth-century artist, done with Chopin's nocturnes in mind? Called *Notturno,* its cool elegance, twilight sensuality, and vaguely apprehensive quality might suggest so.

Franz Liszt (1811–1886)

There are some important composers whose music we unfortunately have to pass over in this book because of space limits. In this box and the one on page 270, we give the biographies of three of them, together with some account of their roles in the history of Romantic music.

Franz Liszt learned music from his father on the Hungarian estate of the princes Esterházy, whom Haydn had once served. At age eleven, the boy gave his first piano concert in Vienna, where he met Beethoven. He later settled in Paris, home of another great émigré pianist-composer, Chopin.

Liszt's dashing looks and personality and his liaisons with married noblewomen—Countess d'Agoult and, later, Princess Sayn-Wittgenstein—dazzled Europe as much as his incredible pianistic technique. No one had heard such virtuosity. He drew crowds like a modern rock star and cultivated a lifestyle to match.

After his relationship with d'Agoult came to a stormy end in 1839, Liszt spent a few years giving sensational concerts all over Europe. Tiring of concert life, he then took a position as conductor and director of the theater at Weimar, in Germany, where there was still a court that supported the arts in the old eighteenth-century manner. There he wrote his most radical and influential music.

Like many other Romantic composers, Liszt was a writer of note, as well as a musician. He was a strong advocate of the music of Richard Wagner; the two men learned much from each other. Both friend and foe linked Wagner's "music dramas" with Liszt's symphonic poems as "Music of the Future." In his personality, however, Liszt was as magnanimous as Wagner was self-centered and devious.

Liszt really had two major careers. The first, at Paris, his career as a fantastic piano virtuoso, underpins a musical ideal that is still alive and well in music conservatories today. It left a mass of fiercely difficult piano music, including the *Transcendental Études* (the name says it all!) and the popular *Hungarian Rhapsodies*—important early products of nationalism in music (see page 298).

Liszt's second career, at Weimar, focused on orchestral music: program symphonies and symphonic poems. We take up these genres on pages 269 and 295.

3   Early Romantic Program Music

The lied and the character piece for piano—the two main forms of early Romantic miniature compositions—were intimately tied up with non-musical, usually poetic, ideas. Furthermore, in a work such as Schumann's *Carnaval*, the various piano portraits are juxtaposed in such a way as to hint at their interaction—hint, that is, at a shadowy story line. Poems, stories, and nonmusical ideas in general were also associated with large-scale instrumental pieces.

As we have seen, *program music* is a term used for instrumental compositions associated with poems, stories, and the like. Program music for orchestra grew up naturally in opera overtures, for even in the eighteenth century it was seen that an overture might gain special interest if it referred to moods or ideas in the opera to come by citing (or, rather, forecasting) some of its themes.

Liszt's phenomenal virtuosity as a pianist inspired many a cartoonist. The sword here refers to his many decorations; he has a halo because he had turned to religion and become an unordained priest. "The Abbé Liszt" was known to break, if not pianos, piano strings, and this helped ruin one Viennese piano maker (Graf).

This happens in Mozart's *Don Giovanni,* in which the next-to-last scene has Don Giovanni carried off to hell by the statue of the murdered Commandant (see page 212). The somber music associated with the statue is first heard in the opera's overture, even before the curtain has gone up. Lively, effervescent music follows; but the serious undertone of Mozart's opera is already loud and clear at the start of the work's overture.

The Concert Overture: Felix Mendelssohn

A further step, conceptually, was the <u>concert overture</u>, never intended to be followed by a stage play or an opera—never intended, indeed, for the theater. Robert Schumann wrote an overture to *Hermann und Dorothea,* by Goethe, which is not a play but an epic poem. Hector Berlioz wrote overtures to literary works of various kinds: plays (Shakespeare's *King Lear*), long poems (*The Corsair* by Lord Byron, a special hero for the Romantics), and novels (*Waverly* by Sir Walter Scott).

Probably the best-known and best-loved concert overtures are by Felix Mendelssohn. He wrote his concert overture to Shakespeare's *A Midsummer Night's Dream* when he was seventeen; the play was a special favorite with both Felix and his sister Fanny. He had no theatrical occasion in mind, though years later the overture was indeed used in productions of the Shakespeare play. At that time Mendelssohn also added other music, and a suite derived from this piece has become a popular concert number.

A work in sonata form, following Classical models quite clearly, the overture to *A Midsummer Night's Dream* nonetheless includes representational features. Music illustrates the delicate, fluttering fairies in the service of King Oberon and Queen Titania, the sleep induced by Puck's magic flower, and the braying of Bottom the Weaver when he is turned into a donkey.

Another fine example by Mendelssohn is the *Hebrides* Overture, an evocative, moody depiction of lonely Scottish islands rich in romantic associations. Surging string music suggests the swell and the spray of waves; woodwind fanfares suggest seabird calls, perhaps, or romanticized foghorns. This is evidently program music, but what makes it an overture? Nothing more than the fact that it follows the standard scheme for overtures at the time—namely, a single movement in sonata form.

Public composer and private composer: Felix Mendelssohn and his sister Fanny

The Program Symphony: Hector Berlioz

PROGRAM OF THE SYMPHONY: A young musician of unhealthy sensibility and passionate imagination poisons himself with opium in a fit of lovesick despair. Too weak to kill him, the dose of the drug plunges him into a heavy sleep attended by the strangest visions, during which his sensations, emotions, and memories are transformed in his diseased mind into musical thoughts and images. Even the woman he loves becomes a melody to him, an *idée fixe* [an obsession], so to speak, that he finds and hears everywhere.

So begins a long pamphlet that the French Romantic composer Hector Berlioz distributed at performances of his first symphony—a symphony which he could justifiably call *Fantastic,* and which to this day remains his most famous work. It certainly represents a more radical approach to program music than that of the concert overture. Berlioz, too, had written several concert overtures, but he now felt the need for a broader canvas. In his <u>program symphonies</u>—entire symphonies with programs spelled out movement by movement—Berlioz set the tone for the grandiose compositions that were to become as characteristic of Romanticism as its musical miniatures.

❝ Love or music—which power can uplift man to the sublimest heights? It is a large question; yet it seems to me one should answer it in this way: Love cannot give an idea of music; music can give an idea of love. But why separate them? They are the two wings of the soul . . ."

From the Memoirs of Hector Berlioz, *1869*

Felix Mendelssohn (1809–1847)

Felix Mendelssohn may be the only great composer who has ever come from an upper-class family, a family of converted Jews who were in banking. Their home was a meeting place for artists and intellectuals over generations. Felix and his sister Fanny were brought up with music and every other advantage that came with a life of privilege. (Felix also became a fine amateur painter.)

By the time he was fifteen Felix was conducting the family orchestra in his own music. He went on to a stellar career, not only as an enormously successful composer, but as a pianist, organist, conductor, educator — he founded the Leipzig Conservatory of Music — and even as a musicologist. His performance of Bach's *St. Matthew Passion* was a landmark in the revival of "early music."

This action was typical, for from the start Mendelssohn showed a great respect for, even deference toward, the classics. His music never goes as far as, say, Schumann or Chopin in acceding to Romantic tendencies, but always keeps a firm foundation of Classical technique.

One of Mendelssohn's most significant fields of activity was the concert overture, an early genre of Romantic program music, discussed on page 269. In his lifetime he was admired even more for his oratorios *St. Paul* and *Elijah,* and for popular sets of piano miniatures he called *Songs Without Words.* His Violin Concerto is a special favorite.

Fanny Mendelssohn (1805–1847)

Fanny Mendelssohn, Felix's older sister, was also a highly prolific composer. The siblings were always very close; music was one of their bonds, for Fanny showed as much talent as her brother. Married to a painter named Wilhelm Hensel, she devoted herself to weekly concerts at the Mendelssohn home in Berlin, for which she composed music of all kinds, including even oratorios.

However, Fanny's music did not pass beyond the threshold of the Mendelssohn mansion. Only a small percentage of it found its way into print, at the end of her short life. Fanny is often seen as a victim of patriarchal society and of the general refusal in the past to take women composers seriously. Like Mozart's sister Nannerl, she watched as her younger brother built a great career while she was expected — indeed, conditioned — to put motherhood and family first, music second. But we should remember that unlike other successful women composers of the nineteenth century — from Louise Farrenc (1804–1875) to Clara Schumann (1819–1896) to Cécile Chaminade (1857–1944) and Ethel Smythe (1858–1944) — Fanny Mendelssohn belonged to the upper class. Few members of this class, male or female, had ever pursued public careers in the arts. They didn't need the rat race. Workaholic Felix was an exception.

Fanny's sudden death at age forty-one devastated Felix, and hastened his own death only six months later.

HECTOR BERLIOZ
Fantastic Symphony: Episodes in the Life of an Artist (1830)

4   1
2–8 38–44

Clearly Berlioz had a gift for public relations, for the program of his *Fantastic* Symphony was not a familiar play or novel, but an autobiographical fantasy of the most lurid sort. Here was music that encouraged listeners to think it had been written under the influence of opium, the drug of choice among the Romantics, which shocked society at large. What is more, half of Paris knew that Berlioz was madly in love (from afar) with an Irish actress, Harriet Smithson, who had taken the city by storm with her Shakespearean roles.

Audiences have never been quite sure how seriously to take it all, but they continue to be bowled over by the sheer audacity of the whole conception and the rambunctious way it is realized. Then there are Berlioz's effects of tone color. He demanded an orchestra of unprecedented size, which he used in the most original and imaginative ways. Also highly original was the notion of having a single theme recur in all the movements as a representation of the musician's beloved — his **idée fixe,** the Shakesperean Smithson. Here is the *idée fixe* theme as it first appears:

Hector Berlioz (1803–1869)

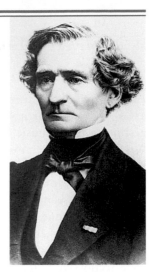

Berlioz was the first great composer who played no standard instrument like violin or piano at all. His father, a country doctor, sent him to medical school in Paris. But, as Berlioz told it, he was so horrified when he entered the dissecting room, where rats were nibbling at the scraps, that he leaped out the window and went to the Paris Conservatory of Music instead.

The anecdote is typical of his emotional and utterly Romantic personality. More than any other composer of his generation, except Wagner, Berlioz thought the unthinkable in music; his grandiose program symphonies had simply no precedent and were not matched in ambition until the time of Gustav Mahler, about 1900. The only instrument he played well was the guitar, but his imagination for orchestral tone color was extraordinary. Like all the Romantic composers, he was inspired by literary models, including especially Shakespeare — his *Lélio* is a meditation on *Hamlet,* and his opera *Béatrice et Bénédict* is taken from *Much Ado about Nothing —* and Virgil. *The Trojans* (1858), his long two-part opera derived from Virgil's *Aeneid,* was seldom performed until modern times, but it is now regarded as his masterpiece.

Berlioz had two unhappy marriages, the first to the Irish Shakespearean actress Harriet Smithson, who is immortalized as the *idée fixe* in the *Fantastic* Symphony. In spite of suffering from constant ridicule from the musical establishment on the one hand, and wretched health on the other, it was a triumph of his impetuous personality that Berlioz ultimately managed to have most of his enormous

compositions performed and to gain a good measure of recognition in musically conservative Paris.

Throughout his life, he was obliged to support himself with musical journalism, at which he was a master; his *Memoirs* is one of the most delightful books ever written about music. He also wrote important treatises on orchestration and conducting. One of the first great conductors, Berlioz toured extensively as a conductor of his own music, especially in Germany, where he was welcomed in progressive circles.

His last years were spent in physical pain and depression. After 1862 he listened to little music and composed none. Berlioz died in Paris in 1869.

Chief Works: Program symphonies: *Fantastic* Symphony, *Harold in Italy, Romeo and Juliet* ■ Concert overtures: *King Lear, The Corsair, The Roman Carnival* ■ Operas: *Benvenuto Cellini, The Trojans* (after Virgil's *Aeneid*) ■ Oratorios: *The Damnation of Faust, The Childhood of Christ* ■ A great Requiem Mass for orchestra, chorus, and four brass bands.

Encore: After the *Fantastic* Symphony, listen to the Symphony *Harold in Italy;* Overture *The Corsair.* Read the *Memoirs.*

This typically Romantic melody takes its yearning quality from its slow struggle to move higher and higher in pitch; from measure 5 on, each phrase peaks a bit above the preceding phrase until the melody reaches its climax at measure 15. Near the end, measure 19 provides a positive shudder of emotion. Notice how many dynamic, rubato, and other marks Berlioz has supplied, trying to ensure just the right expressive quality from moment to moment.

To illustrate his drastic mood swings, Berlioz subjects the *idée fixe* to thematic transformation (see page 252) for all its other appearances in the opium dream. The last movement, for example, has a grotesque parody of the theme. Its new jerky rhythm and squeaky orchestration (using the small E-flat clarinet) thoroughly undermine the original Romantic mood:

Berlioz's expressive terms translate as follows:
Canto espressivo = expressive song;
dolce = sweetly;
poco = somewhat;
poco a poco = bit by bit;
animato = animated;
ritenuto = slowed down (ritardando);
a tempo = back to the original tempo.

First Movement: Reveries, Passions (Largo — Allegro agitato e appassionato assai) We first hear a short, quiet run-in — a typically Romantic touch suggesting that the music has grown up imperceptibly out of silence. Then the "soul-sickness" mentioned in the program is depicted by a halting, passionate melody. A faster section begins with the *idée fixe,* and the music picks up energy (the "volcanic love" of the program).

This fast section follows sonata form, but only very loosely. The *idée fixe* is the main theme, and a second theme is simply a derivative of the first. Some of the finest strokes in this movement run counter to Classical principles — for example, the arresting up-and-down chromatic scale that arrives in the development section without any logical connection to anything else. The recapitulation, too, is extended in a very un-Classical fashion; it actually includes a whole new melody for the oboe.

Near the end, beginning a very long coda, the *idée fixe* returns loudly at a faster tempo — the first of its many transformations. At the very end, slower music depicts the program's "religious consolations."

Second Movement: A Ball (Allegro non troppo)   A symphony needs the simplicity and easy swing of a dance movement, and this ballroom episode of the opium dream conveniently provided one. The dance in question is not a minuet or a scherzo, but a waltz, the most popular ballroom dance of the nineteenth century. The *idée fixe,* transformed into a lilting triple meter, first appears in the position of the trio (**B** in the **A B A** form) and then returns hauntingly in a coda.

Third Movement: Scene in the Country (Adagio)   Invoking nature to reflect human emotions was a favorite Romantic procedure. The "pastoral duet" is played by an English horn and an offstage oboe (boy and girl, perhaps?). At the end, the English horn returns to the accompaniment of distant thunder sounds, played on four differently tuned timpani. Significantly, the oboe can no longer be heard.

In this movement the *idée fixe* returns in a new, strangely agitated transformation. It is interrupted by angry sounds swelling to a climax, reflecting the anxieties chronicled in the program.

Fourth Movement: March to the Scaffold (Allegretto non troppo)   This movement has two main themes: a long downward scale ("gloomy and wild") and an exciting military march ("brilliant and grand"), orchestrated more like a football band than a symphony orchestra. Later the scale theme appears divided up in its orchestration between plucked and bowed strings, woodwinds, brass, and percussion — a memorable instance of Berlioz's novel imagination for tone color. The scale theme also appears in a truly shattering inverted form (that is, moving up instead of down).

Berlioz had written this march or something like it several years earlier. As he revised it to go into the *Fantastic* Symphony, he added a coda that uses the *idée fixe* and therefore only makes sense in terms of the symphony's program. The final fall of the axe is illustrated musically by the sound of a guillotine

THE PROGRAM CONTINUES:
MOVEMENT 1
First he recalls the soul-sickness, the aimless passions, the baseless depressions and elations that he felt before first seeing his loved one; then the volcanic love that she instantly inspired in him; his jealous furies; his return to tenderness; his religious consolations.

Second theme

MOVEMENT 2
He encounters his beloved at a ball, in the midst of a noisy, brilliant party.

MOVEMENT 3
He hears two shepherds piping in dialogue. The pastoral duet, the location, the light rustling of trees stirred gently by the wind, some newly conceived grounds for hope — all this gives him a feeling of unaccustomed calm. But *she* appears again . . . what if she is deceiving him?

MOVEMENT 4
He dreams he has killed his beloved, that he is condemned to death and led to execution. A march accompanies the procession, now gloomy and wild, now brilliant and grand. Finally the *idée fixe* appears for a moment, to be cut off by the fall of the axe.

chop and a military snare-drum roll, right after bars 1–2 of the *idée fixe*. "Berlioz tells it like it is," conductor Leonard Bernstein once remarked. "You take a trip and you end up screaming at your own funeral."

Fifth Movement: Dream of a Witches' Sabbath (Larghetto — Allegro)   Adding a fifth movement to the traditional four of the Classical symphony was a typical Berlioz innovation (although it can be traced back to the Beethoven he so admired). Now the element of parody is added to the astonishing orchestral effects pioneered earlier in the symphony. First we hear the unearthly sounds of the nighttime locale of the witches' orgy. Their swishing broomsticks are heard, and distant, echoing horn calls summon them. Mutes are used in the brass instruments — perhaps the first time mutes were ever used in a poetic way.

As Berlioz remarks, the "noble and timid" *idée fixe* sounds thoroughly vulgar in its last transformation, played in a fast jig rhythm by the shrill E-flat clarinet. (Compare the music examples on pages 271 and 272.) The treatment of the *idée fixe* here is strictly "programmatic": When the theme first arrives, only two phrases are played before the orchestra breaks in, with a "roar of joy" welcoming Harriet Smithson to the orgy to mock her lover's death.

As the merriment is brought to an end by the tolling of funeral bells, Berlioz prepares his most sensational stroke of all — a burlesque of one of the most solemn and famous of Gregorian chants, the *Dies irae* (Day of Wrath). This chant is the centerpiece of Masses for the dead, or Requiem Masses; in Catholic France, any audience would have recognized the *Dies irae* instantly. Three segments of it are used. It makes for a blasphemous, shocking picture of the witches' black mass.

MOVEMENT 5
He finds himself at a Witches' Sabbath.... Unearthly sounds, groans, shrieks of laughter, distant cries echoed by other cries. The beloved's melody is heard, but it has lost its character of nobility and timidity. It is *she* who comes to the Sabbath! At her arrival, a roar of joy. She joins in the devilish orgies. A funeral knell; burlesque of the *Dies irae*.

Original Gregorian chant

Di - es i - rae di - es il - la Sol - vet___ sae - clum _ in fa - vil - la...
Day of wrath, that dreadful day,   *When heaven and earth shall pass away*

Version 1: TUBAS and BASSOONS

Version 2: FRENCH HORNS and TROMBONES

Version 3: WOODWINDS and PIZZICATO STRINGS

The final section of the movement is a "Witches' Round Dance." Berlioz wrote a free fugue — a traditional form in a nontraditional context; he uses counterpoint to give a feeling of tumult and orgiastic confusion. The subject is an excited one:

LISTENING CHART 16

Berlioz, *Fantastic* Symphony, fifth movement

9 min., 59 sec.

4 2–8   3 38–44

INTRODUCTION

2 **38**	0:00	Mysterious orchestral effects
	0:27 *Fanfare*	Like a distant summons: trombones, then flutes plus piccolo echoed by muted French horns
	0:58	Free repetitions: mysterious sounds, fanfare

IDÉE FIXE

	1:39	Prefatory statement: two phrases (only) of the *idée fixe*; note the bass drum. Riotous orchestral response, *ff*
3 **39**	1:59 *Idée fixe*	Entire tune presented in a grotesque transformation, in **6/8** meter, played by "squeaky" E-flat clarinets
0:30	2:29 *Crescendo*	Big climax—the first of many
0:51	2:50 Upward motive	A short, expectant motive (later this motive initiates the fugue subject of the "Round Dance")
0:54	2:53 *Transition*	Quiet descending passage
1:12	3:11 Funeral bells	**Three sets of three bells (the third set is muted); the upward motive also appears**

DIES IRAE

4 **40**	3:37 Segment 1	Segment 1 of the plainchant is played in three versions:
		(1) tubas and bassoons—slow
0:22	3:58	(2) horns and trombones—faster
0:31	4:08	(3) woodwinds—faster still (the rhythm here recalls that of the *idée fixe*)
0:37	4:14 Segment 2	Segment 2 of the plainchant, same three versions
1:00	4:37 Segment 3	Segment 3 (begins like segment 1), same three versions
1:34	5:11 *Transition*	The upward motive is developed; crescendo.

WITCHES' ROUND DANCE (free fugue)

5 **41**	5:29 Exposition	Four entries of the fugue subject
0:27	5:56 *Episode 1*	
0:46	6:15 Subject entries	*Three more entries, in stretto*
6 **42**	6:31 *Episode 2*	A passage starting with a loud rhythmic motive, derived from the subject, comes four times.
0:20	6:51	The music dies down.
0:40	7:11	**Fragments of the *Dies irae***
0:55	7:26	Long transition; crescendo over a drum roll
1:35	8:06 Subject entry	The original subject returns.
7 **43**	8:13 Subject plus *Dies irae*	The two themes together in a polyphonic combination. This is a climax; **trumpets play the *Dies irae* for the first time.**
0:31	8:44 Subject entry	Final appearance of subject: over strings *col legno* (played with the wood, that is, the back of the bow). Some notes are lengthened.
8 **44**	9:19 *Dies irae*	**Segment 1 of the *Dies irae* hastily recollected; big drum strokes**
0:09	9:28 Conclusion	Final passage of cadences: very loud

Witches' Sabbath (detail), by Francisco de Goya (1746–1828), one of a number of dark, unsettling images Goya painted on the walls of his house in his last years. Satan, in the form of a goat, presides over the orgy.

The climax of the fugue (and of the symphony) comes when the Round Dance theme is heard together with the *Dies irae,* played by the trumpets. Berlioz wanted to drive home the point that it is the witches, represented by the theme of their round dance, who are parodying the church melody. The *idée fixe* seems at last to be forgotten.

But in real life Berlioz did not forget; he married Smithson and both of them lived to regret it.

bedfordstmartins.com/listen
▶ Interactive Listening Chart 16

CHAPTER 17

Romantic Opera

An important theme of Romanticism was the surpassing of artistic barriers. The idea of combining music with poetry and other forms of literature, and even with philosophy, made perfect sense to Romantic composers and their audiences. The age that produced the lied—a German song with an important poetic dimension—was also committed to the union of music and drama. The nineteenth century was a golden age of opera, which flourished all over Europe from Germany, France, and Italy to Bohemia and Russia.

Opera in the nineteenth century was affected by another important Romantic theme: the celebration of music as the most profound of all the arts. Opera composers and librettists began thinking seriously about the meaning and message of their work; they came to view opera as a type of serious drama

❝ Carve this into your head, in letters of brass: An opera must draw tears, cause horror, bring death, by means of song.❞

Opera composer Vincenzo Bellini, 1834

The Wolf's Glen Scene from Weber's *Der Freischütz*, most famous of early German Romantic operas (see page 277).

Early Romantic Opera

Romantic opera made its serious start in the 1820s, after the end of the Viennese Classical period. It did not, however, start or flourish in the heartland of Classical music, which was Vienna. In that city, both Beethoven and Schubert felt threatened by the popular rage for the operas of Gioacchino Rossini, a young Italian whose meteoric career left a mark on the whole of Europe.

Gioacchino Rossini (1792–1868)

Rossini is most famous today for crisp, elegant opera buffas in a style that is not all that far from Mozart — the immortal *Barber of Seville* among them. The overtures of these operas, which are popular as concert pieces, are even written in sonata form, the true trademark of Classicism in music.

But in his own day Rossini was admired equally for his serious operas, which established the style and form of Italian Romantic opera. This is sometimes called *bel canto* opera because of its glorification of beautiful singing (*bel canto* means just that — "beautiful song"). Rossini's operas provided models of Romantic emotional melodic expression, such as Desdemona's "Willow Song" from his Shakespeare opera, *Otello*. The same operas are also well stocked with coloratura arias, showcases for the legendary virtuoso singers of that era.

To everyone's astonishment, Rossini gave up opera in 1829 after the success of *William Tell,* his greatest work.

Gaetano Donizetti (1797–1848)

Donizetti, who dominated Italian *bel canto* opera after Rossini's sudden retirement, moved decisively in the direction of simple, sentimental arias and blood-and-thunder action music. Enormously prolific, he wrote more than sixty operas in his short lifetime.

The most famous are *Lucia di Lammermoor,* based on the historical novel by Scott mentioned on page 278, and *Don Pasquale,* a very late example of opera buffa. In the 1970s, the American soprano Beverly Sills starred in a Donizetti trilogy featuring famous queens of English history: *Anna Bolena* (Anne Boleyn, the ill-fated second wife of Henry VIII), *Maria Stuarda* (Mary Stuart — Mary, Queen of Scots), and *Roberto Devereux* (about Queen Elizabeth I and Robert Devereux, Earl of Essex).

Vincenzo Bellini (1801–1835)

Vincenzo Bellini strikes listeners today as the most refined of the three early *bel canto* composers. He wrote many fewer operas than the others, and his most beautiful arias have a unique Romantic sheen. The title role in *Norma,* his finest work, is the final testing ground for sopranos, for it demands highly expressive singing, coloratura fireworks, and great acting, all in unusual quantities.

Verdi often expressed his admiration for the supremely melodious Bellini. All the same, he learned more from the more robust and dramatic Donizetti.

Carl Maria von Weber (1786–1826)

Weber was the founder of German Romantic opera. His most important work, *Der Freischütz* (The Magic Bullet), has the quality of a German folktale or ballad put to music. Max, a somewhat driven young huntsman, sells his soul to the devil for seven magic bullets, but is redeemed by the sacrifice of his innocent fiancée, Agatha.

Two spiritual arias sung by Agatha in this opera show Romantic melody at its best. There are German choruses in folk-song style. A famous scene of devilish conjuration (see the page opposite) features sensational orchestral writing with spooky special harmonic effects.

Supernatural subject matter with a strongly moral overtone — quite unlike the historical subjects chosen by Donizetti, for example — and emphasis on the orchestra became characteristic of German Romantic opera. These features are still evident in the mature works of Richard Wagner, who started out in the 1830s as an opera composer in Weber's mold. Otherwise, however, Wagner's "music dramas" leave early Romantic opera far behind.

Legendary singers of the *bel canto* era: Pauline Viardot (1821–1910; she was also a composer), Maria Malibran (1808–1836), and Giulia Grisi (1811–1869), along with a playbill for one of their favorite showcases, the opera *Norma* by Vincenzo Bellini.

in music, not just a vehicle for song, spectacle, and entertainment, as had often been the case before. Richard Wagner is famous for embracing, publicizing, and indeed co-opting this notion. He put it into action with his "music dramas"—works that fascinated the later nineteenth century. Nevertheless, even when Wagner was still an unknown provincial conductor, he was building on new attitudes toward opera that were developing all over Europe.

Thus many operas took their subjects from highly regarded Romantic novels, such as *Ivanhoe, The Lady of the Lake,* and *The Bride of Lammermoor,* by Sir Walter Scott. Since poets and playwrights were turning with new enthusiasm to Shakespeare's plays, opera composers, too, drew on them widely. Giuseppe Verdi set versions of Shakespeare's tragedies *Macbeth* and *Othello* as well as the comedy *The Merry Wives of Windsor.* Over his long career, Verdi developed his own form of musical drama, which bears comparison with that of Wagner (or anyone else) for seriousness and power.

1   Verdi and Italian Opera

Giuseppe Verdi, the greatest of Italian opera composers, was the dominant figure in nineteenth-century opera houses. For while Wagner's so-called music dramas and his theories of opera attracted much excited attention, Verdi's operas got many more performances. Then as now, people were inevitably drawn to compare and contrast these two masters.

The heart of the contrast lies in Verdi's unswerving commitment to the human voice. In this, he was a faithful follower of the *bel canto* principles of Rossini, Donizetti, and Bellini (see page 277). Verdi never allowed the voice to be overshadowed by the orchestra, and over the course of his long career he learned to write more and more beautiful melodies. Opera was a singing art to Verdi, and generations of Italians before, during, and after his lifetime have enthusiastically agreed with him.

But while audiences have always loved Verdi's melodies, what he himself cared most about was the dramatic quality of his operas. First and foremost, Verdi was interested in people, people placed in situations in which strong, exciting actions bring out equally strong emotions. He sought out dramatic subjects full of stirring action, and he had a genius for finding just the right vocal melody to capture a dramatic situation.

> 66 I want subjects that are novel, big, beautiful, varied and bold—as bold as can be!"
>
> *Giuseppe Verdi, 1853*

Recitative and Aria: The Orchestra

As an opera composer, Verdi never wavered in his commitment to the human voice. That said, however, it must also be said that the orchestra plays a much richer role in Verdi's operas than in those of any of his Italian predecessors. This was all but inevitable in the orchestra-intoxicated nineteenth century.

The role of the orchestra was especially expanded in passages of recitative or near-recitative—the relic or descendant of the recitatives of Baroque opera seria and Classical opera buffa. Italian opera still held roughly to the old division of declamation (recitative) for the action and dialogue portions of an opera, and melody (arias) for reflective, emotional expression. (Ensembles encompassed both.) But plot action and dialogue were now always accompanied by the full orchestra. The orchestra is usually not restricted to the simple chords that were normal in earlier recitative styles; it plays more active, motivic, and excited music that points up the words and urges the singers on.

Giuseppe Verdi (1813–1901)

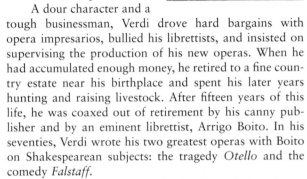

The son of a storekeeper in a tiny village in northern Italy, Verdi had a spotty education. He played church organ and conducted the band of the neighboring little town. A local merchant, Antonio Barezzi, who became a patron and almost a second father to the young man, sent him to Milan to study music.

In those days, the center of musical life in Italy was Milan's opera house, La Scala. (It is still active and world-famous today.) After several discouraging years in that city, Verdi scored a huge success with his biblical opera *Nabucco* (Nebuchadnezzar) when he was twenty-nine years old. For the next ten years he composed operas at a furious rate for opera houses in Italy, Paris, and London. Three great hits in the early 1850s are still his most popular works: *Rigoletto,* which chronicles cynical and deadly court intrigues (the original play was banned), *Il trovatore,* a grisly tale set in the age of chivalry, and—entirely up to date—*La traviata,* about a Parisian courtesan with a noble heart. After this Verdi took more time with his operas, and his later works became richer and more subtle.

Italy was not an independent nation during Verdi's youth. He was an ardent supporter of the Risorgimento, or Italian liberation movement, and many of his early operas had patriotic themes. The most beloved number in *Nabucco* was a nostalgic hymn of the Hebrew slaves in Babylon—a clear reference to the Italians under the heel of the Austrian Empire. In the year of revolution, 1848, Verdi wrote the rousing *Battle of Legnano.* "Verdi" actually became a patriotic acronym for the popular choice for king—Vittorio Emmanuele, *Re d'Italia.* After independence was achieved, the composer was made an honorary deputy in the first Italian parliament.

A dour character and a tough businessman, Verdi drove hard bargains with opera impresarios, bullied his librettists, and insisted on supervising the production of his new operas. When he had accumulated enough money, he retired to a fine country estate near his birthplace and spent his later years hunting and raising livestock. After fifteen years of this life, he was coaxed out of retirement by his canny publisher and by an eminent librettist, Arrigo Boito. In his seventies, Verdi wrote his two greatest operas with Boito on Shakespearean subjects: the tragedy *Otello* and the comedy *Falstaff.*

Verdi's first marriage, to the daughter of his early patron Barezzi, ended when his young wife and two babies died within two years. The composer bore the emotional scars of this tragedy all his life, and it may be that the many moving scenes between fathers and daughters in Verdi's operas served to channel his feelings about fatherhood. He later married a remarkable woman, Giuseppina Strepponi, a singer who had assisted him in his early career and starred in his first success, *Nabucco.* She had been Verdi's mistress for many years.

By the time he died, at the age of eighty-eight, Verdi was a national institution, and he was mourned throughout Italy. Schools closed. Eulogies were delivered in a special session of the senate in Rome. Nearly 300,000 people saw the old man to his grave. His operas remain the most popular of all in the international repertory.

Chief Works: Twenty-four operas, including *Nabucco, Macbeth, Rigoletto, Il trovatore, La traviata, Don Carlo, The Force of Destiny, Aida* ■ Two great Shakespeare operas composed in his seventies, *Otello* and *Falstaff* ■ A Requiem Mass, and a few other choral works; a string quartet

Encore: After *Aida* (Act IV), listen to *Otello* (Act I); *Rigoletto* (Act III).

A popular graffito of the Italian revolution: "Viva VERDI" (meaning "Long live Victor Emmanuel, King of Italy").

"Recitative" is no longer a satisfactory name—though no other name exists—for this action music in Verdi's operas. Highly melodramatic, it is always on the point of merging into a full-fledged melodic style. What distinguishes this music from actual arias is that arias are formally complete and distinct. Unlike passages of Verdian recitative, Verdian arias can be (and often are) extracted and sung separately, as concert numbers.

In arias and duets, the orchestra's role is smaller; here, however, Verdi uses another Romantic resource, that of rich harmonies underpinning melodic high points and climaxes. Many — though by no means all — of Verdi's arias might be described as simple strophic songs in his own exuberant style of Romantic melody. Some of his most famous music consists of timeless tunes such as the tenor aria "La donna è mobile" from *Rigoletto,* the choral hymn "Va pensiero" from *Nabucco,* and the duet "O terra, addio" from *Aida,* which we examine next.

GIUSEPPE VERDI
Aida (1871)

9–12   16–19

*A*ida is one of the most frequently performed of all operas. It includes gorgeous arias — including a tenor favorite, "Celeste Aida" — and grandiose stage display: temples, dancing girls, warriors, even elephants, if available. Egypt is the locale; this work was commissioned for a new opera house in Cairo, for an enormous sum. Egypt was very much in the news at the time, because of a milestone in the history of nineteenth-century capitalism and commerce, the opening of the Suez Canal in 1869. Constructed by a visionary French entrepreneur, this 100-mile freshwater canal created a seafaring trade route from the Mediterranean to India and East Asia, vastly superior to going all the way around Africa.

In view of his commission, Verdi chose an Egyptian subject and wrote some exotic and (as he thought) Egyptian-sounding music. In other hands, perhaps, all this might have been pretty vulgar. But Verdi's arias, display, and exoticism are coupled with an absorbing drama, a drama of credible human beings destroyed by powerful political forces and equally powerful emotions.

Background   The plot of *Aida* is thoroughly romantic (in the amorous sense). A tragic love triangle is acted out against the background of a war between ancient Egypt — controlled by a sinister priesthood — and Ethiopia.

Acts I and II introduce a young Egyptian general, Radames, and a captive Ethiopian slave girl, Aida, who are secretly in love. (The Egyptians don't know that Aida is the daughter of Amonasro, King of Ethiopia.) Unfortunately, Radames has also attracted Amneris, a passionate and jealous Egyptian princess.

In Act III, by a turn of the plot that we need not follow here, Radames is tricked into revealing his country's battle plans to Aida. Amneris discovers their tryst, and in a jealous rage she turns Radames over to the all-powerful priests for judgment as a traitor. Aida escapes in the confusion.

In Act IV Amneris offers to save Radames if he will return her love. To her dismay, he says he would rather die than live without Aida; Amneris realizes too late that she has assured the doom of the man she loves. His trial by the priests, in Act IV, scene i, which she witnesses, is one of the most dramatic scenes in the entire opera. Radames makes no defense and is condemned to be buried alive in a tomb under the temple, sealed in by a huge stone.

Tomb Scene (Act IV, scene ii)   Radames has just been entombed. Verdi called for a stage set divided horizontally: below, a cramped cell containing Radames; above, the Temple of Vulcan, complete with altar, colossal statue of Osiris, and other Egyptian paraphernalia. Although the impact of Verdi's music seldom fails, outside of the theater a special effort is required to envisage the stage and the action, so as to appreciate the full range of Verdi's dramatic art.

" Take great pains with the contrast between the two levels! The lower one is gloomy, with stark colors, bathed in a grey-green light; the temple [above] glows with light, warm colors.

Columns will serve very well to mask the lighting mechanism, which should preferably be gas jets."

Verdi on the visuals in Aida

Recitative The scene opens with quiet, ominous music in the strings—already, in its understated way, a forecast of doom. The first singing consists of three short passages of recitative. Each follows the same general plan. In each recitative passage, simple declamatory singing (with very light orchestral accompaniment) leads to an intense moment of genuine melody, with rich harmonic and orchestral support.

Radames begins singing on a monotone, but works up some emotion when he thinks of Aida and hopes she will be spared knowledge of his fate. Then his more excited second speech is still fragmentary, up to the point when he discovers that Aida has hidden in his tomb to see him once again and die with him. He cries out "You, in this tomb!" on a high note, picking up from an anguished downward scale in the orchestra.

The third recitative passage, Aida's reply, begins simply, over a knell-like orchestral accompaniment. It melts into a beautiful and sensuously harmonized melodic phrase when she tells him she wants to die in his arms.

Ariosos There follow two concise tunelike sections, or *ariosos* (see page 103). In the first of them, sung by Radames, notice the subdued, subservient role of the orchestra. The next arioso is more tuneful yet, with Aida's phrases falling into an almost Classical **a a′ b a′ c** pattern. The harmony is fully Romantic, however, especially in phrase **b**.

Duet (with Chorus) Then Verdi mounts his impressive final scene. At the top level of the stage, priests and priestesses move slowly as they sing a hymn with an exotic, Near Eastern flavor. They are invoking the great god Ptah:

CHORUS OF PRIESTS AND PRIESTESSES (with harp accompaniment)

Im - - menso, immenso Ftha, del mon - - do _ spirito ani - ma - tor ___
Great Ptah, the world's creative spirit

At the bottom level, Aida and Radames begin their final duet, a farewell to the sorrows of earth and a welcome to eternity. It is a famous instance of Verdi's simple and yet expansive melodic style:

Andante

AIDA, then RADAMES

O terra ad - dio addi - o, val - le di pianti,   Sogno di gaudio che in do - lor   sva-nì;   A noi si
Farewell to earth, farewell, vale of tears,   Dream of happiness which vanishes in grief;   The

schiude, si schiude il   ciel, __ si schiude il ciel e l'alme erran - ti ___   Volano al   raggio dell' eter - no dì.
heavens open and our fleeing souls   Escape to the rays of eternal day.

There is an exquisite Romantic harmony at the climax of the melody, in **c** of the **a a′ b a′ c** form—and the final climax, on nearly the highest note in the tenor's range, has to be sung very softly. This gives the melody a uniquely ethereal effect, as befits a couple who are about to die from lack of oxygen.

Other features reinforce this effect: the melodic line that focuses on just a few notes, and the high accompanying haze of string instruments that later swell up ecstatically. We sense that Aida and Radames are already far out of this world, perfectly attuned to each other (they sing the same tune in octaves) in a love that transcends death itself.

Conclusion   Before the final curtain, a figure in mourning enters the temple above the tomb to pray. Drained of all the emotion that she poured out in earlier scenes, Amneris can only whisper on a monotone, "Peace, rest in peace, I pray" *(Pace t'imploro)*. The different psychic states of the characters are made more vivid by simultaneous contrast, a principle we saw at work in Mozart's opera buffa ensembles (see page 211). Amneris's numb grief is set directly against the ecstatic, otherworldly togetherness of Radames and Aida.

High violins take over the duet melody; one can almost visualize the souls of Aida and Radames ascending to "eternal day." And by giving the last words to the chorus of priests—the judges of Radames and the proponents of Egypt's wars—Verdi hands them final responsibility for the threefold tragedy.

LISTEN   Verdi, *Aida,* Tomb Scene, Act IV, scene ii

4   2
9–12   16–19

RECITATIVE: Radames alone, then Aida

Part 1: Radames reflects *Quiet orchestral introduction (strings) sets the mournful mood. Radames sings his first three lines on a monotone. Accompaniment: slow and halting.*

9 16	0:26	Radames:	La fatal pietra sopra me si chiuse;	The fatal stone closes over me;
			Ecco la tomba mia.	This is my tomb.
			Del dì la luce più non vedrò . . .	The light of day I'll never see again.
			Non rivedrò più Aida.	I'll never see Aida.
			Aida, dove sei tu? possa tu almeno	Aida, where are you?
	1:51		Viver felice, e la mia sorte orrenda	Live happily, and never know
			Sempre ignorar!	Of my terrible death.

Part 2: Radames hears a sound *Accompaniment: the rhythm picks up*

	2:04	Radames:	Qual gemito—una larva—un vision . . .	What sound was that? a ghost? a vision?
			No! forma umana è questa . . . Ciel, Aida!	No, a human form . . . Aida!
		Aida:	Son io . . .	Yes . . .
		Radames:	Tu, in questa tomba!	You, in this tomb!

Part 3: Aida explains *Accompaniment: mournful low notes*

	2:43	Aida:	Presago il core della tua condanna,	A presentiment of my heart foretold your sentence;
			In questa tomba che per te s'appriva	This tomb awaited you—
			Io penetrai furtiva,	I hid secretly in it,
			E qui lontana da ogni umano sguardo	And here, far from any human gaze,
			Nelle tue braccia desai morire.	I wanted to die in your arms.

ARIOSO I

10 17	**Radames reacts in despair** *"Con passione"—passionately*			
	3:32	Radames:	Morir! si pura e bella!	Dying, so innocent and beautiful,
			Morir per me d'amore,	Dying, for love of me!
			Degli anni tuoi nel fiore,	So young,
			degli anni tuoi nel fiore fuggir la vita!	so young to give up life!
			T'avea il cielo per l'amor creata,	You were made in heaven for love
			Ed io t'uccido per averti amata!	And I have killed you by loving you!
			No, non morrai, troppo t'amai, troppo	You cannot die! I love you too much,
			sei bella!	you are too beautiful!

ARIOSO II

Aida, "almost in a trance" *Ethereal high strings*

11 **18**	4:49	Aida:	Vedi? di morte l'angelo	See, the angel of death	
			Radiante a noi s'appressa,	Approaches us in radiance,	
			Ne adduce a eterni gaudii	Leading to eternal joys	
			Sovra i suoi vanni d'or.	On his golden wings.	
			Già veggo il ciel dischiudersi;	I see the heavens open;	
			Ivi ogni affano cessa,	Here pain ceases,	
0:40	5:30		Ivi *comincia l'estasi*	Here begins the ecstasy	
			D'un immortal amor.	Of immortal love.	

CHORUS (on the upper stage) with interjections by Radames and Aida
Modal harmonies, harp, and flute

1:13	6:03	Aida:	Triste canto!	Mournful chant!	**Chorus**	*(simultaneously):*
		Radames:	Il tripudio dei sacerdoti . . .	The priestly rites . . .		Immenso Ftha,
		Aida:	Il nostro inno di morte.	Our funeral hymn.		del mondo spirito animator,
		Radames:	Nè le mie forti braccia	All of my strength cannot		noi t'invochiamo.
			Smuovere ti potranno, o fatal pietra!	Move that fatal stone!		
		Aida:	Invan—tutto e finito	In vain—all is finished		Great Ptah,
			Sulla terra per noi.	For us on earth.		the world's creative spirit,
		Radames:	È vero, è vero!	True, it is true.		we invoke thee.

DUET: First Aida, then Radames with Aida *With quiet high strings*

	6:44	Aida and			
		Radames:	O terra, addio, addio, valle di pianti,	Farewell to earth, vale of tears,	
			Sogno di gaudio che in dolor svanì,	Dream of happiness which vanishes in grief;	
			A noi *si schiude* il ciel,	The heavens open,	
			si schiude il ciel e l'alme erranti	And our fleeing souls	
			Volano al raggio dell'eterno dì.	Escape to the rays of eternal day.	

CHORUS (on the upper stage) singing with Aida and Radames
DUET continues: Aida and Radames together (same music) with Amneris and the Chorus

2:39	9:23	Aida and				
		Radames:	O terra addio, addio valle di pianti,		**Chorus**	*(simultaneously):*
			Sogno di gaudio che in dolor svanì,			Immenso Ftha,
			A noi *si schiude* il ciel,			del mondo spirito animator,
			si schiude il ciel e l'alme erranti			noi t'invochiamo.
			Volano al raggio dell'eterno dì.			
4:17	11:02	Amneris:	Pace t'imploro, salma adorata,	Rest in peace, I pray, beloved spirit;		Great Ptah,
			Isi placata, *Isi placata* ti schiuda il ciel,	May Isis, placated, welcome you to		the world's creative spirit,
4:34	11:18		*pace t'imploro, pace . . .*	heaven . . . peace, peace . . .		we invoke thee.

Ends with violins playing the "O terra" tune, Amneris singing "Pace, pace," and the Chorus repeating "Immenso Ftha!"

2 Wagner and Music Drama

Richard Wagner was, after Beethoven, the most influential of all nineteenth-century composers. His strictly musical innovations, in harmony and orchestration, revolutionized instrumental music as well as opera. In terms of opera, Wagner is famous for his novel concept of the "total work of art" (*Gesamtkunstwerk;* see below) and his development of a special operatic technique, that of the "guiding motive" (leitmotiv).

Unlike earlier innovative composers, it seems Wagner could not just compose; he had to develop elaborate theories announcing what art, music, and opera ought to be like. (Indeed, he also theorized about politics and philosophy, with very unhappy results.) Wagner's extreme self-consciousness as an artist was prophetic of attitudes toward art of a later period.

His theory of opera had its positive and negative sides. First, Wagner wanted to do away with all the conventions of earlier opera, especially the

Richard Wagner (1813–1883)

Wagner was born in Leipzig during the turmoil of the Napoleonic Wars; his father died soon afterward. His stepfather was a fascinating actor and writer, and the boy turned into a decided intellectual. Wagner's early interests, literature and music (his idols were Shakespeare and Beethoven), later expanded to include philosophy, mythology, and religion.

As a young man he worked as an opera conductor, and he spent an unhappy year in Paris trying to get one of his works produced at the very important opera house there. The virulent anti-French sentiments in his later writings stemmed from this experience. Back in Germany, he produced the first of his impressive operas, *The Flying Dutchman* and *Tannhäuser*, and wrote *Lohengrin*. Though these works basically adhere to the early Romantic opera style of Carl Maria von Weber, they already hint at the revolutionary ideal for opera that Wagner was pondering.

This he finally formulated after being exiled from Germany (and from a job) as a result of his part in the revolution of 1848–49. He wrote endless articles and books expounding his ideas—ideas that were better known than his later operas, for these were extremely difficult to stage. His book *Opera and Drama* set up the principles for his "music drama" *The Rhinegold*, the first segment of the extraordinary four-evening opera *The Nibelung's Ring*. He also published a vicious essay attacking Felix Mendelssohn, who had just died, and other Jews in music. Fifty years after Wagner's death, his anti-Semitic writings (and his operas) were taken up by the Nazis.

Wagner's exile lasted thirteen years. His fortunes changed dramatically when he gained the support of the young, unstable, and finally mad King Ludwig II of Bavaria. Thanks to Ludwig, Wagner's mature music dramas were at last produced (*The Rhinegold*, completed in 1854, was not produced until 1869). Wagner then promoted the building of a special opera house in Bayreuth, Germany, solely for his music dramas—an amazing concept! These grandiose, slow-moving works are based on myths and characterized by high-flown poetry of his own, a powerful orchestral style, and the use of *leitmotivs* (guiding or leading motives). To this day the opera house in Bayreuth performs only Wagner, and tickets to the yearly Wagner Festival are almost impossible to get.

A hypnotic personality, Wagner was able to spirit money out of many pockets and command the loyalty and affection of many distinguished men and women. His first marriage, to a singer, ended in divorce. His great operatic hymn to love, *Tristan and Isolde*, was created partly in response to his love affair with the wife of one of his patrons. His second wife, Cosima, daughter of Franz Liszt, had been married to an important conductor, Hans von Bülow, who nonetheless remained one of Wagner's strongest supporters. Cosima's diaries tell us about Wagner's moods, dreams, thoughts, and musical decisions, all of which he shared with her. After the death of "the Master," Cosima ruled Bayreuth with an iron hand.

Half con man and half visionary, bad poet and very good musician, Wagner created a storm of controversy in his lifetime that has not died down to this day. He was a major figure in the intellectual life of his time, a thinker whose ideas were highly influential not only in music but also in other arts. In this sense, at least, Wagner was the most important of the Romantic composers.

Chief Works: Early operas: *The Flying Dutchman, Tannhäuser,* and *Lohengrin* ■ Mature "music dramas": *Tristan and Isolde, The Mastersingers of Nuremberg* (a brilliant comedy), *Parsifal,* and *The Nibelung's Ring,* a four-opera cycle consisting of *The Rhinegold, The Valkyrie, Siegfried,* and *The Twilight of the Gods* ■ *Siegfried Idyll,* for small orchestra (based on themes from *Siegfried;* a surprise birthday present for Cosima after the birth of their son, also named Siegfried)

Encore: After selections from *The Valkyrie* listen to "Wotan's Farewell" from the same work (Act III); Prelude and Liebestod (love-death) from *Tristan and Isolde.*

Wagner, Cosima, and their son Siegfried, who followed Cosima as director of the Wagner festivals at Bayreuth.

French and Italian varieties. Opera, he complained, had degenerated from its original form as serious drama in music—Wagner was thinking of ancient Greek drama, which he knew had been sung or at least chanted—into a mere concert in costume. He particularly condemned arias, which were certainly at the heart of Italian opera, as hopelessly artificial. Why should the dramatic action keep stopping to allow for stretches of pretty but undramatic singing?

The Total Work of Art

The positive side of Wagner's program was the development of a new kind of opera in the 1850s, for which he reserved a special name: **music drama.** Music, in these works, shares the honors with poetry, drama, and philosophy—all furnished by Wagner himself—as well as the stage design and acting. Wagner coined the word **Gesamtkunstwerk**, meaning "total work of art," for this powerful concept. He always insisted on the distinction between music drama and ordinary "opera."

Since words and ideas are so important in the *Gesamtkunstwerk*, the music is very closely matched to the words. Yet it is also unrelievedly emotional and intense, as Romantic doctrine required. The dramas themselves deal with weighty philosophical issues, or so at least Wagner and his admirers believed, and they do so under the symbolic cover of medieval German myths and legends.

This use of myths was another Romantic feature, one that strikingly anticipated Freud, with his emphasis on myths (for example, the myth of Oedipus) as embodiments of the deepest unconscious truths. Wagner employed the old romance of Tristan and Iseult, the saga of the Nordic god Wotan, and the Arthurian tale of Sir Perceval to present his views on love, political power, and religion, respectively. Wagner's glorification of Germanic myths in particular made him the semiofficial voice of German nationalism, which in turn paved the way for Hitler.

One of the first great conductors and a superb orchestrator, Wagner raised the orchestra to new importance in opera, giving it a role modeled on Beethoven's symphonies with their motivic development. Leitmotivs (see below) were among the motives he used for this symphonic continuity. The orchestra was no longer used essentially as a support for the singers (which was still the situation, even in Verdi); it was now the orchestra that carried the opera along. Instead of the alternation of recitatives, arias, and ensembles in traditional opera, music drama consisted of one long orchestral web, cunningly woven in with the singing.

Leitmotivs

A **leitmotiv** (guiding, or leading, motive) is a musical motive associated with some person, thing, idea, or symbol in the drama. By presenting and developing leitmotivs, Wagner's orchestra guides the listener through the story.

Leitmotivs are easy to ridicule when they are used mechanically—when, for example, the orchestra obligingly sounds the Sword motive every time the hero reaches for his weapon. On the other hand, leitmotivs can suggest with considerable subtlety what the hero is thinking or feeling even when he is saying something else—or saying nothing. Wagner also became very skillful in thematic transformation, the characteristic variation-like technique of the Romantic composers (see page 252). By transforming the appropriate motives, he could show a person or an idea developing and changing under the impact of dramatic action.

And since, for the Romantics, music was the undisputed language of emotion, leitmotivs—being music—could state or suggest ideas in *emotional* terms, over and above the intellectual terms provided by mere words. This was

> ❝ *Drama* is the most comprehensive work of art; it can only be fully realized when *all the other arts* in their full realization are present in it."
>
> *Wagner pondering the* Gesamtkunstwerk, *1850*

> ❝ The language of music consists only of *feelings* and *impressions.* It expresses to the utmost the emotions . . . independently of the language of words, which has become a purely rational system of communication."
>
> *Wagner in a public letter to his supporters, 1851*

Wagner's theory, a logical outcome of Romantic doctrine about music. Furthermore, the complex web of leitmotivs provided his long music dramas with the thematic unity that Romantic composers sought. On both counts, psychological and technical, leitmotivs were guaranteed to impress audiences of the nineteenth century.

Wagner's *Tristan and Isolde* (1859)

Wagner's first completed music drama was the great love story of Tristan and Isolde, taken from medieval legend. There was already a mystical undertone to the legend, which Wagner, writing the opera's libretto, refined under the sway of Romantic thinking.

The composer was only too pleased to find support in the writings of a contemporary philosopher, Arthur Schopenhauer, who had made his own formulation of the Romantic insight into the central importance of music in emotional life. All human experience, said Schopenhauer, consists either of emotions and drives—which he called "the Will"—or of ideas, morals, and reason, which he downgraded by the term "Appearance." He insisted that the Will always dominates Appearance, and that our only direct, unencumbered sense of it comes through music.

"Through *my* music!" we can almost hear Wagner exclaiming. And in a music drama, what would exemplify the Will better than the strongest human drive that is known, sexual love?

Tristan and Isolde is not just a great love story, then, but something more. It is a drama that presents love as the dominant force in life, one that transcends every aspect of worldly Appearance. Many love stories hint at such transcendence, perhaps, but Wagner's story makes it explicit, on the basis of an actual philosophy that the composer espoused.

The plot shows step by step the growing power of love, and the music—with its hypnotic orchestral web and stirring leitmotivs—grows more and more powerful, too. In Act I, love overpowers Isolde's fierce pride, which had previously made her scorn Tristan as her blood enemy, and also Tristan's chivalry, which had demanded that he escort Isolde safely to her marriage to King Mark of Cornwall, his uncle and liege lord. In Act II, love overcomes the marriage, when the pair meet in the longest unconsummated love scene in all of opera. Their tryst is discovered, and Tristan is mortally wounded—but love overcomes the wound, too. In Act III he simply cannot or will not die until Isolde comes to him from over the seas. Isolde comes; Tristan dies in her arms; she sinks down in rapture and expires also. For both of them, death is not a defeat but an ecstatic expression of love.

At this point (if not earlier) the plot passes the bounds of reality—which was exactly what Wagner wanted to show. Tristan and Isolde, hardly characters anymore but stand-ins for the Will, move in a realm where conventional attitudes, the rules of society, and even life and death have lost their powers. Transcendence is a recurring theme of Romanticism; here passion becomes the ultimate experience, beyond reality. Music, which is itself beyond reality, explores the insecure borderland between love, sensuality, and death.

In Act II of Wagner's opera, Isolde signals Tristan that all is clear for their fatal meeting.

RICHARD WAGNER
The Nibelung's Ring (1848–1874)

Wagner's *Der Ring des Nibelungen* (*The Nibelung's Ring*) is a huge music drama in four parts, stretching over four separate nights of three to five hours each. This work, a quarter-century in the making, surely counts as the supreme example of a Romantic tendency (mentioned on page 251) toward the grandiose. The *Ring* (as it is commonly called) grew so large because of the sprawling material Wagner wanted to cover. It encompasses large portions of the most famous of all Germanic or Norse legends. It involves gods and goddesses, giants and dwarfs, magical prophecies and transformations, a dragon, an invisibility cloak that reminds us of Harry Potter novels — and, in the midst of it all, very human feelings and actions. The *Ring* counts as one of the towering artworks of all time, comparable to the Taj Mahal, the *Iliad* and the *Odyssey,* and Michelangelo's Sistine Chapel (comparisons the megalomaniac Wagner would have enjoyed).

The first night, *Das Rheingold (The Rhine Gold),* shows us events whose consequences will be played out over the following three nights: A precious lump of gold at the bottom of the Rhine River is stolen from its rightful owners, the mermaids of the Rhine, by the dwarf Alberich, and then is taken again from him by the gods. The stolen gold, forged into the ring of Wagner's title by the dwarfs whom Alberich commands, carries with it a curse. It makes all who possess it, even Wotan, the leader of the gods, renounce the love that could save them from its corruption. "Love" is meant here in the broadest sense, to include erotic love, a parent's love for children, and finally human compassion in all its forms.

Over the following three nights of the *Ring* — *Die Walküre (The Valkyrie),* *Siegfried,* and *Götterdämmerung (Twilight of the Gods)* — generations pass. We see the gods, humans, and dwarfs — and a giant, transformed into a dragon — brought to grief by their lust for the gold. An innocent hero, Siegfried, is born who can defy the gods and their corrupt order, but even he dies through treachery arising from everyone else's pursuit of the ring.

Wagner employs all this elaborate mythology to tell a simple modern tale. His basic theme is the moral decline of the world, brought about by greed for money and hunger for power. In the guise of Norse gods, gnomes, and warriors, one group after another of nineteenth-century society is shown destroying itself in the pursuit of gold. Even the renunciation of love entailed in possessing the ring is an allegory, turning the old myth into an indictment of bourgeois biases toward work and discipline and away from emotion.

The English playwright and music critic George Bernard Shaw accurately described the *Ring* as an immense critique by a Romantic artist of the middle-class capitalist values of the day. (The critique might still have something to tell us now.) Wagner was a revolutionary activist in his youth and had been thrown out of Germany as a result (see page 241). This enormous work is one outcome of his early political passions.

The Valkyrie (1851–56), Act I, scene i   *The Valkyrie* is the second of the four nights of the *Ring*. Much of the opera concerns a subplot in the complex machinations of Wagner's tale. This story within a story brings together Siegmund and Sieglinde, two of Wotan's numerous children, a brother and sister separated in early childhood. Their irresistible attraction to each other results in an incestuous union (at the end of Act I), doubly illicit since Sieglinde is already married to Hunding. In Act II Hunding fights a duel with Siegmund.

❝ By the mid-sixties *The Lord of the Rings* [by J.R.R. Tolkien; film trilogy by Peter Jackson, 2001–] was probably the most influential fantasy story in the Western world, occupying the same position *Star Wars* did in the late seventies and Wagner's *Ring* cycle did toward the end of the nineteenth century."

Film critic Marion Gostlyn, 1986

Wotan, for reasons stemming from his fateful involvement with the ring, is powerless to intervene to help his son, and Siegmund is killed—another playing out of the renunciation of love. Sieglinde escapes, however, to bear their child: the hero Siegfried, protagonist of the last two nights of the *Ring*.

The first scene of Act I shows us the meeting of Siegmund and Sieglinde. He stumbles into her dwelling, worn to exhaustion by a pack of enemies pursuing him in a raging thunderstorm. The storm is depicted by the orchestral prelude that opens the work; see our own Prelude on pages 4–6 and listen again to this opening. Siegmund collapses on the hearth to the sound of a leitmotiv we quickly come to associate with him, a descending scale that is a transformed, more emotional version of the scale theme of the storm. This musical connection shows us, directly and without words, that the storm is in Siegmund's soul as much as it is out in the elements.

Sieglinde enters from the back room and is startled, but also curious and concerned, to find a stranger unconscious on her floor. As she bends over him, the violins sound her leitmotiv—it rises up gently and falls back—while cellos underneath continue to play Siegmund's. Wagner's orchestral music has already joined the two characters.

What follows is one of the great portrayals of love at first sight in all of opera. Or nearly at first sight: Siegmund and Sieglinde's attentions are riveted to each other almost from the moment he regains consciousness, but the intensity of their emotional connection grows quickly during this scene. By the time it ends, only about fifteen minutes into the drama, the audience has a pretty clear idea that their union is destined and inevitable.

General Features   Along the way the audience witnesses the primary features of Wagner's revolutionary music drama.

❧   The orchestra, carrying the leitmotivs, plays a role far beyond merely accompanying the singers. It seems to depict for us the characters' thoughts and especially their feelings, even when they are not singing. It yields a sense of psychological depth and complexity in the characters—a sense conveyed, in typical Romantic fashion, more by music than by words.

❧   The leitmotivs hardly ever appear in exactly the same way twice but instead are transformed slightly for each new appearance. In this way their psychological portrayal shifts along with the drama. This probing, shifting depiction of the characters' feelings is one of the hallmarks of Wagnerian drama.

❧   The singers, meanwhile, do not as a rule sing the leitmotivs, and their melodies show none of the tunefulness or lyrical song forms of Verdi's duet from *Aida*. Instead they deliver a free-formed declamation of the words, something like recitative, that blossoms forth now and then to approach tunefulness but never gives way to full-fledged aria.

The First Drink   As Sieglinde leans over him, Siegmund awakes and cries out for a drink. She hurries outside to fill a drinking horn for him. While she does so the orchestra takes over, welling up to a miniature climax before falling back; in its music we still hear the combination of Siegmund's and Sieglinde's leitmotivs. Siegmund drinks, and his eyes fix on Sieglinde for the first time. A new melody grows in the orchestra, warmly scored for solo cello and other low strings, and richly harmonized. It is the leitmotiv of their blossoming love: Now the characters exchange information, for their benefit and the audience's.

Stage directors and designers have no hesitation about altering the original concept or milieu of an opera, especially with a work as myth-laden as *The Valkyrie*. *Above:* costume sketches for Siegmund and Sieglinde as conceived by Wagner. *Below:* Act I in a 2003 production. Compare this stage set with the traditional one shown on page 6.

SOLO CELLO

very tenderly

Sieglinde tells him that she is Hunding's wife; he tells her how he came to her home. (When he mentions the storm, the scale theme from the opera's prelude makes another appearance.) He speaks finally of the relief from his misery she has brought him: "Now the sun smiles on me anew."

The Second Drink   At this, Sieglinde spontaneously hurries to her storeroom to fill a horn with honeyed mead for him. This action, an intensified version of her fetching water earlier, summons from the orchestra an intensified version of the climax it had risen to then. Listen to and compare the similar music of these two passages, the first and second orchestral climaxes referred to in the listening guide on pages 291–92.

14,16 21,23

The lovers share the mead, their eyes now fixed on each other, and the love motive sounding in the orchestra also intensifies—until Siegmund rouses himself with a deep sigh accompanied in the orchestra by a loud dissonant chord. He is ill-fated, misfortune follows wherever he goes (Wagner sets the crucial, repeated word *Misswende* to additional dissonant chords), and he would not for the world bring such misery on her (Love motive); he must leave. Sieglinde cannot let him go. She stops him in his tracks with an impulsive and intimate confidence: She is as ill-fated as he!

Communion   At Sieglinde's last word a hesitant new melody begins low in the orchestra, one clearly meant to be interpreted as an affirmation of the deep empathy they already feel for each other. It is played first in sequence—a favorite Wagnerian technique for developing his leitmotivs. Then, when Siegmund announces he will stay, the orchestra cannot restrain itself; it pours forth a lush, Romantic harmonization of the new melody, the soon-to-be lovers regarding each other all the while. If you listen carefully, you can hear other leitmotivs in this beautiful passage: First Sieglinde's, later the Love motive, and at the end Siegmund's drooping scale.

Sorrow/empathy Motive

The passage comes to no cadence—another favorite trick of Wagner's—but is cut off by a new, brusque leitmotiv in the low brasses, contrasting with everything we have heard so far. It announces Hunding's return, and with it the beginning of the second scene.

Wagner's drama often moves at an enormous, slow pace, and it has sometimes been criticized for this. (And lampooned, too; there is a Bugs Bunny cartoon in which the *Ring* is reduced to three minutes of singing and action.) In the first scene of *The Valkyrie* we have the sense that searching looks, eyes meeting or avoiding one another, and sighs are stretched out to great length—a length that is almost painful for impatient, push-ahead listeners. Action is at a minimum; other than Sieglinde's fetching two drinks for Siegmund, the scene contains very little conventional stage action at all. At the same time, however, especially because of his orchestra with its leitmotivs, Wagner manages to pack a lot into the minimal gestures of his characters. By the end of scene i, barely a quarter hour into the drama, we have been introduced to two protagonists and gained knowledge of their history and a subtle sense of their emotional lives. And, before our eyes and ears, they have fallen in love.

❝ *Monday, July 17* First act of *Valkyrie,* Fräulein Scheffsky [Sieglinde] terrible! Herr Niemann [Siegmund] does it well. R. very tired, little demand for seats. *Tuesday, July 18* Second act of *Valkyrie,* Frl. Scheffsky even more horrible; at lunch an excess of ungainliness and gracelessness! Conference over whether to get rid of her. . . .

—*from the 2000-page* Diary of Cosima Wagner: *rehearsals for the premiere* of The Nibelung's Ring *at Bayreuth, 1876*

))) | **LISTEN** | **Wagner, *The Valkyrie*, Act I, scene i**

4 2
13–18 20–25

The inside of a dwelling, built around a huge ash tree in its midst; to the right a hearth, and behind it an inner storeroom. Siegmund, exhausted, enters from outside as the storm subsides.

13 20	0:09	**Siegmund:** Wess' Herd dies auch sei, hier muss ich rasten	Whoever's hearth this may be, I must rest here.

He sinks back and lies motionless. Sieglinde enters, thinking her husband has returned; she is surprised to find instead a stranger. Hesitantly she approaches him closer and closer.

Siegmund Motive

		Sieglinde: Ein fremder Mann?	A stranger here?
		Ihn muss ich fragen.	I must ask him:
		Wer kam ins Haus	Who has come into this house
		und liegt dort am Herd?	and lies on the hearth?
		Müde liegt er von Weges Müh'n:	He's weary and travel-worn.
	1:31	schwanden die Sinne ihm?	Is he unconscious?
		Wäre er siech?	Could he be sick?
		Noch schwillt ihm der Atem;	No, he is still breathing;
		das Auge nur schloss er.	he's only sleeping.
		Mutig dünkt mich der Mann,	He seems to me valiant,
		sank er müd' auch hin.	even though he's exhausted.

Sieglinde Motive

		Siegmund: *(suddenly raises his head)* Ein Quell! Ein Quell!	A drink! A drink!
		Sieglinde: Erquickung schaff' ich.	I'll bring some water.

14 21	2:17	**FIRST ORCHESTRAL CLIMAX**

She quickly takes a drinking horn and goes out. She returns with the horn filled and offers it to Siegmund.

	Labung biet' ich dem lechzende Gaumen: Wasser, wie du gewollt!	Moisten your dry lips with this drink I've brought: water, as you wished!

1:04	3:32	*Siegmund drinks and gives the horn back. As he nods his head in thanks, his eyes fix on her face with growing interest.*

Love Motives

2:14	4:32	**Siegmund:** Kühlende Labung	The water brings me
		gab mir der Quell,	cooling relief;
		des Müden Last	it lightens
		machte er leicht;	my weary load;
		erfrischt ist der Mut	my heart is refreshed,
		das Aug' erfreut	my eyes relish
		des Sehens selige Lust.	a beautiful, glorious sight.
		Wer ist's, der so mir es labt?	Who is it who so revives me?

15 22	5:34	**Sieglinde:** Dies Haus un dies Weib	This house and this wife
		sind Hundings Eigen;	belong to Hunding;
		gastlich gönn' er dir Rast:	he'll welcome you as guest;
		harre, bis heim er kehrt!	wait here until he returns!

		Siegmund: Waffenlos bin ich:	I am weaponless;
		dem wunden Gast	a wounded guest will
		wird dein Gatte nicht wehren.	not threaten your husband.

	Sieglinde: Die Wunden weise mir schnell!	You're wounded? Where?

0:30	6:04	**Siegmund:** Gering sind sie,	It's nothing,
		der Rede nicht wert;	pay no heed;
		noch fügen des Leibes	my body is still
		Glieder sich fest.	strongly knit.
		Hätten halb so stark wie mein Arm	If my shield and spear had been
		Schild und Speer mir gehalten,	half as strong as my body,
		nimmer floh ich dem Feind;	I never would have fled my foe.
		doch zerschellten mir	But spear and shield
		Speer und Schild.	were shattered;

0:50	6:24	Der Feinde Meute hetzte mich müd', Gewitterbrunst brach meinen Leib; doch schneller, als ich der Meute, schwand die Müdigkeit mir; sank auf die Lider mir Nacht, die Sonne lacht mir nun neu.	the horde of enemies chased me down, the thunderstorm broke body and spirit; but now—faster than I fled my weariness flees from me! Darkness sank on my eyes, but now the sun smiles on me anew!	Storm Motive

<table>
<tr><td>16
23</td><td>7:01</td><td colspan="3">SECOND ORCHESTRAL CLIMAX
Sieglinde goes to the storeroom and fills a horn with mead; she returns and offers it to Siegmund.</td></tr>
<tr><td></td><td></td><td>Sieglinde:</td><td>Des seimigen Metes süssen Trank
mög'st du mir nicht verschmähn.</td><td>Surely you'll not refuse
a sweet drink of honeyed mead.</td></tr>
<tr><td></td><td></td><td>Siegmund:</td><td>Schmecktest du mir ihn zu?</td><td>Would you not taste it first?</td></tr>
</table>

17 24	8:06		**LOVE MOTIVES RETURN**	

*Sieglinde drinks from the horn and gives it back. Siegmund takes a long drink, watching her all the while with growing warmth. At **1:06** he sighs deeply and his eyes sink to the ground.*

		Siegmund:	Einen Unseligen labtest du: Unheil wende der Wunsch von dir! Gerastet hab' ich und süss geruht: weiter wend ich den Schritt.	You've helped an unhappy man; may I keep Ill-fate from you! I have rested—rested sweetly; now I must go on my way.
		Sieglinde:	Wer verfolgt dich, dass du schon fliehst?	Who follows you, making you flee?
1:55	10:01	Siegmund:	Misswende folgt mir, wohin ich fliehe; Misswende naht mir, wo ich mich zeige.	Ill-fate follows me, wherever I run; Ill-fate approaches, wherever I linger.
2:29	10:35		Dir, Frau, doch bleibe sie fern! Fort wende ich Fuss und Blick.	You, wife, keep your distance! I must turn my path from you.

He turns to leave. She calls after him impetuously.

Sorrow/empathy Motive

18 25	10:48	Sieglinde:	So bleibe hier! Nicht bringst du Unheil dahin, wo Unheil im Hause wohnt!	No, remain here! Ill-fate is nothing new here, where Ill-fate makes its home!

He turns back, looks searchingly at her; she lowers her eyes in sadness and shame.

		Siegmund:	Wehwalt hiess ich mich selbst: Hunding will ich erwarten.	I myself named me Wehwalt— Woebound; I'll wait for Hunding.

EMPATHY MOTIVE DEVELOPED

Hunding Motive

*He rests against the hearth, his eyes fixed on her; she raises her eyes to his, and they regard each other with deep emotion. At **2:08** Sieglinde starts as she hears Hunding outside.*

bedfordstmartins.com/listen
▶ Quizzes and Flashcards

CHAPTER 18

The Late Romantics

The year 1848 in Europe was a year of failed revolutions in France, Italy, and in various of the German states. Political freedom, which for the Romantics went hand in hand with freedom of personal expression in life and art, seemed further away than ever. While not all the early Romantics lived in free societies, at least by today's standards, freedom was an ideal they could take seriously as a hope for the future. We recall Beethoven's enthusiasm for Napoleon as a revolutionary hero, reflected in the *Eroica* Symphony of 1803, one of the landmarks of nineteenth-century music. In the 1820s, artists and intellectuals thrilled to the personal role of one of them—Lord Byron, a poet— in the struggle for Greek independence. Then they lamented his death near the field of battle.

But the failure of the revolutions of 1848 symbolized the failure of so many Romantic aspirations. In truth, those aspirations had had little to nourish them since the days of Napoleon. Romanticism lived on, but it lived on as nostalgia.

The year 1848 is also a convenient one to demarcate the history of nineteenth-century music. Some of the greatest early Romantic composers—Mendelssohn, Chopin, and Schumann—died between the years 1847 and 1856. By a remarkable coincidence of history, too, the 1848 revolution transformed the career of Richard Wagner. Exiled from Germany for revolutionary activity, he had no opera house to compose for. Instead he turned inward and—after a long period of philosophical and musical reflection—worked out his revolutionary musical ideas. Wagner's music dramas, written from the 1850s on, came to dominate the imagination of musicians in the second part of the century, much as Beethoven's symphonies had in the first part.

Romanticism and Realism

European literature and art from the 1850s on was marked not by continuing Romanticism, but by realism. The novel, the principal literary genre of the time, grew more realistic from Dickens to Trollope and George Eliot in Britain, and from Balzac to Flaubert and Zola in France. In French painting, there was an important realist school led by Gustave Courbet. Thomas Eakins was a realist painter in America; William Dean Howells was our leading realist novelist. Most important as a stimulus to realism in the visual arts was that powerful new invention, the camera.

Realists in the arts of the nineteenth century tended toward glum or grim subject matter. The Philadelphia artist Thomas Eakins was so fascinated by surgery that he painted himself in among the students attending a class by a famous medical professor, Dr. S. D. Gross *(The Gross Clinic,* 1875).

There was a move toward realism in opera at the end of the nineteenth century, in France as well as in Italy. On the other hand, the myth-drenched music dramas of Wagner were as unrealistic as could be. (Wagner thought he was getting at a deeper, psychological realism.) And what would "realism" in orchestral music be like? Given music's nature, it was perhaps inevitable that late nineteenth-century music assumed a sort of inspirational and emotional escape function—an escape from political, economic, and social situations that were not romantic in the least.

Perhaps, too, music serves a similar function for many listeners of the twenty-first century. Significantly, concert life as we know it today, with its emphasis on great masterpieces of the past, was formed for the first time in the late nineteenth century.

1 Late Romantic Program Music

Late Romantic program music took its impetus from an important series of works called *symphonic poems,* composed in the 1850s by Franz Liszt. A **symphonic poem** is a one-movement orchestral composition with a program, in a free musical form. By using the word *poem,* Liszt insisted on the music's programmatic nature.

It is not often that a great virtuoso pianist such as Liszt, who started out composing études and other miniatures of the kind cultivated by Chopin and Schumann, turns himself into a major composer of large-scale orchestral works. Liszt's formula was simply to write a one-movement piece for orchestra associated in one way or another with a famous poem, play, or narrative. Unlike a Berlioz program symphony, a symphonic poem is in one movement, and unlike a Mendelssohn concert overture, it is not in sonata form or some clear derivative of sonata form. Symphonic poems, so-called or under some other name, became very popular in the later nineteenth century.

Among Liszt's symphonic poems are *Hamlet, Orpheus, Prometheus,* and *Les Préludes,* the latter loosely connected with a poem by the French Romantic poet Alphonse de Lamartine. But except for *Les Préludes,* these works are heard less often today than other symphonic poems written by composers influenced by Liszt's example. The most popular of later symphonic poems are those by Pyotr Ilyich Tchaikovsky and Richard Strauss (see page 354).

PYOTR ILYICH TCHAIKOVSKY
Overture-Fantasy, *Romeo and Juliet* (1869, revised 1880)

19–30   1–12

Tchaikovsky wrote several symphonic poems, including one on a subject already used by Liszt and Berlioz, Shakespeare's *Hamlet.* Rather than "symphonic poem," he preferred the descriptions "symphonic fantasia" or "overture-fantasy" for these works. They are lengthy pieces in one movement, with free forms adopting some features from sonata form, rondo, and so on.

In his *Romeo and Juliet,* Tchaikovsky followed the outlines of the original play only in a very general way, but one can easily identify his main themes with elements in Shakespeare's drama. The surging, romantic string melody clearly stands for the love of Romeo and Juliet. The angry, agitated theme suggests the vendetta between their families, the Capulets and the Montagues. More generally, it suggests the fate that dooms the two "star-cross'd lovers," as Shakespeare calls them. The hymnlike theme heard at the very beginning of the piece (later it sounds more marchlike) seems to denote the kindly Friar Laurence, who devises a plan to help the lovers that goes fatally wrong.

Slow Introduction   The slow introduction of *Romeo and Juliet* is already heavy with drama. As low clarinets and bassoons play the sober Hymn theme, the strings answer with an anguished-sounding passage forecasting an unhappy outcome. The wind instruments utter a series of solemn announcements, interspersed by strumming on the harp, as though someone (Friar Laurence?) was preparing to tell the tale. This sequence of events is repeated, with some variation, and then both the woodwind and string themes are briefly worked up to a climax over a dramatic drum roll.

> 66 The kernel of a new work usually appears suddenly, in the most unexpected fashion . . . All the rest takes care of itself. I could never put into words the joy that seizes me when the main idea has come and when it begins to assume definite shape. You forget everything, you become a madman for all practical purposes, your insides quiver . . . "
>
> *Tchaikovsky writes to Mme. von Meck about his composing, 1878*

Pyotr Ilyich Tchaikovsky (1840–1893)

Tchaikovsky was born in the Russian countryside, the son of a mining inspector, but the family moved to St. Petersburg when he was eight. In nineteenth-century Russia, a serious musical education and career were not accorded the social approval they received in Germany, France, or Italy. Many of the famous Russian composers began in other careers and only turned to music later in life, when driven by inner necessity.

Tchaikovsky was fortunate in this respect, for after working as a government clerk for only a few years, he was able to enter the brand-new St. Petersburg Conservatory, founded by another Russian composer, Anton Rubinstein. At the age of twenty-six he was made a professor at the Moscow Conservatory. Once Tchaikovsky got started, after abandoning the civil service, he composed prolifically — six symphonies, eleven operas, symphonic poems, chamber music, songs, and some of the most famous of all ballet scores: *Swan Lake, Sleeping Beauty,* and *The Nutcracker.* Listen to a dance from *Nutcracker* on the Companion DVD.

Though his pieces may sometimes sound "Russian" to us, Tchaikovsky was not as devoted a nationalist as some other major Russian composers of the time (see page 299). Perhaps because of this, he had greater international renown than they. Of all the nineteenth-century Russian composers, Tchaikovsky had the most success in concert halls around the world. His famous Piano Concerto No. 1 was premiered in 1875 in Boston, and he toured America as a conductor in 1891.

Tchaikovsky was a depressive personality who more than once attempted suicide. He had been an extremely delicate and hypersensitive child, and as an adult he worried that his homosexuality would be discovered and exposed.

In an attempt to raise himself above suspicion, he married a highly unstable young musician who was in love with him. The marriage was a fiasco; in a matter of weeks, Tchaikovsky fled and never saw his wife again. She died in an asylum.

For many years Tchaikovsky was subsidized by a wealthy, reclusive widow named Nadezhda von Meck. She not only commissioned compositions from him but actually granted him an annuity. By mutual agreement, they never met; nevertheless, they exchanged letters regularly over the thirteen years of their friendship. This strange arrangement was terminated, without explanation, by Madame von Meck.

By this time Tchaikovsky's position was assured, and his music widely admired. By a tragic mishap, he died after drinking unboiled water during a cholera epidemic.

Chief Works: Symphonies No. 4, 5, and 6 *(Pathétique)*; a very popular Violin Concerto and Piano Concerto ▪ Operas: *The Queen of Spades* and *Eugene Onegin,* based on works by the Russian Romantic poet Alexander Pushkin ▪ Symphonic poems: *Romeo and Juliet, Hamlet, Overture 1812* (about Napoleon's retreat from Russia in that year) ▪ Ballet scores: *Swan Lake, Sleeping Beauty, The Nutcracker*

Encore: After *Romeo and Juliet,* listen to the *Nutcracker* Suite; Symphony No. 4; Violin Concerto.

Allegro   The tempo changes to allegro, and we hear the Vendetta or Fate theme. It is made up of a number of short, vigorous rhythmic motives, which Tchaikovsky at once begins to develop. Then the Vendetta theme returns in a climax punctuated by cymbal claps.

The highly romantic Love theme (illustrated on page 247) is first played only in part, by the English horn and violas — a mellow sound. It is halted by a curious but affecting passage built out of a little sighing figure:

After the Love theme dies down at some length, a lively development section begins (a feature suggesting sonata form). Confronted by various motives from the Vendetta theme, the Hymn theme takes on a marchlike character. We may get the impression of a battle between the forces of good and evil.

LISTENING CHART 17

Tchaikovsky, Overture-Fantasy, *Romeo and Juliet*

18 min., 39 sec.

INTRODUCTION (Andante)

19 1	0:00	**Hymn theme**	Low woodwinds, *pp*
	0:34	**String motives**	Anguished quality; contrapuntal
	1:26	**Strumming harp**	With "announcements" in the high woodwinds
20 2	2:07	**Hymn theme**	High woodwinds with pizzicato strings. Followed by the string motives and harp; the "announcements" are now in the strings.
1:50	3:57	**Buildup**	Ends with drum roll, *f*
21 3	4:31	**Preparation**	Prepares for the main section; *p,* then *crescendo*

MAIN SECTION (Allegro)

22 4	5:01	**Vendetta theme**	Full orchestra, *f*
0:21	5:23		Development of the Vendetta theme; contrapuntal
0:46	5:47		Reaches a climax: cymbals
0:57	5:59	**Vendetta theme**	Full orchestra, *ff*
1:17	6:18		Relaxes, in a long slowdown
1:57	6:58		Prefatory statement of Love theme (English horn): phrase **a**
23 5	7:13		"Sighing" theme; muted strings, *pp*
24 6	7:52	**Love theme**	Form is **a b a**, in woodwinds, with the sighing motive played by the French horn.
0:59	8:51		Harp. Cadences; the music dies down and nearly stops.

DEVELOPMENT

25 7	9:52	**Developmental combination**	Vendetta theme fragments are combined with the Hymn theme, which now sounds more like a march than a hymn.
26 8	11:07		This works up to a climax, marked by a cymbal clash.
0:23	11:30	**Hymn theme**	Played by trumpets; syncopated rhythm in the cymbals

CYMBALS

FREE RECAPITULATION (abbreviated)

27 9	11:58	**Vendetta theme**	Full orchestra, *ff*
0:23	12:21		Sighing theme
1:00	12:58	**Love theme**	**a b a**; ecstatically in the strings, with the sighing motive again in the French horn; the last **a** is *ff.*
28 10	14:01		Fragments of the Love theme
0:25	14:26	**(Love theme)**	Sounds like another ecstatic statement, but is interrupted
0:35	14:36		Interruption by the Vendetta theme: conflict! Cymbals
0:49	14:50	**Developmental combination**	Vendetta theme fragments combined with the Hymn theme; Build up to *fff*
1:21	15:22		Then dies down, rather unwillingly; ends on drum roll, *f*

CODA (Moderato)

29 11	15:59	**Love theme**	A broken version of the Love theme, with muffled funeral drums. The music seems to be ending.
30 12	16:37	**New theme**	Woodwinds; ends with a transformation of the sighing motive
1:06	17:43	**Love theme**	Section **a** in a slow cadential "transcendent" version. The strumming harp of the slow introduction has returned.
1:40	18:17		Final cadences; a drum roll and solemn ending gestures

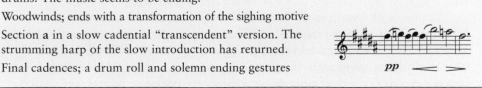

A famous Juliet of Tchaikovsky's time: Mrs. Patrick Campbell in an 1895 London production of Shakespeare's play.

The Vendetta theme returns in its original form (suggesting a sonata-form recapitulation). The sighing motive and the lengthy Love theme also return, but the end of the latter is now broken up and interrupted—a clear reference to the tragic outcome of the drama. At one last appearance, the Vendetta theme is joined more explicitly than before with the Hymn theme.

Coda (slow)   A fragment of the Love theme appears in a broken version over funeral drum taps in the timpani. This must depict the pathos of Romeo's final speeches, where he refers to his love before taking poison. A new, slow theme in the woodwinds is really a transformation of the sighing motive heard earlier.

But the mood is not entirely gloomy; as the harp strumming is resumed, the storyteller seems to derive solace and inspiration from his tale. Parts of the Love theme return in a beautiful new cadential version, surging enthusiastically upward in a way that is very typical of Tchaikovsky. Doesn't this ecstatic surge suggest that even though Romeo and Juliet are dead, their love is timeless— that their love transcends death? The influence of Wagner's *Tristan and Isolde* (see page 286) was felt here as everywhere in the later nineteenth century.

bedfordstmartins.com/listen
▶ Interactive Listening Chart 17

2 Nationalism

One legacy of Romanticism's passion for freedom played itself out all through the nineteenth century: the struggle for national independence. The Greeks struggled against the Turks, the Poles rose up against Russia, the Czechs revolted against Austria, and Norway broke free of Sweden.

As people all over Europe became more conscious of their national characters, they also came to prize their distinctive artistic heritages more and more. This gave rise to a musical movement, **nationalism** in music. The characteristic feature of this movement is simply the incorporation of national folk music into concert pieces, songs, and operas. Symphonic poems or operas were based

"The art of music is above all other arts the expression of the soul of a nation. The composer must love the tunes of his country and they must become an integral part of him."

Nationalist composer Ralph Vaughan Williams

on programs or librettos that took up national themes — a hero of history such as Russia's Prince Igor; a national literary treasure such as the Finnish Lemminkaïnen legends; even a beloved river such as the Vltava (Moldau) in Bohemia. Such national themes were reinforced by actual musical themes taken from folk song. The result was music that stirred strong emotions at home, and often made an effective ambassador abroad.

Although in the nineteenth century political nationalism was certainly a major factor all over Europe, composers in Germany, Italy, and France are not categorized with the musical nationalists. For musical nationalism also strove to make local music independent of Europe's traditional cultural leaders. Nationalist composers often deliberately broke the traditional rules of harmony, form, and so on. They did this both in a spirit of defiance and also in an effort to develop new, genuinely local musical styles.

Exoticism

Audiences came to enjoy hearing folk music at symphony concerts, whether it was their own folk music or somebody else's. We have seen that Verdi wrote Egyptian music, in the priest's hymn in *Aida*. French composers wrote Spanish music, Russians wrote Italian music, and Czechs wrote American music (George Bizet's opera *Carmen,* Tchaikovsky's orchestra piece *Capriccio Italien,* and Antonín Dvořák's famous *New World* Symphony, with its reference to spirituals). Such music cannot be called nationalistic, since its aim was not national self-definition. Perhaps the best name for it is "exotic."

Yet even this nonpolitical, exotic music had the effect of emphasizing the unique qualities of nations. In the later nineteenth century, Romantic individuality had become a national ideal as much as a personal one.

The Russian *Kuchka*

A close group of five Russian nationalist composers were nicknamed (by one of their critic friends) the *kuchka* — sometimes translated as the "Mighty Five," but actually meaning a group or clique. They were an interesting and

Nationalism: for Finland chafing under the rule of Russia, the epic poem *Kalevala* became a nationalist icon, drawn upon again and again by composer Jean Sibelius as well as the Finnish painter Akseli Gallen-Kallela. In our picture, Kullervo, one of the saga's heroes, rides off to war; *Kullervo* by Sibelius is a grandiose symphonic poem.

exceptionally talented group—even though they included only one trained musician, Mily Balakirev (1837–1910). Alexander Borodin (1833–1887) was a distinguished chemist, César Cui (1835–1918) an engineer, Nikolai Rimsky-Korsakov (1844–1908) a navy man, and Modest Musorgsky (1839–1881) an officer in the Russian Imperial Guard.

What held this group together was their determination to make Russian music "Russian," their deep interest in collecting folk song, and their commitment to self-improvement as composers, relatively late in life.

MODEST MUSORGSKY
Pictures at an Exhibition (1874)

31–34 26–29

The title of this interesting work refers to a memorial exhibit of pictures by a friend of Musorgsky's who had recently died, the Russian painter Victor Hartmann. Like Musorgsky, Hartmann cared deeply about getting Russian themes into his work. *Pictures at an Exhibition* was originally written for piano solo, as a series of piano miniatures joined in a set, like Robert Schumann's *Carnaval*. In 1922 the set was orchestrated by the French composer Maurice Ravel, and this is the form in which it has since become popular.

31
26
Promenade [1]   To provide some overall thread or unity to a set of ten different musical pieces, Musorgsky hit upon a plan that is as simple and effective as it is ingenious. The first number, "Promenade," does not refer to a picture, but depicts the composer strolling around the picture gallery. The same music returns several times in free variations, to show the promenader's changes of mood as he contemplates Hartmann's varied works.

The promenade theme recalls a Russian folk song:

Ravel orchestrated this forceful theme first for brass instruments, later for woodwinds and strings. Quintuple meter (**5/4**: measures 1, 3, and 5) is a distinct rarity, and having this meter alternate with **6/4** (measures 2, 4, and 6) rarer still. The metrical anomaly gives the impression of blunt, unsophisticated folk music—and perhaps also of walking back and forth without any particular destination, as one does in a gallery.

32
27
Gnomus   "Gnomus" is a drawing of a Russian folk-art nutcracker. The gnome's jaws crack the nut when his legs (the handles) are pulled together; the same grotesque figure, which could frighten a little child, comes to life and dances in Tchaikovsky's well-known Christmas ballet *The Nutcracker*. Musorgsky writes music that sounds suitably macabre, with a lurching rhythm to illustrate the gnome's clumsy walk on his handle-legs, and striking dissonant harmonies.

The lurching rhythms and dissonance of "Gnomus" and the **5/4** meter of "Promenade" are among the features of Musorgsky's music that break with the norms of mainstream European art music, in a self-consciously nationalistic spirit.

33
28
Promenade [2]   Quieter now, the promenade music suggests that the spectator is musing as he moves along . . . and we can exercise our stroller's prerogative and skip past a number of Hartmann's pictures, pictures that are not nationalistic in a Russian sense. Some refer to other peoples, and Musorgsky

The Great Gate at Kiev

follows suit, writing music we would call exotic: "Bydlo," which is the name of a Polish cattle-cart, and "Il Vecchio Castello," Hartmann's Italian title for a conventional painting of a medieval castle, complete with a troubadour serenading his lady.

34
29

The Great Gate at Kiev The last and longest number is also the climactic one. It illustrates — or, rather, spins a fantasy inspired by — a fabulous architectural design by Hartmann that was never executed.

Musorgsky summons up in the imagination a solemn procession with clashing cymbals, clanging bells, and chanting Russian priests. The Promenade theme is now at last incorporated into one of the musical pictures; the promenader himself has become a part of it and joins the parade. In addition, two real Russian melodies appear:

The ending is very grandiose, for grandiosity forms an integral part of the national self-image of Russia—and, unfortunately, of many other nations.

Modest Musorgsky (1839–1881)

Musorgsky (pronounced MOO-sorgsky) was the son of a well-to-do landowner. The social class into which he was born dictated that he become an officer in the Russian Imperial Guard. Musorgsky duly went to cadet school and joined a regiment after graduation, but he could not long ignore his deep-seated desire to become a composer.

In the meantime, the emancipation of the serfs and other political and economic changes in Russia caused the liquidation of his family estate. For a time Musorgsky tried to help run the family affairs, but in his twenties he was obliged to work at a clerical job. Meanwhile, he experimented with musical composition, struggling to master the technique of an art that he had come to late in life. It was around this time that he joined the circle of Russian nationalist composers that was dubbed the *kuchka* (the Group; see page 299).

Musorgsky never felt secure in his technique and relied on his skillful *kuchka* friend, Nikolai Rimsky-Korsakov, to criticize his work. But his intense nationalism formed his vision of what he wanted his work to be— truly Russian music. His masterpiece, the opera *Boris Godunov*, is based on the story of the sixteenth-century tsar as told by the great Russian poet Alexander Pushkin.

It hardly had the success it deserved when it was finally revised and performed in St. Petersburg. Indeed, this and other works by Musorgsky only succeeded some time later, after their orchestration had been touched up (some say glamorized) by Rimsky-Korsakov.

Musorgsky led a rather grim life; his was a personality filled with self-doubts, and his instability was a constant concern to his friends. He became an alcoholic early in life. Musorgsky died of alcoholism and epilepsy in an army hospital at the age of forty-two.

Chief Works: Operas: *Boris Godunov* and *Khovanschina* ■ Orchestral program compositions: *Pictures at an Exhibition* (originally for piano) and *Night on Bald Mountain* ■ Songs, including the very impressive song cycles *The Nursery* and *Songs and Dances of Death*

Encore: After *Pictures*, listen to *Boris Godunov*, Coronation Scene (scene ii).

3 Responses to Romanticism

At the beginning of this chapter, we remarked that European art and literature after the 1850s were marked not by continuing Romanticism, but by realism, which was in fact a reaction against Romanticism. In music, an art that can hardly be realistic in the usual sense, the anti-Romantic reaction came later— at a time when realism was no longer an ideal in the other arts.

After 1850, music continued to develop along Romantic lines but came to seem out of phase with a no-nonsense world increasingly devoted to industrialization and commerce. In the world of Victorian morality, people devoted to the work ethic denied themselves and others the heady emotion that the Romantics had insisted on conveying in their art. There is probably some truth to the contention that late nineteenth-century music assumed the function of a sort of never-never land of feeling. Music was an emotional fantasy world for a society that placed a premium on the suppression of feeling in real life.

The work of the two greatest late nineteenth-century German composers can be viewed in terms of their responses to this situation. Johannes Brahms, though a devoted young friend of Robert Schumann, one of the most Romantic of composers, turned back to the Classicism of the Viennese masters. Evidently he saw this as a way of tempering the unbridled emotionalism of Romanticism, which he expressed only in a mood of restraint and resignation.

A younger composer, Gustav Mahler, reacted differently. Lament was his mode, rather than resignation; his music expresses an intense, bittersweet nostalgia for a Romanticism that seems to have lost its innocence, even its credibility. The lament for this loss is almost clamorous in Mahler's songs and symphonies.

Other Nationalists

Nationalism enjoyed new life after 1900. Some of the most impressive nationalists were also among the earliest modernists, among them Béla Bartók in Hungary and Charles Ives in the United States. We examine this new nationalism in Chapters 20 and 21, restricting ourselves here to a listing of some of the main late-Romantic nationalists outside of Russia.

⁊ *Bohemia* Bohemia, as the Czech Republic was then called, produced two eminent national composers: Bedřich Smetana (1824–1884), who wrote the symphonic poem *Vltava* (The Moldau) and the delightful folk opera *The Bartered Bride,* and Antonín Dvořák (1841–1904), composer of the popular *Slavonic Dances* as well as important symphonies and other large-scale works. Dvořák also spurred nationalist music in a distant land he visited—the United States of America. See page 395.

⁊ *Scandinavia* The Norwegian composer Edvard Grieg (1843–1907) wrote sets of piano miniatures with titles such as *Norwegian Mountain Tunes*, which were very popular at the time; also a well-known suite of music for *Peer Gynt*, the great drama by the Norwegian playwright Henrik Ibsen.

Jean Sibelius (1865–1957), a powerful late-Romantic symphonist, produced a series of symphonic poems on the folklore of his native Finland: *The Swan of Tuonela, Kullervo, Finlandia,* and others.

⁊ *Spain* Among Spanish nationalists were Enrique Granados (1867–1916), Joaquín Turina (1882–1949), and Manuel de Falla (1876–1946), best known for his *Nights in the Gardens of Spain* for piano and orchestra. Spain was a favorite locale for exotic compositions with a Spanish flavor written by Frenchmen—among them Bizet's opera *Carmen* and orchestral pieces by Emmanuel Chabrier *(España)*, Claude Debussy *(Ibéria)*, and Maurice Ravel *(Boléro)*.

⁊ *Great Britain* The major English nationalist in music was Ralph Vaughan Williams (1872–1958). His *Fantasia on a Theme by Thomas Tallis* is a loving meditation on a psalm tune that was written by a major composer from Britain's national heritage at the time of Queen Elizabeth I.

Less well known is Irish composer Sir Charles Villiers Stanford (1852–1924), who wrote *Irish Rhapsodies* for orchestra and the opera *Shamus O'Brien*.

The Renewal of Classicism: Brahms

Born in the dour industrial port city of Hamburg, Johannes Brahms gravitated to Vienna, the city of Haydn, Mozart, and Beethoven. The move seems symbolic. For Brahms rejected many of the innovations of the early Romantics and went back to Classical genres, forms, and, to some extent, even Classical style.

Brahms was a serious man; this is one of the few pictures of him smiling. He is sketched with some bachelor friends at his favorite Vienna tavern, the Red Hedgehog.

Brahms devoted his major effort to traditional genres such as string quartets and other chamber music works, symphonies, and concertos. In these works, he found new life in the Classical forms — sonata form, theme and variations, and rondo. The only typical Romantic genre he cultivated was the miniature — the lied and the characteristic piano piece; he never contemplated grandiose works such as philosophical program symphonies or mythological operas. Almost alone among the important composers of his time, he made no special effort to pioneer new harmonies or tone colors.

What impels a great composer — and Brahms *was* a great composer, not a timid traditionalist — to turn back the clock in this way? One can only speculate that he could not find it in himself to copy or continue the enthusiastic, open-ended striving of the early Romantics. In the late nineteenth century, this type of response no longer rang true, and Brahms recognized it.

On the other hand, the nobility and power of Beethoven inspired him with a lifelong model. Seen in this way, Brahms's effort was a heroic one: to temper the new richness and variety of Romantic emotion with the traditional strength and poise of Classicism.

> ❝ Brahms, without giving up on beauty and emotion, proved to be a progressive in a field that had not been cultivated in half a century [i.e., the Classical tradition]. He would have been a pioneer if he had simply returned to Mozart. But he did not live on inherited wealth; he made a fortune of his own."
>
> *Modernist composer Arnold Schoenberg, 1947*

Johannes Brahms (1833–1897)

The son of an orchestral musician in Hamburg, Brahms was given piano lessons at an early age. By the time he was seven, he was studying with one of Hamburg's finest music teachers. A little later he was playing the piano at dockside taverns and writing popular tunes.

A turning point in Brahms's life came at the age of twenty when he met Robert and Clara Schumann. These two eminent musicians befriended and encouraged the young man and took him into their household. Robert wrote an enthusiastic article praising his music. But soon afterward, Schumann was committed to an insane asylum — a time during which Brahms and Clara (who was fourteen years his senior) became very close. In later life Brahms always sent Clara his compositions to get her comments and suggestions.

With another musician friend, Joseph Joachim, who was to become one of the great violinists of his time, the young Brahms signed a foolish manifesto condemning the advanced music of Liszt and Wagner. Thereafter he passed an uneventful bachelor existence, steadily turning out music — chamber music, songs, and piano pieces, but no program music or operas. He was forty-three before his first symphony appeared, many years after its beginnings at his desk; it seemed that he was hesitating to invoke comparison with Beethoven, whose symphonies set a standard for the genre. In fact, this symphony's last movement contains a near-quotation from Beethoven's Ninth Symphony that is more like a challenge. When people pointed out the similarity, Brahms snarled, "Any jackass can see that," implying that it was the differences between the two works that mattered, not their superficial similarities.

Brahms would eventually write four magnificent symphonies, all harking back to forms used by Beethoven and even Bach, but thoroughly Romantic in their expressive effect.

For a time Brahms conducted a chorus, and he wrote much choral music, including *A German Requiem*, a setting of sober texts in German from the Bible. As a conductor, he indulged his traditionalism by reviving music of Bach and even earlier composers, but he also enjoyed the popular music of his day. He wrote waltzes (Johann Strauss, the "Waltz King," was a valued friend), folk song arrangements, and the well-known *Hungarian Dances*.

Chief Works: Four symphonies, *Tragic* Overture, and a rather comical *Academic Festival* Overture ▪ Violin Concerto, Double Concerto for Violin and Cello, and two piano concertos ▪ Much chamber music — including quartets, quintets, and sextets; a trio for French horn, violin, and piano; a beautiful quintet for clarinet and strings ▪ Piano music and many songs ▪ Choral music, including *A German Requiem* and *Alto Rhapsody* ▪ Waltzes, *Hungarian Dances*

Encore: After the Violin Concerto, listen to the Clarinet Quintet; Symphony No. 3.

JOHANNES BRAHMS
Violin Concerto in D, Op. 77 (1878)

Concertos are always written to show off great virtuosos—who are often the composers themselves, as with Mozart, Chopin, and Liszt. Brahms wrote his one violin concerto for a close friend, Joseph Joachim, a leading violinist of the time and also a composer. Even this late in life—Brahms was then forty-five—he accepted advice about certain details of the composition from Joachim, and Joachim wrote the soloist's cadenza for the first movement.

We can appreciate Brahms's traditionalism as far as the Classical forms are concerned by referring to the standard movement plan for the Classical concerto, on page 205. Like Mozart, Brahms wrote his first movement in double-exposition sonata form; this must have seemed extremely stuffy to writers of Romantic concertos who had developed new and much freer forms. Also, Brahms's last movement is a rondo—much the most common Classical way to end a concerto. If it is a relatively simple movement, by Brahms's standards, that is because the last movements of Classical concertos were typically the lightest and least demanding on the listener.

Third Movement (**Allegro giocoso, ma non troppo vivace**)   *Giocoso* means "jolly"; the first theme in this rondo, **A,** has a lilt recalling the spirited gypsy fiddling that was popular in nineteenth-century Vienna. Imitating gypsy music in this work and others counts as an exotic feature in Brahms's music (see page 299).

The solo violin plays the theme (and much else in the movement) in *double stops,* that is, in chords produced by bowing two violin strings simultaneously. Hard to do well, this makes a brilliant effect when done by a virtuoso.

The theme falls into a traditional **a a b a′** form; in Brahms's hands, however, this becomes something quite subtle. Since the second **a** is identical to the first, except in instrumentation, the last **a** (**a′**) might be dull unless it were varied in an interesting way. Brahms manages to extend it and tighten it up at the same time, by compressing the main rhythmic figure:

Such "cross-rhythms" have the effect of fitting 3/8 in for a moment within 2/4. They are a characteristic fingerprint of Brahms's style. There are other examples in this movement.

The first rondo episode, **B,** a theme with a fine Romantic sweep about it, begins with an emphatic upward scale played by the solo violin (high double stops in octaves). This is answered by a *downward* scale in the orchestra in a lower range. When the orchestra has its turn to play **B,** timpani are added; the

Violinist Joseph Joachim, for whom Brahms wrote his Violin Concerto, playing with another Brahms friend, Clara Schumann (see page 263).

upward scale is transferred down to the low register, and the downward scale up to the high register.

The second rondo episode, **C,** involves another rhythmic change; this charming melody—which, however, soon evaporates—is in **3/4** time:

The coda presents a version of the **a** phrase of the main theme in **6/8** time, in a swinging march tempo. Again the timpani are prominent. Most of the transitions in this movement are rapid virtuoso scale passages by the soloist, who is also given two short cadenzas prior to the coda.

bedfordstmartins.com/listen
▶ Interactive Listening Chart 18

Romantic Nostalgia: Mahler

If, like Brahms, Gustav Mahler felt ambivalent about the Romantic tradition, he expressed this ambivalence very differently. He eagerly embraced all the excesses of Romanticism that Brahms had shrunk from, writing huge program symphonies (though he vacillated on the question of distributing the programs to his audiences) and symphonies with solo and choral singing. Mahler once said that a symphony is "like the world." Again and again his works set out to encode seemingly profound metaphysical or spiritual messages.

Yet it would appear that Mahler felt unable to enter freely into this Romantic fantasy world. There is an uneasy quality to his music that sets it apart from other late Romantic music. For while we may feel that the emotion expressed in Tchaikovsky's music, for example, is exaggerated, we do not feel that Tchaikovsky himself thought so. Mahler's exaggeration seems deliberate and self-conscious.

❝ A symphony must be like the world, it must embrace everything."

Famous dictum of Gustav Mahler

))) LISTENING CHART 18

Brahms, Violin Concerto, third movement

Rondo. 7 min., 43 sec.

1	0:00	**A (Tune)**	The entire tune is presented.
	0:00	**a**	Solo violin, with double stops
	0:11	**a**	Orchestra
	0:22	**b**	Solo violin
	0:35	**a′**	Orchestra
	0:46		The solo violin begins the cadences ending the tune, which lead into a transition.
	1:04		Fast scales prepare for **B**.
2	1:14	**B (Episode 1)**	Melody (emphatic upward scale) in the violin, with inverted motive below it, in the orchestra
0:20	1:34		Melody in the orchestra, with inverted motive above it
0:35	1:50		Cadential passage (orchestra), *f*
3	2:00	**A′**	
	2:00	**a**	Solo
0:11	2:11	**a″**	Orchestra
0:20	2:21		Transition (orchestra and solo), *p*
4	2:38	**C (Episode 2)**	Lyrical tune (solo and orchestra), *p*
0:33	3:11		Expressive climactic section, solo
0:44	3:22		Orchestra interrupts, *f*.
0:48	3:27		Scales prepare for **B**.
0:57	3:35	**B**	
5	4:23	**A″**	Starts with **b′** (solo)
0:20	4:43	**a‴**	In orchestra, extended; the real feeling of "return" comes only at this point.
0:46	5:09	**Short cadenza**	Solo, double stops again; orchestra soon enters.
1:02	5:25		Solo trills and scales; motive ♩♩♩♩
1:31	5:54		Passage of preparation: motive ♩♩♩♩ in low French horns
6	6:09	**Short cadenza**	
0:11	6:20	**Coda**	Mostly in **6/8** time. Starts with a marchlike transformation of phrase **a** (solo), over a drum beat
0:35	6:44		References to **B**
1:07	7:16		Final-sounding cadences
1:19	7:28		The music dies down and ends with three loud chords.

From Brahms's score of his Violin Concerto

Gustav Mahler (1860–1911)

Mahler's early life was not a happy one. Born in Bohemia to an abusive father, he lost five of his brothers and sisters to diphtheria, and others ended their lives in suicide or mental illness. The family lived near a military barracks, and the many marches incorporated into Mahler's music—often distorted marches—have been traced to his childhood recollections of parade music.

After studying for a time at the Vienna Conservatory, Mahler began a rising career as a conductor. His uncompromising standards and his authoritarian attitude toward the orchestra musicians led to frequent disputes with the authorities. What is more, Mahler was Jewish, and Vienna at that time was rife with anti-Semitism. Nonetheless, he was acknowledged as one of the great conductors of his day and also as a very effective musical administrator. After positions at Prague, Budapest, Hamburg, and elsewhere, he came to head such organizations as the Vienna Opera and the New York Philharmonic.

It was only in the summers that Mahler had time to compose, so it is not surprising that he produced fewer pieces (though they are very long pieces) than any other important composer. Ten symphonies, the last of them unfinished, and six song cycles for voice and orchestra are almost all he wrote. The song cycle *The Song of the Earth* of 1910, based on translated Chinese poems, is often called Mahler's greatest masterpiece.

He married a famous Viennese beauty, Alma Schindler, who after his death went on to marry the great architect Walter Gropius and later the novelist Franz Werfel and then wrote fascinating memoirs of her life with the composer. By a tragic irony, Gustav and Alma's young daughter died of scarlet fever shortly after Mahler had written his grim orchestral song cycle *Songs on the Death of Children*.

Mahler's life was clouded by psychological turmoil, and he once consulted his famous Viennese contemporary, Sigmund Freud. It has been said that his disputes with the New York Philharmonic directors, which discouraged him profoundly, may have contributed to his early death.

Chief Works: Ten lengthy symphonies, several with chorus, of which the best known are the First, Fourth, and Fifth ■ Orchestral song cycles: *The Song of the Earth, Songs of a Wayfarer, The Youth's Magic Horn* (for piano or orchestra), *Songs on the Death of Children*

Encore: After Symphony No. 1, listen to the Adagietto from Symphony No. 5; *Songs of a Wayfarer*.

From the score Mahler was working on at his death—the unfinished Symphony No. 10.

Exaggeration spills over into another characteristic feature, distortion. Mahler tends to make more or less slight distortions of melody, motive, and harmony. Sometimes these distortions put a uniquely bittersweet touch on the musical material; sometimes they amount to all-out parody. The parody does not seem harsh, however, but affectionate, nostalgic, and ultimately melancholy. Distortion for Mahler was a way of acknowledging his inability—and the inability of his generation—to recapture the lost freshness of Romantic music.

To give an example: The slow movement of his Symphony No. 1 quotes the cheerful children's round, "Frère Jacques," strangely distorted so as to sound like a funeral march. Mahler explained that this march was inspired by a well-known nursery picture of the time, *The Huntsman's Funeral Procession*, showing forest animals shedding crocodile tears around the hearse of a hunter (see p. 310). But an innocent children's song was not distorted in this way in order to mock childhood or childish things. If anything, Mahler used it to lament his own lost innocence, and that of his time.

Mahler's Symphony No. 8, called "Symphony of a Thousand," represents a peak in the nineteenth-century tradition of grandiose compositions (see page 251). One early performance (in Philadelphia) did indeed use 1,069 orchestral players, chorus singers, and soloists.

GUSTAV MAHLER
Symphony No. 1 (1888)

5   3

7–14   13–20

Mahler's first symphony went through as complicated a process of genesis as any major work of music. It started out as a symphonic poem in one movement, grew to a five-movement symphony, and was finally revised into four movements. As is also true of several of his other symphonies, Symphony No. 1 includes fragments from a number of earlier songs by Mahler, songs about lost love. The program that Mahler once published for the whole symphony, but then withdrew, concerns the disillusion and distress of disappointed love, with the hero pulling himself together again in the finale.

An important general feature of Mahler's style is a special kind of counterpoint closely tied up with his very individual style of orchestration. He picks instruments out of the orchestra to play momentary solos, which are heard in counterpoint with other lines played by other "solo" instruments. The changing combinations can create a fascinating kaleidoscopic effect, for the various bright strands are not made to blend, as in most Romantic orchestration, but rather to stand out in sharp contrast to one another.

Third Movement   (Feierlich und gemessen, ohne zu schleppen — "With a solemn, measured gait; do not drag")   This ironic funeral march is also a personal

Chinese Opera

What we know as Beijing opera, the most famous variety of Chinese musical drama, is in China called **jingju** (chéeng-chu), meaning "theater of the capital." It is one of more than three hundred different local varieties of traditional Chinese musical drama, each identified by the province or district of its origin. Beijing opera is a rich amalgam of song, spoken dialogue, instrumental music, dance, elaborate costume, and martial arts. In a nation of vast size and immense cultural diversity, the "theater of the capital" comes closest to being a national tradition of musical drama.

Beijing opera is a relatively recent product of a long, complex history. Some of its stylistic features were introduced to the capital by provincial theater troupes at the end of the eighteenth century, while others developed through much of the nineteenth. Only by the late 1800s did Beijing opera assume the form we know today, and even that form has more recently undergone striking changes, especially during the Communist period of the last half-century.

Voice Types in Beijing Opera

In European opera, different voice types have been habitually associated with specific character types. In Romantic opera, tenors usually play young, vital, and amorous characters (for example, Radames in Verdi's *Aida*), and sopranos play their female counterparts (Aida herself); most often the two are star-crossed lovers. The lower female voice is often reserved for a character who conspires against the soprano and tenor (Amneris), while the low male voices, baritone and bass, can variously have fatherly, comic, or evil associations.

Such conventional connections of voice and character type are highly developed in Beijing opera, too — but the voice types are different. Young men of romantic, dreamy inclination sing in a high register and usually in falsetto. Older, bearded men, trusted and loyal advisors of one sort or another, sing in the high baritone range. Warriors sing with a forced, throaty voice; in addition they must be skilled acrobats in order to enact lively, athletic battle scenes.

Two other special male roles are the male comic, who speaks more than he sings, and the *jing* or face-painted role, who may be a warrior, a dashing bandit, or even a god. His face is painted more elaborately than those of the other actors, with patterns whose colors symbolically reveal much about his character. The *jing* sings in a loud, hoarse manner that takes years to master, like the other voice types here — and like the equally artificial voice types of European opera.

The female roles in Beijing opera were, until the Communist era, almost always sung by male impersonators. They include a mature, virtuous woman, sung in a refined, delicate falsetto (when women sing these roles today, they imitate that male falsetto). A younger woman, lively and flirtatious, is sung in a suggestive, innuendo-laden falsetto. There is also an acrobatic female warrior.

The Orchestra

The small orchestra of Beijing opera consists of a group of drums, gongs, and cymbals, a few wind instruments, and a group of bowed and plucked stringed instruments. These are all played by a handful of versatile musicians who switch from one instrument to another during the performance.

The percussion group is associated especially with martial music, accompanying battle scenes. But it also fulfills many other roles: It can introduce scenes, provide special sound effects, use conventional drum patterns to announce the entrances and social status of different characters, and play along with the frequent songs. The most important function of the stringed instruments is to introduce and accompany the songs.

Beijing Opera Songs

In a way that is somewhat akin to the Western contrast of recitative and aria, Beijing opera shows a wide range of vocal styles, from full-fledged song through more declamatory song to stylized speech and even, for comic and minor characters, everyday speech. In general, the songs of Beijing opera

Beijing opera: a female character and a *jing*

A Beijing opera orchestra: The player in front holds the banjo-like *yueqin;* behind him are an *erhu* player and, standing, percussion players.

are, like the arias of Italian opera, the musical heart of the drama, marked off from the other singing around them by their lyrical style. The songs suggest the feelings and internal psychological states of their singers.

Unlike Italian opera, however, these Chinese arias are not composed anew for each new opera. Instead, their music is chosen from a stock collection of melodies and percussion patterns and fitted to the song-texts of each new libretto added to the repertory. Sometimes whole songs are fitted to new texts in standard poetic forms; at other times, looser musical patterns are taken over and adapted to texts of freer poetry. The foremost concern in this fashioning of arias is to choose melodies and rhythms that convey effectively the emotional situation of a particular song-text.

The Prince Who Changed into a Cat

6
29

Our recording presents the beginning of a scene from *The Prince Who Changed into a Cat,* one of the most famous of Beijing operas. The story concerns an Empress who is banished from Beijing through the machinations of one of the Emperor's other wives. (Her new-

born son, the prince of the title, is stolen from his cradle and replaced by a cat.) The present scene takes place many years later, when a wise and just Prime Minister meets the Empress and determines to restore her to her rightful position.

First the percussion plays, and then string instruments, along with a wooden clapper, introduce an aria sung by the Prime Minister (0:25). There are only three stringed instruments: a high-pitched, two-string fiddle played with a bow called a *jinghu* (chéeng-hoo), a similar but lower-pitched fiddle called *erhu* (ár-hoo), and a plucked lute called *yueqin* (yuéh-chin). All three play the same melody, the erhu doubling the jinghu an octave below while the yueqin adds characteristic repeated notes created by the quick, banjo-like strumming of a string.

Finally, the singer enters (0:41). He sings the same melody as the stringed instruments, though he pauses frequently while they continue uninterrupted. This heterophonic texture (see page 29) is typical of Beijing opera arias. The Prime Minister is a bearded old-man role and sings in the appropriate high baritone range.

The Twentieth Century and Beyond

T his unit, which deals with music from around 1900 on, brings our survey up to the present. Looking back to the year 1900, we can recognize today's society in an early form. Large cities, industrialization, inoculation against disease, advertising, processed food, the first automobiles, telephones, movies, and phonographs—all were in place by the early years of the twentieth century.

Hence many of the phenomena treated in this unit will strike us as fairly familiar, compared to those of earlier centuries. For one thing, the wide availability of art to mass audiences—not just to the various select groups, as in the past—is something we take for granted. The new mass audience emerged because of sociological factors, as mobility between social classes became easier and more common, along with technological factors—the amazing developments of the phonograph, radio, television, and the Internet. We also take for granted the split that has occurred between classical music and popular music. A rift that had widened in the nineteenth century became a prime factor of musical life in the twentieth.

We are also aware of the force of American popular music, whose characteristic features emerged, once again, around the year 1900. With the evolution of ragtime and early jazz, a vital rhythmic spring derived from African-American sources was brought into the general American consciousness. This led to a long series of developments: swing, bebop, rhythm and blues, rock, rap. After World War II, when the United States began to play a commanding political role in the world at large, our popular music became a world language.

Looking Forward and Looking Back

What happened to classical music in this same period? It experienced its own split. On the one hand, there was music that we call "modernist," on the other hand, music of a more traditional nature.

The term modernist requires a word of explanation. It is not the same as modern or contemporary, terms that refer to anything at all that happens to take place in the present; the -ist at the end of the word modern gives it an extra twist. The modernists of 1900 were artists and intellectuals who insisted on a particular kind of modernity: anti-traditionalism. They formed *a specific movement marked by radical experimentation. Though its roots go back earlier, this movement first peaked during the years 1890 through 1918— a period of breakthrough works by such figures as novelists Marcel Proust and James Joyce, poets Ezra Pound and T. S. Eliot, and painters Pablo Picasso and Henri Matisse.*

The chief composers associated with the modernist movement in this early phase were Claude Debussy, Arnold Schoenberg, and Igor Stravinsky. Sometimes they are referred to as members of the "avant-garde"; **avant-garde**— *meaning "vanguard"—was originally a military term, but it has long been embraced by radical artists and intellectuals to denote the forefront of their activity. Later, about 1950, a second phase of musical modernism set in, involving a new generation of avant-garde composers.*

Some twentieth-century artists and composers resisted modernism from the start, and others, after experimenting with modernism, turned back from it. They found they could comfortably continue in the general spirit of late Romanticism, or even look back to earlier styles. Though the avant-gardists often claimed that the old principles of art had been "used up," there was still plenty of potential left in more traditional forms and styles.

Through the twentieth century, phases of assertive modernism alternated with reactions of a more traditional nature. The heady avant-garde experiments of 1900–1920 gave way to a period of consolidation in the 1920s and 1930s; the new wave of modernism after 1950 turned, in the last decades of the century, to a reaction sometimes called Neoromanticism. In this unit we study the music of modernism and also the reaction against modernism. Our final chapter deals with America's characteristic music, jazz and rock.

CHAPTER 19

Prelude
Music and Modernism

The period from about 1890 to 1940 saw profound changes in European and American societies and the art they created. These changes were outgrowths of trends whose beginnings we traced in Chapter 18 — trends such as the collapse of Romantic political aspirations in 1848, accelerating industrialization, and increasingly pronounced nationalism. They came to a climax in the first half of the new century, with the cataclysms of World War I (1914–18) and World War II (1939–45).

The artists of this period responded in ways generally familiar also from the nineteenth century. Some pushed forward with ever bolder expression and technique (think of Wagner). Others searched for new vitality in modes of expression that by now seemed traditional (think of Brahms).

The first of these groups, the modernists, riveted the attention of the artistic world in the period leading up to World War I because of the excitement (many thought scandal) generated by their experimentation and innovation. We take up these innovations in this Prelude and the following Chapter 20. The second, more traditional group came into its own especially in the period between the world wars as a kind of response to the challenges and difficulties of modernism. We consider a sampling of these composers in Chapter 21.

1 Progress and Uncertainty

Industrialization is one of two overriding historical facts of the nineteenth century. The other one, the emergence of the modern nation-state, we spoke of earlier; see pages 298–300. Ever since the first so-called age of science in the seventeenth century, technological discoveries had come faster and faster, and industry was transformed. The harnessing of steam power in the eighteenth century was matched by the capturing of electricity in the nineteenth. Europe and America were crisscrossed with railroads, built for the benefit of industry and commerce. By the early twentieth century, automobile and air travel were in their early stages of development, as were telephones, movies, and sound recordings.

What had been essentially rural societies, controlled by stable aristocracies, turned into modern nations, dominated by urban centers and run by self-made entrepreneurs. These changes occurred at breakneck speed, as people saw at the time. Yet no one could have forecast how the stresses caused by such social changes would lead on the one hand to the disturbing artistic-intellectual movement known as modernism, and on the other to the catastrophe of World War I.

For at the heart of nineteenth-century culture was a sense of confidence in progress. Progress in science and technology, it was thought, would be matched in due time by progress in human affairs. And although anyone could see evidence to the contrary — for example, in the appalling conditions of the new industrial poor, as exposed by the novels of Charles Dickens and the political writings of Karl Marx — this evidence was easily ignored by the rich and powerful who were profiting from technology's advances.

Another dark side of progress became evident in the development of weaponry. The deadly novelty of the American Civil War was the rifle, effective over five times the range of previous shoulder weapons. In World War I, tanks, submarines, and chemical weapons showed technology's terrible potential for destruction: an estimated forty million military and civilian dead from war, famine, and epidemic, and twenty million wounded. With World War I, nationalism reached its first, horrifying climax, as modern nation-states pitted themselves against one another. Nineteenth-century confidence in progress — a response to the successes of technology — was thrown into question by technology itself.

By this time, however, the groundwork for such loss in confidence had already been laid by science in other areas. Men and women were shaken in their most basic assumptions about life by startling advances in physics, biology, and psychology.

¶ The impact of Einstein's theory of relativity made its own contributions to the technology of weaponry later in the century, with the invention of nuclear weapons. At first, however, it was more philosophical than practical in nature. The idea that things depend on the standpoint of the observer, and cannot be counted on according to the objective rules of Newtonian physics, rocked people's sense of certainty.

¶ For many, this uncertainty deepened a crisis in religion that the Victorians had already experienced as a result of scientific theories of evolution. Here the key figure was Charles Darwin. Were human beings created by God in God's image, as the Bible teaches, or did they evolve by an impersonal process from lower animals? The disturbance that this idea caused in people's sense of stability is still reflected in today's disputes about creationism and "intelligent design."

¶ Meanwhile the psychological theories of Sigmund Freud suggested that in spite of what people thought they were doing or feeling, they were in fact controlled by unconscious drives. The idea of men and women in the grip of irrational forces of their own (or their parents') making was, again, very disturbing. At the same time, the prospect of working out one's problems through psychotherapy gave the new century its paradigm for personality change.

2   The Response of Modernism

If the traditional laws of physics, biblical authority, and psychological certainty could no longer be accepted, it seemed a small enough step to question the rules and assumptions surrounding the arts.

Cubism was one of the earliest forms of abstract or near-abstract art, developed around the time of World War I by Pablo Picasso, Georges Braque, and others. In this Braque painting, one can discern a guitar and the score of *Socrate,* a work by the modernist composer Erik Satie.

One such assumption was that visual art had to represent something from the external world. Once this idea was questioned, and then abandoned, the materials of painting and the other arts could be used for themselves — and a world of abstract painting opened up (it is also called "nonrepresentational"). Avant-garde artists developed whole new languages for art — for example, the language of cubism, shown in the painting by Georges Braque, above.

In literature, the basic assumption was that poets and novelists would use ordinary sentence structure, syntax, and grammar. Freedom from these assumptions opened up a whole new sphere of suggestion in tune with Freud's ideas about the mind's unconscious and irrational impulses. James Joyce's novel *Ulysses* of 1922 is one of the most famous instances of the so-called stream-of-consciousness method of writing. His last novel, *Finnegans Wake,* makes use of a language that is half-English and half words he invented.

In music, the basic assumptions concerned the composing of melody and its close associates harmony and tonality. These assumptions too were thrown into doubt, and the logic of earlier musical styles was questioned or even rejected. Some avant-garde composers turned away from conventional presentation of rhythm and meter, while others wrote melodies that carried to new lengths the most complex of late-Romantic melodic designs. Still others devised new harmonies more complicated and dissonant than those of earlier generations, or even harmonies derived from new scales, different from the major and minor.

There was a tendency around this time for artists of various kinds to gravitate together in formal or informal groups, both for mutual encouragement and for the exchange of ideas. Thus Claude Debussy was friends with several avant-garde poets. Schoenberg, himself a painter as well as a musician, associated with a group of artists who set forth their ideas in *The Blue Rider,* a magazine named after a picture by the pioneer nonrepresentational painter Wassily Kandinsky (see page 327). Stravinsky and Maurice Ravel belonged to a group who called themselves the Apaches. With all this interchange, it is not surprising that one can sometimes detect similar tendencies in music and the other arts.

3 Literature and Art before World War I

The new languages for art were unquestionably (and unapologetically) difficult. To this day, few people understand *Finnegans Wake*. Avant-garde art became detached from music's ordinary public, and hence abstracted from a base in society.

At the same time, the modernists' concentration on artistic materials led to abstraction of another kind, the separation of technique from expression. This emphasis on technique was welcomed by some as a relief from the over-heated emotionality of late Romantic music of Tchaikovsky, Mahler, and the like. Especially in the 1920s, "objectivity" was an ideal espoused by many artists. Only too often, their works struck the public as abstract in a cold, dry sense.

Characteristic of this phase of the avant-garde were experiments with schematic, even mathematical devices in the arts. The Dutch painter Piet Mondrian made pictures out of straight lines at right angles to one another and juxtaposed planes of bright color. Among composers, Igor Stravinsky was known for his provocative statements extolling objectivity and attacking Romantic music — and certainly the brisk, mechanistic rhythms that characterize Stravinsky's style are diametrically opposed to rubato (see page 246), the rhythmic stretching that contributes so much to nineteenth-century music's emotionality.

Several lesser composers, fascinated by machine rhythms, even tried to evoke machinery in their works: the American George Antheil (*Ballet mécanique*), the Russian A. V. Mosolov (*The Iron Foundry*), and the Swiss Arthur Honegger (*Pacific 231* — a locomotive). An Italian group called the Futurists — more famous for their well-publicized proclamations than for any actual music —

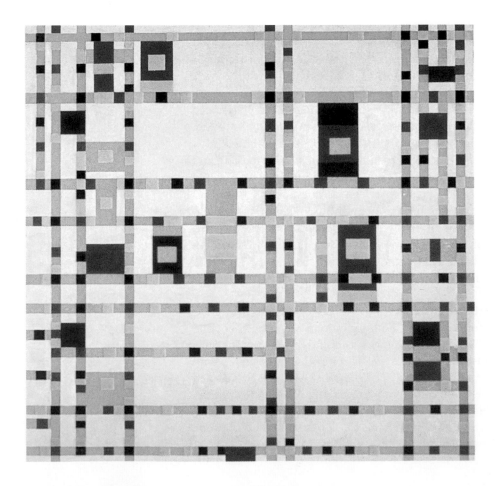

Broadway Boogie-Woogie by Piet Mondrian — a tribute to the "mechanical" rhythms of jazz (as he perceived them) by a premier abstract painter.

In the Boat, an impressionist painting by Edouard Manet (1832–1883). Does nature imitate art? This snapshot of Debussy (second from the left) and some friends is startlingly similar in mood to the (earlier) painting by Manet.

called for "music of the machine age" and composed with industrial noises. They invented a mechanized "noise intoner" with dozens of categories ranging from explosions and crashes to crackles and howls.

Impressionists and Symbolists

As we have already remarked, modernism got its start in the late nineteenth century and then peaked in the twentieth. The best-known modernist movement, **impressionism,** dates from the 1870s, when people were astonished by the flickering network of color patches used by impressionist painters to render simple scenes from everyday life (as in Edouard Manet's *In the Boat,* above). These painters claimed that they had to develop such a technique to catch the actual, perceived quality of light. They proudly called themselves "realists," in reaction to the idealized and overemotional art of Romanticism. Remember Claude Monet's multiple pictures of Rouen Cathedral, on page 190; they emphasize (even exaggerate!) how differences in daylight define the impressionist painter's reality.

Symbolism, a consciously *un*realistic movement, followed soon after impressionism. Symbolist poets revolted against the "realism" of words being used for reference—for the purpose of exact definition or denoting. They wanted words to perform their symbolizing or signifying function as freely as possible, without having to fit into phrases or sentences. The meaning of a cluster of words might be vague and ambiguous, even esoteric—but also rich, "musical," and endlessly suggestive.

Musical was exactly what the symbolists called it. They were fascinated by the music dramas of Richard Wagner, where again musical symbols—Wagner's leitmotivs—refer to elements in his dramas in a complex, ambivalent, multilayered fashion. All poets use musical devices such as rhythm and rhyme, but the symbolists were prepared to go so far as to break down grammar, syntax, and conventional thought sequence to approach the elusive nonreferential quality of music.

Claude Debussy is often called an impressionist in music because his fragmentary motives and little flashes of tone color seem to recall the impressionists'

With pure nails brightly
    flashing their onyx
Anguish at midnight
    holds up (Lucifer!)
A multitude of dreams
    burnt by the Phoenix
. . .

*Opening of a symbolist
sonnet (Stéphane Mallarmé)*

Horses and riders, painted by Wassily Kandinsky over a four-year period, show his path toward nonrepresentational painting. In the first picture, the figures are quite clear; in the last, they could be missed entirely. Top left: *Couple on Horseback* (1907); top right: *Blue Mountain* (1909); bottom: *Romantic Landscape* (1911).

painting technique. Debussy can also—and more accurately—be called a symbolist, since suggestion, rather than outright statement, is at the heart of his aesthetic. Famous symbolist texts inspired two famous Debussy works: the orchestral *Prelude to "The Afternoon of a Faun"* (a poem by Stéphane Mallarmé) and the opera *Pelléas et Mélisande* (a play by Maurice Maeterlinck), where Debussy's elusive musical symbols and Maeterlinck's elusive verbal ones combine to produce an unforgettable effect of mysterious suggestion.

Expressionists and Fauves

In Paris and Vienna—artistic centers which were also centers of avant-garde music—two émigré artists pursued separate but parallel paths toward completely abstract painting.

Our horse-and-rider pictures to the left by the Russian-born painter Wassily Kandinsky (1866–1944) show step by step how the process was accomplished. Kandinsky belonged to a German movement in the arts called expressionism— not to be confused with impressionism—which sought to express the most extreme human feelings by divorcing art from everyday literalness. Anguish, even hysteria, could be conveyed by the harsh clashing of strong colors, irregular shapes, and jagged lines. What seems to be conveyed is not something external but the artist's inner turbulence—most violently in the last Kandinsky picture, *Romantic Landscape,* which is almost entirely abstracted from the outer world.

Parallel to the expressionists was a short-lived group in Paris dubbed *Les fauves,* "the wild beasts." The fauves experimented with distorted images bordering on the grotesque; they also employed motifs from what they called "primitive" art as though in defiance of a decadent European culture. In Pablo Picasso's famous painting *Les Demoiselles d'Avignon* of 1907 (Avignon was a street in the red-light district of Barcelona), the quality of abstraction is evident in the angular bodies and the African-mask-like heads—a complete break with conventional European rules of human portrayal (see page 328). Picasso took a further step toward abstraction later when he turned to cubism.

There is violence in both Kandinsky's and Picasso's work of this period. Certainly that is how it struck a generation used to the nonthreatening art of the impressionists—painters of flickering summer landscapes, soft-edged nudes, and diaphanous action pictures of the ballet. Composers, too, courted violence in their music. The Hungarian composer Béla Bartók wrote a "barbarous" piano piece entitled *Allegro barbaro.* Stravinsky, in his ballet *The Rite of Spring,* depicted human sacrifice in the fertility ceremonies of primitive Slavic tribes.

4 Modernist Music before World War I

The art of music never enjoyed (or suffered) a link to the tangible world that was comparable to representation in painting, or to the reference of words in literature. But it did have its own stable, generally accepted set of principles, its own traditional internal logic. This rested upon elements that we have discussed many times in this book: tune, motive, harmony, tonality, tone color, and rhythm.

The music of Bach, Beethoven, and Brahms was based on this logic, and so was the entire stream of Western European folk songs, popular songs, dances, military marches, and the rest. Modernist music moved away from this norm.

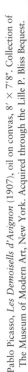

Pablo Picasso, *Les Demoisells d'Avignon* (1907), oil on convas, 8′ × 7′8″. Collection of The Museum of Modern Art, New York. Acquired through the Lille P. Bliss Bequest.

Picasso's famous shocker *Les Demoiselles d'Avignon* (1907). Picasso and other abstract painters designed sets for the Diaghilev Ballets Russes, sponsor of Stravinsky and other modernist composers.

Like abstract, nonrepresentational painting, music worked out new principles based on the materials of the art itself.

With European music before World War I, we can lay our main emphasis on developments in melody, harmony, and tonality, for on the whole, these features were the main preoccupations of avant-garde composers in that period. Developments in tone color and rhythm—or, more broadly, musical sonority and musical time—dominated a later stage of modernist music, after World War II.

Experiment and Transformation: Melody

Melody, harmony, and tonality all work closely together. In historical terms, harmony arose as a way of supporting and adorning melody, and tonality first arose as a means of clarifying both melody and harmony; later tonality functioned as a more general way of organizing music. Each of these functions was transformed in the early twentieth century.

We have seen the Viennese Classical composers bring tunes to the fore in their music, and the Romantics capitalize on tunes as the most emphatic means of conveying powerful emotion. Yet Wagner, despite the melodic quality of many of his leitmotivs, was criticized for the confusing quality of his singing lines, and Mahler's audiences were puzzled and irritated by the bittersweet distortions that he applied to folklike tunes. In his later works, his long melodies surge, swoop, and yearn in a strange, almost painful manner.

By that time another Viennese composer, Arnold Schoenberg, was writing even more complex melodies that simply made no sense to contemporary listeners. The intense rhythms and the anguished intervals of Romanticism were there, but the actual notes did not appear to fit together at all.

Schoenberg, *Pierrot lunaire*

Outside of Vienna, the disintegration of traditional melody was accomplished in other ways. In many (not all) of his works, Claude Debussy used only the most shadowy motives—a constant suggestion of melody without clear tunes. A little later Igor Stravinsky, writing in Paris, seized upon Russian folk songs but whittled them down (or abstracted them) into brief, utterly simple fragments, blank and "objective," as his theories demanded.

New Horizons, New Scales

We have mentioned the influence of African masks on Picasso's *Demoiselles*. Non-European musics, too, began to make inroads into European classical music. At a World's Fair that fascinated Paris in 1889—the fair for which the Eiffel Tower was built—Debussy heard his first non-Western music played by native musicians, under simulated native conditions. He tried to recapture the sounds of the Indonesian gamelan (see page 220) in several compositions, even taking a Balinese melody for the theme of a concerto movement.

Debussy sensed a resonance between his own music and the unique timbres of the gamelan, and also the scales used in Indonesian music. The traditional diatonic scale had served as the foundation of Western music for so long that it was almost regarded as a fact of nature. But now composers were beginning to reconsider the basic sound materials of music. Notable among these experimenters was Charles Ives, in America. New scales were employed for themes or even whole movements, first among them the **pentatonic scale,** a five-note scale playable on the black notes of the keyboard. Imported from folk song and Asian music, this scale was tried in all the usual genres, not only (as before) in nationalist or other folk-derived compositions.

Three other new scales introduced at this time are (significantly enough) abstract constructions, which anyone can figure out by systematically analyzing the total chromatic scale. The **whole-tone scale** divides the octave into six equal parts—all of its intervals are whole steps; again, Debussy worked with this resource in many pieces. The **octatonic scale**—a specialty with Stravinsky—fits eight pitches into the octave by alternating whole and half steps.

Less used, the **quarter-tone scale** employs all the pitches of the chromatic scale plus the pitches that come halfway between each pair of them.

More important as a means of composition than the use of any of these scales was **serialism,** the "new language" for music invented in the 1920s by Arnold Schoenberg. As we will see in the next chapter, serialism in effect creates something like a special scale for every serial composition.

"The Emancipation of Dissonance"

As melody grew more complex, more fragmentary, or more vague, harmony grew more and more dissonant. The concepts of consonance and dissonance, as we noted on page 28, rest on the fact that certain chords (consonant chords)

Pentatonic scale

Debussy, *Clouds*

Whole-tone scale

Octatonic scale

Quarter-tone scale

sound stable and at rest, whereas others (dissonant chords) sound tense and need to resolve to consonant ones. In a famous phrase, Schoenberg spoke of "the emancipation of dissonance," meaning emancipation from that need to resolve. Dissonance was to be free from the rule that says it must always be followed by the appropriate consonance.

Tonality, as we know, is the feeling of centrality, focus, or homing toward a particular pitch that we get from simple tunes and much other music. As melody grew more complex and harmony grew more dissonant, tonality grew more indistinct. Finally, some music reached a point at which no tonal center could be detected at all. This is **atonal** music.

However, just as consonance and dissonance are not open-and-shut concepts, neither are tonality or atonality. Most Baroque music sounds firmly rooted in its key, for example, whereas certain Romantic music seems rather to hover around a general key area. Much early twentieth-century music that was once criticized as "atonal" can be heard on careful listening to have a subtle sense of tonality after all.

Melody, harmony, tonality: All are closely related. Beleaguered conservatives around 1900 referred to them jokingly as the "holy trinity" of music. The "emancipation" of melody, harmony, and tonality all went together. This joint emancipation counts as the central style characteristic of the first phase of twentieth-century avant-garde music.

bedfordstmartins.com/listen
  ▶ Quizzes and Flashcards

CHAPTER 20

The Twentieth Century: Early Modernism

The first major phase of avant-garde music—what we now call modernist music—took place in Paris and Vienna from around 1890 to 1914. Claude Debussy, Igor Stravinsky (a young Russian working in Paris), and Arnold Schoenberg were the leading figures in this brilliant era. And there were strong modernist rumblings in Russia, Hungary, Italy, and the United States.

It was a period of rapid development in all the arts, as we have seen, in which the basic tenets of nineteenth-century art were everywhere challenged. In music in particular, nineteenth-century ideas of melody, harmony, tonality, rhythm, and tone color came under attack. Above all, it was the revolution in tonality—which went along with a radical reconsideration of melody and harmony—that caught the imagination of the early twentieth century.

1 Debussy and Impressionism

Claude Debussy occupies the border area between late nineteenth- and early twentieth-century styles. His investigation of sensuous new tone colors for orchestra and for piano, his development of new rich harmonies, and his search for new ways to express emotion in music—all remind us of the Romantics. Yet while in some ways his work seems tied to Romanticism, in others it represents a direct reaction against it.

Debussy's tone colors avoid the heavy sonorities that were usual in late Romantic music, merging instead into subtle, mysterious shades of sound. His themes and motives are usually fragmentary and tentative, his harmonies sound strangely vague, and the tonality of his music is often clouded. His themes often draw on the vague-sounding new scales mentioned in Chapter 19.

Debussy's orchestral sound differs sharply from that of his contemporary, Gustav Mahler, another great innovator in orchestration. Mahler treated the orchestra more and more contrapuntally; each instrument tends to stand out from the others like a Romantic hero striving for his own say in the world. Debussy's orchestra is more often a single, delicately pulsing totality to which individual instruments contribute momentary gleams of color. In this it reminds us of an impressionist picture, in which small, separate areas of color, visible close up, merge into unified color fields as the viewer stands back and takes in the painting as a whole (see page 325).

> " (. . . Sounds and perfumes sway in the evening air)"
>
> Title of a Debussy "miniature" for piano; the parentheses and dots are his.

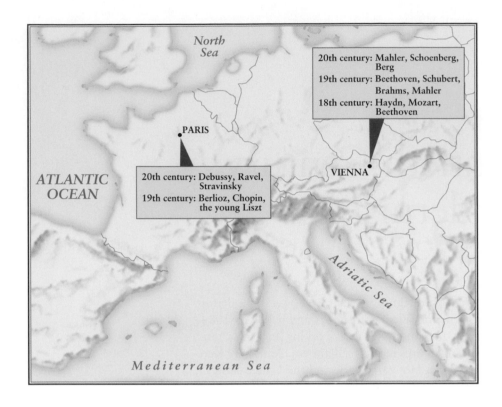

North
Sea

20th century: Mahler, Schoenberg,
    Berg
19th century: Beethoven, Schubert,
    Brahms, Mahler
18th century: Haydn, Mozart,
    Beethoven

•PARIS

ATLANTIC
OCEAN

20th century: Debussy, Ravel,
    Stravinsky
19th century: Berlioz, Chopin,
    the young Liszt

VIENNA•

Adriatic Sea

Mediterranean Sea

Paris and Vienna as musical
centers.

CLAUDE DEBUSSY
Three Nocturnes (1899)

5   2
15–20 30–35

> ❝ The title "Nocturnes"
> should be taken here in a
> more general and especially
> in a more decorative sense.
> . . . *Clouds:* the unchanging
> aspect of the sky, the slow,
> melancholy motion of the
> clouds, fading away into
> agonized grey tones, gently
> tinged with white."
>
> *Claude Debussy*

Debussy's Three Nocturnes, like most of his orchestral works, might be described as impressionist symphonic poems, though they have no narrative programs. They suggest various scenes without attempting to illustrate them literally.

The title "nocturne" evokes a night-time scene, the great examples before Debussy being the piano nocturnes of Chopin (see page 266). But in fact Debussy's reference was to famous atmospheric paintings by an artist who was close to the impressionists, James McNeill Whistler (see opposite page). The first of the nocturnes, *Clouds*, is a pure nature picture, the least nocturnal of the three. The second, *Festivals*, depicts mysterious nighttime fairs and parades. The third Nocturne, *Sirens*, includes a women's chorus along with the orchestra, singing not words but just vowels and adding an unforgettable timbre to the usual orchestra. The women's voices evoke the legendary maidens of the title, who tempt lonely sailors and pull them into the deep.

Clouds We first hear a quiet series of chords, played by clarinets and bassoons, that circles back on itself repeatedly. They seem to suggest great cumulus clouds, moving slowly and silently across the sky.

As a theme, however, these chords do not function conventionally. They make no strong declarations and lead nowhere definitive. This is also true of the next motive, introduced by the English horn—a haunting motive that occurs many times in *Clouds*, with hardly any change. (It is built on an octatonic scale; see page 329.) Yet even this muted gesture, with its vague rhythm and its fading conclusion, seems sufficient to exhaust the composition and bring it to a near halt, over a barely audible drum roll:

After this near stop, the "cloud" music begins again, leading this time to a downward passage of remarkably gentle, murmuring chords in the strings—chords all of the same complex structure:

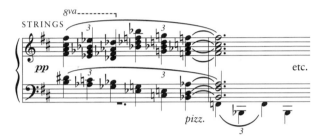

These rich chords slip by without establishing a clear sense of tonality; gorgeous in themselves, they are not functionally significant. This use of parallel chords is one of Debussy's finest and most famous innovations.

Clouds might be said to fall into an **A B A'** form—but only in a very approximate way. Debussy shrinks from clear formal outlines; the musical form here is much more fluid than that of **A B A** structures observed in earlier music. Such fluidity is something to bear in mind when following *Clouds* and other avant-garde music with Listening Charts. By design, avant-garde composers break down the sharp and (to them) oversimple divisions of older musical styles. If they avail themselves of form types such as rondo, sonata form, and so on, they do so in very free, imaginative ways.

In the **A** section of *Clouds,* the return of the cloud theme after a more active, restless passage suggests an internal **a b a'** pattern as well. The next idea, **B,** sounds at first like a meditative epilogue to **A;** it is built on a pentatonic scale (see page 329, again). But when the little pentatonic tune is repeated several times, it begins to feel like a substantial section of contrast. The return, **A',** is really just a reference to some of **A**'s material, notably the English-horn figure. Then at the end the bassoons play a dim, disturbed fragment of the cloud theme; the flute hovers for a moment on the **B** tune; and the drum roll is extended—so as to suggest distant thunder, perhaps.

bedfordstmartins.com/listen
▶ Interactive Listening Chart 20

Nocturne—Grey and Gold by James McNeill Whistler (1834–1903). The American-born expatriate artist painted many more "Nocturnes" and other pictures with musical titles: "Symphony," "Harmony," and "Variations."

Claude Debussy (1862–1918)

Claude Debussy went through the strict curriculum of the famous Paris Conservatory of Music, which he entered at the age of ten. He did not do well in the piano exams, or at least not well enough, but won various awards in theory and composition. He was finally awarded the coveted Grand Prix (Top Prize)—a three-year fellowship to study in Rome.

Before this, Debussy took a job with Madame von Meck, the eccentric patron of Tchaikovsky, playing in a trio at her house in Moscow. Russian music (music of the *kuchka:* see page 299) was one of several vivid influences on the young composer; another was the Indonesian gamelan (see page 220), which he encountered at the World's Fair in Paris in 1889. Visits to Bayreuth, the shrine of Wagner's music dramas, afforded another, even stronger influence. But Debussy soon turned against Wagner and German music in general. He felt it was stifling modern music in France.

Debussy settled into Parisian café life, becoming a familiar bearded figure in his broad-brimmed hat and flowing cape. A long-term relationship with a mistress came to a bad end, as did Debussy's first marriage, when he eloped with a married woman, who later became his wife. They had a daughter—Debussy wrote the well-known *Children's Corner* Suite for her before she was old enough to play the piano.

In his early thirties Debussy seems to have rather suddenly crystallized his musical style, reflecting the influences of the French symbolist poets and impressionist painters. One remarkable work after another was given its premiere, greeted with a flurry of controversy, and then generally accepted by the critics and the public. His one opera, *Pelléas et Mélisande* (1902), written directly to the words of a play by the prominent symbolist Maurice Maeterlinck, exasperated the author. But today Maeterlinck's play is remembered mainly because of Debussy's opera.

Debussy is famous for his innovations in orchestration and in piano writing; his Preludes and Études for the piano are the most impressive "miniatures" since the time of the early Romantics. Some would say the same for his songs. One of his later works, music for the ballet *Jeux* (Games), dissolves melody, theme, and rhythm so far that it was taken up as a model by the avant-garde after World War II.

For a short time Debussy wrote music criticism, in which he expressed in pungent prose the anti-German attitudes that were already manifest in his music. Debussy died of cancer in Paris during World War I, while the city was being bombarded by the Germans he hated.

Chief Works: For orchestra, *Prelude to "The Afternoon of a Faun"* (a famous poem by the French symbolist poet Mallarmé), Three Nocturnes, *La Mer* (The Sea), *Ibéria, Jeux* (Games) ■ The opera *Pelléas et Mélisande* ■ For piano: Preludes and Études, *Children's Corner* Suite, and *Suite bergamasque,* including "Clair de lune" ■ Songs to poems by Baudelaire, Verlaine, and Mallarmé ■ A string quartet and other chamber music ■ *Syrinx* for solo flute

Encore: After *Clouds,* listen to *Fêtes* (Festivals), *Prelude to "The Afternoon of a Faun,"* "Clair de lune."

2 Stravinsky: The Primacy of Rhythm

Stravinsky's earliest work followed from that of his teacher, the nationalist composer Rimsky-Korsakov. But in three famous ballet scores written for the Ballets Russes in Paris, Stravinsky rapidly developed his own powerful, hard-edged avant-garde style, a style that can be compared to the contemporary fauve style in French painting (see page 327). These ballets reveal a fascinating progression toward a more and more abstract use of folk tunes. Compare the development of abstraction in art by Kandinsky and Picasso, which we spoke of earlier.

The first ballet, *The Firebird* (1910), spins a romantic fairy tale about the magical Firebird, the ogre Kastchei, and Prince Ivan Tsarevitch, son of the tsar. Its rich, half-Asian setting is matched by beautifully colored folk music and orchestral sound worthy of Debussy himself. But in the next ballet, Stravinsky moved from the steppes to the urban marketplace, to Mardi Gras

LISTENING CHART 20

Debussy, *Clouds*

7 min., 0 sec.

5 **2**
15–20 30–35

15 30	0:00	**A** **a**	Cloud theme: clarinets and bassoons	
	0:15		English-horn motive	
	0:20		Quiet timpani roll—music almost stops	
16 31	0:34		Cloud theme: high strings	ENGLISH HORN
	0:47		Downward chord passage	
0:15	1:02		Further development: strings	
0:34	1:21		English-horn motive, with a new echo in the French horn	
1:02	1:49		Downward chord passage	
17 32	2:10	**b**	Rising section, more restless: woodwinds added	
0:30	2:41		Brief climax	
0:37	2:48		English-horn motive (with new even-note rhythm accompaniment) is repeated several times, until it dies away.	
18 33	3:38	**a′**	Cloud theme, with new solo viola counterpoint	
0:16	3:54		Downward chord passage	
19 34	4:12	**B**	A new tune enters tentatively, but then repeats itself; flute and harp	FLUTE
0:27	4:40		Tune in strings and solo violin	
0:44	4:56		Tune in flute and harp	
		(A′)	*Not a real "return" of* **A,** *only of selected elements standing in for* **A**	
20 35	5:19		English-horn motive, with its echo	
0:31	5:51		Quiet timpani and low strings—prominent until the end	
			Recollection of thematic fragments:	
0:54	6:13		Cloud theme: bassoons, then cellos	
1:13	6:32		**B** tune	
1:21	6:40		French-horn echo to the English-horn motive	

in St. Petersburg. *Petrushka* (1911), the story of a carnival barker and his puppet, encouraged him to put a hard, satirical edge on his folk material. Then in *The Rite of Spring* (1913), Stravinsky boldly and brutally depicted the fertility cults of prehistoric Slavic tribes. Here Russian folk music, broken down into repeated, fragmentary motives, is treated as the source of primitive rhythmic and sexual energy, rather than picture-postcard charm.

The musical style that Stravinsky brought to a head in the *Rite* has many features that struck listeners of the time as barbaric, apart from its use of deliberately crude folk-tune fragments. The music was abstract in the sense that it sounded utterly unemotional, by Romantic standards. It was grindingly dissonant. It emphasized meter in a very heavy, exciting way, and the rhythms themselves were dazzling and unpredictable. Finally, the score is enormously loud: It demands a colossal orchestra, as though the composer wanted to show how he could control—and transform—the chief powerhouse of musical Romanticism.

Stravinsky, drawn by Picasso during the period when they were associated at the Ballets Russes.

IGOR STRAVINSKY
The Rite of Spring (1913): Part I, "The Adoration of the Earth"

The first performance of *The Rite of Spring* caused a riot; the audience was shocked and infuriated by the violent, dissonant sounds in the pit and the provocative choreography on the stage, suggesting rape and ritual murder.

The ballet has no real story, and Stravinsky even said that he preferred to think of the music as an abstract concert piece. However, inscriptions on the score specify a series of ancient fertility rites of various kinds, culminating in the ceremonial choice of a virgin for sacrifice. After this she is evidently danced to death in the ballet's second part, entitled "The Sacrifice."

Introduction   The halting opening theme is played by a bassoon at the very top of its normal register. Avant-garde composers strained all the elements of music, including the ordinary capabilities of instruments. The bleating bassoon is joined by odd hootings on other woodwinds, gradually building up an extraordinary polyphony that is highly dissonant. The instrumental parts sound rather like a static series of preliminary fanfares (or perhaps like the calls of prehistoric wildlife?).

"Omens of Spring" — "Dance of the Adolescents"   After a brief introduction, in which the dancers presumably register an awareness of spring's awakening, the "Dance of the Adolescents" commences with a famous instance of Stravinskian rhythmic irregularity. (Probably the original audience started their cat-calls at this point.) A single very dissonant chord is repeated thirty-two times in even eighth notes—but with heavy accents reinforced by short, fat chords played by eight (!) French horns on the most unexpected beats:

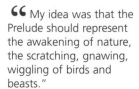

> **"** My idea was that the Prelude should represent the awakening of nature, the scratching, gnawing, wiggling of birds and beasts."
>
> *Igor Stravinsky, reminiscing in 1960 about* The Rite of Spring

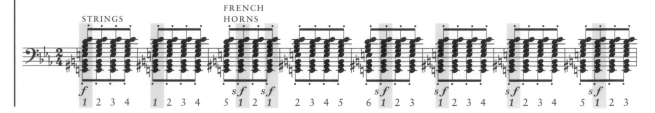

The climax of
The Rite of Spring

))) LISTENING CHART 21

Stravinsky, *The Rite of Spring,* from Part I

Ballet score. 10 min., 41 sec.

21 **21**	0:00	**Introduction**	Bassoon "fanfare," *p,* twice interrupted by English horn	
	1:04		Fanfares in oboe, high (E♭) clarinet, bass clarinet	
	1:41		Buildup	
22 **22**	2:04		New motive in the oboe and E♭ clarinet	
0:29	2:33		Stop; return of the bassoon fanfare, *p*	
0:37	2:41	**Omens of Spring**	Dance of the Adolescents is foreshadowed; the music stops and starts, ending with a high violin chord.	
0:58	3:02		Tempo is established; trill, ♩♩♩♩ rhythm introduced.	
23 **23**	3:08	**Dance of the Adolescents**	Loud rhythmic passage with irregular accents (French horns); various motives are introduced.	
0:36	3:44		Rhythmic passage again	
24 **24**	3:53		Folk-song fragment no. 1—bassoons and contrabassoon, etc.	
0:28	4:21		Abrupt interruption of the regular rhythm	
0:37	4:30		Return of the introductory "Omens" music	
0:53	4:46		Folk-song fragment no. 2—French horn, flutes	
1:27	5:20		Folk-song fragment no. 3—trumpets (triangle)	
1:50	5:44		Folk-song fragment no. 2—piccolos; big buildup	
25 **25**	6:16	**The Game of Abduction**	Faster; frantic rhythms. Brass is prominent; sliding horn calls	
0:56	7:12		Ending passage: alternation between scurrying figures in the winds and heavy booms in the drums	
26 **26**	7:33	**Round Dances of Spring**	Slower; introduction: flute trills, clarinet melody	
0:34	8:08		The main slow dance rhythm is introduced; woodwind motive	
27 **27**	8:45		Folk-song fragment no. 3 (slower than before)—violas, *mf*	
0:53	9:39		Folk-song fragment no. 3, *ff,* with cymbals	
1:16	10:01		Climactic passage—brass	
1:33	10:19		Short coda: faster, with violent rhythmic interjections	
1:50	10:34		Brief return of the slow introduction, *p*	

no. 1

no. 2

no. 3

Very fast
ff

Slow
mf

Musical sketches for
The Rite of Spring

These accents completely upset ordinary meter. Instead of eight standard measures of four eighth notes — **1** *2 3 4,* **1** *2 3 4,* etc. — Stravinsky makes us hear **1** *2 3 4,* **1** *2 3 4 5,* **1** *2,* **1** *2 3 4 5 6,* **1** *2 3,* **1** *2 3 4,* **1** *2 3 4 5,* **1** *2 3.* (For a truly bewildering experience, try beating time to this passage.) Yet these irregular rhythms are also exhilarating, and they certainly drive the music forward in a unique way.

The repeating chords are now overlaid with new motives, derived from Russian folk song. The motives are repeated with slightly different rhythms and at slightly different lengths. This is Stravinsky's distinctive type of ostinato, a technique we have met with in many other kinds of music (pages 106, 112, 137); the ostinato is indicated by brackets on the example below. Like Debussy, Stravinsky tends to concentrate on small melodic fragments, but whereas Debussy soon abandons his fragments, Stravinsky keeps repeating his in this irregular, almost obsessive way.

"The Game of Abduction"   New violence is introduced with this section, a whirlwind of brilliant rhythms, with much frantic pounding on the timpani.

"Round Dances of Spring"   After a moment of respite, a short, quiet introduction conveys a remarkably desolate, empty feeling, partly as a result of its novel orchestration: a high (E♭) clarinet and low (alto) flute playing two octaves apart. Then a slow dragging dance emerges, built out of the third folk-tune fragment from the "Dance of the Adolescents."

The strong downbeat makes the meter hypnotic — but one or two added or skipped beats have a powerful animating effect. The dance reaches a relentless climax with glissando (sliding) trombones, gong, cymbals, and big drum. After a sudden fast coda, the primordial introduction returns to conclude the section.

bedfordstmartins.com/listen
▶ Interactive Listening Chart 21

Four more sections follow our selection in Part I of *The Rite of Spring*. The dynamic "Games of the Rival Tribes" introduces two more folk-tune fragments. A huge masked figure is borne aloft by the male dancers in a slower section, the "Procession of the Sage"; the Sage then performs a brief ceremony, "Adoration of the Earth." The concluding orgiastic "Dance of the Earth" is built on a fast and furious ostinato.

What is conspicuously absent from any of this is emotionality. Tough, precise, and barbaric, it is as far from old-line Romantic sentiment as it is from the delicate, shadowy vision of Debussy. In Stravinsky's later works the barbarism was tamed, but the dry, precise quality remained, and so did the exhilarating irregular rhythms. Throughout his long career they provided him with a powerful strategy for movement, unlike that of any other composer. It was the primacy of rhythm that produced Stravinsky's "new language" for music.

Igor Stravinsky (1882–1971)

The son of an important opera singer, Igor Stravinsky studied law and did not turn seriously to music until he was nineteen. He was fortunate to be able to study with Nikolai Rimsky-Korsakov, a survivor of the nationalist *kuchka* (see page 299) who was still composing actively.

Rimsky's brand of nationalism served young Stravinsky well in the famous (and still outstandingly popular) ballet scores *The Firebird, Petrushka,* and *The Rite of Spring,* which he wrote for the Ballets Russes, a Russian company centered in Paris. This enormously dynamic organization, run by a brilliant producer and man-about-the-arts named Sergei Diaghilev, astonished the blasé Parisian public with its exotic spectacles combining the newest and the most sensational in dance, music, scenery, and costume design. Among Diaghilev's dancers were Vaslav Nijinsky, also choreographer of *The Rite,* and Anna Pavlova; among his designers were Pablo Picasso and Henri Matisse.

After World War I Stravinsky composed more ballets for Diaghilev, as well as other works in a dazzling variety of styles, forms, and genres. One of his most impressive scores, *The Wedding,* was choreographed by Bronislava Nijinska, Nijinski's sister, who was less famous as a dancer than her brother but much better as a choreographer. Among the first classical composers to be interested in jazz, Stravinsky wrote *Piano Ragtime* in 1917 (and, much later, *Ebony Concerto* for clarinetist Woody Herman's jazz band; clarinets are made of ebony). He became an outspoken advocate of "objectivity" in music, the rejection of Romantic emotionality. For many years after World War I he modeled his music on pre-Romantic composers such as Bach, Handel, and Mozart, transforming the music by his own unique rhythmic and harmonic style. This style is sometimes called **Neoclassicism.**

His final work in this vein was an opera, *The Rake's Progress,* which is a modern transformation of Mozart's *Don Giovanni.* This was written in America (to English words), where Stravinsky moved in 1939. After World War II his music grew more abstract and formal in style.

For a quarter of a century people had regarded Stravinsky (and he regarded himself) as the leading Neoclassical composer in the French orbit, at the opposite pole from Schoenberg and the Viennese serialists (see page 347). So he created yet another sensation when, in his seventies, he produced a remarkable group of late compositions employing serial technique. One of the first of these, *Agon,* was written for the great choreographer George Balanchine of the New York City Ballet, who had worked on Stravinsky's Neoclassical *Apollo* twenty-five years earlier with the Ballet Russes.

After some scary stays in American hospitals, on which the composer's comments were particularly sardonic, Stravinsky died at his home in New York in 1971. He is buried in Venice, near the grave of Diaghilev.

Chief Works: Ballet scores, including *The Firebird, Petrushka, The Rite of Spring, The Wedding, Orpheus, Agon* ▪ *The Soldier's Tale,* an unusual chamber-music piece with narrator ▪ An "opera-oratorio," *Oedipus the King; The Rake's Progress,* an opera in English (words by the poet W. H. Auden) ▪ Two symphonies; concertos; *Symphony of Psalms* for orchestra and chorus ▪ Other religious works: a Mass, *Requiem Canticles*

Encore: After *The Rite of Spring,* listen to *Petrushka* and *Symphony of Psalms.* Read *Conversations with Stravinsky* by Robert Craft, a protégé of Stravinsky for many years.

3 Expressionism

Even as Stravinsky was rejecting Romantic sentiment, in Austria and Germany composers pressed forward with music that was increasingly emotional and complex. As though intent on taking Romantic fervor to its ultimate conclusion, they found themselves exploiting extreme states, extending all the way to hysteria, nightmare, even insanity. This movement, known as *expressionism,* shares its name with important parallel movements in art and literature (see page 327).

These years also saw the publication of the first works of Sigmund Freud, with their new analysis of the power of unconscious drives, the significance of dreams, and the central role of sexuality. Psychoanalytic theory had a clear impact on German expressionism; a vivid example is *Erwartung* (Anticipation),

Nightmarish images recur in expressionist art. Perhaps the most famous expressionist image is *The Scream*, by the Norwegian artist Edvard Munch (1863–1944).

a monologue for soprano and orchestra written by Arnold Schoenberg in 1909. In it, a woman comes to meet her lover in a dark wood and spills out all her terrors, shrieking as she stumbles upon a dead body she believes to be his. One cannot tell whether *Erwartung* represents an actual scene of hysteria, an allegory, or a Freudian dream fantasy.

Schoenberg was the leading expressionist in music. He pioneered in the "emancipation of dissonance" and the breakdown of tonality, and shortly after World War I he developed the revolutionary technique of serialism (see page 346). Even before the war, Schoenberg attracted two brilliant Viennese students who were only about ten years his junior, and who shared almost equally in his innovations. Schoenberg, Anton Webern, and Alban Berg are often referred to as the Second Viennese School, by analogy with the earlier Viennese triumvirate of Haydn, Mozart, and Beethoven.

ARNOLD SCHOENBERG
Pierrot lunaire (1912)

5 3
28–29 28

This highly influential song cycle sets poems by a minor symbolist poet, Albert Giraud. Like many artists of the time—poets as well as composers—Giraud is not easy to figure out at once. Pierrot is the eternal sad clown, and hence perhaps also the alienated artist; but why is he called "lunar"? In poems that are dotted with Freudian imagery, we hear about his obsession with the moon, his amorous frustrations, his nightmarish hallucinations, his pranks and his adventures.

To match all this, Schoenberg wrote music that utterly lacks the tunes one might expect to find in a set of songs. The soprano does not exactly sing or exactly speak, but performs in an in-between style of Schoenberg's invention called *Sprechstimme* ("speech-song"). **Sprechstimme** is an extreme example of the avant-garde composers' search through the most basic artistic materials for new expressive means—here, sound that is not even fully organized into pitches. Through *Sprechstimme*, Giraud's strange moonstruck poems are somehow magnified, distorted, parodied, and haunted all at the same time.

Pierrot lunaire calls for five instruments: flute, clarinet, violin, cello, piano. Three of their players double on other instruments; that is, the flutist sometimes switches to piccolo, the clarinetist to bass clarinet, and the violinist to viola. Not all the songs involve all the players, so nearly every song has its own unique accompaniment, ranging from a single flute in No. 7 to all eight instruments in No. 21 (the players switching within this one). Schoenberg's dazzling variety of instrumental effects compensates for the inherent sameness of the *Sprechstimme*.

We will examine two songs vastly different in expressive tone—both unsettling in their distinctive ways.

28 *No. 8: "Night"* (voice, piano, bass clarinet, cello) The poem presents the nightmarish aspect of expressionism; we could easily imagine the screaming figure of Edvard Munch's famous painting (on the opposite page) responding to a vision of this sort:

Finstre, schwarze Riesenfalter	Sinister giant black butterflies
Töteten der Sonne Glanz.	Eclipse the blazing disk of sun.
Ein geschlossnes Zauberbuch,	Like a sealed-up book of wizard's spells
Ruht der Horizont—verschwiegen.	The horizon sleeps—secretly.
Aus dem Qualm verlorner Tiefen	From dank forgotten depths of Lethe
Steigt ein Duft, Erinnrung mordend!	A scent floats up, to murder memory.
Finstre, schwarze Riesenfalter	Sinister giant black butterflies
Töteten der Sonne Glanz.	Eclipse the blazing disk of sun.
Und vom Himmel erdenwarts	And from heaven downward dropping
Senken sich mit schweren Schwingen	To the earth in leaden circles,
Unsichtbar die Ungetüme	Invisible, the monstrous swarm
Auf die Menschenherzen nieder . . .	Descends upon the hearts of men,
Finstre, schwarze Riesenfalter.	Sinister giant black butterflies.

Schoenberg used the lowest instruments of his ensemble to depict these ominous insects, weighty in a way utterly unlike real butterflies. Through the last section of the poem we can hear their swarm settling heavily downwards, blotting out the light of day.

Schoenberg called this song a *passacaglia*, recalling a type of ostinato piece from the Baroque period (see page 110). If you listen closely you will hear that his music is dominated by the three-note ostinato shown in the margin.

The ostinato is announced at the very beginning by the piano, then taken up by the cello and bass clarinet; it also ends the song. Throughout, the instrumental accompaniment is largely constructed from overlapping versions of it, moved freely to various pitch levels. The soprano is even asked to sing it, at the eerie bottom of her range, on the word *verschwiegen* (secretly)—the only moment in the entire song cycle when Schoenberg has her abandon *Sprechstimme* for conventional song.

Note, however, that the ostinato is chromatic in essence, its last pitch set a half-step below its first. From such simple materials, Schoenberg can both unsettle conventional tonality and match the scary tone of Giraud's words.

29
28 *No. 18: "The Moonfleck"* (voice, piano, piccolo, clarinet, violin, cello) The piano plays a short introduction, or transition from the previous number. Listen to this piano passage several times. Dense, dissonant, atonal, and alarmingly intense in its motivic insistence, the passage gives us Schoenberg's uncompromising version of musical modernism in a nutshell. It also seems devised to recall the loudest, scariest moments of "Night," one of many such musical connections across Schoenberg's cycle.

> **❝** I only know that on the two occasions I heard *Pierrot lunaire* I was conscious of the most profound impression I have ever experienced from a work of art, and that the enigmatic power of these pieces has left *permanent* traces on my innermost being. But when I look at the score it still remains completely mysterious. . . ."
>
> *Letter to Schoenberg from student Alban Berg, 1914*

In the song itself, the tone shifts abruptly from this intensity; now it is not horror but the nagging bother of an obsession. Pierrot can neither forget nor bear the moonfleck that has soiled his tuxedo:

Einen weissen Fleck des hellen Mondes
Auf dem Rücken seines schwarzen Rockes,
So spaziert Pierrot im lauen Abend,
Aufzusuchen Glück und Abenteuer.

With a fleck of white—bright patch of moonlight—
On the back of his black jacket,
Pierrot strolls about in the mild evening air
On his night-time hunt for fun and good pickings.

Plötzlich stört ihn was an seinem Anzug,
Er beschaut sich rings und findet richtig—
Einen weissen Fleck des hellen Mondes
Auf dem Rücken seines schwarzen Rockes.

Suddenly something strikes him as wrong,
He checks his clothes over and sure enough finds
A fleck of white—bright patch of moonlight—
On the back of his black jacket.

Warte! denkt er: das ist so ein Gipsfleck!
Wischt und wischt, doch—bringt ihn
    nicht herunter!
Und so geht er, giftgeschwollen, weiter,
Reibt und reibt bis an den frühen Morgen—
Einen weissen Fleck des hellen Mondes.

Damn! he thinks, There's a spot of plaster!
Rubs and rubs, but can't get rid of it.

So goes on his way, his pleasure poisoned,
Rubbing and rubbing till dawn comes up—
At a fleck of white, a bright patch of moonlight!

In his setting Schoenberg explores timbres completely different from those of "Night." He uses high-pitched, quicksilver motives, scattered through the whole ensemble, to depict flickering moonlight. Simultaneous fugues and canons are at work, but what the listener perceives is a fantastic lacework of sounds, with hardly a hint of tonality, as Pierrot frantically but in vain brushes at himself. "The Moonfleck" uses extremely complicated technical means to achieve a unique sonorous effect.

An expressionist Pierrot by Georges Rouault (1871–1958).

Arnold Schoenberg (1874–1951)

Arnold Schoenberg grew up in Europe's most intense musical environment, the Vienna of Johannes Brahms and Gustav Mahler. He was largely self-taught in music, though he found a mentor in the conductor and composer Alexander von Zemlinsky, whose sister became Schoenberg's first wife. (His second wife also had a musical brother, the leader of an important string quartet—a quartet that featured Schoenberg's music.) A man of unusual versatility, Schoenberg produced important books on music theory, painted (and gave exhibitions of) pictures in expressionist style, and wrote the literary texts for many of his compositions.

His early music—notably *Transfigured Night* of 1899, still his best-known work—followed from the late Romantic tradition of Brahms and Mahler. But Schoenberg soon came to feel that he was destined to carry this tradition through to its logical modern development, by way of increasing chromaticism and atonality. Listeners felt otherwise, and Schoenberg's revolutionary compositions of the 1900s probably met with more hostility than any other works in the entire history of music. At the same time, they attracted the sympathetic interest of Mahler and Richard Strauss, and drew a coterie of brilliant young students to Schoenberg.

Schoenberg's music grew progressively more and more atonal, but he was nearly fifty before he developed the twelve-tone (or serial) system (see page 346). Of all the "new languages" for music attempted by the early avant-garde composers, serialism was the most radical and also the most fruitful. After World War II, even though some leading radicals rejected Schoenberg's music, they still used his fundamental idea of a serial language for music.

As a Jew, Schoenberg was forced to leave Germany when the Nazis came to power, and he spent the rest of his life in Los Angeles, becoming a U.S. citizen in 1941. His unfinished opera *Moses and Aaron* of 1933 is both a Judaic epic and an allegory of the problem of modernist communication with the public. *A Survivor from Warsaw* was written in memory of the slaughter that occurred in the Warsaw Jewish quarter when the Nazis crushed the uprising there in 1943.

Arnold Schoenberg was a strange personality: gloomy, uncompromising, inordinately proud, and also highly superstitious. Of all the major composers, he was the first great teacher since Bach; besides his close associates of the Second Viennese School, he strongly influenced many other musicians who sought him out as a teacher. Near the end of his life he taught at UCLA.

Chief Works: An early "symphonic poem" for string sextet, *Transfigured Night;* Five Orchestral Pieces; two chamber symphonies, a piano concerto and a violin concerto; five string quartets ▪ *Erwartung* ("Anticipation"), an expressionist monodrama for one singer and orchestra; the unfinished opera *Moses and Aaron* ▪ *A Survivor from Warsaw* ▪ Songs, including *The Book of the Hanging Gardens,* to texts by the German symbolist poet Stefan George; *Pierrot lunaire* ("Moonstruck Pierrot")

Encore: After *Pierrot lunaire,* listen to *Verklärte Nacht* ("Transfigured Night") and Five Orchestral Pieces.

ALBAN BERG (1885–1935)
Wozzeck (1923)

30–34   5–6

After Schoenberg, the most powerful exponent of expressionism in music was his student Alban Berg. Berg's opera *Wozzeck,* first conceived during World War I, was completed in 1923. In general plan, this opera can be described as Wagnerian, in that it depends on musical continuity carried by the orchestra. It uses leitmotivs, and contains no arias. Its musical style owes much to Schoenberg's *Pierrot lunaire.*

Background   Berg set a remarkable fragmentary play by the German dramatist Georg Büchner, a half-legible draft that was discovered after his death in 1837. In a series of brief, savage scenes spoken in the plainest vernacular, Büchner presents an almost paranoid vision of the helpless poor oppressed by society. Berg's music for the play's dialogue is all highly intense, and he kept

Wozzeck, Marie, and their child—before the murder

the tension up by writing continuous orchestral interludes during the blackouts between all the scenes, five in each of the opera's three acts.

Franz Wozzeck is an inarticulate and impoverished soldier, the lowest cog in the military machine. He is troubled by visions and tormented for no apparent reason by his captain and by the regimental doctor, who pays him a pittance for serving as a human guinea pig in bizarre experiments. Wozzeck's lover, Marie, sleeps with a drum major, who beats Wozzeck up when he makes some objection. Finally Wozzeck murders Marie, goes mad, and drowns himself.

Act III; Interlude after scene ii   Scene ii is the murder scene. When Wozzeck stabs Marie, she screams, and all the leitmotivs associated with her blare away in the orchestra. It is said that all the events of our lifetime flash before our eyes at the moment of dying.

A blackout follows, and the stark interlude between the scenes consists of a single pitch played by the orchestra in two gut-bursting crescendos. Don't turn the sound down if this passage hurts your ears—it's supposed to.

Scene iii   The lights snap on again. In a sordid tavern, Wozzeck gulps a drink and seeks consolation with Marie's friend Margret. Berg's idea of a ragtime piano opens the scene—one of many signs that European music of the 1920s had woken up to American influences. But it is a distorted, utterly dissonant ragtime, heard through the ears of someone on the verge of a breakdown.

The music is disjointed, confused, shocking. When Margret gets up on the piano and sings a song, her song is distorted, too:

Suddenly she notices blood on Wozzeck's hand. It smells like human blood, she says. In a dreadful climax to the scene, the apprentices and street girls in the inn come out of the shadows and close in on Wozzeck. He manages to escape during another blackout, as a new orchestral interlude surges frantically and furiously.

The whole of scene iii is built on a single short rhythm, repeated over and over again with only slight modifications—*but presented in many different tempos.* This twitching "master rhythm" is marked above the two previous examples, first at a fast tempo, then at a slow one; we first heard it in the timpani in the interlude between scenes ii and iii. Another obvious instance comes when Margret first notices the blood:

Here is yet another kind of ostinato—very different from Stravinsky's kind (see page 338). Even though this master rhythm may elude the listener in a good many of its appearances, its hypnotic effect contributes powerfully to the sense of nightmare and fixation.

Scene iv   Fatefully, Wozzeck returns to the pond where he murdered Marie. The orchestra engages in some nature illustration; we can even hear frogs croaking around the pond. Wozzeck's mind has quite cracked. He shrieks for the knife (in powerful *Sprechstimme* reminiscent of *Pierrot lunaire:* see page 340), discovers the corpse, and sees the blood-red moon and the pond, too, seemingly filled with blood. He walks into the water to wash himself.

At this point, his principal tormenters walk by. The captain and the doctor hear the macabre orchestral gurgles and understand that someone is drowning, but like people watching a mugging on a crowded city street, they make no move to help. "Let's get away! Come quickly!" says the terrified captain—in plain, naturalistic speech, rather than the *Sprechstimme* used by Wozzeck.

In the blackout after this scene, emotional music wells up in the orchestra, mourning for Wozzeck, Marie, and humanity at large. Here Berg adopts and even surpasses the late Romantic style of Gustav Mahler. Anguished leitmotives from earlier in the opera, mainly in the brass, surge into a great climax, then subside.

Scene v   Berg (following Büchner) has yet another turn of the knife waiting for us in the opera's final scene. Some children who are playing with Wozzeck's little son run off to view his mother's newly discovered corpse. Uncomprehending, he follows them. The icy sweetness of the music here is as stunning as the violent music of the tavern scene and the weird pond music. In turning Büchner's visionary play fragment into an expressionist opera, Berg created one of the great modernist theater pieces of the twentieth century.

For once, a composer picture that's different: Alban Berg looks out over a lifesized portrait of himself painted by Arnold Schoenberg.

Schoenberg and Serialism

Of all early twentieth-century composers, Arnold Schoenberg (1874–1951) was the most keenly aware of the problem caused by ever-broadening dissonance and atonality. The problem, to put it simply, was the clear and present danger of chaos. In the early 1920s Schoenberg found a way that he felt would impose order or control over the newly "emancipated" elements of music.

This resulted in the **twelve-tone system,** defined by Schoenberg as a "method of composing with the twelve tones solely in relation to one another"—that is, *not* in relation to a central pitch, or tonic, which is no longer the point of reference for music. This method became known as **serialism.** Serialism can be regarded as a systematization of the chromaticism developed by Romantic composers, especially Richard Wagner (see page 248).

The Twelve-Tone System

Schoenberg's method of composing with the twelve pitches of the chromatic scale held them to a *fixed ordering.* An ordered sequence of the twelve pitches is called a **twelve-tone row,** or **series:** hence the term *serialism.* For any composition, he would determine a series ahead of time and maintain it (the next piece would have a different series).

What does "maintain" mean in this context? It means that *Schoenberg composed by writing notes only in the order of the work's series,* or of certain carefully prescribed other versions of the series (see below). As a general rule, he went through the entire series without any repetitions or backtracking before starting over again. However, the pitches can appear in any octave, high or low. They can stand out as melody notes or blend into the harmony. They can assume any rhythm: In the example below, pitch 10 lasts sixteen times as long as pitch 7.

And what are those "versions" of the series? The series can be used not only in its original form, but also *transposed,* that is, the same note ordering can start from any note in the chromatic scale. The composer can also present the series *backward* (called "retrograde") or *inverted,* that is, with the intervals between notes turned upside down. The basic idea of serialism may seem to impose order with a vengeance by putting severe limits on what a composer can do. But once the versions are taken into consideration, an enormous number of options becomes available.

Phrase of a Schoenberg melody using a twelve-tone series.

LISTEN   Berg, *Wozzeck,* Act III, scenes iii and iv

5   DVD
30–34   5–6

SCENE iii: A tavern

| 30 | 0:30 | Wozzeck: | Tanzt Alle; tanzt nur zu, springt, schwitzt und stinkt, es holt Euch doch noch einmal der Teufel! | Dance, everyone! Go on, dance, sweat and stink, the devil will get you in the end. |

(Gulps down a glass of wine)
(Shouts above the pianist:)

			Es ritten drei Reiter wohl an den Rhein,	Three horsemen rode along the Rhine,
			Bei einer Frau Wirtin da kehrten sie ein.	They came to an inn and they asked for wine.
			Mein Wein ist gut, mein Bier ist klar,	The wine was fine, the beer was clear,
			Mein Töchterlein liegt auf der . . .	The innkeeper's daughter . . .

| | | | Verdammt! Komm, Margret! | Hell! Come on, Margret! |

(Dances with her)

			Komm, setzt dich her, Margret!	Come and sit down, Margret!
			Margret, Du bist so heiss. . . . Wart' nur,	Margret, you're hot!
			wirst auch kalt werden!	Wait, you too will be cold!
			Kannst nicht singen?	Can't you sing?

(She sings:)

Serialism and Unity

Part of the point of twelve-tone composition is that each piece has its own special "sound world" determined by its series. This permeates the whole piece. The next piece has a new series and a new sound world.

Serialism can be regarded as the end result of an important tendency in nineteenth-century music, the search for ever stronger means of unity within individual compositions. We have traced the "principle of thematic unity" in music by Berlioz, Wagner, and others (see page 252). A serial composition is, in a sense, totally unified, since every measure of it shares the same unique sound world. On its own special terms, Schoenberg's serialism seemed to realize the Romantic composers' ideal of unity.

The Second Viennese School

The two composers after Schoenberg quickest to adopt his serialism, Anton Webern and Alban Berg, had both studied with him in Vienna before World War I. Together the three are sometimes referred to as the Second Viennese School. They were very different in musical personality, and serialism did not really draw them together; rather it seems to have accentuated the unique qualities of each composer.

Anton Webern (1883–1945) was an unspectacular individual whose life revolved around his strangely fragile artistic accomplishment. Despite his aristocratic background, he became a devoted conductor of the Vienna Workers' Chorus, as well as holding other rather low-profile conducting positions.

From the start, Webern reacted against the grandiose side of Romanticism, as represented by the works of Richard Strauss and Gustav Mahler. He turned his music about-face, toward abstraction, atomization, and quiet: so quiet that listening to his music, one listens to the rests almost as much as to the notes themselves. His compositions are all extremely brief and concentrated (we discuss one of them on page 374). Webern's entire musical output can fit on three CDs.

But both Webern's vision of musical abstraction and his brilliant use of serialism made him a natural link between the first phase of modernism, around World War I, and the second. Though he was killed in 1945, shot in error by a member of the American occupying forces in Austria, his forward-looking compositions caught the imagination of an entire generation of composers after World War II.

Alban Berg (1885–1935), in contrast, looked back; more than Schoenberg and certainly more than Webern, he kept lines of communication open to the Romantic tradition by way of Mahler. Berg's first opera, *Wozzeck,* was an immediate success on a scale never enjoyed by the other "Second Viennese" composers. His second opera, *Lulu* (1935), is now also a classic, though it made its way slowly—Berg had only partly orchestrated Act III when he died, and both operas were banned by the Nazis.

Like Webern, Berg met a bizarre end: he died at the age of 50 as a result of an infected insect bite. After his death, it came out that he had been secretly in love with a married woman, and had employed a musical code to refer to her and even to address her in his compositions—among them a very moving Violin Concerto (1935), his last work, which also refers to two other women.

1:44	Margret:	In's Schwabenland, da mag ich nit, / Und lange Kleider trag ich nit. / Denn lange Kleider, spitze Schuh, / Die kommen keiner Dienstmagd zu.	But Swabia will never be / The land that I shall want to choose, / For silken dresses, spike-heeled shoes, / Are not for servant girls like me.
	Wozzeck:	Nein! keine Schuh, man kann auch blossfüssig in die Höll' geh'n! Ich möcht heut raufen, raufen. . . .	No shoes! You can go to hell just as well barefoot! I'm feeling like a fight today!
2:29	Margret:	Aber was hast Du an der Hand?	But what's that on your hand?
	Wozzeck:	Ich? Ich?	Me? My hand?
	Margret:	Rot! Blut!	Red! Blood!
	Wozzeck:	Blut? Blut?	Blood? Blood? / (People gather around)
	Margret:	Freilich . . . Blut!	Yes, it is blood!
	Wozzeck:	Ich glaub', ich hab' mich geschnitten, da an der rechten Hand. . . .	I think I cut myself, on my hand. . . .
	Margret:	Wie kommt's denn zum Ellenbogen?	How'd it get right up to the elbow, then?

31

		Wozzeck:	Ich hab's daran abgewischt.	I wiped it off there. . . .
		Apprentices:	Mit der rechten Hand am rechten Arm?	Your right hand on your right arm?
		Wozzeck:	Was wollt Ihr? Was geht's Euch an?	What do you want? What's it to you?
		Margret:	Puh! Puh! Da stinkt's nach Menschenblut!	Gross! It stinks of human blood! *(curtain)*

Confusion. The people in the Inn crowd around Wozzeck, accusing him. Wozzeck shouts back at them and escapes.

SCENE iv: A pond in a wood

32 3:41 Wozzeck:

Das Messer? Wo ist das Messer? Ich hab's dagelassen . . . Näher, noch näher. Mir graut's! Da regt sich was. Still! Alles still und tod . . . Mörder! Mörder! Ha! Da ruft's! Nein, ich selbst.	The knife! Where is the knife? I left it there, around here somewhere. I'm scared! Something's moving. Silence. Everything silent and dead . . . Murderer! Murderer! Ah, someone called! No, it was just me.
Marie! Marie! Was hast Du für eine rote Schnur um den Hals? Hast Dir das rote Halsband verdient, wie die Ohrringlein, mit Deiner Sünde? Was hangen Dir die schwartzen Haare so wild?	Marie, Marie! What's that red cord around your neck? A red necklace, payment for your sins, like the earrings? Why is your dark hair so wild?

1:03 4:44

Mörder! Mörder! Sie werden nach mir suchen. . . . Das Messer verrät mich! Da, da ist's!	Murderer! Murderer! They will come look for me. . . . The knife will betray me! Here, here it is.
So! da hinunter! Es taucht ins dunkle Wasser wie ein Stein. Aber der Mond verrät mich . . . der Mond ist blutig. Will denn die ganze Welt es ausplaudern?! — Das Messer, es liegt zu weit vorn, sie finden's beim Baden oder wenn sie nach Muscheln tauchen.	There! Sink to the bottom! It plunges into the dark water like a stone. But the moon will betray me. . . . The moon is bloody. Is the whole world going to betray me? The knife is too near the edge — they'll find it when they're swimming or gathering mussels.
Ich find's nicht . . . Aber ich muss mich waschen. Ich bin blutig. Da ein Fleck . . . und noch einer.	I can't find it. But I have to get washed. There's blood on me. Here's one spot . . . here's another. . . .
Weh! Weh! Ich wasche mich mit Blut! Das Wasser ist Blut . . . Blut. . . .	Oh, woe! I am washing myself in blood! The water *is* blood . . . blood. . . . *(drowns)*

33 6:21

Captain:	Halt!	Wait!
Doctor:	Hören Sie? Dort!	Don't you hear? There!
Captain:	Jesus! Das war ein Ton!	Jesus! What a sound!
Doctor:	Ja, dort.	Yes, there.
Captain:	Es ist das Wasser im Teich. Das Wasser ruft. Es ist schon lange Niemand entrunken. Kommen Sie, Doktor! Es ist nicht gut zu hören.	It's the water in the pond, the water is calling. It's been a long time since anyone drowned. Come away, Doctor! This is not good to hear.
Doctor:	Das stöhnt . . . als stürbe ein Mensch. Da ertrinkt Jemand!	There's a groan, as though someone were dying. Somebody's drowning!
Captain:	Unheimlich! Der Mond rot und die Nebel grau. Hören Sie? . . . Jetzt wieder das Achzen.	It's weird! the red moon, the gray mist. Now do you hear? . . . That moaning again.
Doctor:	Stiller, . . . jetzt ganz still.	It's getting quieter — now it's stopped.
Captain:	Kommen Sie! Kommen Sie schnell!	Let's get away! Come quickly! *(curtain)*

34 7:53 ORCHESTRAL MUSIC (LAMENT)

4 Modernism in America: Ives

As we have seen, Paris and Vienna, centers of intense activity in all the arts, were also the first centers of modernist music. Echoes of modernism, some loud, some soft, were heard elsewhere in Europe: in Italy, where there was a short-lived movement called Futurism, and in Germany, Russia, Hungary, and England.

It is nevertheless amazing that a major modernist composer should have emerged in the United States as early as around 1900; for at that time America had no rich tradition of classical music, and what we did have was resolutely conservative. "Emerged" is not quite the word, for what also amazes is that Charles Ives worked in isolation, composing in his spare time. His music was scarcely performed until the 1950s.

Many of Ives's compositions have American subjects, such as *Central Park in the Dark* and *Some Southpaw Pitching*. His *Holidays* Symphony includes movements titled "The Fourth of July," "Thanksgiving," and so on. These pieces

Charles Ives (*1874–1954*)

Charles Ives was the son of a Civil War military bandmaster and music teacher from Danbury, Connecticut, near New York City. Ives senior was an extraordinary character who enjoyed musical games such as playing two tunes simultaneously in different keys. His father's unconventionality—and his association with popular music—left a lasting impression on Charles.

Ives was a church organist as a teenager, and then went on to Yale, where he was a popular undergraduate (with a D+ average). He absorbed everything that his professor, the eminent composer Horatio Parker, had to teach him. But the American musical climate in the 1890s was basically hostile to modern trends; Parker wrote in a dull, traditional style. For Ives, this was not only dull but somehow also unmasculine. His vision was of a much more vigorous, rough-grained, enthusiastic, experimental kind of music.

So when he got his B.A. he hedged his bets and took a job in insurance as well as another church organist position. After a few years he relegated music entirely to his spare time, while pursuing a very successful and innovative business career during the day. He seldom mixed with musicians and for years made little effort to get his works performed or published.

All the while Ives was developing his unique mystical notions about music, notions that have been linked to nineteenth-century New England transcendentalism. To Ives, the actual sound of music seems to have counted less than the idea of music making as a basic human activity. All kinds of music were equally valid, then, whether popular or sophisticated, whether simple or wildly dissonant, whether played in or out of tune. What mattered was people's communal joy in music making. Believing also

that all musical experiments have equal validity, Ives launched into visionary projects that no other composer of the time would have considered.

Ives's late years were clouded by pathos, for after 1920 he gave up music almost entirely due to discouragement and bad health. He also sometimes tinkered with his old music to make it appear even more revolutionary than it was—though the music as he originally wrote it still amazes music historians. For his last thirty years Ives lived in quiet affluence with his wife, Harmony, the sister of a college friend—he had taken her to his junior prom; Harmony seems to have had a strong influence on her husband's ideas about music and life. They lived long enough to see his music admired first by a growing number of American musicians and then by the public at large.

Chief Works: For orchestra, 4 symphonies and the *Holidays* Symphony, several "Orchestral Sets," *Central Park in the Dark* and *The Unanswered Question* ▪ *Concord* Sonata for piano (movements entitled "Emerson," "Hawthorne," "The Alcotts," "Thoreau") ▪ *Variations on "America"* for organ (written at age 17; best known in its arrangement for orchestra) ▪ Chamber music, much of it programmatic ▪ Church music, choral music, and important solo songs, among them "General William Booth enters into Heaven"

Encore: After Orchestral Set No. 2, listen to *The Unanswered Question, Putnam's Camp, The Fourth of July.*

regularly employ American music: folk songs, popular songs by Stephen Foster, gospel hymns, and ragtime are all quoted, sometimes in great profusion. Ives especially favored the hymns he remembered from his youth.

Ives was our first important nationalist composer. But he was also more than that: a true American original, a man with amazingly radical ideas about music, and an insatiable experimenter with musical materials. Ives anticipated many of the most talked-about musical innovations of the early part of the twentieth century—and of the later part, too.

Writing highly dissonant music was the least of it. He also wrote music for pianos tuned to quarter tones, and several works in which certain elements can be played, or not played, or played differently, depending on the performer's choice. For the whole length of his *Psalm 90*, for chorus, organ, and bells, low C sounds continuously in the organ pedals—for nearly eleven minutes. In one of his major works, the *Concord* Sonata of 1915, the pianist has to use his elbow and a special wooden block that holds sixteen notes down at a time.

To get an idea of the extraordinary range of Ives's work, we should examine two works—one of them little known, the other very famous.

> " I remember, when I was a boy—at the outdoor Camp Meeting services in Redding (Conn.), all the farmers, their families and field hands, for miles around, would come afoot or in their farm wagons. I remember how the great waves of sound used to come through the trees . . . There was power and exaltation in those great conclaves of sound from humanity."
>
> *Charles Ives*

A revival meeting

CHARLES IVES
Second Orchestral Set, second movement:
"The Rockstrewn Hills Join in the People's Outdoor Meeting" (1909)

35–36   29–30

This orchestral piece is the second of three that make up Ives's Second Orchestral Set. Ives wrote four symphonies; if his orchestral sets are thought of as (very) informal examples of the same genre, this movement would count as the scherzo. For all its obscurity, the title has a true Ivesian ring: The grandeur of nature joins a human festivity, apparently some sort of revival meeting.

The piece begins with several false starts, as though any effort to formulate a melody is bound to be defeated by other sounds, rhythms, and bits of tunes coming from this way and that. A dance fragment, first in the strings, then in the woodwinds, is interrupted by snatches of brass band music and piano ragtime. The hubbub gets more and more dissonant and atonal.

Gradually this array of "sound bites" builds up to a passage of forceful irregular rhythms. We catch a fragment of a cakewalk, a ragtime dance of the 1890s. At the climax, the confused superimposition of various ideas gives way for just a moment to homophony; the irregular pounding rhythms here remind us of Stravinsky's *The Rite of Spring*—a work written four years after Ives wrote this one. There is a slowdown and a quiet pause.

A new section begins with a fragmentary march in the trombones. Then at last a phrase of a hymn tune begins to crystallize. Only at the fourth try does the melody become clear. "I am coming, Lord!," the rousing chorus from one of Ives's favorite hymns, is orchestrated like a march:

A gospel hymn book of the time, open at the hymn used in Ives's Second Orchestral Set.

Hymn, "I Hear Thy Welcome Voice"

I am coming, Lord!   Com-ing now to Thee!   Wash me, cleanse me, in the blood That flowed on Calva-ry.

Ives

Slow, swinging tempo

(tune fades)

After this collapses, the piano can be heard playing four-note segments of the whole-tone scale (a hallmark of Debussy—but Ives probably learned it from his inquisitive father, not from the French composer). The outdoor meeting ends on an intense but quiet dissonance that is strangely serious, even spiritual—a characteristic Ivesian gesture.

Whole-tone scale

bedfordstmartins.com/listen
▶ Interactive Listening Chart 22

LISTENING CHART 22

Ives, "The Rockstrewn Hills"
4 min., 43 sec.

5   3
35–36   29–30

35 29	0:00	Introductory
	0:17	Dance fragment, strings; interrupted
	0:29	Dance fragment, woodwinds; interrupted
	0:49	Ragtime fragment, piano
		Kaleidoscopic array of fragmentary ideas; buildup
	1:27	Brass becomes prominent.
	1:58	Cakewalk fragment
	2:07	Climax: homophony
	2:34	Slowdown and pause (solo stringed instruments)
	2:44	March fragment, trombones
	3:00	The hymn is prefigured.
36 30	3:14	Dance fragment from beginning, brass—collapse
0:13	3:27	Hymn, clearer
0:43	3:57	At last the hymn emerges clearly: "I am coming, Lord!"
0:54	4:08	Fades: a fragmentary whole-tone scale in the piano

❝ Get up and try to use your ears like a man!"

Charles Ives

CHARLES IVES
The Unanswered Question (1906)

6
1

This famous work—utterly quiet, serene, and solemn—is as different as could be from the cheerful clatter of "The Rockstrewn Hills." It requires two conductors. We cannot describe it better than Ives did himself:

> The strings play *ppp* throughout, with no change in tempo. They represent "The Silences of the Druids" who know, see, and hear nothing. The trumpet intones "The Unanswered Question of Existence" and states it in the same tone of voice each time. But the hunt for "The Invisible Answer" undertaken by the flutes and other human beings [Ives is personifying the other woodwind instruments] gradually becomes more active and louder. The "Fighting Answerers" seem to realize a futility, and begin to mock "The Question"—the strife is over. . . . After they disappear, "The Question" is asked for the last time, and the "Silences" are heard beyond in "Undisturbed Solitude."

What is so novel here—what rivals in innovativeness any of the experiments of the European modernists of the time—is the concept of three distinct, independent levels of music. The smooth string choir, playing consonant harmonies, is one. Another is provided by the dissonant woodwinds, a more and more taunting modernist challenge to the strings. Then there is the single trumpet, sounding like a voice, all the more solemn and haunting for asking its Question only about half a dozen times in the whole composition.

These simultaneous levels do not fit together in the least, in terms of traditional polyphony. Their precise rhythmic or contrapuntal relationship is left to chance. Yet this unusual nondialogue between "Silences," "Questioner," and "Answerers" proves to be both coherent and poignant: a foretaste, perhaps, of our own age, an age marked by the quiet desperation of noncommunication.

LISTEN

IVES
The Unanswered
Question

1:51 Question, *ppp*
      (trumpet)
2:45 Question
again at 3:41, 4:17, 4:58
5:43 Question, *f*
6:34 Question, *ppp*

TRUMPET

bedfordstmartins.com/listen
▶ Quizzes and Flashcards

CHAPTER 21

Alternatives
to Modernism

I n music, as in all the arts, modernism was a primary source of creative energy in the period from before World War I until after World War II. The vision of new "languages" to express the new conditions of modern life was a powerful one, even if the public at large often found those languages hard to understand. The success of some avant-garde works of art—Alban Berg's opera *Wozzeck,* for one—shows that they met with a deep response from minds and hearts battered by the events of the early twentieth century.

Not everyone was as successful as Berg, however; most modernist music played to a small, esoteric audience. A figure like Schoenberg, convinced that music's progress depended on his leadership, could accept this and hold uncompromisingly to modernist principles. Many others, too, never blinked—including, after Ives, several modernists here at home, chief among them Carl Ruggles (1876–1971), Roger Sessions (1896–1985), and Edgard Varèse (1883–1965; Varèse came to America from France).

Twentieth-Century Traditionalism

Other composers, both here and abroad, took a more ambivalent view of modernism. No one could escape its influence, and not many wanted to; but not everyone wanted to accept it fully. The force of Romantic tradition was still strong. Some famous twentieth-century names never joined the avant-garde at all and kept on mining the reliable quarries of Romanticism for their own private veins of (they hoped) musical gold. One area where this tendency is particularly clear, as we will see, is early film music.

Other composers worked with the ideas of Schoenberg or Stravinsky, selectively adopting no more than they needed to fulfill their own creative needs. Still others started out wholeheartedly in the avant-garde, only to turn back to stylistic amalgams of one kind or another between the modern and the more traditional. American figures who fall somewhere in this spectrum are Charles Griffes (1884–1920), William Grant Still (1895–1978), Samuel Barber (1910–1981), and William Schuman (1910–1992), as well as Aaron Copland (1900–1990), whom we come to at the end of this chapter. Both Still, the first important African American composer in the concert music tradition, and Copland also recall nineteenth-century nationalism in their use of American musical idioms.

Opera in the Early Twentieth Century

As we have seen in Chapter 17, late nineteenth-century opera was dominated by the towering figures of Giuseppe Verdi in Italy and Richard Wagner in Germany. It's remarkable that each country produced a younger opera composer, working under the shadow of these masters, whose works today are almost as much admired as theirs: Giacomo Puccini and Richard Strauss.

Both produced their main operas in the period from 1895 to 1915—the breakthrough years for Stravinsky, Schoenberg, and the rest of the avant-garde. Each found his own, very different alternative to modernism. Puccini kept his distance, selecting just a few modernist techniques that he could incorporate into his relatively conservative style. Strauss started out as a musical radical second to none, only to pull back later in life.

Giacomo Puccini (1858–1924)

Growing up in Italy, the land of opera, Puccini composed operas and not much else—like Verdi. For Italians, opera means melody, and Puccini was the only composer of his time whose melodies could stand comparison to Verdi's. This, together with an exceptional gift for all things theatrical, resulted in a stream of operas that bowled over international audiences in his day, and still do today.

Puccini is especially moving in his musical depiction of afflicted women: the abandoned Cio-Cio San (*Madame Butterfly*), Mimi, dying of consumption (*La Bohème*), and Floria Tosca, who fights off a lecherous police chief (*Tosca*).

Modernism, which arose in France and Germany, was never kind to melody. So the world of Italian opera paid it little attention. Nonetheless, Puccini found he was able to incorporate certain modernist techniques for striking effects in his operas. One such technique was harmony of the kind developed by Debussy (see page 331). It is prominent in two Puccini operas: *La Fanciulla del West* (The Girl of the Golden West, 1910) and *Il Tabarro* (The Cloak, 1918).

Puccini also made a careful study of non-Western music for use in operas set in Japan and China: *Madame Butterfly* (1904) and *Turandot* (completed after his death by another composer, 1926).

Richard Strauss (1864–1949)

The career of Richard Strauss could hardly have been more different. In the 1890s, when Schoenberg and Stravinsky were still youngsters, Strauss was *the* modernist discussed by everyone, resented by many, and attacked by some. He first raised eyebrows with sensational symphonic poems and symphonies, but the climax of his early career was a pair of operas that still have the power to shock, *Salome* (1905) and *Elektra* (1909).

They owe this power both to their librettos and to their music. *Elektra* revisits the most dreadful of all the old Greek myths: Clytemnestra, murderer of her husband Agamemnon, is slain in turn by her son Orestes, egged on by her almost maniacally vengeful sister Electra. The music is often violent and distorted. It verges on and sometimes slips into atonality.

But after 1909, to the astonishment of the musical world, Strauss pulled sharply back from such extremes. His later operas are either frankly Romantic or Neoclassical. *Der Rosenkavalier* (The Knight of the Rose, 1911), still another opera favorite, is a delightful, dizzy mixture of Mozart, Wagner, and Johann Strauss, the Waltz King (no relation). With *Der Rosenkavalier,* coming soon after *Elektra,* it feels as though the composer were bluntly criticizing modernism.

Strauss ended his career in 1948 with some of the loveliest songs (for soprano and orchestra) ever written in the Romantic style.

Giacomo Puccini and Richard Strauss, with contemporary posters of *Madame Butterfly* and *Elektra*.

Ravel (right) with the legendary dancer Vaclav Nijinsky, the star of his ballet *Daphnis and Chloé* in 1912. A year later Nijinsky was responsible for the riot-inducing choreography of Stravinsky's *Rite of Spring*.

Of the many impressive composers active in the first half of the twentieth century, several have maintained and even increased their hold on audiences up to the present day — including the opera composers Puccini and Strauss (see opposite page). Two major composers were Russians who (like Stravinsky) fled the Russian Revolution of 1917: Sergei Prokofiev, who is discussed on page 369, and Sergei Rachmaninov (1873–1943). Rachmaninov was one of the greatest pianists of his time, and his Piano Concertos Nos. 2 and 3 are among the most popular works in the concert repertory. There is a section from Rachmaninov's *Rhapsody on a Theme by Paganini,* a concerto-like work for piano and orchestra, on our DVD.

13

1 Maurice Ravel

Maurice Ravel, born in 1875 in the south of France, was later attracted to Paris. From the very start, his music was marked by refinement, hyperelegance, and a certain coolness; musicians admire him for his superb workmanship and high style. As Debussy occupied the middle ground between Romanticism and modernism, Ravel carved out a place for himself between impressionism and Neoclassicism. While his harmonies and chord progressions often remind us of Debussy, he favored clarity, precision, and instant communication, qualities he found in earlier musical forms and styles.

Few composers have ranged as widely in imagination as Ravel. His music visited Spain, Madagascar, Asia, ancient Greece, America, and — again and again — the world of childhood. He even evoked Vienna, in a bitter anti-German parody of waltz music, *La Valse,* right after World War I (1919).

Maurice Ravel (1875–1937)

Maurice Ravel was born in a little town in the south of France, two miles from the Spanish border, and was brought to Paris at an early age. His mother came from the Basque region of Spain, and many of his compositions have exotic Spanish resonances — *Boléro,* most famously, also *Habanera, The Spanish Hour,* and others.

Ravel spent no fewer than sixteen lackluster years at the Paris Conservatory, the gateway to French musical life in those days, while his older contemporary Claude Debussy emerged as a leader in the music of modernism. When Debussy died in 1918, Ravel was acknowledged as the leading composer of war-ravaged France. Ravel hated Germany and German music, and he was young enough to volunteer for military service against the Germans in World War I, despite his frail body and retiring personality.

From the time of his first major success, with the impressionistic piano piece *Jeux d'eau* (*Fountains;* 1901), it was clear Ravel had an amazing ear for sonority, and the magical sound of his music for piano or orchestra is unmatched. In the following years he belonged to a group of modernist artists and writers who called themselves the Apaches (a name with fauve overtones: see page 327), but he never really warmed to the modernist spirit. He was the most meticulous and exquisite of composers, and his aim was for clarity above all. Some of his most famous compositions make use of classical forms, such as the *Sonatine* for Piano and the Piano Concerto in G.

Ravel never married, seems to have had no close relationships, and lived an uneventful life at his home in Paris. His one big trip, in 1928, was to America; here he met George Gershwin (and Charlie Chaplin) and came back with a small fortune. In 1932, Ravel contracted a rare brain disease; he died five years later. The Piano Concerto in G of 1931 was his last work but one.

Chief Works: Orchestral works: *Mother Goose Suite, La Valse,* the ballet scores *Boléro* and *Daphnis and Chloé* ■ One-act operas: *L'Heure espagnole* (The Spanish Hour) and *L'Enfant et les sortilèges* (The Child Bewitched), a delightful childhood fantasy ■ Piano concertos; *Gaspard de la nuit,* one of the hardest pieces ever written for piano; *Jeux d'eau;* and a charming piano *Sonatine* ■ Songs; a string quartet ■ Many arrangements for orchestra, including Musorgsky's *Pictures at an Exhibition* (see page 300)

Encore: After the first movement of the Piano Concerto in G, listen to the second movement; *Boléro; Sonatine* for Piano.

MAURICE RAVEL
Piano Concerto in G (1931)

A light-hearted piece for piano and small orchestra, the Piano Concerto in G is Ravel's tribute to jazz (his most outspoken tribute, but not his first; like Debussy and Stravinsky, Ravel was fascinated by jazz long before he came to the United States in 1928 and haunted night-spots in Harlem). Americans like George Gershwin and Aaron Copland incorporate jazz accents in their compositions in a fairly direct way (see page 409). With Ravel everything is slightly skewed, as through a special filter, with a delicacy and elegance that we think of as characteristically French, perhaps, and that Ravel projects more clearly than any other composer.

First Movement (Allegramente)   The first theme is *not* jazzy. A long, lively, folklike tune is presented in the sort of fabulous orchestration that is this composer's hallmark: After a whiplash — literally — a piccolo plays the tune with syncopated *pizzicato* (plucked) string chords and the piano shimmering in the background. But the tune really belongs to a special high trumpet (trumpet in C), with the syncopated chords barked out by the other brass.

PICCOLO

LISTENING CHART 23

Ravel, Piano Concerto in G, first movement

Free sonata form. 8 min., 12 sec.

37–41

37	**EXPOSITION**

0:00 **Theme 1**, piccolo, syncopated strings *pizzicato*

0:24 **Theme 1**, trumpet, syncopated brass

0:36 Sudden modulation

Second group

0:44 **Theme 2**, piano: slower; interrupted by the "break"

38	1:40 **Theme 3**, piano
0:37	2:17 **Theme 3**, orchestra—bassoon, trumpet
0:55	2:35 Vigorous, driving music for the piano
1:14	2:54 Break
1:47	3:27 Approach to a cadence
39	3:36 **Retransition:** upward scales in the piano

RECAPITULATION

| 0:09 | 3:45 **Theme 1**, piano, *ff;* returns to the tonic key |
| 0:21 | 3:57 Sudden modulation |

Second group

0:29	4:05 **Theme 2**, piano—with gong
40	4:30 Dreamlike episode: **theme 2**, harp
0:38	5:08 Break; melody continues in the French horn
1:14	5:44 "Cadenza": **theme 3**, with extensive trills
2:04	6:34 **theme 3**, piano and orchestra
2:34	7:05 Piano: vigorous, brilliant
3:07	7:37 Approach to a cadence

CODA

| 41 | 7:42 Orchestra (trumpet), *f*, in the original tonic key, with motives derived from **theme 1** |
| 0:17 | 7:59 *ff* |

The piano now introduces a second theme that recalls the blues—not directly, but clearly enough. A third theme suggests romantic torch songs of the 1930s. Typical of early jazz is Ravel's use of short *breaks*, instrumental interludes between lines of a song lasting just one or two measures (see page 396). He catches this device perfectly with the high clarinet (E-flat clarinet) and a muted trumpet cutting into theme 2, with swishing sounds from the piano and the harp.

At a later point, the harp plays theme 2 itself, in a dreamlike episode that brings this busy movement to a state of near suspension.

After the piano and orchestra have presented themes 2 and 3, the piano engages in vigorous, propulsive music of the sort that often leads to cadences in concertos (see page 206). A new syncopated motive strongly implies that a cadence is coming, though the actual resolution is disguised.

Ravel uses the classical form for a concerto first movement (see page 205), but in the freest possible way. He skips both the orchestra exposition and the development section entirely. A passage that he labels "cadenza" resembles a true cadenza in that it comes near the end of a concerto first movement and the piano plays entirely solo, yet it feels nothing like a free improvisation; in fact, the unaccompanied piano plays theme 3. Ravel drew on classical tradition but at the same time invented his own super-clear and listener-friendly form for the Piano Concerto in G.

At the very end of the first movement, Ravel borrows a favorite device invented by Debussy, a long series of parallel chords. The effect could hardly be more different: Debussy's chords—in *Clouds*, for example; see page 332—are *piano*, legato, silky, vague, and atmospheric; Ravel's are *fortissimo* and staccato, crisp and clear.

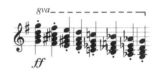

bedfordstmartins.com/listen
▶ Interactive Listening Chart 23

2 Béla Bartók

Growing up in Hungary in the 1890s, the young Béla Bartók was first swept away by the international avant-garde leaders Debussy and especially Richard Strauss. Later in his career he was also influenced by his close contemporary

Bartók collecting folk songs: He was using recording equipment just a few years after commercial recordings began coming out. Around 1906, these rural Hungarians seem less amazed by the primitive phonograph than by the camera.

Béla Bartók (1881–1945)

Béla Bartók showed unusual talent as a pianist and composer at an early age. Music was the avocation of his father, who was principal of an agricultural school in Hungary; after his death Bartók's mother worked as a piano teacher, tirelessly promoting her son's career.

Few musicians have ever had as varied a career as Bartók. He was a prolific composer and a fine pianist, as was his second wife; they appeared as a two-piano team. (Both of his wives had been his students.) In conjunction with another important Hungarian composer, Zoltán Kodály, he directed the Budapest Academy of Music, where the two men tried out new ideas in music teaching. An outcome of this side of Bartók's career is his *Mikrokosmos*, a series of 153 graded piano pieces starting with the very easiest. Well known to most piano students today, the *Mikrokosmos* has probably done more than any other work to introduce modernism to large numbers of musicians in their impressionable years.

Also with Kodály, Bartók undertook a large-scale investigation of Hungarian (and other) folk music, writing several standard books on the topic. He published many folk-song and folk-dance arrangements, and his other compositions are saturated with folk rhythms, modes, and melodic turns. The outstanding nationalist composer of the twentieth century, Bartók left a body of work that equals or surpasses that of any of the nineteenth-century nationalists.

Bartók was strongly opposed to the Nazis. After they came to power in Germany, he refused to concertize there and switched away from his German publisher. And his liberal views caused him a good deal of trouble from right-wingers in Hungary. In 1940, after the outbreak of World War II, Bartók came to America, but he was not well known here and there was little interest in his music. His last years were a struggle to complete his Third Piano Concerto and the Viola Concerto. Ironically, his important works earned a wide, enthusiastic audience shortly after his death.

Chief Works: Concerto for Orchestra, 3 piano concertos, Violin Concerto, Music for Strings, Percussion, and Celesta (for small orchestra) ■ Six string quartets; a fascinating Sonata for Two Pianos and Percussion ■ An opera, *Bluebeard's Castle*, and a ballet, *The Miraculous Mandarin* ■ *Mikrokosmos* and other works for piano ■ Many folk-song arrangements for various ensembles, including Six Rumanian Dances

Encore: After Music for Strings, Percussion, and Celesta, listen to the Violin Concerto and Quartet No. 6.

Stravinsky. Bartók was, however, a man of multiple careers—pianist, educator, and musicologist as well as composer. His deep commitment to folk music—much deeper than Stravinsky's—and his professional involvement with it as a collector had a decisive impact on his music. Many would say that Bartók was more successful in integrating folk music into classical music than any other composer.

Folk music assured that Bartók's music would never (or seldom) become as abstract as much modernist music was. There is always an earthy feel to it; even at its most dissonant, there will be an infectious folk-dance swing or a touch of peasant melody. This is true even in works of his most modernist period, around 1925–35. The austere String Quartet No. 4 of 1928 is often regarded as Bartók's masterpiece.

After that time Bartók's music gradually became more accessible, and the references to folk songs in it became more mellow and, often, more poignant. He now used established forms such as sonata form and rondo; this made his music easier to follow for listeners already accustomed to these forms from eighteenth- and nineteenth-century music. And many of his last works include passages reminiscent of Romanticism: Violin Concerto No. 2, the popular Concerto for Orchestra, and Quartet No. 6 of 1939—another good candidate for Bartók's greatest composition.

> " The right type of peasant music is most perfect and varied in its forms. Its expressive power is amazing, and at the same time it is devoid of all sentimentality and superfluous ornaments. It is simple, sometimes primitive, but never silly. . . . A composer in search of new ways cannot be led by a better master."
>
> *Béla Bartók*

BÉLA BARTÓK
Music for Strings, Percussion, and Celesta (1936)

This interesting composition can be thought of as an informal symphony in the usual four substantial movements, composed for a specially constituted small orchestra. Much of the time the instruments are divided into two sections that answer each other back and forth.* Besides strings, Bartók includes piano, harp, celesta (see pages 38 and 42), timpani—very important—and other percussion. We do not learn this all at once, however. The celesta makes its first entrance with an exquisite effect halfway through the first movement. The piano and harp arrive in the second, and the xylophone only in the third.

Second Movement (Allegro)   The music bubbles over with variety, an exhilarating rush of little melodic tags, rhythms, folk-dance fragments, and novel percussion sounds. It is all held together by sonata form.

A "preface" played by *pizzicato* (plucked) strings precedes theme 1:

> ❝ We've rehearsed a lot . . . the conductor and orchestra have all worked with me showing the greatest affection and devotion; they claim to be very enthusiastic about the work (I am too!). A couple of spots sound more beautiful and startling than I had imagined. There are some very unusual sounds in it!❞
>
> *Bartók writes to his wife about rehearsals for the premiere of* Music for Strings, Percussion, and Celesta

The preface, theme 1, and the contrapuntal bridge passage—all are energized by motive **a.** One thinks of Beethoven's Fifth Symphony (page 231). Bartók's motive works especially well in the timpani, which play a very powerful role in this movement.

There is a full stop after the bridge, so self-conscious that one wonders if Bartók is making fun of sonata-form conventions. The second theme group contains at least three very short themes. Theme 3 has a folk-dance lilt about it:

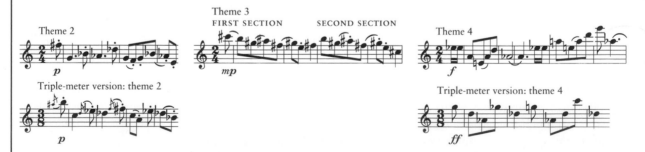

Suddenly the piano enters with a theme containing odd note-repetitions. Since the pianist has hardly played at all up to this point, this new theme feels more like a beginning than like a conclusion. Still, it functions as a cadence theme; very soon the *exposition* ends with another exaggerated cadence.

The timpani introduce the *development section.* Motive **b,** played *pizzicato,* comes in for an extensive workout. After a moment the strings drop down into an accompaniment for an amazing passage for piano, snare drum, and xylophone, punching out syncopated notes. This must have been inspired by the riot-

*This is a principle that goes back at least as far as Giovanni Gabrieli in the early Baroque era: See page 97.

LISTENING CHART 24

Bartók, Music for Strings, Percussion, and Celesta, second movement (Allegro)

Sonata form. 6 min., 59 sec.

2	0:00 Theme 1	With pizzicato "preface"	
	0:23	Held note, drum	
	0:26 **Bridge**		
		CADENCE Big stop, after drumbeat	
3	**Second group**		
	0:56 **Theme 2**		
0:13	1:10 **Theme 3**	Folklike tune, strong beat	
		Developmental	
0:36	1:32 **Theme 4**	Over a string trill	
1:08	2:05 **Cadence theme**	Piano	
4		CADENCE Exaggerated cadence; drumbeat	
	DEVELOPMENT		
	2:24 **Section 1**	Irregular rhythms: piano and percussion, leading to the Stravinskian passage (see below)	
0:49	3:14 **Section 2**	Pizzicato scales, from the "preface"	
5	3:34	New folklike tune	
		Drum prepares:	
0:31	4:05 **Section 3**	Crescendo	
1:20	4:54 **(retransition)**	Drum grows insistent; slowdown ⟶	
	RECAPITULATION		
6	5:10 **Theme 1**	With timpani; meter change	
0:18	5:28 **Bridge**		
7	**Second group**		
	5:40 **Theme 2**	Transformation: triple meter	
0:11	5:51	New continuations	
0:24	6:04 **Theme 4**	Transformation: triple meter	
0:44	6:24 **Cadence theme**	Piano, as before	
	CODA		
8	6:32	New fast dialogue on theme 1	

producing "Dance of the Adolescents" in Stravinsky's *The Rite of Spring* (see page 336).

PIANO, ORCHESTRA—GROUP 1

ORCHESTRA—GROUP 2
(with Harp)

Next, pizzicato string scales in imitative polyphony weave endless new knots and tangles. The scales blend into another folklike tune, similar to theme 3, which is repeated very freely. Introduced by the timpani, a fugue starts up in the lowest register, preparing for the recapitulation. The fugue subject is derived from theme 1, with the meter askew.

And when the <u>recapitulation</u> comes, after much signaling from the timpani, and after an expectant slowdown, the meter is changed throughout. Theme 1 vacillates between duple and triple meter, and the second group tips the balance: themes 2 and 4 each return in swinging triple meter (as shown in the examples on page 360). Theme 3 returns more freely. It takes the piano's odd "cadence theme" to bring us back to the solid duple meter of the start. As a *coda*, Bartók stages a fast, intense dialogue on theme 1.

bedfordstmartins.com/listen
▶ Interactive Listening Chart 24

3   Aaron Copland

America's leading composer of the generation after Charles Ives was Aaron Copland. (Ives was active from around 1895 to 1920; Copland wrote his main works from 1925 to 1950.) Young composers after World War I found many more options open to them than Ives had around 1900. The musical climate was much more favorable to new ideas, partly because the United States had been growing more aware of all things European, including European new music. Like important American writers who lived abroad—Gertrude Stein, T. S. Eliot, Edith Wharton, Ernest Hemingway—composers now associated themselves with European modernism in a way that their predecessors never did.

A worker, a farmer, and a boss are shown "harmonizing": a political allegory by New York painter Ben Shahn (1898–1969), a friend of Copland.

The chief modernist influence on Copland was Stravinsky, and one of Copland's most impressive works is a strenuous set of twenty Variations for Piano (1930) that reflects Stravinsky's dry rhythmic style and his "objective" aesthetic. But after this, Copland's music grew more traditional. Like Strauss, Bartók, and most other composers of the time, he held back from the most extreme manifestations of modernism and forged his own style using such elements of modernism as he needed.

Music for Americans

Again like Bartók, Copland adopted a nationalist agenda. From the start he felt that as an American, he should write music that would speak to his fellow Americans. Copland reached out for American music of all kinds, regions, and ages.

He first turned to jazz, in orchestral pieces called *Music for the Theater* and *El salón México*. Later he incorporated cowboy songs in the ballets *Rodeo* and *Billy the Kid*, an old Shaker melody in *Appalachian Spring*, and square dancing in *The Tender Land*, an opera about growing up in the corn belt. Old hymns make an appearance in his song cycle *Twelve Poems of Emily Dickinson*. In this eclectic attitude we can perhaps again trace the influence of Stravinsky, who over his long career also tapped many musical sources, from Russian folk song to Bach, Tchaikovsky, and Schoenberg.

> ❝ It bothers me not at all to realize that my range as a composer includes both accessible and problematic works. To have confined myself to a single compositional approach would have enhanced my reputation for consistency, no doubt, but would have afforded me less pleasure as a creator."
>
> *Aaron Copland, 1941*

AARON COPLAND
Appalachian Spring (1945)

5 3
42–45 31–33

T he ballet *Appalachian Spring* was choreographed and danced by Martha Graham, a towering figure in American modern dance. She conceived of "a pioneer celebration in spring around a newly built farmhouse in the Pennsylvania hills in the early part of the last century." From his ballet music, Copland arranged a concert suite in six continuous sections. Our recording is conducted by the composer.

42 / 31 *Section 1*   The ballet begins with a very still, clear, static passage of a kind that Copland made very much his own. It seems to catch the spirit of a vast silent landscape at dawn, perhaps, or just before dawn. Solo instruments play meditative figures in counterpoint; an occasional solemn pulse is heard in the harp.

43 / 32 *Section 2*   Here "the bride-to-be and the young farmer husband enact the emotions, joyful and apprehensive, their new domestic partnership invited." The celebration of their new house starts with a lively square dance. Soon a new slower melody—something like a hymn—looms up in counterpoint to the dance figures, first in the wind instruments and then in the strings:

'Tis the gift to be simple,
 'tis the gift to be free,
'Tis the gift to come down
 where you ought to be,
And when we find our-
 selves in the place just
 right
'Twill be in the valley of
 love and delight. . . .
When true simplicity is
 gained
To bow and to bend we
 shan't be ashamed,
Turn, turn will be our
 delight,
Till by turning, turning we
 come round right.

"Simple Gifts"

Allegro   WINDS: Hymn

STRINGS, PIANO: Square Dance

Aaron Copland (1900–1990)

Aaron Copland was the son of Russian-Jewish immigrants living in Brooklyn. After a solid musical education at home, he went abroad to study in Paris. Like many other overseas students, Copland was fortunate to be able to work with a remarkable musician named Nadia Boulanger (1887–1979). For fifty years Boulanger was a revered teacher and mentor of composers, even though she gave up composition herself in deference to the talent of her sister Lili, also a composer, when Lili died tragically at the age of twenty-four. Boulanger encouraged Copland's interest in Stravinsky, whose avant-garde style influenced him greatly.

Back in America, Copland tirelessly promoted American music. He organized an important series of concerts (with another composer, Roger Sessions) to showcase new American scores, wrote articles and books, and formed a Composer's Alliance. Like many artists and writers of the 1930s, he was attracted by leftist ideology and the idea that art should "serve the people." Many works drawing on American folk materials stem from this period of Copland's career, as does his high-school opera *The Second Hurricane*. During World War II he wrote *A Lincoln Portrait* and *Fanfare for the Common Man*, patriotic works, and *Appalachian Spring*, a celebration of traditional American values.

After 1940 Copland headed up the composition faculty at the important summer school at Tanglewood, Massachusetts, in association with the Boston Symphony Orchestra, but his output as a composer decreased. Among his students was Leonard Bernstein. Devoid of the egoism characteristic of so many artists, Copland was one of the most beloved figures of modern American music.

Chief Works: For orchestra: 3 symphonies, *A Lincoln Portrait* (with a speaker), *El salón México* (incorporating South American jazz), a favorite Clarinet Concerto, written for jazzman Benny Goodman ▪ Film scores: *Of Mice and Men* and *Our Town* ▪ Operas: *The Second Hurricane* and *The Tender Land*; ballet scores *Billy the Kid*, *Rodeo*, *Appalachian Spring* ▪ For piano: Variations (Copland's outstanding modernist work; 1930), a sonata, Piano Fantasy (a fine late work; 1957) ▪ A song cycle to poems by Emily Dickinson

Encore: After *Appalachian Spring*, listen to *El salón México* and Clarinet Concerto.

After a section of irregular rhythm, reminiscent of Stravinsky, the music dies down into a prayerful version of the hymn. We also hear little fragments of the dance.

Sections 3 and 4   The next two sections pick up the tempo: Section 3 evokes another whirling square dance and section 4 is a danced sermon by a revivalist and his followers. Both sections include quiet statements of the hymn.

Section 5   The next dance is choreographed to a set of variations on a Shaker song, "Simple Gifts." The Shakers, a religious sect adhering to celibacy and common ownership of property, founded scattered communities from New York to Kentucky in the late eighteenth century.

LISTEN		
COPLAND		
Appalachian Spring		
SECTION 5		
0:00	5:14	Theme
0:36	5:51	Variation 1
1:05	6:19	Variation 2
1:51	7:05	Variation 3
2:31	7:45	Variation 4

44
33

The four variations are little more, really, than playings of the tune or part of the tune by different instruments, in different keys, and in different tempos. Sometimes melodic phrases are heard in imitation.

45 | *Section 6*   Finally, after some music that the program says is "like a prayer," the hymn and the landscape music return once again. We realize that Copland has ingeniously made one grow out of the other. The ballet concludes very quietly. Perhaps the housewarming celebrations have gone on all night, and we are now experiencing another clear gray dawn, a reminder of the many lonely dawns the pioneer couple will face together in the years to come.

Modern dance is, with jazz, one of the great American art forms. Martha Graham (1894–1991), who commissioned and choreographed Copland's *Appalachian Spring,* was one of the legendary group of women who created modern dance in the early twentieth century.

4 The Rise of Film Music

From the early twentieth century on, film music has provided a fertile terrain for composition in many styles. Avant-garde modernism, minimalism, jazz, pop music, rock, and rap have all found a place on film soundtracks. Most prevalent of all, however, have been soundtracks employing the symphony orchestra in styles reminiscent of late Romanticism. Film music, in other words, has been a chief outlet for orchestral music in traditional styles.

This connection of film music to Romanticism was natural, given the Romantics' interest both in opera and in program music. It began with the earliest history of cinema—when some late Romantic styles were still new. In the era of silent film (especially the 1910s and 1920s), live musicians were hired by theaters to provide music to accompany films as they were projected. Pianists or organists would improvise, responding moment by moment to the images on-screen; but their improvisations were often based on published catalogues of favorite themes from Romantic symphonies and operas. In matching these themes to the situations on-screen, the musicians produced something akin to Wagner's leitmotiv technique (see page 285), and indeed many of the melodies in their catalogues were drawn from Wagner's operas.

When new technologies in the late 1920s allowed for soundtracks to be recorded on the filmstrip itself, this leitmotivic procedure evolved. Now composers wrote more-or-less continuous scores for full orchestra, teeming with leitmotivs synchronized precisely to the filmed action. An early monument to this new relation of music and film is the horror classic *King Kong* of 1933, with a soundtrack by the most important of early Hollywood composers, the Viennese émigré Max Steiner. This leitmotivic style has remained prominent in cinema composition ever since. (Many films you might see at the movie theater use it in some form, but it is particularly apparent in mythic blockbusters such as the *Lord of the Rings* series or the 2005 remake of *King Kong*.)

Composers for Film: Prokofiev

Composers who lavish attention on film music tend not to turn up in textbooks such as this one, yet they represent an important strain of twentieth-century orchestral composition. Along with Max Steiner, who composed the score for *Gone with the Wind* in addition to *King Kong*, we might point to the Italian Nino Rota, who collaborated with Federico Fellini on many films and with Francis Ford Coppola on *The Godfather*; to Tōru Takemitsu, collaborator with the giant of Japanese cinema, Akira Kurosawa (rent *Ran* at your local video store); and to John Williams, whose scores for the *Star Wars* films have been excerpted to create a regular repertory piece for pops orchestras across the United States.

Meanwhile, twentieth-century concert, or classical, composers have often turned to film as a creative outlet. In the Soviet Union Sergei Prokofiev devoted much energy to the new medium; so did his younger compatriot Dmitri Shostakovich. (Shostakovich had started his career as a silent-film pianist.) Prokofiev fell into a rewarding collaboration with the greatest of Soviet filmmakers, Sergei Eisenstein (1898–1948). In America Aaron Copland and Leonard Bernstein, whom we come to in Chapter 23, both wrote soundtracks. Copland's work in this vein, for example *Our Town,* strongly evokes the American heartland; in this it is related to his ballet *Appalachian Spring.* Bernstein brought a harder edge, and with it a tint of modernism, to his soundtrack for *On the Waterfront* (1954).

Music and Totalitarianism

European composers of the early twentieth century found their lives profoundly affected by the economic, political, and military upheavals of the time. Besides the sheer threat of annihilation in a time of war, other, more subtle difficulties loomed. Many institutions that composers' careers depended on—orchestras, opera companies, and the like—disappeared or fell into disarray. Some were victims of changing governments with new priorities. Others did not survive staggering inflation in parts of Europe in the 1920s, worldwide depression in the 1930s, or war in the 1940s.

Modernist composers in particular faced threats that were not only physical and social but also *ideological*— that is, threats made not on their lives or livelihoods but on their ideas, including musical ideas. This was most evident in (though not restricted to) the two most powerful repressive totalitarian regimes of the era. In Nazi Germany and Stalin's Soviet Union, artistic modernism in most of its guises was rejected and banned.

In each country the rationale for repression was the same distorted outgrowth of nineteenth-century nationalism: Art ought to speak straightforwardly to the national "folk" and give voice to its aspirations and history. This tenet was foreign to modernist art's emphasis on originality and individualism, its formal intricacies, and its experimentation—its elitism, as the culture czars in Russia and Germany saw it. For Nazis and Stalinists alike, modernist art had no reason to exist.

Nazi Germany

Hitler's regime promoted music of the great German masters; Beethoven and Wagner were special favorites. But it banned explicitly modernist music, supporting instead the latter-day Romanticism of the aging Richard Strauss, for example (see page 354). Meanwhile Jewish composers and other musicians faced extermination. Those who could fled to countries all over the world, many of them to the United States. Arnold Schoenberg is the best known of these refugees (see page 343), but there were many others, including Kurt Weill, composer of "Mack the Knife," who established a second career on Broadway. Béla Bartók, who was not Jewish but also decided to emigrate when his native Hungary finally joined with Hitler, had a harder time (see page 359).

The Soviet Union

Perhaps the most famous victim of ideological muzzling was one of Russia's greatest composers, Dmitri Shostakovich (1906–1975; Shos-ta-kó-vich). Growing up under Communism, he originally followed the dictates of the state without question. Shostakovich was certainly no radical modernist of the Schoenberg sort; but his music did show novel tendencies, including especially strong

dissonant harmonies. A darling of the regime in the early 1930s, he nevertheless walked a perilous path.

With his opera *Lady Macbeth of the Mtsensky Region* of 1934, when he was twenty-eight, he went over the edge. Subject matter and music were equally shocking. The worldwide clamorous success of this work brought Stalin himself to see it. Two days later the official Communist Party newspaper condemned the work and issued a scarcely veiled threat to the composer: "The power of good music to affect the masses has been sacrificed to a petty-bourgeois, formalist attempt to create originality through cheap clowning. It is a game of clever ingenuity *that may end very badly.*"

In fact, Shostakovich was back in favor a year afterwards. But his troubles were not over; he was condemned again ten years later—only to be rehabilitated once more when Stalin died. To what extent Shostakovich accommodated the regime, or criticized it by means of half-secret musical signals in his later compositions—signals recognized by his audiences—is a fascinating question still debated.

Dmitri Shostakovich (left), on one of his rare trips to the West (1962). Looming over him is the Communist Party functionary who came along.

SERGEI PROKOFIEV
Alexander Nevsky (1938)

Eisenstein's *Alexander Nevsky* ranks among the most monumental and innovative of early sound films. It is also a propaganda piece. The title names a Russian culture-hero from the thirteenth century who, having already defeated marauding Vikings, was called upon to unite Russian forces against invading Germans. The film was produced at a moment when tensions between Germany and the Soviet Union were on the rise. In case its allegory was not clear, the last words of the film are Nevsky's proclamation, "He who comes to Russia with a sword, shall die by the sword."

A year after *Alexander Nevsky* was made, Prokofiev refashioned his sound-track music as a cantata so that it could be performed in concert. Our excerpts (which stay especially close to the original soundtrack) come from the beginning of the climactic scene in the film, when the Russians and the Germans meet in battle on the frozen surface of Lake Chudskoe. The reenactment is the most astonishing battle scene anywhere in early cinema. At its end the Germans, fleeing in disarray, crash through the ice and perish, to a harrowing score for percussion only—which Prokofiev omitted, however, from his cantata.

From the music we get a series of vivid sound-pictures of the action, interspersed with moments when the orchestra stops entirely in favor of the noise of battle itself. Prokofiev begins with the frozen lake and apprehensive Russians watching in silence for the German army (compare the still morning landscape of Copland's *Appalachian Spring*). Sustained, minor-mode string chords, ominous drum rolls, a rising tremolo melody in the cellos, and strange, scraping noises from the violas set the shivering tone.

The mood is broken by a battle call in the distance—the signal for the Germans to advance; Prokofiev specifies a muted trombone, played backstage. The last six notes of this call will be heard again and again in the brass, sometimes in long note-values and sometimes in quicker ones, as the Germans move forward (see the example in the margin). The energy picks up with the

German invaders and Russians square off in the battle on ice from Eisenstein's *Alexander Nevsky*—a spectacular sequence that set a high standard for later cinematic war-scenes.

Sergei Prokofiev (1891–1953)

Sergei Prokofiev was a child prodigy who became a concert pianist, conductor, and enormously versatile, productive, and popular composer.

Born in present-day Ukraine, he spent many years at the St. Petersburg conservatory (like Debussy and Ravel in Paris). His early reputation was as a radical, and one ambitious work was written under the direct influence of Stravinsky's *Rite of Spring*. But he made an about-face a year later with his *Classical Symphony*, a gentle parody of a Haydn symphony. Easy to hear in Prokofiev's music is a sound that's hard to describe — within a clear ("Haydnish") tonal framework, the use of very simple chords placed in an unexpected way. The *Classical Symphony* was a forerunner of Neoclassicism, which Stravinsky also embraced after World War I, when both Russian composers lived in Paris, keeping their distance.

Prokofiev moved away from modernist extremes and toward clear tonality, tunefulness, and the use of Russian folk themes. But the good-humored parody of *Classical Symphony* turned into a sharper satirical style that could become positively grotesque in scherzos — another Prokofiev characteristic ("scherzo," remember, means joke).

By the 1930s Prokofiev was a recognized star worldwide, but his thoughts turned back to his Soviet homeland, which had been tempting him with many commissions. He returned to live in Russia in 1936, to much acclaim. He must have known that his freedom of expression would be limited, but he cannot have anticipated how much. Even pieces he wrote to exalt Stalin and the Soviet Union ran into trouble, increasingly so with the approach of World War II. Time and again the ever-fluent Prokofiev rewrote his works, but only too often they were never approved or performed. Twelve years after his welcome back to Russia, his music was publicly denounced by a Soviet arts commissar and performances were banned.

After years of ill health, Prokofiev died on the same day as Stalin — within the hour. His impressive opera based on Tolstoy's *War and Peace,* begun with official support in 1941, was still in limbo at his death.

A slight but much-loved work by Prokofiev is *Peter and the Wolf,* a narrated children's story with orchestral interludes; each of the characters is represented by his or her own instrument and leitmotiv. The hero, needless to say, is a sturdy little Russian.

Chief Works: Operas *The Love of Three Oranges* and *War and Peace* ■ Ballet scores *Romeo and Juliet* and *Cinderella* ■ Film scores for *Alexander Nevsky, Lieutenant Kije,* and others ■ Seven symphonies, including the *Classical Symphony,* piano sonatas and concertos, a beautiful violin concerto (No. 2) ■ *Peter and the Wolf* for children (of all ages)

Encore: Listen to *Lieutenant Kije* and *Classical Symphony.*

LISTENING CHART 25

6
9–10

Prokofiev, *Alexander Nevsky* Cantata, 5: "The Battle on Ice"

FIRST EXCERPT

9

0:00 The frozen lake; the Russians wait.

1:19 The German battle call: muted, offstage trombone

1:45 Staccato eighth notes in strings, drum

1:53 Tuba and saxophones state battle call, overlapping.

2:13 Trumpet and tuba state three-note threat motive; then descending chromatic melody for trumpet and violins

2:55 German chant

4:50 Climactic statements of battle call

4:08 The armies meet.

SECOND EXCERPT

10

0:00 The Russians close in.

introduction of steady eighth notes in the strings and percussion, while the brass—tuba and horns, later trumpets and trombones also—present the call motive and alternate it with another motive, using three chromatic notes out of order.

Gradually the dynamics swell and the texture grows. A chorus is heard singing over and over a homophonic phrase; it is the Germans, intoning a liturgical hymn associated with their cruelty earlier in the film. At the climax, finally, the armies meet. Prokofiev's music abruptly breaks off, and only the noise of battle is heard.

After more than three minutes of cinematic sword-to-sword combat, the Russian trick is revealed: They have lured the Germans onto the lake while keeping much of their force in reserve on the flanks. Now Nevsky gives the order for the flanks to close in ("For Russia! For Russia!"). Prokofiev's music strikes up again, with none of the threatening German sounds from before but now with several new, rousing melodies of victory, alternating helter-skelter in violins, brasses, and other instruments.

TUBA

TRUMPET AND TUBA
(TWO OCTAVES LOWER)

bedfordstmartins.com/listen
▶ Interactive Listening Chart 25

CHAPTER 22

The Late Twentieth Century

Only twenty-one years, from 1918 to 1939, separated the two cataclysmic wars of the twentieth century. It was an uneasy period. The devastation of World War I had stunned artists as well as everybody else, and the sorts of extravagant experimentation that had marked the prewar period no longer seemed appropriate. There was a turn back to earlier styles and genres — the alternatives to modernism we examined in Chapter 21 — and also a search for solid standards and norms.

These efforts were undercut by a new round of devastating events. First came the economic depression, worldwide and protracted, that began in the late 1920s. Then, in the 1930s, the ominous rise of Hitler and the unbelievable (and, by many, disbelieved) tyranny of Stalin led to a second world war. With the Japanese attack on Pearl Harbor at the end of 1941, the United States was thrown into this war to an extent that made our involvement in World War I seem minor. The occupation of France, the siege of Leningrad, the bombings of London, Dresden, and Tokyo, the mass murders in the concentration camps, the detonation of atom bombs over Hiroshima and Nagasaki — these events were virtually impossible for human beings (including artists) to take in. History seemed to be showing that all human conceptions or representations of the world were inadequate.

In music, these events and uncertainties helped to prompt a new phase of experimental modernism in the 1950s and 1960s. In some respects this phase was even more radical and searching than the avant-garde before World War I. Just as with that earlier avant-garde, however, the challenge of new ideas stimulated a consolidating, consoling reaction. By the 1970s yet another set of styles had begun to appear, turning away from the most extreme implications of the second phase of modernism. Today the avant-garde of the 1950s is a somewhat distant memory, and concert music composition is dominated by the styles that arose in reaction to it. In this chapter we sample both of these stylistic waves.

1 Modernism in Music: The Second Phase

Modernism reemerged as the driving force in music during the third quarter of the twentieth century, modernism in a new, more extreme phase. It was a fascinating phase — and no less fascinating because two of its main tendencies seem almost contradictory.

First of all, highly intellectual constructive tendencies came to the fore, inspired by Schoenberg's serialism, but going far beyond it. There were even efforts to "serialize" rhythm, dynamics, and timbre—that is, to set up predetermined series of note durations or tone colors or dynamic levels and compose with them in a fixed order. Never before had such complex mathematical theories been advanced to compose and explain music.

Meanwhile, other composers moved in the opposite direction, relinquishing control over some elements of musical construction and leaving them to chance. (We have already discussed an early anticipation of this move, *The Unanswered Question* by the ever-original Ives.) Some of these same composers also worked toward an extreme simplification of musical materials, offering a stark alternative to the cerebral complexities of post–World War II "total serialism."

It may seem strange to find composers who followed such different paths grouped together under the same general rubric of avant-garde modernism. However, both groups, the complex constructivists and the chance composers, pursued the same goal: They all wanted to question the most fundamental premises that had guided music composition before them. Debussy might have blurred the identity of

The Pianist by Pablo Picasso

melodic themes, Stravinsky might have undermined the regularity of musical meter, and Schoenberg might have dispensed altogether with tonality. But mainstream modernism after 1945 questioned every one of these features of the musical tradition at once and others as well—to the point of even questioning the composer's role in structuring a work at all.

New Sound Materials

In this light another general tendency of modernist composers after World War II is not at all surprising: their demand for new sound materials. The ordinary orchestra, even as expanded by Debussy, Stravinsky, and others, now struck them as stiff and antiquated. They explored new sonorities—nonmusical noises, unexpected new sounds squeezed out of old instruments, and an infinite range of musical materials produced not by instruments at all, but by electronics.

It began with composers making new demands on the standard sources of music. Singers were instructed to lace their singing with hisses, grunts, clicks, and other "nonmusical" noises. Pianists had to stand up, lean over the piano, and pluck the strings or hit them with mallets. Using a special kind of breath pressure, clarinetists learned to play chords called *multiphonics*—weird-sounding chords by conventional standards but fascinating to those attuned to the new sound universe.

Western orchestras and chamber music groups had always been weak in percussion, as compared to their counterparts in many non-Western cultures, notably the gamelans of Indonesia, as we have seen (page 220). Even more to the point, Western art music had been weak in this respect as compared to jazz. Marimbas, xylophones, gongs, bells, and cymbals of many kinds—percussion instruments that had been used only occasionally in the art music of earlier times—became standard in the postwar era.

However, the truly exciting prospect for new sonorities in music emerged out of technology developed during the war: the production of music by electronic means.

Electronic Music

Recording equipment can *reproduce* sounds of any sort—music, speech, and all the sounds and noises of life. Electronic sound generators can *generate* sounds from scratch—in principle, any sounds that can be imagined, or calculated using formulas derived from the science of acoustics.

A technological breakthrough during World War II, the development of magnetic tape, made the storing and handling of sound much easier. It also opened up exciting possibilities for modifying it by manipulating the tape: making tape loops, changing speed, cutting and splicing, and so on. Across the second half of the twentieth century, we can discern three stages in the evolution of electronic music, each of them defined by new technological possibilities:

◗ *Musique concrète* Shortly after World War II composers began incorporating the sounds of life into their compositions. This they called "concrete"

Electronic music: from a synthesizer of the 1960s to a mixing board of the 2000s. Violinist Chee-Yun, center, and pianist Akira Eguchi, right, stand in front of the board.

The latest opera by John Adams, *Doctor Atomic* (2005), deals with political and ethical issues raised by nuclear warfare. "Doctor Atomic" is a nickname for physicist J. Robert Oppenheimer, the so-called father of the A-bomb.

STEVE REICH (b. 1936)
Music for 18 Musicians (1974–76)

17–18

Steve Reich, a philosophy major at Cornell, studied music subsequently and has become the acknowledged old master of the minimalist style. A keyboardist, he has performed his work with his own special group—a practice that a number of other contemporary composers follow, including Glass. Though much of his early music was rather abstract, one of his most impressive works, *Different Trains* (1988), introduced recorded speech and personal memories, and Reich went on to write operas—*The Cave* (1998) and *Three Tales* (2002)— with his wife, video artist Beryl Korot. *Music for 18 Musicians* is regarded as one of the early classics of the minimalist style.

The eighteen musicians include four singers (they sing no words, but only syllables like "doo" and "ah"), a cellist, a violinist, two clarinetists (who sometimes switch to bass clarinets), and a large percussion group: four pianos, three marimbas, two xylophones, and a vibraphone (see page 42). This ensemble produces a timbre favored by the early minimalists—a percussive sound alternating between ringing and dry and brittle, reminiscent of the gamelan orchestras of Indonesia (see pages 220–22). Reich was much influenced by their music; *Music for 18 Musicians* is directed not by a conductor but by the resonant vibraphone, and Reich likened this procedure to the role

LISTENING CHART 27

Reich, *Music for 18 Musicians,* beginning

8 min., 00 sec.

17	**INTRODUCTION**	
	0:00	Neutral pulse
	0:19	First harmony
	0:40	Second harmony
	0:58	Third harmony
	1:16	Fourth harmony
		etc.
18	**SECTION 1**	
0:00	3:47	Neutral pulse
0:04	4:01	Theme begins to emerge.
0:26	4:23	Vibraphone cue: Theme extended, cello prominent
0:44	4:41	Vibraphone cue: Theme extended again, voices prominent
1:16	5:14	Vibraphone cue: cello shifts harmony slightly; pulsing clarinets
		MIDPOINT
2:31	6:28	Clarinets resume theme (with voices).
2:51	6:48	Vibraphone cue: Disassembly of theme begins
		etc.
4:01	7:58	Vibraphone cue begins Section 2.

of the drummers who direct gamelans. Throughout *Music,* each time the vibraphone plays it cues changes in the melodies and harmonies.

The piece is rigorously, almost schematically, organized. It falls into an introduction, twelve connected sections lasting about four minutes each, and a conclusion mirroring the introduction—all adding up to almost an hour of performance time. We will listen to the first eight minutes or so, the introduction and first section.

Steve Reich

Introduction   *Music for 18 Musicians* begins with another feature beloved by minimalist composers: a regular, repeating pulse, seemingly objective and cool—a pulse that will continue for the whole work. Over this pulse, the introduction presents a set of rich harmonies on which the later sections of the work are based. But it does not present them in a conventional manner, as a harmonic progression that might accompany a melody. Instead the musicians linger over each harmony, repeating it over the even pulse for fifteen or twenty seconds or more before shifting to the next one. This is our first hint that musical time for the minimalists moves differently than for conventional composers. The most notable event in the midst of each harmony is contributed by the bass clarinets, which fade in and out twice with their own quick pulses.

Section 1   This four-minute section is based on a single harmony, the first harmony of the introduction, repeated by the pulsing instruments throughout the section. Reich compared this huge extension of a single harmony to the technique of the medieval organum composer Pérotin, who took individual notes of a Gregorian chant as the basis for long sections of polyphony (see pages 68–69).

Minimalism in music and art:
Chant II by Bridget Riley
(b. 1931).

As the pulsing of the percussion instruments smoothly continues, the clarinets, joined later by the voices, begin to present the section's melodic material. A theme builds up gradually from fragments to something much more continuous; it also rises gradually to higher and higher pitch levels. Each change to greater continuity and higher pitch is cued by the vibraphone.

When the theme, which has a lively, syncopated feel, is completely assembled, the clarinets give it over entirely to the voices and play even pulses, fading in and out, as they did in the introduction. This is the midpoint of the section.

Soon the clarinets take up the main theme again, with the voices. Now the process of assembly we heard before is reversed; at each cue from the vibraphone the theme moves lower in pitch and grows more fragmentary, until little is left. Finally it drops out altogether. All that remains is the endless background pulse, before another cue from the vibraphone signals the beginning of the second section.

Two more general features of much minimalist music emerge from our listening to this section of *Music for 18 Musicians*. First is the minimalists' love of *symmetrical musical forms*. The gradual assembly and disassembly of the theme of this section, with the midpoint of the pulsing clarinets, yields an arch form of the sort that could be diagrammed **A B C B A**; most of the other sections of *Music* are similarly symmetrical.

Second is the minimalists' ability to make us hear *musical process* in a new way, or at least with a new concentration. The incessant repetition of musical materials focuses our attention on the gradual changes they undergo; we hear this music as a process of slow building and unbuilding. This kind of listening is not a regular feature of European classical music, though it is well known in many traditions. Its hypnotic effect is particularly prized in trance-inducing music the world over.

A New Expressionism

Many composers at the end of the twentieth century, as we have noted, exploited experimental and unconventional techniques pioneered by the modernists but with a clarity and poignancy of emotional expression that recalls earlier styles. Often this emotion explored dark reaches of the psyche and recalled the anxiety, paranoia, and terror of the expressionists from the beginning of the century (see page 339).

The composer George Crumb (b. 1929), whose works were especially prized during the 1970s and 1980s, offers many examples of this new expressionism. He has a special fondness for the disturbing and surreal poetry of the Spaniard Federico García Lorca (1898–1936), which he has set to music in works exploring novel timbres and instrumentation (a toy piano and a musical saw, for instance) and presented with theatrical trappings such as masks and dance. His most famous work, *Ancient Voices of Children* (1970), is a song cycle setting Lorca's verse; the complete text of one song reads (in translation): "Every afternoon in Granada a child dies." The song transforms Lorca's reaction to the atrocities of the Spanish civil war of the 1930s (in which he was murdered) into Crumb's response to Vietnam.

KAIJA SAARIAHO (b. 1952)
From the Grammar of Dreams (1988)

6
19–21

3
35–37

The Finnish composer Kaija Saariaho represents a generation of European composers who have combined the experimentation of earlier modernism with a resistance to its most arcane complexities and a frank emotive expression. Her modernist pedigree is clear; she works often at IRCAM, a famous center for electronic music in Paris directed by the older modernist Pierre Boulez, where her husband also works. But her special interest is vocal music, particularly the soprano voice. Saariaho has written the operas *L'Amour de loin* (Love from Afar), which received its U.S. premiere in 2002, and *Adriana Mater* (2006).

From the Grammar of Dreams is a cycle of five songs for two unaccompanied sopranos. The songs set words of Sylvia Plath, a moving American poet who struggled with depression and took her own life at an early age in 1963. The words of the songs bring together prose excerpts from Plath's most famous work, the novel *The Bell Jar,* and a multistanza poem entitled "Paralytic." The poem recounts the impressions and sensations of a polio patient lying in an iron lung. (This was a huge medical machine, all too common in the years before vaccinations, that pumped air in and out of the lungs of patients paralyzed by polio.)

Saariaho departs in a number of ways from a conventional musical setting of these words. First, she scatters the stanzas of the poem unevenly across her five songs. Songs 1 and 3 set stanzas 1–4 and 8, respectively. Second, Saariaho often superimposes two different texts sung simultaneously, a treatment rarely encountered in songs. (For one genre that did it as a matter of course, see the isorhythmic motet of the late Middle Ages, page 72.) Finally and most strikingly, Saariaho employs her restricted performing forces with great versatility, presenting a miniature catalogue of unorthodox—and vividly expressive—vocal techniques.

Kaija Saariaho

LISTEN   Kaija Saariaho, *From the Grammar of Dreams*

SONG 1

Soprano 1 ("Paralytic," stanzas 1–4)

It happens. Will it go on? —
My mind a rock,
No fingers to grip, no tongue,
My god the iron lung
    That loves me, pumps
My two
Dust bags in and out,
Will not
    Let me relapse
While the day outside glides by like ticker tape.
The night brings violets,
Tapestries of eyes,
    Lights,
The soft anonymous
Talkers: "You all right?"
The starched, inaccessible breast.

Soprano 2 (from *The Bell Jar*; sung simultaneously with soprano 1)
A bad dream.
I remembered everything.

SONG 3

Sopranos 1 and 2 ("Paralytic," stanza 8 — the last stanza)
The claw
Of the magnolia,
Drunk on its own scents,
Asks nothing of life.

SONG 4

Soprano 1 (*The Bell Jar*)
I thought I would swim out

until I was too tired to swim back.
As I paddled on, my heartbeat
boomed like a dull motor in my ears.
I am I am I am

Soprano 2 (*The Bell Jar*)
I took a deep breath and listened
    to the old brag of my heart.
I am I am I am

Song 1   The more active soprano here sings stanzas 1–2 of "Paralytic" to a violent, leaping, swooping melody. At first she tears apart the words, as in some sort of bizarre verbal dissection, delivering the sounds of individual letters and word fragments with distorted emphasis: for "happens" we hear *huh — huh — appp — enzzzzzzz,* and so on. Meanwhile the other soprano unfolds a gentler line in counterpoint, filled with warbling trills, in which we gradually come to hear words from *The Bell Jar:* "A bad dream. I remembered everything." Is she casting the experience of the paralytic as a nightmare, and nothing more?

Finally, at about 1:20, the violent soprano begins to shift to her partner's more lyrical style (stanza 3). In the end, each soprano is reduced in turn to deliberate, monotonal speech, accompanied by a lingering trill from the other singer.

Song 3   This is the lyrical and emotional heart of the cycle — and also its most conventional song. Its words, the last stanza of "Paralytic," are sung by both voices. The singers, like the poetic image of their words, seem to convey a calm, quiet renunciation (of struggle against the iron lung? of the attempt to touch an unreachable world?) — perhaps even a renunciation of life altogether. The song is organized around an arch of shifting pitch levels, as the voices gradually rise to a climax (at 1:35), then fall back to their starting places.

It is organized also by a technique we have heard often since the Renaissance: imitative polyphony. Listen for this especially in the half-step motives at the beginning and end, which wind together like the clawed tree roots and branches alluded to in the poem, or at the repeated word *magnolia* starting at 1:01.

Song 4   Here images from *The Bell Jar* eerily summon up Plath's own suicidal thoughts, only to turn to the life force of a beating heart. We can hear this song as a free **A B A′** form, with the **A** section formed of harsh, impassioned panting. The longer, fully sung **B** section (starting at 0:19) rises steadily to an ecstatic, almost unbearable climax on "I am I am I am"; along the way, the panting from **A**, now sung, returns. An abrupt collapse (at 1:25) ushers in **A′**, made up of fading, panting repetitions of "I am" in heartbeat-like rhythms. Song 4 seems to affirm that the renunciation of life, desire, and self hinted at in Song 3 does not come without struggle.

Back to the Future

Concert music composition around the turn of the millennium points in many directions. Most composers are now far from avant-garde modernism. Many have embraced a frank emotional expression akin to Saariaho's while using whatever new techniques can aid them in achieving it. Others have turned back to premodernist styles and genres; their music, in its clear tonality, rich instrumentation, and impassioned melodies, has been termed Neoromantic.

Today's compositional scene is most noteworthy for three tendencies: its eclecticism, that is, its free juxtaposing of many different styles and gestures; its self-conscious reference to earlier styles and genres; and its strong, straightforward expression. The forbidding, challenging attitude of high modernism is a thing of the past, replaced by a more welcoming, approachable stance. All these tendencies remind some observers of analogous trends in architecture and the visual arts termed *postmodern*. Postmodern composers are not exactly *anti*-modernist; rather, they pick and choose from modernist and many other styles in order to achieve their expressive ends.

JOHN ADAMS (b. 1947)
El Niño (2000)

7–9

John Adams is doubtless the premier concert music composer in America today. He has emerged as a true American original, and however different from Ives and Copland, he ranks along with them. Raised (like Ives) in New England, he moved west to San Francisco in 1971. At first he was strongly influenced by Steve Reich's minimalism; we have already mentioned Adams's early opera *Nixon in China* as a foremost work from the minimalist camp. Many of his other works also have American themes — most recently, *On the Transmigration of Souls*, a powerful memorial for September 11, and *Doctor Atomic*, about J. Robert Oppenheimer and the testing of the first atom bomb at Los Alamos. A scene from *Doctor Atomic* is shown on page 382.

But Adams always showed a tendency to range more widely in his musical tastes than the hard-core minimalists. His music (again like that of Ives) is inspired by vernacular as well as cultivated styles and genres; we can hear in it echoes of the classical tradition from Bach through Schoenberg and Stravinsky,

Postmodern architecture: the Sony building in Manhattan (1984), designed by Philip Johnson. Unlike modernist skyscrapers (see page 51), this building looks back knowingly on history. Its alternating wide and thin stripes recall early skyscrapers like the Empire State Building, and its topmost ornaments gesture toward antique furniture—a highboy or a grandfather clock.

brushing up against marches, dance-band music, rock, rap, and even cartoon music. Whatever else it means, being an "American original" suggests this kind of eclecticism.

Adams's *El Niño* returns to a genre we haven't mentioned since our discussion of the late Baroque period: the oratorio. However, oratorios continue to be written and played to large, appreciative audiences long after Handel's *Messiah* (see page 161)—and *El Niño*, in its postmodern way, is directly modeled on this most famous of all Handel's works (and of all oratorios). The *niño* (child) of Adams's title is the infant Christ, and his work, like Handel's, consists of separate numbers involving vocal soloists, chorus, and orchestra presenting events from Christ's life. Whereas Handel concentrated on the prophecies around Christ's birth and his resurrection, Adams turns to other episodes: the divine impregnation of Mary; King Herod's attempt to kill the baby, whom he fears as a challenge to his rule, by slaughtering all the male children of Bethlehem; and the flight of Joseph, Mary, and Jesus from Bethlehem to escape the massacre.

For his text Adams pieced together passages from scripture, supplemented with poems from other sources, especially poems in Spanish from Mexican female poets. Eclectic indeed: the bilingual libretto for *El Niño* carries a multicultural message that was clearly important for the composer in conceiving the work. In its first performances, noted opera director Peter Sellars emphasized this multiculturalism by presenting the work on two separate levels. Onstage the

LISTEN | John Adams, El Niño

DVD
7–9

7 | **1. PUES MI DIOS HA NACIDO A PENAR**

1—Pues mi Dios ha nacido a penar,
    déjenle velar.

Because my Lord was born to suffer,
let him stay awake.

2—Pues está desvelado por mi,
    déjenle dormir.

Because he stays awake for me,
let him sleep.

3—Déjenle velar,
    que no hay pena, en quien ama
    como no penar.

Let him stay awake,
for there is no suffering for him who loves,
as if there were no pain ever.

4—Déjenle dormir,
    que quien duerme, en el sueño
    se ensaya a morir.

Let him sleep,
for one who sleeps, in his dreaming
rehearses his own death.

5—Silencio, que duerme.

Silence, let him sleep!

6—Cuidado, que vela.

Take care, let him stay awake!

7—¡No le despierten, no!

Don't wake him, no!

8—¡Si le despierten, si!

Yes, wake him, yes!

9—¡Déjenle velar!

Let him stay awake!

10—¡Déjenle dormir!

Let him sleep!

8 | **2. WHEN HEROD HEARD**

Now when Jesus was born in Bethlehem of Judaea,
in the days of Herod, the king, behold, there came wise
men from the east to Jerusalem, saying,

Where is he that is born King of the Jews? for we have
seen his star in the east, and are come to worship him.

Now when Herod had heard these things, he was troubled,
and he privily called the wise men, inquired of them diligently
what time the star appeared. And he sent them to Bethlehem,
saying,

Go and search diligently for the young child, and when you
have found him bring me word again, that I may come and
worship him also.

— Matthew 2

9 | **3. WOE UNTO THEM THAT CALL EVIL GOOD**

Woe unto them that call evil good, and good evil; that put darkness for light and light for darkness; that put bitter for sweet and sweet for bitter!

Woe unto them that are wise in their own eyes, and prudent in their own sight!

Woe unto them that seek deep to hide their counsel from the Lord, and their works are in the dark, and they say, Who seeth us? and who knoweth us?

I will also choose their delusions, and will bring forth their fears upon them.

— Isaiah 5; 29; 66

John Adams

much of the energy of early American musicians was devoted to the composition of new psalm and hymn tunes, and to the teaching and improvement of church singing.

William Billings (1746–1800) of Boston is often mentioned as our first composer. He wrote hymns and **fuguing tunes,** which are simple anthems based on hymns, with a little counterpoint. (An anthem is a choral piece in the vernacular for use in Protestant services.) When sung with spirit, fuguing tunes sound enthusiastic, rough, and gutsy.

Billings's more secular-minded contemporaries enjoyed the Classical music of the era. Benjamin Franklin, who tried his hand at most everything, also tried composing. But without well-established musical institutions, there was not much support for native composers outside the church. The problem in those years is hardly that of distinguishing between cultivated and vernacular music. The problem is finding written music to listen to and talk about at all.

The Cultivated Tradition

As cities grew, first on the East coast and then farther west, more and more concerts appeared, and with them faithful concertgoers. One such was a New York lawyer and civic leader named George Templeton Strong, who left a four-and-a-half-million-word diary discussing (among other things) all the symphonies, oratorios, and organ music he heard, in unending enthusiastic detail.* By the mid-1800s, all our major cities had their concert halls and opera organizations and amateur choral societies. The 1860s saw the foundation of our first conservatories of music, in Boston, Cincinnati, and elsewhere.

Americans eagerly bought tickets to hear traveling celebrities from Europe, and skilled native composers and performers began to appear. The first American musicians to gain worldwide reputations were the immigrant German composer Anthony Philip Heinrich (1781–1861), a quirky early Romantic, and the Louisiana piano virtuoso Louis Moreau Gottschalk (1829–1869).

On the whole, however, Americans were content to look to Italy for opera and to Germany for instrumental music. That the cultivated tradition in American music was essentially German in orientation is not surprising. Ever since the time of Mozart and Beethoven, German music had achieved wonders and had earned enormous prestige all over Europe. The mid-nineteenth-century immigration from Germany brought us many musicians who labored for the cause of music in this country. We can hardly blame them for their German bias.

- Vivaldi's concertos in parts
- Bach's songs 2nd collection
- Handel's Coronation anthems
- Heck's art of playing the harpsichord
- Hayden's [sic] cantatas . . .

In 1783 Thomas Jefferson's music library contained these and a hundred other items.

"Cultivated" music in America: a scene from Philadelphia society of the 1890s, *The Concert Singer,* by Thomas Eakins.

*Bits of Strong's diary are cited on pages 232 and 234.

A concert at New York's Castle Garden in 1850, in a print issued by Currier & Ives. Their hand-colored lithographs are famous for vividly illustrating nineteenth-century America.

There were significant native composers at the end of the nineteenth century: John Knowles Paine, Arthur Foote, and Henry Chadwick of the so-called Boston School, and Edward MacDowell of New York. They wrote symphonies, piano miniatures, and so on, in a competent but conservative German Romantic style. Time has not been kind to their work, despite recent efforts to revive it.

The music of Amy Beach (1867–1944), in particular, has stirred interest in recent years. Active as both a composer and a pianist, she made her debut with the Boston Symphony Orchestra at the age of seventeen. "Mrs. H. H. A. Beach" (as she always signed her works) contributed to many established genres, such as the piano concerto, the piano quintet, and the symphony. Her *Gaelic* Symphony of 1896 was the first symphonic work ever composed by an American woman.

The emergence of Charles Ives in the midst of this conservative tradition seems like a miracle of music history (see page 349). Yet Ives profited more than he sometimes cared to admit from the grounding in European concert music he received from his German-trained professor, Horatio Parker.

Music in the Vernacular

We might well count the psalms and hymns mentioned above as vernacular music, for in colonial days everybody who could carry a tune sang them at church and in the home, and later they were widely sung at revival meetings and the like. Nineteenth-century

Amy Beach

Global Perspectives 6

African Drumming

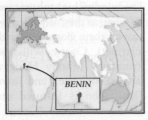

BENIN

We said before that the syncopated rhythms of ragtime, blues, and jazz derived from traditional African music, particularly drumming. We don't know enough about African or African American music in the nineteenth century to detail this connection in all its stages, but we can surmise that the rhythmic complexities of modern jazz and today's African drumming are connected in a history that reaches back centuries.

Listen now to our recording of a drum ensemble from Benin, a small West African nation situated be-

tween Ghana and Nigeria. The drummers play music used in the worship of ancestral spirits among the Yoruba people—one of a wide variety of religious and nonreligious uses of drumming in the region.

Syncopation and Polyrhythms

The rhythms of this music cannot be said to *swing* precisely in the manner of jazz, but they show a complexity and vitality related to jazz rhythms and not found in the European classical music tradition through the nineteenth century.

These rhythms are related to what we have termed *beat syncopation* in jazz (see page 397). A single drum

A drumming club in another West African country, Ghana.

lays down a basic, fast, four-plus-four pulse; each group of four feels like a beat, and two groups of four take about a second. (This quick pulse is heard all the way through the recording, except for three brief moments: This drummer speeds up momentarily at 1:09, 1:46, and 2:33, with stunning, energizing effect, fitting six strokes into the space usually taken up by four.)

Against the main drum's consistent pulse, the other drums play a variety of different rhythms. Sometimes they underscore the main drum's even pulse, or even duplicate it. Often, however, they play off it with more complicated and varied rhythms, including extensive syncopation within the groups of four (or beats), and occasionally they boldly contradict it.

Such overlapping of varied patterns with the main pulse is essential in West African drumming. Since several rhythmic formulas can be heard at once, it is sometimes called *polyrhythm*. From its polyrhythms the musical whole gains an extraordinary richness of rhythmic profile. And from the syncopations within the beat it derives its irresistible vitality (irresistible also to the ancestral spirits invoked).

A Closer Look

To study this recording more closely, listen for a few clear polyrhythmic interactions:

❧   One drummer aligns a regular syncopated formula against the main pulse, in this manner:

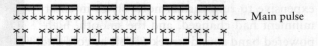
— Main pulse

Listen for this four times in the recording, at 0:23–0:29, 0:50–0:53, 1:23–1:28, and 2:13–2:19.

❧   Another drummer plays an even 3 + 3 pulse against the main 4 + 4, seeming to contradict its duple meter with a triple orientation. This occurs prominently twice, at 0:41–0:44 and again at 2:22–2:26.

❧   One drummer in particular departs freely from the main pulse all the way through this recording. He is the soloist, so to speak, improvising against the more regular and predictable playing of his ensemble-mates. His drum is recognizable by its wooden, clickety-clack timbre and by the fact that it plays two distinct pitches (the higher pitch is more wooden-sounding than the lower).

One good way to listen for his distinctive, irregular syncopations is to clap along with the main pulse as you listen, once every four strokes. You will be clapping about twice a second. Then compare the regularity of your own clapping with the seemingly free fantasy of the clickety-clack drum.

The Jimi Hendrix Experience, on the cover of their first album, dressed in their Carnaby Street best.

In the wake of the 1970s it is wise to remember that even the music that seems to rage loudest "against the machine" is usually brought to you by a multinational communications conglomerate.

Trends since 1980: Punk, Rap, and Post-Rock

Despite—or perhaps because of—this commercialization, rock has survived. Indeed the last thirty years or so have brought something of a rejuvenation. Three trends can be pointed to:

❧ The youthful disaffection that set in by the end of the 1960s, as the idealistic counterculture began to sense its impotence, hardened in the next decade. Its most influential expression was the nihilistic alienation of *punk rock.* In New York City and Britain, groups like the Patti Smith Group ("Gloria"), the Ramones ("Blitzkrieg Bop"), and the Sex Pistols ("Anarchy in the UK") reacted against the commercial flashiness of much rock with what we might call an anti-aesthetic: All expression was possible, including no expression. All musical expertise was acceptable, including none. (Some of the punks were fully aware that in this move they were following the lead of arch-modernists like John Cage; see page 380.)

The punk approach gave strong impetus to a kind of populist movement in rock, encouraging the formation of countless "garage bands" and today's *indie rock,* distributed on small, independent labels. Some punk singers also pioneered an alienated, flat vocal delivery that contrasts both with the impassioned singing of earlier rock and with the streetwise cool of rap. In these features punk looked forward to the unpolished, moving, but somehow distant style of *grunge rock,* led by Kurt Cobain (until his death in 1994) and his band Nirvana ("Lithium," "Smells Like Teen Spirit").

❧ First emerging about the same time as punk, *hip-hop* or **rap** has compiled a thirty-year history as a primary black rhetorical and musical mode. Early on, its influence was transmitted, with stunning postmodern quickness, around the

Kurt Cobain

globe. Rap is now a strong undercurrent sweeping through world pop-music traditions. Its influence is heard in the vocal delivery of countless rock groups.

The early 1990s marked rap's moment of highest notoriety in the American mass media. One strain of rap—the violent, misogynist variety known as *gangsta rap*—figured centrally in the public debate, which was marked not only by justifiable distaste at the vision of these rappers but also by unmistakable racist undertones. However, the debate tended to miss two important points: First, while rap originated as a pointed expression of black urban concerns, it was marketed successfully to affluent whites, especially suburban teens. Second, the clamor against gangsta rap ignored the wider expressive terrains that rap as a whole had traveled. Already in 1980 rap was broad enough to embrace the hip-hop dance numbers of the Sugarhill Gang ("Rapper's Delight") and the trenchant social commentary of Grandmaster Flash ("The Message"). By the 1990s, rap could range from the black empowerment messages of Public Enemy ("Don't Believe the Hype") through sensuous love lyrics and tongue-twisting word games to Queen Latifah's assertions of women's dignity and strength ("Latifah's Had It Up 2 Here"). And the 2000s would bring Eminem, the first white superstar of rap.

Missy Elliott, leading hip-hop artist of the new century

❼ Around 1990 a new, experimental rock movement began to take shape; soon it was dubbed *post-rock*. Early post-rock groups (for example, Slint: "Good Morning Captain") emerged from the indie rock movement. They typically employed rock instrumentation and technology in a style that features hypnotically repeated gestures (especially bass ostinatos), juxtaposition of contrasting plateaus of sound, slow transitions and buildups, free improvisation, and emphasis of instruments rather than voice. (When a voice is present, it often doesn't so much *sing* as recite fragments of poetry in front of the instrumental backdrop.) This thumbnail sketch alone is enough to reveal post-rock's relation to two other musical movements we have encountered: minimalism (page 381) and avant-garde jazz (page 407).

And just as jazz and classical music purists questioned those styles, some listen to post-rock and wonder, "But is it rock'n'roll?" The question grows more pressing still with post-rock groups that feature acoustic rather than electrified instruments and even avoid the foremost trait of rock: a strong beat (for instance Godspeed You Black Emperor!; "Storm").

Questions of style, it seems to us, are not a matter of pre-set categories but of fluid affiliations, changing always as new music develops. Rock will accommodate post-rock, just as jazz accommodated fusion, just as classical concert music accepted minimalism. But it will be transformed in the process. In fact, the transformation is already well under way. One of the most widely noticed rock bands of the late 1990s, Britain's Radiohead, began around 2000 to expand its earlier, song-oriented style with traits of post-rock ("Pyramid Song").

Global Perspectives   7

Global Music

We have seen in Global Perspectives 2 (page 93) that European efforts to colonize foreign lands never resulted in the simple substitution of European cultures for native ones, but rather in new, complex mixed cultures. Such is the way of all meetings of distinct cultures and distinct musics. An Andean chorus singing Catholic Church polyphony to Quechua words and accompanying itself on Inca flutes and drums is the perfect example of such mixture.

But a funny thing happened to mixed musical cultures on their way through the twentieth century: recorded sound. Around the globe, the impact on music of technologies that store and play back sound has been nothing short of revolutionary. Combined with radio and TV broadcasts, and with the modern ease of travel and commerce, it has given musicians and listeners from all parts of the world access to a much wider variety of music than ever before. Nothing in the whole history of culture, probably, has ever traveled more widely and easily than certain kinds of music do today.

Complexities of Globalism

Two opposing tendencies have arisen from this situation. The first works toward the worldwide *homogenization* of musics. Huge stretches of the sonic landscape are now inhabited by styles that are similar in certain basic features: electrified instruments, especially guitars; strong percussive presence; extensive syncopation; and relatively brief song-form presentation.

These features spread out from the American and especially African American pop-music revolution that occurred in the decades after World War II. Since the 1960s the dispersion of styles such as rhythm and blues, rock, soul, and rap has been powerful. Musical currents have, to be sure, flowed in both directions. *Reggae,* to take one example, was formed in the 1960s from a merger of native Jamaican styles with American rhythm and blues and soul, but by the late 1970s it had crossed back over to exert a great influence on American rock itself. The global dispersion has been enabled by a recording industry that has grown

A choir—not for isicathamiya, given the many women participating—rehearses in South Africa. The beauty of the singers' costumes contrasts with the stark landscape of Soweto Township behind them.

Isicathamiya praktisa:
a rehearsal at the Beatrice
St. YMCA, Durban, South
Africa, 1996.

increasingly rich, increasingly multinational, and increasingly influential in determining our musical tastes. It is enough to make one observer of these developments speak — with some worry — of a "universal pop aesthetic."

There is another tendency, however, opposing this move toward sameness, a move to *localize* music making. People never simply take on foreign things without in some way making them their own. Even as musicians around the world have felt the influence of American pop styles, they have combined these styles in their local musics to forge new, distinct styles. (Reggae is one example of this process.)

Pop music is now, in some general way, recognizable worldwide. We know it when we hear it, and we easily distinguish it from traditional folk musics like Andean panpipe groups or Appalachian fiddling and traditional elite musics like Japanese gagaku or European classical music. Nevertheless, what we recognize as pop music comes in an immense variety of distinct idioms derived from specific interactions of global and local tendencies.

South African Choral Song: Isicathamiya

A South African musical tradition with a difficult name, *isicathamiya* (ees-ee-zaht-ah-mée-ah), pro-

SOUTH
AFRICA

vides an example reaching back many decades of this diversity-within-sameness. It has become familiar to listeners worldwide through the recordings of the singing group Ladysmith Black Mambazo. Isicathamiya is an all-male, *a cappella* song style that arose among an impoverished class of black, mostly Zulu-speaking migrant laborers. A chief diversion in the laborers' camps were Saturday-night contests among singing groups, and for the musical styles the performers looked back to earlier, complex international roots.

Standing behind isicathamiya are traditions of choral polyphony native to the Zulus and other groups of the region. In the nineteenth century, these traditions seem to have merged readily with the four-part harmony of Christian hymn-singing brought to the area by European and American missionaries. Then another ingredient was added to the mix: American vaudeville or minstrel shows, with their syncopated, ragtime songs (see page 395 and the picture on page 411). An enormously influential African American minstrel — not a white minstrel in blackface — named Orpheus McAdoo toured South Africa extensively in the 1890s, to the great acclaim of black audiences.

By the 1930s, these musical influences were put together by the first recording stars of the local Zulu singing scene, Solomon Linda and the Evening Birds. Their greatest hit, "Mbube" or "Lion," known to most of us today as "The Lion Sleeps Tonight," was originally recorded around 1939. Then it was re-recorded by pop singers and became a top-40 hit in the 1960s. Most recently it was featured in Disney's film and musical *The Lion King*.

"Anoku Gonda"

Solomon Linda's song "Anoku Gonda" ("You Must Understand This"), from the same period as "Mbube," combines two distinct styles that are still heard today in isicathamiya. The first is a richly harmonized, homophonic style that recites the text freely and shows no clear or consistent sense of meter—*choral declamation,* we can call it. We hear two phrases of choral declamation, each stated and repeated in the pattern **a a b b a a.** Notable here, and frequent in isicathamiya, is the slide in all voices from high to lower pitches.

Then, after about a minute, the music takes on a clear meter. This is the second style common in isicathamiya. It is still organized in repeating phrases, but now the texture departs from the simple homophony of the recitational opening section. It uses call-and-response techniques (see page 395), pitting Linda against the rest of the group at first; later the basses in the chorus sing against the group as a whole. The call-and-response phrases alternate with a falling cadential phrase sung by the whole chorus.

))) LISTEN   ⬤ 6 / 31

"Anoku Gonda"

0:00	Unmetered choral declamation
0:00	a
0:13	a
0:25	b
0:30	b
0:35	a
0:47	a
0:57	Metrical call and response: Solomon Linda against the full chorus
1:27	Metrical call and response: Basses against the full chorus

6 Conclusion

Just a few words in conclusion: not so much as a conclusion to this chapter, but rather to our total effort in this book as a whole.

We might recall what was said near the end of the introductory unit, on page 53. Our basic goal has been to learn how to listen better, in order to understand and appreciate music—music of the European art tradition, mostly, but also other musics, other musical traditions. Some musical terminology has been introduced that should help clarify listening, and a somewhat rapid trip has been conducted through the history of Western music from Hildegard of Bingen to John Adams, by way of Bach, Mozart, Beethoven, Wagner, Stravinsky, and Ellington. There have been side trips beyond Europe, offering us perspectives on music around the globe. The most important thing we've done, by far, is *listen:* listen with some care to numerous individual pieces of music. Not all, but many of them are famous works that listeners have found rewarding over a period, in most cases, of many generations.

Rewarding is a pale, neutral term that will cover beautiful, fascinating, profound, exciting, comforting, and any other adjective that may correspond to something deep in your personal experience. Feelings of this kind about music tend to last a long time. If you have come to appreciate and love some of the music this book has introduced you to, it may be forever. Consider yourself ahead.

❝ [Music] takes us out of the actual and whispers to us dim secrets that startle our wonder as to who we are, and for what, whence and whereto."

Ralph Waldo Emerson, 1838

Scale: A selection of ordered pitche
terial for music *(16)*

Scherzo (scáir-tzo): A form develo
minuet to use for movements in larg
times used alone, as by Chopin *(231*

Score: The full musical notation for
many performers *(23)*

Secco recitative: See *recitative (156)*

Second group: In *sonata form,* the gro
bridge, in the second key *(184)*

Second theme: In *sonata form,* one the
nent among the second group of them

Semitone: Same as *half step (19)*

Sequence: (1) In a melody, a series of frag
their placement at successively higher or
in the Middle Ages, a type of *plainch*
phrases of text receive nearly identical m

Serialism, serial: The technique of comp
erally a twelve-tone series *(346)*

Series: A fixed arrangement of pitches
throughout a serial composition *(346)*

Sforzando: An especially strong accent; t
in musical notation *(sf* or *>) (12)*

Shamisen (shah-mée-sen): A Japanese thre
accompaniment in *kabuki (315)*

Sharp: In musical notation, a sign (♯) indi
precedes is to be played a *semitone* higher.
occasionally used to indicate that a note is
higher *(18)*

Sho: A Japanese mouth reed-organ with se
in *gagaku (218)*

Siciliana: A Baroque dance type in *compou*

Simple meter: A meter in which the main
vided, or are subdivided into two, e.g., **2/4,**

Sixteenth note: A note one-sixteenth the length

Slur: In musical notation, a curved line over
cating that they are to be played smoothly, or

Solo exposition: In Classical concerto form,
expositions, played by the soloist and the orc

Sonata: A chamber-music piece in several mo
for three main instruments plus *continuo* in th
and for only one or two instruments since the

Sonata form (sonata-allegro form): A form
Classical composers and used in almost all the
of their symphonies, sonatas, etc. *(183)*

Song cycle: A group of songs connected by a
story, and sometimes also by musical unifying d

Sonority: A general term for sound quality, eith
tary chord, or of a whole piece or style *(77)*

Soprano: The high female (or boy's) voice

Spiritual: Religious folk song, usually among Afr
(called "Negro spiritual" in the 19th century) *(39*

Sprechstimme: A vocal style developed by Scho
tween singing and speaking *(340)*

Passion: A long, oratorio-like co[...]
Jesus' last days, according to one [...]

Pavan (pa-váhn): A slow, 16th-cent[...]
(91)

Pedal board: That keyboard of an o[...]
feet *(46)*

Pentatonic scale: A five-note *scale* [...]
playable on the black notes of a key[...]

Phrase: A section of a melody or a t[...]

Piano; pianissimo: Soft; very soft *(p;* [...]

Piano trio: An instrumental group [...]
cello, and piano; or a piece composed [...]
players themselves

Pitch: The quality of "highness" or "l[...]
plied ("a pitch") to any particular pitch [...]

Più: More (as in *più forte,* louder) *(8)*

Pizzicato (pit-tzih-cáh-toe): Playing a s[...]
normally bowed by plucking the string[...]

Plainchant, plainsong: Unaccompani[...]
without fixed rhythm or meter, such as [...]

Poco: Somewhat (as in *poco adagio* o[...]
slow, somewhat loud)

Point of imitation: A short passage of *im[...]
on a single theme, or on two used togeth[...]

Polonaise: A Polish court dance in a mod[...]

Polyphony, polyphonic: Musical texture [...]
melodic lines are played or sung simulta[...]
homophony or *monophony (29)*

Prelude: An introductory piece, leading [...]
fugue or an opera (however, Chopin's l[...]
tended to lead to anything else)

Premiere: The first performance ever of a pie[...]

Presto; prestissimo: Very fast; very fast ind[...]

Program music: A piece of instrumental mu[...]
story or other extramusical idea *(249)*

Program symphony: A symphony with a pr[...]
(269)

Quarter note: A note one-quarter the length [...]

Quarter-tone scale: A 24-note scale, used in [...]
consisting of all the *semitones* of the *chro*[...]
quarter tones in between the semitones *(329)*

Quartet: A piece for four singers or players; [...]
string quartet

Quintet: A piece for five singers or players [...]

Qur'anic recitation: An Islamic tradition in wh[...]
of the prophet Muhammad gathered in the Q[...]
are chanted in Arabic *(73)*

Ragtime: A style of American popular music an[...]
ally for piano, which led to *jazz (399)*

Range: Used in music to mean "pitch range," i.e[...]
from the lowest to the highest pitch in a piece, a p[...]